Quantitative Methods in Marketing

Second Edition

Graham J. Hooley
and
Michael K. Hussey

INTERNATIONAL THOMSON BUSINESS PRESS
I(T)P® An International Thomson Publishing Company

London • Bonn • Johannesburg • Madrid • Melbourne • Mexico City • New York • Paris
Singapore • Tokyo • Toronto • Albany, NY • Belmont, CA • Cincinnati, OH • Detroit, MI

Quantitative Methods in Marketing

Copyright © 1999 International Thomson Business Press

I(T)P® A division of International Thomson Publishing Inc.
The ITP logo is a trademark under licence

British Library Cataloguing-in-Publication Data
A catalogue record for this book is available from the British Library

First published by Academic Press Limited 1994
Reprinted by the Dryden Press 1995

Second edition published 1999 by International Thomson Business Press

Typeset by LaserScript Limited, Mitcham, Surrey
Printed in the UK by TJ International, Padstow, Cornwall

ISBN 1–86152–417–X

International Thomson Business Press
Berkshire House
168–173 High Holborn
London WC1V 7AA
UK

http://www.itbp.com

Table of contents

Foreword

I am delighted to have been invited to write a foreword to this the second edition of Graham Hooley and Michael Hussey's *Quantitative Methods in Marketing*.

Some readers may recall that the first edition of this book was originally published as a Special Issue of the *Journal of Marketing Management* (Volume 10, Jan/Feb/April 1994). The Special Issue marked an increase in the frequency of publication of *Journal of Marketing Management* from four to eight issues per year. It was also the first specially invited triple issue addressing a specific theme and sub-field within marketing. This innovation has since been continued and in 1999 the sixth in the series addressed the theme of Brand Reality and was edited by Chris Macrae.

As noted in the Foreword to the first edition the decision to adopt a thematic, monograph approach covering three issues of the journal was prompted by a number of considerations. First, by identifying the specific sub-field of marketing one can achieve a degree of focus atypical for a journal positioned to attract contributions from the whole spectrum of marketing management. Second, the selected focus can concentrate upon a topic which may have received only limited exposure and discussion by generalists due to the perception that it is the exclusive domain of 'experts'. Third, by introducing a degree of focus and specialization one can promote the exchange between theory and practice which is the *Journal of Marketing Management*'s primary aim. Finally, the special issue is capable of being reprinted as a book and so made available to students or others who may have a particular interest in the topic and want a copy but are not regular subscribers to the journal itself.

The success of this formula is clearly reflected in the appearance of this second edition. Many of the original contributions have been retained, updated where necessary to take into account recent developments, and have been complemented by a number of new chapters which are described by the Editors in their Introduction. These new chapters reinforce and extend the original objective of making *Quantitative Methods in Marketing* accessible and understandable to anyone willing to put in a little effort to read them. They clearly demonstrate that quantitative analysis is an essential tool of the professional marketer and that one does not need an advanced degree in mathematics to be able to understand and apply these techniques.

Michael J. Baker
Editor
Journal of Marketing Management

About the Authors

J. Scott Armstrong received his Ph.D. from MIT and is currently Professor of Marketing at The Wharton School, University of Pennsylvania. He has held visiting positions in many countries including Sweden, Switzerland, New Zealand, South Africa, Thailand, Argentina and Japan. Scott was a founding editor of both the *Journal of Forecasting* and the *International Journal of Forecasting*. In 1996, he was named as one of the first six 'honorary fellows' for distinguished contributions to forecasting by the International Institute of Forecasters. An independent survey ranked him among the top 15 marketing professors in the US. He is currently engaged in a project to forecast the sales effectiveness of advertising. His research on forecasting is summarized on http://hops.wharton.upenn.edu.

Neil Barnard is Visiting Research Associate at South Bank University, London and a consultant in market analysis and advertising evaluation.

Steve Baron obtained graduate and postgraduate qualifications in mathematics and statistics. Since working on a year's secondment for P & O Shopping Centres Ltd. he has been actively involved in marketing research for shopping centre owners and managers over the past seven years. He has specialized in the development of models of pedestrian flow and the monitoring of customer attitudes. He is associate editor of *OR Insight*, co-author of textbooks on retailing and services marketing and the joint editor of the Macmillan *Dictionary of Retailing*.

Patrick Barwise is Professor of Management and Marketing at London Business School. He directs the London Business School's Centre for Marketing and the Future Media Research Programme. His latest book is *Strategic Decisions*, co-edited with Vassilis Papadakis (Kluwer, 1997).

Amanda Broderick is Lecturer in Marketing at Aston Business School, a visiting senior research fellow at De Montfort University and a visiting lecturer at the College of Charleston, South Carolina. Her main research interests lie in international targeting and modelling. She publishes in the areas of consumer behaviour at the point of sale and competitive positioning and regularly contributes papers to international conferences. She is Director of Aston Business School's Marketing Management Programme.

Roderick J. Brodie is Professor and Head of the Department of Marketing at the University of Auckland, New Zealand. In the last two decades he has held teaching and visiting research positions in a number of North American and European universities, including Warwick University, the Helsinki School of Economics and Vanderbilt University. Professor Brodie's university teaching and research experience is in the areas of marketing research, marketing science and forecasting. His publications have appeared in many leading international journals. He is currently on the editorial board of the *International Journal of Research in Marketing*, the *Journal of Services Research*, the *International Journal of Forecasting* and the *Australasian Journal of Marketing*.

Stephen Castleberry received his Ph.D. from the University of Alabama. He is currently Professor of Marketing at the University of Minnesota, Duluth. He has held positions at the University of Georgia, where he was the Professor of Sales and Marketing, and Northern Illinois University. He has served as a consultant and sales trainer for a number of firms. Dr Castleberry has published in the main US and European journals. His research interests include the informal sales organization and sales person listening.

David Coates is Lecturer in Management Science in the Business School at Loughborough University. His interests include applied statistics, time series analysis and digital signal processing.

Bruce Curry is Lecturer in Computing at Cardiff Business School, University of Wales College of Cardiff. His research and professional interests include information systems, business applications of artificial intelligence and expert systems, as well as the emerging technologies of multimedia computing.

Mark A.P. Davies is Lecturer at Loughborough Business School, having formerly held positions in performance analysis. He is an active researcher, having authored three books and numerous academic papers, contributing to national and international conferences. His current research interests include relationship marketing and cross-cultural research applied to marketing communications and marketing behaviour.

Adamantios Diamantopoulos is Professor of Marketing and Director of Research in the Business School at Loughborough University. He previously held a professorial position at the European Business Management School, University of Wales, Swansea. He has held previous full-time academic posts at the University of Edinburgh and the University of Strathclyde and has been visiting associate professor at the University of Miami. His research interests are in pricing, sales forecasting, marketing research and international marketing and he is the author of approximately 100 publications in these areas. He has presented his research at numerous international conferences and his work has appeared, among others, in the *International Journal of Research in Marketing, Industrial Marketing Management, Journal of Forecasting, Journal of the Market Research Society, European Journal of Marketing* and *Journal of Marketing Management.*

Neil Doherty is Lecturer in Management Information Systems in the Business School at Loughborough University. His interests include the application of expert systems to managerial decision making.

Andrew Ehrenberg is Research Professor of Marketing at South Bank University Business School, London. He has published widely in business and statistics and is perhaps best known for his ground breaking theories of repeat buying behaviour.

Gordon Foxall is Professor of Consumer Behaviour in the Department of Management, and Honorary Professor in Psychology, at Keele University. He is a graduate of both the University of Birmingham (Ph.D. in industrial economics and business studies) and of the University of Strathclyde (Ph.D. in psychology), and holds a higher doctorate of the University of Birmingham (D.Soc.Sc.). He is the author of fifteen books on consumer behaviour and related themes including the critically-acclaimed *Consumer Psychology in Behavioral Perspective* (Routledge, London and New York, 1990) and the best-selling text *Consumer Psychology for Marketing,* co-authored with Ron Goldsmith (Routledge, London and New York, 1994). In addition, he has authored some 250 refereed articles, chapters and papers on consumer behaviour and marketing. His previous professorial appointments have been at the Universities of Strathclyde, Birmingham and the Cardiff Business School, when he was Distinguished Research Professor in Consumer Psychology; he has also held posts at Cranfield University and the University of Newcastle upon Tyne. Professor Foxall's research interests lie in the psychological theory of consumer behaviour, consumer innovativeness, and micro-micro analysis of intra-firm behaviour.

Alan French is a Lecturer in Management Science in the Business School at Loughborough University. His interests include the application of computer science techniques to management problems.

Gordon E. Greenley is Professor of Marketing and Head of the Marketing Group at Aston Business School, Aston University, UK. He has published widely in many journals, including the *European Journal of Operational Research, International Journal of Research in Marketing, Journal of Business Research, Journal of Management Studies, Omega: the International Journal of Management Science* and the *Strategic Management Journal*. He is a fellow of the British Academy of Management and was the founding editor of the *Journal of Strategic Marketing*. His research interests are in marketing planning and strategy, competitive advantage, market and stakeholder orientation, slack resources and consumer behaviour response to marketing planning.

Paul Hackett is Reader in Health Studies, University College, Worcester, where he conducts research into aspects of health and caring. He holds a doctorate in environmental psychology (Ph.D. University of Aston in Birmingham, 1989). He is a chartered psychologist, an associate fellow of the British Psychological Society and a member of both the American and Texas Psychological Associations. He is author of the book *Conservation and the Consumer: Understanding Environmental Concern* (Routledge, London, 1995) and is the originator of Facet Mapping Therapy. He has authored many refereed articles and papers on various aspects of applied social psychology. Dr Hackett's research interests are in situated human behaviour, environmental concern, Facet Mapping Therapy, scale development and multidimensional data analysis.

Graham J. Hooley is Professor of Marketing and Director of Research at Aston Business School, Aston University, UK. Prior to taking up his appointment at Aston he held academic appointments at Warwick Business School and Bradford Management Centre in the UK and the University of Otago Business School in New Zealand. He has senior managerial experience in the publishing and marketing research industries and runs his own management consultancy specializing in providing strategic marketing help to both national and international companies. He has published widely in international journals in the fields of marketing, marketing strategy and quantitative methods.

Mike Hussey is Lecturer in Marketing Research at Aston Business School. Besides a generic concern for the improved application of quantitative models in business situations, his research interests include service quality tracking, brand image measurement and the role of risk in consumer choice modelling.

David Jobber is Professor of Marketing at the University of Bradford Management Centre. He has published over 100 articles on various aspects of marketing research, marketing strategy, selling and sales management. His industrial experience was with the TI Group and he has acted as a consultant to a number of national and international companies. He is a visiting lecturer at the University of Aston and the University of Warwick. He is a member of the editorial board of the *International Journal of Research in Marketing*.

Pirjo Karppinen gained a postgraduate degree in marketing. Since then she has pursued a marketing research career and is now a marketing manager responsible for marketing and product management in the ISKU Group, a leading furniture manufacturer in Scandinavia.

Simon Knox is Professor of Brand Marketing at Cranfield School of Management, Cranfield University, UK. Upon graduating, he followed a career in the marketing of international brands with Unilever plc, initially in detergents then convenience foods. As lead country manager for Europe, he launched Cup-a-Soup Special with a beverage positioning which was subsequently adopted by other country managements across Europe. Since joining Cranfield School of Management, Simon has published over 50 papers on branding and customer purchasing styles. He is the director of the institute for Advanced Research in Marketing in the School and is currently leading research into brand loyalty and customer equity issues for a consortium of companies.

Charles Marshall lectured in statistics at Silsoe College, Cranfield Institute of Technology. After graduating, Charles worked for the Agricultural and Food Research Council designing experiments for research. He publishes in statistical journals on modelling yield loss and statistical hypothesis. Charles is a member of the Royal Statistical Society.

K.E. Kristian Möller is Professor of Marketing and Head of the Marketing Department at the Helsinki School of Economics and Business Administration.

Formerly president of the European Marketing Academy, Dr Moller is an active member of the academic marketing network in Europe. His current research is focused on business marketing from a relationship and network perspective, on marketing capability and business strategy, and on theory development in marketing.

Luiz Moutinho is Professor of Marketing at University of Glasgow Business School. He was previously employed as professor of marketing at the Cardiff Business School. Having obtained his Ph.D. from the University of Sheffield, he has also held posts at a number of universities in both the UK and the USA. He has published widely and is author of many books and numerous published papers, as well as being a member of the editorial board of several international journals.

Deon Nel is Professor of Marketing at the Graduate Business School, University of Cape Town. Deon's past academic posts include a period at Aston Business School, UK and before that a position as associate professor of marketing at the University of Pretoria. He is the co-author of a marketing casebook, and has published a large number of papers in journals, such as the *Journal of Business Ethics,* the *European Journal of Marketing,* and *Industrial Marketing and Purchasing.* In recent years Deon has also presented papers at the AMA Educators' Conference: World Marketing Congress and the Pi Sigma Epsilon National Sales Management Conference in the USA. His research areas are in international marketing of services, specializing in service quality measurement and management. Currently he is a consultant to major international companies on measuring service quality.

Dianne Phillips has graduate and postgraduate qualifications in sociology and mathematical statistics. As the director of the Social Information Technology Unit at the Manchester Metropolitan University, she is responsible for the provision of design and analysis support for a wide range of social science research projects, including quality assessment and evaluation reports for external organizations. She is also chairperson of ASSESS, the SPSS Users Group. Research interests include the appraisal of categorical techniques for the measurement and analysis of social attitudes and the philosophy of statistics.

Leyland F. Pitt is Professor of Marketing at the Cardiff Business School, UK. He was formerly Professor of Management Studies at Henley Management College, UK and before that Associate Professor of Marketing at the Graduate School of Business, University of Cape Town. He has also held executive positions in industry and has taught marketing at other universities in Europe,

South Africa, Australia, South-East Asia, and the USA. Leyland Pitt has published many papers in professional and academic journals, including *Omega, The Journal of Direct Marketing, Industrial Marketing Management,* the *European Journal of Marketing* and *Psychological Reports.* His current research interests are in the area of service quality measurement, marketing organization and internet marketing.

Francesca Dall'Olmo Riley is currently Senior Lecturer at Kingston Business School, having previously worked for the Open University Business School as a research fellow. Before receiving her Ph.D. from the London Business School, she held several managerial positions in marketing in Italy, the US and the UK. Her research has been published in the main European journals.

John Saunders is Professor of Marketing and Head of Aston Business School, Aston University. Before joining Aston he was Director of the Loughborough Business School. Previous experience includes working for Bradford University Management Centre, the University of Warwick, the Pacific-Asian Management Institute (Hawaii) and the Hawker Siddeley Group. Research interests include marketing strategy, South-East Asia computer and model assisted marketing. Publications include several books, business games and many articles in leading professional journals. As a senior consultant he has worked with many companies and institutions. These include Unilever, ICI, TI, THF, Dixons, Woolworth, British Standards Institute, the Asian Development Bank and the Singapore Government.

Richard Speed is Associate Professor in Marketing at the Melbourne Business School, the University of Melbourne. His research interests and publications centre on how firms create and sustain a market orientation, decision making for marketing strategy and the use and management of brands. He is leader of the sponsorship Excellence Research Project, a major project supported by a consortium of businesses that is seeking to better understand the impact of sponsorship activity.

Marco Vriens received a masters degree in psychology from Leiden University and he received his Ph.D. degree from the University of Groningen, both in the Netherlands. He served on the faculty of both the University of Groningen and Tilburg University (the Netherlands). Currently, he is affiliated as client services director, management sciences at Research International Inc, USA. His research has appeared in international journals such as the *Journal of Marketing Research,* the *International Journal of Research in Marketing, Marketing Letters, Journal of Direct Marketing, Journal of Product Innovation Management, Journal of Marketing*

Management, Journal of Information Science, and the *Journal of the Market Research Society.*

David Walker has a Ph.D. in consumer behaviour from Cranfield School of Management. He began his career with the European Brands Group in the food brokerage division from where he has experience in research and planning in FMCG markets, notably mineral waters, pet food and confectionery. He then spent three years as a researcher at Cranfield School of Management investigating the effects of consumer involvement on repeat purchase patterns, brand loyalty and advertising recall. David joined The Planning Business in 1992 and was involved in a broad range of research and consultancy projects including pan-European NPD research, strategic brand planning, price modelling and forecasting. He is proficient in most current multivariate analysis techniques and specializes in multi-country data analysis, interpretation and modelling. He has published widely in the consumer behaviour literature. Since 1996 he has been working as a strategic planner for Coca-Cola, UK.

Trevor Webb worked in the UK electricity supply industry for more than 30 years. He is a qualified electrical engineer and is experienced in all aspects of distribution and supply of electricity, having held increasingly senior positions at many locations throughout the Midlands.

Andreas H. Zins is Associate Professor at the Institute for Tourism and Leisure Studies at the Vienna University of Economics and Business Administration (where he received his doctorate). He lectures in international marketing, business administration, tourism marketing planning, consumer and travel behaviour models. Dr Zins is active in research in the fields of tourist behaviour, marketing research, cost-benefit analyses, social impacts, computer assisted interviewing, theme parks and related leisure attractions. He has served as Project Manager of the National Austrian Guest Survey since 1988. Books on leisure attractions (1991), strategic management for tourism organisations (1993) and tourism expenditures (1996) appeared under Austrian publishers in the German language. Articles on behavioural and psychographic issues of tourism are published in the *Journal of Marketing Management, Journal of Business Research,* and *Journal of Travel Research.*

Introduction to the Second Edition

Welcome to the Second Edition of *Quantitative Methods in Marketing*. Since the publication of the first edition, the speed, power and capacity of PCs have increased many times with a resulting increase in the availability of sophisticated data analysis software.

In Lewis Carroll's book, *Through the Looking-Glass*, the nineteenth century mathematician has the Red Queen remark:

> Now, here you see, it takes all the running you can, to keep in the same place. If you want to get somewhere else, you must run at least twice as fast as that.

The Red Queen's words are certainly true of recent developments in quantitative methods but the proposition behind the second, revised edition of this book is that it is not just a question of how fast you run but, perhaps even more importantly, the direction in which you are heading.

Since the publication of the first edition, the authors have carried out extensive research across Europe to determine the most up-to-date types of quantitative techniques being used by companies, service industries and business. A summary of this research is presented in Chapter 2 but its principal findings are also reflected in the choice of new material for this expanded edition.

Of course, this does not mean that all of our original material has been discarded. Much has been retained, and basic techniques remain valid. After all, we are still using Pythagoras' theorem to calculate Euclidean distances in brand map construction – and both Pythagoras and Euclid have not been around for at least a couple of millennia.

Table 0.1 sets out some information on the uses of quantitative methods in marketing. One of the top application areas is sales forecasting and we have

TABLE 0.1 Uses of Quantitative Methods in Marketing
(n = 433 European Companies)

	Total (433)	Consumer Goods (134)	Indust Goods (113)	Consumer Services (89)	Indust Services (97)
Application areas					
Sales forecasting	72%	81%	83%	55%	60%
Market segmentation	72%	78%	74%	66%	67%
Consumer behaviour	55%	76%	35%	60%	43%
Pricing decisions	54%	63%	58%	49%	39%
Sales promotion	36%	49%	31%	24%	34%
Advertising decisions	33%	47%	20%	30%	30%
Sales force allocation	21%	25%	19%	19%	23%
Data analysis techniques used					
Data tables	83%	90%	82%	76%	81%
Graphical representation	84%	84%	87%	81%	81%
Summary statistics	79%	76%	81%	81%	77%
Tests of significance	26%	35%	17%	32%	20%
Simple regression (2 vars)	36%	46%	31%	36%	28%
Multivariate methods	29%	39%	22%	29%	21%

been fortunate to secure an accomplished contribution from world experts Scott Armstrong and Rod Brodie entitled Forecasting for Marketing (Chapter 6). Unlike many contemporary articles on forecasting which introduce Baysean smoothing and cross-spectral density estimation within the first couple of lines, Armstrong and Brodie's approach provides an invaluable plain English guide to the best forecasting techniques to use in any given situation. This article alone is worth the price of the book.

Within the multivariate methods category, multiple regression analysis proved to be the most popular technique employed (18 per cent). Much larger figures of 45 per cent and 60+ per cent were recorded for other surveys (see Chapter 2).

Not wishing to ignore these findings but conscious that there are many well written accounts of straightforward regression in other texts, we have opted to include an introduction to the topical area of hierarchical moderated regression analysis. Gordon Greenley provides a very well organized exposition of the necessary theory in Chapter 9, and with co-author Gordon Foxall, gives a first rate example of how this controversial technique can be applied in practice by investigating the relationship between stakeholder orientation and company performance in Chapter 19.

During the qualitative stages of the research described in Chapter 2, a number of marketing and marketing research directors and managers were interviewed. Overall their comments were very illuminating but the following quotation caused us some concern: *'The intelligent interpretation of data has declined since the 1960s'.*

To compensate directly for this view we have included a paper in the applications section on consumer choice in the motion picture industry. The authors of Chapter 15, Kris Moller and Pirjo Karppinen, provide a very articulate account of how a portfolio of multivariate techniques including factor analysis and discriminant analysis can be employed to provide a rich picture of the consumers' attribute variables and motives.

Another comment from our qualitative researches suggested that hard and soft marketing techniques are increasingly being used to complement each other. This is well illustrated in Chapter 8 by Paul Hackett and Gordon Foxall which uses Facit theory to model consumer motives and place evaluation within a conference centre.

The final chapter by Amanda Broderick was written specifically to complement the original erudite theoretical guide to Linear Structural Relationships (LISREL) written by Diamantopoulos – by describing a practical application of this popular technique in respect of validating the results from cross-national research.

Table 0.1 also shows that consumer goods marketers tend to make greater use of quantitative methods for various market modelling applications and in particular use the more sophisticated techniques. This is not surprising as many of the original applications of these techniques, reported in the marketing literature, occur in the consumer field and reinforces the suggestion that analysis requirements are more powerful drivers of the diffusion of new quantitative techniques in marketing, rather than technological (new technique) developments.

The editors were encouraged that the results of their research supported many of the assertions put forward in Chapter 1 of the original edition of *Quantitative Methods in Marketing*. For example: 'Familiarity with computing skills should not be confused with expertise in evaluating data.' And finally: '. . . advanced analysis techniques can enhance the value of good quantitative data. But people, expertise and experience are even more important.'

We hope that you enjoy reading this revised and expanded edition of *Quantitative Methods in Marketing*.

Michael Hussey
Graham Hooley
Aston Business School

■ □ ▨ ■ Part 1

■ □ ■ ■ 1

Quantitative Methods in Marketing: The Multivariate Jungle Revisited

Graham J. Hooley and Michael K. Hussey

Introduction

Anyone considering carrying out a word-association test using the cue 'marketing' as a stimulus might expect responses to include 'flair', 'entrepreneur', 'vision', 'instinct', 'creativity' etc.

The term 'quantitative' would come fairly low on most commentators' list of expectations. Outside of the physical sciences and astro-mathematics, however, the commercial imperative has ensured that marketing is one of the leading players when it comes to the application of quantitative methods. Now that the meteoric improvement in PC technology has brought substantial computing power to the desktops of all managers and other marketing professionals, this vast arsenal of quantitative methods – for so long the province of the 'expert' – is widely available to all who wish to experiment.

The aim of the following articles is to provide readers with a guide to some of the most recent and popular techniques currently in use as well as including typical applications to support the theoretical discussions.

Many observers (e.g Fox and Long, 1990) agree that the so called modern revolution in quantitative methods can be traced back to a paper by the statistician John Tukey (Tukey, 1962) in which the ideas of exploratory data analysis are discussed. In order to supplement the more formal testing of statistical models – often constructed under the most rigid and restrictive of assumptions – Tukey argued for a more enquiring role for quantitative methods.

In a later publication, Tukey (1977) uses the analogy of a criminal court case to illustrate his ideas. In this example the jury – deciding between guilt or innocence – are seen to be applying the more traditional hypothesis testing approach to quantitative methods. It is the investigating officers, searching for new evidence, however, who can be considered to be employing the more flexible and creative modern philosophy of exploratory analysis.

In marketing literature two publications provide useful points of reference. More than two decades ago, Sheth (1971) first chronicled what he called the 'multivariate revolution in marketing'. Although the title of the publication speaks for itself, it should be noted that the emphasis in Sheth's article was on the classical use of statistical techniques to test models that had been specified fairly rigidly.

Nearly a decade later, Hooley (1980) provides a snapshot of the contemporary 'state of the art' regarding the use of quantitative methods in marketing, while highlighting the gulf between academic theory and marketing practice.

Since the early 1980s, the exponential rise in power of microcomputers has meant that not only have new and more powerful techniques been developed but that they are available to all at relatively low cost.

This collection of articles has been written by marketing experts in the hope of bridging the gap with managers and other marketing professionals. Although accuracy is maintained at all times the paramount aim is that of explanation as opposed to definition. To quote Alt (1990): 'Definitions are the last refuge of a scoundrel; what is needed is an explanation.'

It is hoped that readers already familiar with the use of empirical techniques will enjoy 'visiting old friends' – i.e. reviewing the contemporary use of established techniques as well as exploring the more up-to-the-minute developments in second generation quantitative methods. Less experienced readers are provided with a stimulating but relatively painless guide through the main tracks, hidden paths and occasional snakepits of the quantitative jungle.

The following material could have been arranged in a number of ways, including the traditional split between predictive and descriptive techniques. However, as all of the articles contained both theoretical and applied components it was decided to organize the contents of this collection so that the first part includes those papers in which the main focus is theoretical while the second part comprises those articles with a more applied flavour. Several other themes run through the collection and these are explored in the following sections.

Graphical and pictorial presentation of data

The prime objective of any data analysis is to convert data into information. It is often said that we live in a period of 'information explosion'. We do not. In fact we live in a period where there is a 'data explosion' with more and more bits of data becoming available every second. What is important from the managerial perspective is to convert that data into something that can aid decision making. Quantitative analysis techniques act as a lens through which data can be focused to provide information. At their most basic (and often most useful) level they simply present the data in an easily assimilated and understood form.

The extra impact provided by the presentation of data in a pictorial rather than tabular format is highlighted throughout this volume. Although most of the standard devices, the bar chart, line graph and pie chart were originally invented by William Playfair, a Scottish engineer, at the end of the seventeenth century, their introduction did not pass off without some resistance No less a body than the Royal Society requested that the graphs of an early weather clock should be:

> reduce(d) into writing . . . that the society might have a specimen of the weather clock's performance before they proceed to the repairing of it
> (Hoff and Geddes, 1962; cited in Spence and Lewandowsky, 1991)

It is comforting to know that things have not changed too much. Baron and Phillips report a similar response from their modern day clients regarding the presentation of CHAID results from their shopping centre study described in Chapter 10.

There appear to be two important but distinct uses for graphical methods in the presentation of data. The first is principally to display data in a simpler or more meaningful fashion: to provide extra insights or a more holistic appreciation of the information content of the original data. The second use of pictorial methods is as an aid to making decisions regarding the next phase of analysis. Saunders' use of star plots for determining clusters (Chapter 3) or Hackett and Foxall's use of scree diagrams to select the optimum number of factors (Chapter 8) represent examples of this type of application.

For display purposes the three dimensional MDS plot of 15 competing leisure facilities provided by Zins (Chapter 17) is of considerable interest. Despite the large amounts of information contained in the diagram, readers may find themselves wishing for a couple of simpler two dimensional printouts. Somehow we get used to thinking of 'flat' illustrations and the addition of an extra dimension may provide information overload.

As well as being used to represent data, spatial illustrations may of course be used to represent relationships between variables as well as decision rules. Speed's useful flow diagram for the implementation of small sample re-use techniques (Chapter 11) is an example of the latter, while Diamantopoulos's path diagrams – which bear some similarity to the circuit diagrams used in the days of analogue computing – provide an example of the former (Chapter 12).

The use of facial icons to represent multivariate data as described by Nel, Pitt and Webb (Chapter 21) may signal the way ahead for new applications of graphical methods. The idea that separate facial features can map the individual variables in a multivariate study raises many interesting and exciting possibilities. In the area of computerized interviewing, for example, it would be fairly straightforward to program the PC to cycle through the whole range of different faces. The respondent might then be asked to pause the display when the screen showed a face which most nearly corresponded to his/her attitude on a particular question. There are, of course, some minor difficulties such as allowing for the interviewee's response time but these should not be insurmountable.

More substantial questions need to be faced in terms of a comprehensive validation of readers' reactions to these faces: how easy is it to distinguish between different faces? And how consistent is the interpretation of a single face from one observer to the next? Before long, desktop PCs could well be displaying video-fit faces both to describe multivariate data and to elicit respondents multidimensional attitudes.

Computing considerations

Nearly all of the methods described in the following pages require a computer and suitable software for their successful application. As far as software is concerned, SPSS is still the market leader in the academic sector. The recent introduction of SPSS for Windows Version 8.0 with its much improved graphics capabilities can only serve to consolidate this position. Jobber (Chapter 4) used SPSS for his logit analysis as did Baron and Phillips for their investigation of shopping centre survey data using CHAID. Zins' MDS study, could have been accomplished using SPSS, which also has a conjoint analysis option as described by Vriens (Chapter 5). Knox, Walker and Marshall (Chapter 13) used GENSTAT, a favourite with professional statisticians.

As far as the commercial sector is concerned, and particularly in the USA, STATGRAPHICS seems to be becoming the most popular data analysis package (Hussey, 1991).

Outside the world of proprietary software packages, the program disks that accompany text books can include both useful and powerful sources of analysis. Davies's example on AHP (Chapter 7) could have been conveniently automated using the software from Dyer and Forman, (1991), and Green, Carmone and Smith, (1989), in their book on multidimensional scaling, provide a comprehensive suite of programs on related techniques.

Another fruitful source of economy software for marketing applications is the shareware or public domain collections, but it should be noted that for some applications suitable software is not always readily available. Speed suggests that this is the case in respect of the jackknife and bootstrapping methods. Here it may be necessary to write one's own routines for a spreadsheet package such as Lotus or Excel.

Despite the amazing increase in the power of microcomputers over the past decade, still more is needed. Clearly, future marketing managers are not only going to need a powerful PC to do their job properly but also a comprehensive software toolkit.

Assumptions and presumptions

Throughout the collection of papers a number of assumptions are made, tested and challenged. For instance, Zins considers the traditional problem of comparing the attributes of 15 different leisure outlets. Using MDS he concludes that consumer preferences can be measured on only three separate dimensions. This reasoning can only be valid, however, if it is known that all target consumers use the same criteria to evaluate the attributes of each of the 15 locations. In segmented markets it is likely that not only do criteria vary from segment to segment, but so do perceptions and preferences.

Hackett and Foxall's factor analytic study, on the other hand, comparing the criteria used to judge two very different shopping areas, seems to suggest that this theory of homogeneous criteria is not correct. This conclusion may cause some problems for analysts who embrace a gravity theory of retail site attraction assuming homogeneous criteria.

At the level of optimal redevelopment of a single shopping centre, Baron and Phillips use chi-square automatic interaction detection (CHAID) to explore shoppers' preferences for leisure facilities. Their findings that age, and to a lesser extent, gender, influence choices is not altogether surprising. Things get interesting, however, when these two variables are combined to show, for example, that most women in the age group 25–44yrs would favour a children's fun area while nearly all men of any age are indifferent to such a facility.

Taking a closer look at grocery brands, Knox, Walker and Marshall adapt techniques developed for the measurement of consumer involvement with the purchase of durable goods to investigate levels of involvement with fast moving consumer goods. They conclude that while tinned tomatoes and kitchen towels are products engendering fairly low levels of involvement, detergents and toothpaste generate considerably higher consumer involvement. The important question, of course, is just how differing levels of involvement might affect consumer buying decisions such as increased purchasing frequency. Barnard, Barwise, Castleberry, D'O Riley and Ehrenberg also use toothpaste as one of the product categories in their study (Chapter 4), which demonstrates that individual consumer's attitudes do, in fact, vary considerably over time.

Taken together, the above findings would seem to indicate that any comprehensive model of consumer choice should include a hierarchy of stochastic variables if it is to be realistic. Whilst it would not be too difficult to specify such a model, possible techniques for solution might provide the subject matter for a volume similar to this in another ten years time.

Snapshots and overviews

The first part of this collection features articles on cluster analysis, logit modelling, conjoint analysis, analytical hierarchy process, CHAID and LISREL. The theoretical focus papers also contain a discussion of analysis techniques dealing with small sample problems.

Saunders' well reasoned article on cluster analysis emphasizes the importance of using graphical methods to ensure that the clusters generated make sense in business terms. Because the mechanical application of clustering algorithms will always generate clusters, however artificial, Saunders' nine point plan for obtaining reliable and valid cluster solutions is most welcome.

Jobber presents a fascinating introduction to the use of logit models in marketing. Logit models are examined as special cases of the log–linear model when the dependent variable is dichotomous. Of particular interest is the contrary interpretation of the critical or significant probability when (a) using minimum likelihood ratio chi-square to fit a logit model and (b) when examining incremental changes in the likelihood ratio function in order to select the model of best 'fit'.

Vriens explores the well researched area of conjoint analysis from a fresh viewpoint. By segmenting the various applications of conjoint analysis into six different clusters that are meaningful to marketeers, he provides a powerful guide for marketing professionals on just how conjoint analysis might be used to solve their problems.

Davies introduces the analytical hierarchy process (AHP) as a technique for facilitating multicriteria decision making. Using a mixture of qualitative and quantitative methods, a customized hierarchy is constructed so that the key components of any decision problem can be identified. A helpful amount of detail is included in the worked example which enables the reader to obtain a much better overall perspective of the process. Comparisons between AHP and the more widely accepted trade-off technique of conjoint analysis provide added interest.

Baron and Phillips deal with chi-square automatic interaction detection (CHAID). Explaining that the technique is easy to use, produces intuitively appealing results and is statistically valid, the authors recommend CHAID as an exploratory technique. Once the most relevant predictor variables have been identified then methods like log–linear analysis might be employed. This is one of the few papers to report client response to the analysis.

Speed draws attention to the problem of using regression techniques when sample sizes are small in Chapter 11. The issue of validating the fit of a particular model by sample re-use techniques is addressed with the utmost clarity. Both the jackknife and bootstrapping methods are considered in such a way that any marketing manager with a sample size problem will be anxious to learn more of these techniques.

Diamantopoulos (Chapter 12) provides a 'tour de force' by navigating readers through the sometimes deep waters of linear structural relationships (LISREL). LISREL, or covariance structure analysis as it is more properly called, is an example of a second generation multivariate analysis technique. In the same way that first generation multivariate techniques grew out of bivariate statistical analysis, the second generation techniques represent generalizations and extensions of first generation methods. In practice, all first generation techniques are particular cases of second generation methods (Fornell, 1987). A feature of particular importance with respect to second generation methods is their greater flexibility in terms of the interaction between theoretical constructs and empirical results.

The second part of the collection presents applications focused papers. Knox, Walker and Marshall (Chapter 13) present the first article in this section. Recent work on the development of causal models that distinguish between forms and sources of consumer involvement for consumer durables is discussed. The authors then extend their investigation to fast moving grocery products by developing a refined measuring device. Initial results of this exploratory study suggest that significant differences do indeed exist in the levels of involvement across grocery product categories.

Barnard, Barwise, Castleberry, D'O Riley and Ehrenberg (Chapter 14) describe the results of their extensive investigation into the way in which individuals' attitudes vary over time. Anyone who has had occasion to administer a questionnaire containing attitude scales will find their novel conclusions of interest. Working with large samples in both the UK and USA the authors conclude that whilst attitudinal responses to brands are generally steady in aggregate – a finding supported by panel surveys – there is considerable variation at the individual level. What effect, if any, these results have on the validity or application of Ehrenberg's models of repeat purchasing behaviour (Ehrenberg, 1988) is not clear.

Hackett and Foxall (Chapter 16) use factor analysis to investigate what considerations influence shoppers' choice of retail location for two very different settings – the first a modern shopping mall and the second a traditional city centre shopping area. Their results suggest that very different factors operate in the two situations and thus call into question the validity of the findings from more traditional gravity based models. The authors further argue that factor analysis has proved to be a very suitable tool for exploring customers' location specific values. The set of notes accompanying this chapter will be very much appreciated by readers not familiar with the technique of factor analysis.

In Chapter 17, Zins describes the results of a study which uses non-metric multidimensional scaling techniques to explore day-trippers' attitudes to 15 different types of leisure facilities ranging from archaeological sites and museums to sporting events and a zoo. Despite a rich variety of different views, three principal influencing 'factors' were determined. These might be described as (1) a cost-benefit factor; (2) a good-life factor; and (3) a gravity-transport factor.

Moutinho and Curry (Chapter 18) report on research aimed at using neural network (NN) techniques to model consumer attitudes. Employing the results from a survey of bank customers using Automatic Telling Machines (ATMs), the authors argue that their application of NNs confirms the widely held hypothesis that consumers' previous expectations about the performance of ATMs influences their level of continuing satisfaction with the financial service. More general findings about new product design and the need for continuously monitoring customer satisfaction are also reported.

Coates, Doherty and French (Chapter 20) provide a fascinating insight into the world of large marketing databases and the methods that companies use to extract meaningful information from the vast mass of data at their disposal. The authors review a number of computer based heuristic techniques which arise from applications outside the marketing field. These include simulated annealing, branch and bound and expert system methods. Many of the recent advances described in this paper will be of great interest to marketing managers.

Nel, Pitt and Webb (Chapter 21) introduce the intuitively appealing idea of using facial icons to represent multivariate service quality data. The concept underlying these graphics, or Chernoff Faces as they are called, after the statistician who first introduced them, is that each facial feature can be used to represent a different variable. The authors conclude that using such devices provides a more holistic view of the service quality position.

Finally, Amanda Broderick (Chapter 22) describes the challenges posed by increasing globalization of brands and how quantitative methods may be used with confidence in cross-national research. The chapter describes a statistically valid model which covers five European countries.

Health warning

This collection of articles has been written by marketing experts whose enthusiasm for their chosen topics is infectious. Anyone with a desktop PC and a decent statistics package can, after reading the software manual for an hour or two, have access to most of these techniques. It is important to remember, however, that all statistical models make assumptions about such matters as the method of sampling used, the functional structure of the data and the distribution of any 'error' terms. If any of these assumptions are violated then the output from such models should be interpreted with care.

Should readers be in any doubt, they may be well advised to adopt the 'Seven Commandments' approach as recommended by Sheth (1971), and reiterated by one of the editors in an earlier publication (Hooley, 1980).

For the new millennium, given the rapid increase in both computer power and availability on the desks of researchers and managers alike, the original seven dicta of the old testament might usefully be replaced or expanded by the following ten new-age commandments:

1. **Do not be technique oriented**. Focus the problem on the needs of management, then select the appropriate analytical tool, and not vice-versa. As Young (1973), put it two decades ago: 'The danger we must always avoid is becoming pedlars of techniques in search of problems rather than problem solvers in search of techniques.'
2. **Consider multivariate models as information for management**. Any model produced from multivariate techniques is an aid to managerial decision making and not a substitute for managerial judgement. The

techniques and models do not themselves make decisions, they merely provide information to help decision making.

3. **Do not substitute multivariate methods for researcher skill and imagination**. Use common sense to evaluate the results of quantitative analyses. Do not rely on statistical measures of robustness alone. Recognize the fact that data analysis is part science, part art. (See Chapter 3 by Saunders.)

4. **Develop communication skill**. Learn how to communicate findings to management in a non-technical way wherever possible. Adoption of findings as information inputs to decisions depends on management feeling confident about how the information was derived.

5. **Avoid making statistical inferences about the parameters of multi-variate models**. Beware of generalizations to populations when the nature of the sample is unclear. Most techniques make some assumptions about the nature of the sample. Make sure that these assumptions are both known and upheld.

6. **Guard against the danger of making inferences about market realities when such inferences may be due to the peculiarities of the method**. Do not take results at face value. Even where high levels of statistical significance can be attached to the findings, ensure that the results have a sound theoretical and common sense basis. Where possible use split samples to validate models developed on fresh data. (See Chapter 11 by Speed.)

7. **Exploit the complementary relationship between descriptive and predictive methods**. Don't use techniques in isolation where other techniques may add to the information obtained, or further validate findings. Often techniques can helpfully be used in sequence.

8. **Avoid the temptation to over analyse**. Resist using the power of the computer to analyse to the nth degree issues which might be better approached through simpler techniques. Frequency counts and bar charts are still very powerful ways of conveying information. There may be no need to adopt more sophisticated techniques just because they are on the desktop.

9. **Start at the beginning**. The correct place to commence any data analysis exercise is well before any of the numbers have been collected. By thinking through the main features of the proposed analysis *a priori*, many potential problems involved in the execution of a particular technique can be avoided.

10. **Keep an eye on the cost-benefit factors**. Collecting information costs money. Do not collect data just because 'it would be nice to know'.

Resources used to collect and analyse redundant data might be more profitably used for other marketing activities.

Used appropriately and with care the vast array of quantitative techniques now available can enrich and enlighten the marketing decision-making process. Used inappropriately or sloppily they can confuse or even mislead. It is hoped that this collection of papers will contribute to a better understanding both of their potential and their limitations.

References

Alt, M. (1990), *Exploring Hyperspace*, Maidenhead: McGraw-Hill

Dyer, R.F. and Forman, E.H. (1991), *An Analytical Approach to Marketing Decisions*, Englewood Cliffs: Prentice-Hall

Ehrenberg, A.S.C. (1988), *Repeat Buying: Facts, Theory and Applications*, London: Charles Griffen and Co. Ltd

Fornell, C. (1987), A second generation of multivariate analysis: classification of methods and implications for marketing research. In M.J. Hountan (Ed.), *Review of Marketing*, American Marketing Association, pp. 407– 450

Fox, J. and Long J.S. (1990), Eds, *Modern Methods of Data Analysis*, Newbury Park: Sage

Green, P.E., Carmone, F.J. Jnr and Smith, S.M. (1989), *Multidimensional Scaling: Concepts and Applications*, Needham Heights: Allyn and Bacon

Hair, J.F. Jnr, Anderson, R.E., Tatham, R.L. and Black, W.C. (1992), *Multivariate Data Analysis*. (3rd Edn), New York: Macmillan

Hoff, H.E. and Geddes, L.A. (1962), The beginnings of graphic recording, *Isis*, Vol 33, pp. 287–324

Hooley, G.J. (1980), Ed. A guide to the use of quantitative techniques in marketing. *European Journal of Marketing*. (Special Issue), Vol 14, pp. 379– 448

Hussey, M.K. (1991), Painting by numbers, *PC Today*, Vol 5, pp. 148–152

Kass, G., (1980), An exploratory technique for investigating large quantities of categorical data, *Applied Statistics*, Vol 29, pp. 127–129

Maren, A., Harston, C. and Pap, R. (1990), *Handbook of Neural Computing Applications*, London: Academic Press, Inc

Saaty, T.L., (1980), *The Analytic Hierarchy Process*, New York: McGraw-Hill, pp. 165–192

Sheth, J.N., (1971), The multivariate revolution in marketing research, *Journal of Marketing*, January 1971, pp. 13–19

Spence, I., and Lewandowsky, S. (1991), Graphical perception, In R.F. Dyer and E.H. Forman (Eds), *Modern Methods of Data Analysis*, Newbury Park: Sage, pp. 13–57

Tukey, J.W. (1962), The future of data analysis, *Annals of Mathematical Statistics*, Vol 3, pp. 1–67

Tukey, J.W. (1977), *Exploratory data analysis*, Reading, MA: Addison-Wesley

Young, S. (1973), Pitfalls down the primrose path of attitude segementation, *European Research*, November 1973, pp. 157–73

■ □ ▣ ■ 2

The Diffusion of Quantitative Methods into Marketing Management

Michael K. Hussey and Graham J. Hooley

This paper investigates the extent to which various quantitative techniques are employed in marketing across Europe. Marketing practitioners, marketing services providers and marketing educators were all surveyed in a pan-European study aimed at uncovering the extent of diffusion into practice of quantitative methods. The impact of the PC revolution and its subsequent effect on the use of quantitative methods in marketing was a common theme with practitioners, marketing researchers and educators alike. Most see this as a positive development making more sophisticated and potentially useful data analysis techniques more widely available. There is a minority, however, who are more sceptical and warn of the dangers such computing power puts into relatively inexperienced hands. Despite the increased use of computers, and the wider availability of modelling software, the most popular quantitative techniques are still the most basic data summary and presentation methods. Marketing students receive only a limited exposure to advanced quantitative methods and practitioners typically find little use for the more sophisticated techniques.

Introduction

The application of quantitative techniques to business has long been a subject of contention. For the quantitatively literate they offer a wealth of opportunities to explore data afresh and gain new insights into marketing phenomena. For the 'quantitatively challenged' they produce scepticism or strike downright fear into the heart. It has long been so. In Elizabethan times an unknown scholar penned the lines:

Multiplication is vexation,
Division is as bad;
The Rule of three doth puzzle me,
And practice drives me mad.

(Anon, 1570)

A few decades later the most advanced data analysis techniques of the day were being mobilized in an effort to consolidate the first shoots of a commercial renaissance that resulted in the first Industrial Revolution (Swertz, 1987).

As far as marketing is concerned, this polarization of views was still very much in evidence during the 1960s and still exists to this day. Adler (1967) suggested the following caricature of a marketing executive, which might now be recognized as the seeds of postmodernism in marketing thought (see Brown, 1994):

> A good many marketing executives, in the deepest recesses of their psyches, are artists, not analysts. For them, marketing is an art form, and in my opinion, they really do not want it to be any other way. Their temperament is antipathetic to system, order, knowledge. They enjoy flying by the seat of their pants – though you will never get them to admit it. They revel in chaos, abhor facts and fear research. They hate to be trammelled by written plans. And they love to spend but are loath to assess the results of their spending.
>
> (Adler 1967; cited in Lilien and Kotler 1983)

Despite the evidence for relatively low levels of quantitative sophistication amongst marketing managers, Rivett (1972) suggested that it is hard to see how (marketing) executives of the future will succeed without a grounding in mathematics, probability and statistics.

Today, even the most cursory survey of the academic marketing literature will reveal a continuing polarization between those employing quantitative methods in their research, typically pursuing 'scientific', or 'modern' paradigms, and those eschewing quantitative rigour in favour of the more eclectic post-modern perspective. For the scientists, the PC revolution, putting computers on the desks of managers, researchers, academics and students alike, has afforded substantially increased opportunities to use the more sophisticated and advanced techniques, once the preserve of the expert with access to proprietary, and often obscure, software. For the post-modernist it has resulted in over analysis of the inherently unanalysable.

The purpose of this study is to examine the extent to which quantitative methods are used in marketing. No judgement is made about the relative merits of the competing paradigms nor indeed about the relevance of the individual techniques as a means to understanding marketing phenomena. The objective is simply to examine the use of quantitative methods in practice.

Methodology

The research process commenced with a series of in-depth, semi-structured interviews with marketing and marketing research practitioners to explore their views on and use of quantitative methods. Twelve interviews were conducted to shed light on their awareness and knowledge of statistical jargon and their level of use of individual techniques.

As a result of these exploratory interviews three sets of questionnaires were drawn up, one for each of the three main constituencies in the research: marketing practitioners; marketing research providers; and marketing educators. Figure 2.1 shows the research framework adopted.

The starting point was to examine what is taught to marketing students on marketing courses. These students are the marketing executives of the future and it might be expected that what they learn will diffuse into practice with them. Some of these graduates may go into marketing research jobs, while others may pursue careers as marketing managers. Hence the flow from education into both other constituencies of individuals, theory and advice.

This first survey was of marketing professors in leading European universities and business schools. The sample was drawn from the membership

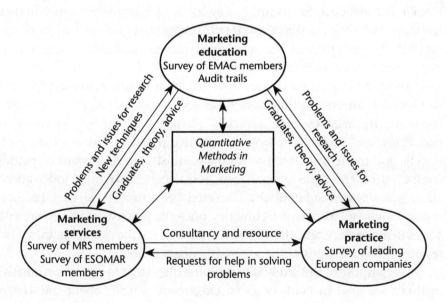

FIGURE 2.1 The research framework

lists of EMAC, the European Marketing Academy, now widely considered the premier marketing academic body in Europe. Responses were obtained from 37 members in total, a response rate of 21 per cent (see the Appendix to this chapter for methodology).

Second, marketing research professionals were surveyed. As gatherers, analysers and interpreters of marketing data these professionals might be expected to be at the leading edge of application of the newer, more advanced quantitative techniques. The research providers interact with marketing practitioners by providing expertise and consultancy services. They may also interact with marketing education by having input into syllabus design, suggesting areas for educational emphasis and also providing issues for academic research. This part of the survey drew on the mailing lists of the European Society for Opinion and Market Research (ESOMAR). Responses were obtained from 20 European countries. (See the Appendix for more detailed methodology). In total 247 companies replied to the questionnaires, a response rate of 37 per cent.

Third, marketing practitioners were questioned about what techniques they use. Clearly their needs for the more advanced techniques are likely to be more limited than the research professionals and their focus more on decision making than on data analysis or interpretation. Marketing practitioners set the agenda for marketing research through requests for help in solving problems. They may also interact with marketing education through input to syllabus design and to research agendas in the same way that research professionals do.

Surveys were conducted of leading businesses in six European countries, the United Kingdom, Germany, Belgium, the Netherlands, France and Spain with Japan being included for comparison purposes (see the Appendix for methodology). In total 435 companies replied, representing an average response rate of 11 per cent, from a wide spectrum of backgrounds presenting a comprehensive and unique picture of European marketing.

Results

The initial interviews showed that for most marketing professionals and researchers the bottom line was either solving their own problems or producing solutions to their client's problems. Few had much interest in quantitative methods for their own sake – they were a means to an end rather than an end in themselves. However, because marketing systems tend to be highly complex, models, summaries and approximations are widely used to help simplify decision making.

While many respondents expressed interest in seeing new techniques developed and implemented, there was a degree of cynicism over how new many techniques really are. One research director put forward the following, somewhat cynical, verbal model for the cyclical reinvention of some more advanced quantitative methods:

> A new technique tends to be adopted in a small way. Once successful it attracts 'followers' and soon becomes mainstream. Sooner or later its popularity leads to overuse and then to misuse with a consequent falling from favour. Such techniques (e.g. AID) are then consigned to the wilderness where they languish for seven or eight years before being re-invented and the cycle repeated.

Virtually all of the models employed tended to be either iconic/graphical or symbolic/mathematical in nature. The most popular type of modelling technique appeared to be to use the computer to interrogate a complex symbolic model and then to use a graphical user interface to present the results. This would seem to reinforce the theme of a general preference for pictures as opposed to numbers which tended to be echoed throughout the investigation.

The modelling process

Most research professionals interviewed emphasized the importance of good modelling skills in the solution of their client's quantitative problems. The choice of data analysis technique was thought to be only a part of the overall model selection process. Smaller companies would tend to use a specialist modelling expert to help develop their conceptual model. Most larger companies had their own in-house expert. Many respondents felt that qualitative and quantitative methods were now seen as complementary – with both having important parts to play in the overall modelling process.

The low costs and substantially increased power specification of modern PCs mean that many marketing research companies now carry out their own data analysis. It is not just a matter of economics but more a matter of control. Desktop PCs enable analysts to work interactively – something that is not possible if work is processed in batch mode by an outside data processing bureau.

When it comes to presenting the final outcome of a project all clients will expect an interpretative report telling them what the numbers mean in marketing terms. Almost always, someone in the client company will want to be taken through the technical report. This might be the manager who has actually commissioned the work or a technical expert.

Sometimes marketing research companies are able to provide their clients with a working model. This might occur, for example, in a study using conjoint analysis where the final part-worths determined by the model are downloaded into a spreadsheet for the client to carry out their own 'what if' type of investigation.

Most respondents felt that the choice of model was a heuristic trial and error or matching process in which alternative model formulations were paired with different types of data analysis technique and evaluated against the different data collection and communication possibilities. A visual representation of this process is shown in Figure 2.2.

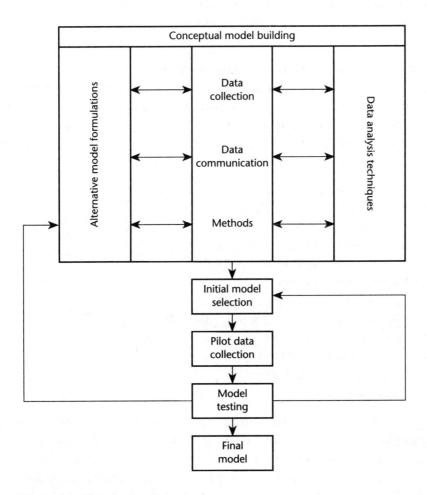

FIGURE 2.2 Conceptual model building

Perceptions of quantitative methods within a modelling framework

In order to try to determine the dimensions used by professional researchers in their appreciation of the different types of quantitative techniques available to them within the modelling process, triadic elicitation, on the lines of the Kelly repertory grid, was used. After a prior qualitative check to verify the suitability of the terms used, respondents were presented with 18 cards with the following element names written on them:

Statistical significance tests	Conjoint analysis	Multidimensional scaling
Correspondence analysis	Factor analysis	Frequency tables
Cross-tabulations	Graphical representation	Exponential smoothing
Two variable lin. regression	Cluster analysis	ARIMA modelling
LISREL	Multiple regression	Summary statistics
AID	Discriminant analysis	Log-linear analysis

They were first asked to remove any elements with which they were not familiar. The remaining cards were then presented to them in random triads and they were asked to divide each triad into a pair and a single element in such a way that the pair differed from the remaining card in a particular way. The most popular constructs obtained by this method are listed below together with the frequency of mentions:

1. Pictures – Numbers (6)
2. Data display – Data analysis (3)
3. Established – Recent (4)
4. One Variable – Many variables (4)
5. People – Variables (3)
6. Original data – Extended data (4)
7. Routine – Special use (6)
8. Agency suggestion – Client suggestion (3)
9. Low cost – High cost (4)
10. Data reduction – Data extension (3)
11. Exploring – Deciding (3)
12. Sorting – Explaining (3)

A further dozen or so varied but less popular constructs were given. Clearly, constructs numbered 7, 8 and 9 relate to the way companies see quantitative methods in terms of their professional practice. From informal analyses carried out on statistically sophisticated third parties (quantitative academics and researchers), constructs 3, 7 and 9 seem to be very highly correlated. In other words, established techniques are carried out as a matter of routine largely because they have a relatively low cost base. An informal cluster analysis on the same elements suggested that the different quantitative techniques might be grouped in the following fashion:

Group 1   Statistical significance tests

Group 2   Graphical representation of data, Summary statistics, Frequency tables, Cross-tabulations

Group 3   Factor analysis, Cluster analysis, MDS, Discriminant analysis, AID, Log-linear analysis, LISREL

Group 4   Two variable linear regression, multiple regression, exponential smoothing, ARIMA

The first group might be considered to represent deciding techniques. They are used to decide whether one set of findings differ from another. The second group represent basic data summary techniques whilst group 4 refers to 'explaining' methods. Group 3 seems to consist of a mixture of sorting and describing techniques. Many respondents would group these together as 'multivariate'.

The spread of quantitative methods in modelling

The four main sources of new quantitative ideas for companies in the marketing and marketing research industries are represented in Figure 2.3.

New ideas from staff usually come about as a result of external training courses or staff being recruited from other (marketing research) companies. Overall, the marketing research industry takes professional training very seriously and it is not unusual for companies to send their analysts on updating courses every 6–12 months.

New recruits to the profession are usually graduates but come from a wide variety of subject backgrounds. The most popular qualification for recently recruited quantitative analysts seemed to be, perhaps surprisingly, a languages degree. It is unlikely that new graduates contribute very much in the way of new data analysis techniques to an established marketing research company.

Occasionally clients will request the use of a particular technique – over and above the routine data tables, summary statistics and graphical devices that they will expect as a matter of course. Sometimes this will arise because of repeat business where either the current agency or one that the client used previously has suggested a particular form of analysis and the client wants the same analysis techniques to be used. Very occasionally a client will request the use of a particular data analysis technique just because it is fashionable.

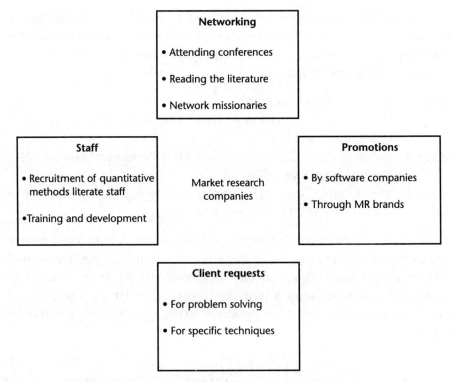

FIGURE 2.3 Sources of new quantitative techniques

Software companies' promotion of their products plays a large part in the adoption of new quantitative techniques by marketing research companies. Research executives are constantly bombarded by literature, demonstration disks and offers of places on training courses by promoters of statistical packages such as SPSS, SAS and STATGRAPHICS. Once the research company has bought the software, further new techniques are discovered by experimenting with the various program options.

Another type of promotion involves specialist software companies or the larger marketing research companies selling 'branded' quantitative methods. Here, the particular basic raw technique has been packaged with a user-friendly interface in a form that is more directly relevant to marketing research applications. Sometimes the research company using such branded products will supply a qualitative front and back end service.

Perhaps the most important source of new quantitative ideas is networking. Often, new quantitative techniques will be introduced into a company via a director who has met a colleague at a seminar or conference and bought or licensed a particular software package. Again, senior managers are often approached directly by network contacts with a view to acquiring new software. It is worth noting at this stage that virtually all new quantitative techniques of relevance to marketing research are PC driven.

Network missionaries also play a significant part in the spread of new techniques but their influence may not be altogether beneficial. Network missionaries are 'evangelists', who spread the word about the particular technique which is the subject of their current obsession with an almost religious fervour. They are not necessarily motivated by commercial gain but more by a desire to convert more followers to their cause. These pedlars of quantitative techniques are best avoided as they are usually more interested in redefining a problem to fit their technique rather than the other way round.

Most companies in the UK keep in touch with current developments in the applications of quantitative techniques to research by reading the Market Research Society's publications. In Europe, most companies quoted ESOMAR publications and the US *Journal of Marketing Research* as their staple source of reference. Besides reading the popular weekly marketing magazines, *Marketing*, *Marketing Week* and *Campaign* in the UK, most companies were likely to read magazines in the area in which they specialize, e.g. finance, health, telecommunications and cars.

Overall, marketing research companies see themselves as very much the passive partner when it comes to the adoption of new data analysis techniques. Pressure from the various players mentioned above means that they rarely have to go looking for something new but can afford to be reactive when it comes to facing a novel quantitative challenge.

The questioning of respondents in the present survey sought to identify the time it takes for new techniques to filter through from initial publication to practical use. A very wide variety of answers was found ranging from '2–3 months', through '2–3 years' to 'over 10 years' or even 'never'. Clearly the diffusion time is dependent on the particular technique and its relevance to solving practical marketing problems.

The modal figure was around three years but specific variations were pointed out in that correspondence analysis was developed in the 1960s but not used widely (apart from in France) until the 1980s and neural networks were initially mentioned in the early editions of *Star Trek* but are only now beginning to be used in a tentative fashion in marketing. Cluster analysis, on the other hand, was thought to have been first published in 1967 and applied to marketing problems in the same year.

The point was made that some of the larger marketing research companies both undertake and publish a fair amount of original research. However, they are unlikely to publish while their technique still affords them some measure of competitive advantage. As one respondent said: 'We do not publish our new (methodological) work for some time. Only by constant technical development can we stay ahead of the game.' Several comments related to the 'fashion' element in the use of new quantitative techniques: '(The use of quantitative techniques) definitely goes in waves – certain techniques being "hot-news" and others keep being re-invented' or 'New techniques can die within a year. Where has trade-off analysis gone to?' The consensus opinion seemed to agree that certain techniques were prone to be rediscovered every eight to ten years.

Quantitative methods used in marketing research and industry

Data from the quantitative surveys are now presented and discussed. Data are drawn from the samples of marketing research professionals (the ESOMAR respondents) and leading European businesses. Findings discussed in this section are presented under three main headings:

- Market modelling applications
- Data analysis techniques used
- The impact of computers.

General results across Europe are considered and, where appropriate, differences in use between countries are highlighted.

Market modelling applications

The first part of Table 2.1 shows the areas of marketing in which practitioners report the use of quantitative techniques (for a recent review of the arena of market modelling see Lilien, 1994). Results have been broken down by country of the respondent.

Consumer behaviour applications were much more likely amongst German, Spanish and UK companies than the sample average. They were less likely amongst Japanese, Belgian and Dutch companies. Market segmentation applications were most common amongst Spanish, French, German and UK companies. Sales forecasting applications were most common in the UK and Germany while pricing applications were most likely in Spain and the UK. Distribution applications were much more likely in Germany and the Netherlands, and advertising applications in Germany and Spain. Advertising applications were much less likely in Japan where only 9 per cent of companies reported their use compared to a whole sample average of 33 per cent. As with advertising applications, sales promotion uses were most likely in Germany

TABLE 2.1 Country variations in application of quantitative techniques (survey of leading European companies)

	Total (435) %	UK (112) %	Germany (72) %	Belgium (59) %	Netherlands (53) %	France (44) %	Spain (63) %	Japan (32) %
Market modelling applications								
Consumer behaviour	55	58	74	44	45	50	60	34
Market segmentation	72	75	76	63	62	80	81	59
Sales forecasting	72	79	78	63	62	73	70	69
Pricing decisions	54	60	54	53	47	41	64	41
Distribution decisions	29	24	47	24	42	25	22	19
Advertising decisions	33	30	58	22	21	25	44	9
Sales promotion	36	37	54	25	25	16	48	31
Sales force allocation	21	37	19	25	17	0	24	19
Data analysis techniques used								
Data tables	83	88	89	83	83	96	83	44
Graphical representation	84	90	90	81	74	96	79	59
Summary statistics	79	88	82	78	60	82	79	66
Tests of significance	26	45	15	22	28	18	22	13
Simple regression (2 vars)	36	40	42	29	38	32	33	31
Multivariate methods	29	37	29	22	25	32	27	19
Regular use of								
Correspondence analysis	12	10	9	14	9	24	21	27
Regression analysis	18	20	20	10	19	18	33	27
Cluster analysis	15	20	17	16	21	8	18	9
Factor analysis	12	12	18	20	12	18	0	18
Discriminant analysis	8	5	9	14	9	18	6	0
Multidimensional scaling	6	5	10	8	7	3	3	0
Conjoint analysis	4	8	3	6	0	0	3	0
Trade-off analysis	6	11	5	4	7	0	3	0
Simulation	9	10	8	6	16	11	12	18
LISREL	0	0	3	0	0	0	0	0

and Spain but much less likely in France. Sales force allocation applications were most common in the UK and to a lesser extent Belgium and Spain.

Overall it can be seen that German, UK and Spanish companies tend to make greater use and application of quantitative techniques for marketing modelling while the Japanese, French and Belgians make less use.

Variations in the use of data analysis and presentation techniques were not particularly marked. In all cases, however, the UK companies reported a consistently greater application of techniques than the overall sample average. Similarly the Japanese companies reported lower application levels.

More striking differences were found in the application of specific multivariate techniques. Correspondence analysis, for example, recently introduced into the English speaking world by American academics has a relatively high usage rate in France and Japan. Indeed, the set of techniques that comprise correspondence analysis have long been used in France as a means of graphically portraying relationships between objects and variables. It has been the French equivalent of multidimensional scaling. Because applications had been written up and published in French, however, their use in predominantly English speaking countries had been limited. Multi-dimensional scaling applications have, on the other hand, been more widely used in Germany, Belgium and the Netherlands.

Regression techniques are particularly widely used in Spain while applications of conjoint analysis and its allied techniques of trade-off analysis seem more popular in the UK. Discriminant analysis was more widely applied in France than the other countries. Simulation methods were most widespread in Japan. Germany reported the only incidences (2 companies) of the regular use of the relatively new LISREL technique.

Data analysis techniques used by marketing services companies

Table 2.2 shows relatively similar levels of usage of the simpler univariate statistics by market researchers across the seven countries in the survey. At the bivariate analysis level, however, differences begin to emerge with the Dutch increasingly using more sophisticated techniques such as regression and the French and Spanish using correspondence analysis.

With regard to multivariate techniques the Dutch were again the heaviest users overall, on average reporting twice the usage levels of the UK respondents. The next biggest users of multivariate techniques were the Germans and the French, followed by the Belgians. Across this sample the UK respondents appeared less likely to use the more advanced techniques than their Continental counterparts.

The impact of computers

In 1979, before the PC revolution had really begun, the following prophetic words forecast what was likely to happen in the ten years ahead:

> an order-of-magnitude increase in the amount of marketing data used; a similar tenfold increase in the computer power available for

TABLE 2.2 Use of data analysis techniques by marketing research companies by country (ESOMAR sample)

ESOMAR sample	Total (182) %	UK (54) %	Germany (43) %	Belgium (12) %	Netherlands (15) %	France (22) %	Spain (15) %	Italy (21) %
Univariate techniques								
Frequency counts	86	82	95	75	80	91	100	71
Graphical representation	85	80	98	67	73	96	93	76
Summary statistics	86	87	95	75	73	82	100	76
Bivariate techniques								
Correlation	60	43	81	42	80	59	80	43
Cross tabulation	88	89	98	75	80	86	100	71
Two variable regression	37	22	49	25	67	32	60	29
ARIMA modelling	3	2	2	0	7	5	7	0
Exponential smoothing	11	9	9	8	7	32	7	5
Correspondence analysis	44	37	21	42	53	77	73	48
Multivariate techniques								
Multiple regression	45	35	49	33	60	55	60	38
Cluster analysis	60	52	67	58	73	68	47	62
Factor analysis	62	48	63	58	87	73	67	62
Discriminant analysis	39	22	47	42	60	55	27	38
Conjoint analysis	36	33	35	34	67	36	20	33
Log-linear analysis	9	9	14	0	13	9	7	0
Multidimensional scaling	13	11	16	17	40	5	7	0
AID	10	17	5	17	27	0	0	5
LISREL	4	0	7	0	33	0	0	0

marketing analysis: a shift from market-status reporting to market-response reporting; and a new methodology for supporting strategy development (Little, 1979)

Now that most of the above predictions have come to pass and if anything seem conservative, a major focus of this research is to assess their impact both on marketing management and marketing research. A number of attitudinal statements, generated from prior qualitative research, were presented to respondents and they were asked to indicate the strength of their agreement or disagreement with each.

There was a great deal of variation in response to many of the statements given. Broad agreement was reached, however, with respect to the following:

- First, it is generally agreed that more sophisticated modelling is now carried out (76 per cent agree or strongly agree) and that multivariate techniques of data analysis are now used more extensively (73 per cent agree or strongly agree).
- Second, it is also generally agreed that wider availability of computers has increased client expectations in terms of the speed of response to their needs (79 per cent agree or strongly agree).

The other questions posed showed often bi-polar responses, some respondents agreeing while others disagreed. To clarify the data the full sample was submitted to a cluster analysis, based on the responses to these attitudinal statements. The clustering was carried out using K-means method under SPSS for Windows and cluster clarity was assessed using discriminant analysis and cross-tabulation (chi-square) techniques.

The clustering process was carried out on the full five point scales for each statement but for clarity of presentation the scale has been shortened to three points: agree; no opinion; and disagree. In total 19 respondents were deleted from the analysis due to incomplete data hence the usable sample was 228.

Four clusters emerged from the analysis:

1. Problem solvers
2. Cautious enthusiasts
3. Computer sceptics
4. Efficiency gainers.

The clusters are presented in Table 2.3.

The four clusters can be interpreted as follows:

Cluster 1: Problem solvers

This group, comprising just over one fifth of the usable sample (21 per cent), strongly agree that more sophisticated modelling is now being carried out and that multivariate techniques are more extensively used. Perhaps surprisingly, and differentiating them dramatically from the remainder of the sample, they disagree that more computers mean more data analysis. This suggests that the group believe the increase in sophistication of modelling and in the use of multivariate techniques has not been fuelled specifically by the availability of computer hardware and software. Further work with these respondents suggests their view is that wider use of quantitative techniques has been driven more by the problems researchers have set out to solve, rather than by the availability of computer hardware and software.

TABLE 2.3 Clustering of respondents on attitude statements (ESOMAR Sample)

Statement		Usable sample (228) %	Cluster 1 (49) %	Cluster 2 (72) %	Cluster 3 (53) %	Cluster 4 (54) %
More computers mean more data analysis	Agree	56.1	6.1	84.7	39.6	79.6
	N/Op	12.3	18.4	11.1	7.5	13.0
	Disagree	31.6	75.5	4.2	52.8	7.4
More sophisticated modelling is now carried out	Agree	79.4	89.8	94.4	81.1	48.1
	N/Op	12.3	8.2	4.2	9.4	29.6
	Disagree	8.3	2.0	1.4	9.4	22.2
Multivariate techniques are now used more extensively	Agree	74.6	95.9	95.8	71.7	29.6
	N/Op	10.5	2.0	2.8	13.2	25.9
	Disagree	14.9	2.0	1.4	15.1	44.4
Increased computing power leads to better marketing research	Agree	61.4	61.2	95.8	22.6	53.7
	N/Op	9.2	8.2	2.8	13.2	14.8
	Disagree	29.4	30.6	1.4	64.2	31.5
Computers have lowered the costs of marketing research studies	Agree	57.9	89.8	50.0	1.9	94.4
	N/Op	8.8	10.2	12.5	7.5	3.7
	Disagree	33.3	0.0	37.5	90.6	1.9
Wider availability of computers leads clients to expect a faster response	Agree	82.5	87.8	87.5	66.0	87.0
	N/Op	7.5	2.0	9.7	5.7	11.1
	Disagree	10.1	10.2	2.8	28.3	1.9
There is a current backlash against quantitative techniques	Agree	14.0	6.1	13.9	15.1	20.4
	N/Op	28.1	22.4	36.1	24.5	25.9
	Disagree	57.9	71.4	50.0	60.4	53.7
Wider availability of hardware and software leads to dangers of misuse	Agree	39.0	22.4	55.6	35.8	35.2
	N/Op	19.7	20.4	20.8	11.3	25.9
	Disagree	41.2	57.1	23.6	52.8	38.9

The group also strongly believe that computers have lowered the costs of marketing research and they are the group who disagree most with the statement that wider availability of hardware and software leads to dangers of their misuse.

Cluster 2: Cautious enthusiasts

The second grouping to emerge represents nearly one third of respondents (32 per cent). This group strongly agree that the advent of computers has increased the amount of data analysis carried out and that there is more sophisticated modelling carried out together with the more extensive use of multivariate techniques. The group are labelled 'enthusiasts' because they generally believe that increased computer power leads to better research. They are labelled 'cautious' because they also agree with the statement that wider availability of hardware and software leads to dangers of misuse or inappropriate use.

Cluster 3: Computer sceptics

The third grouping, a further quarter of the total sample (23 per cent), agree that there is more sophisticated modelling taking place and that multivariate techniques are now more extensively used. They typically disagree, however, that increased computing power leads to better marketing research and disagree that computers have lowered the costs of marketing research. This group were also more likely than the sample as a whole to disagree with the statement that more computers mean more data analysis.

Cluster 4: Efficiency gainers

The final grouping, again one quarter (24 per cent) of the total sample, report generally diverse views on many of the questions raised. Indeed a larger sample might have resulted in a subclustering of this group. Where they do agree, however, is that computers have lowered the costs of marketing research studies and allow clients to expect faster response to their individual needs.

The four clusters described above demonstrate that opinions on the impact of computers do vary somewhat even across even a relatively homogeneous community such as the market research industry. One possible explanation for this might be the different views expressed by companies whose work is largely qualitative as opposed to others who may specialize in more quantitative techniques. To some extent company size is a surrogate for the type of techniques in which a company might choose to specialize, with smaller companies tending to favour the softer, more qualitative approaches. In other words, the variations in attitude to the impact of PCs may simply be a reflection of company size.

The teaching of quantitative methods on marketing courses

Having examined the mix of quantitative methods used in companies and the marketing services sector, it is sensible to question how well the academic sector (the service provider) mirrors this mix.

With this end in mind the link between what is taught and researched in the universities and business schools and what finally filters into commercial practice, was also investigated at the supply end of the chain, by surveying members of the European Marketing Academy (EMAC). At the undergraduate level quantitative methods are extensively used on marketing research courses and, where offered, on sales forecasting courses, but figure less in straight marketing courses. It is primarily at the postgraduate level, however, that specific courses in quantitative methods in marketing are generally offered. This is typically in specialist MSc courses rather than MBAs. Table 2.4 shows which quantitative methods are taught on marketing courses and by whom they are taught.

TABLE 2.4 Quantitative methods taught on marketing courses (EMAC Sample n=37)

Technique	Taught by marketing staff %	Taught by non-marketing staff %	Not taught to marketing students %
Univariate techniques			
Frequency counts	45.9	70.3	2.7
Graphical Representation	43.2	70.3	2.7
Summary statistics	45.9	78.4	0.0
Bivariate techniques			
Correlation	54.1	70.3	0.0
Cross tabulation	59.4	73.0	0.0
Regression	56.8	67.6	0.0
ARIMA modelling	10.8	37.8	27.0
Exponential smoothing	24.3	59.5	10.8
Correspondence analysis	35.1	13.5	24.3
Multivariate techniques			
Multiple regression	62.2	64.9	2.7
Cluster analysis	64.9	27.0	13.5
Factor analysis	73.0	29.7	5.4
Discriminant analysis	64.9	27.0	10.8
Conjoint analysis	64.9	18.9	10.8
Log-linear analysis	16.2	35.1	32.4
Multidimensional scaling	64.9	13.5	10.8
AID	27.0	10.8	25.1
LISREL	29.7	10.8	32.4

Basic quantitative methods such as univariate and bivariate techniques are usually taught to marketing students by non-marketing staff (typically statistics specialists). Multivariate techniques, however, are more often taught by marketing staff. At first sight this may seem strange but reflects the more specialized nature of these techniques and their more immediate application in marketing.

Student exposure to all types of computers is widespread but the increased use of PCs is especially significant. The research showed that quantitative skills were considered by academic respondents to be equally important to creative, general analytical, strategic planning and financial skills for those considering future careers in marketing. They are generally considered less important, however, than the soft, interpersonal and communication skills so necessary in management in general and marketing in particular.

The role of academics in stimulating the introduction and use of new quantitative techniques in marketing is more limited than was first anticipated. As discussed above, new graduates are generally unlikely to have studied the techniques to any depth on marketing courses (and the preliminary qualitative research interviews showed that many graduate recruits to both marketing and marketing research jobs do not even specialize in marketing at undergraduate level anyway).

Links between the marketing research companies and academics is limited, with some new techniques being developed by practitioners and then filtering back to academics, rather than vice versa. There is, however, evidence of stronger links between leading commercial companies and academic institutions and indeed the impact of recent graduates on these institutions is also greater.

A mismatch in perceptions between marketing academics and marketing research practitioners as to the speed of diffusion of new data analysis methods was found. Academics generally believe that it takes longer for practitioners to adopt new techniques than the practitioners themselves believe. This may be due to academics becoming aware of techniques earlier (in the less 'practitioner accessible' scientific journals) or may simply reflect a limited view of practice by academics. Across all of the studies a modal value of some 3–5 years for the period between the publication of a new technique and its use by marketing practitioners was evident. It is recognized, however, that there will be a wide variation in this figure depending on the ease of implementation and immediate usefulness of any new technique.

Conclusions and implications

Access to computers is widespread with marketing managers, research analysts and most marketing academics benefiting from what amounts to a 'one per desk' information technology policy in many organizations. The most popular applications – apart from the ubiquitous word processing – tended to be spreadsheets and databases, with many of the research agencies using proprietary survey analysis packages or their own in-house versions. For more sophisticated data analysis and market modelling, SPSS was the favourite off the shelf package with SAS coming second a good way behind.

When it comes to the type of data analysis methods actually used by companies and research agencies, the most familiar and commonly used were the basic techniques of frequency counts, graphical representation, summary statistics and cross tabulation. These were used by as many as 80 per cent of the respondents.

More sophisticated analyses – often using multivariate techniques – were popular with the larger research firms. Cluster analysis and factor analysis were the most widely used with regression analysis, conjoint analysis and discriminant analysis also receiving numerous mentions. Smaller agencies tended more towards a qualitative focus as a means of supporting their basic data analysis.

Occasionally, conflicting messages were obtained from the different surveys in respect of country comparisons. The survey of leading European companies suggested that marketing departments in German, UK and Spanish companies tended to make greater use of quantitative techniques for market modelling, while the Japanese, French and Belgians made less use. French use tended to be dominated by the presentational analytical techniques such as correspondence analysis. The European research agencies survey, however, highlighted the Netherlands as the country most likely to make use of advanced analysis techniques. The Germans and French were also noted as fairly heavy users. In other words, the problems to be solved drive the use of techniques rather than the techniques driving the problems. Analysis techniques that are most used and most useful are those which allow further interpretations to be gained from existing data rather than those which prompt whole new areas of marketing research.

Overall, it seems that it is the techniques that are most generally applicable, rather than narrow in their application, that have been most widely adopted. These are the techniques that typically allow for analysis, modelling and presentation of existing data in new ways rather than requiring the collection of fresh, specific data that would not otherwise have been collected.

Generally, close links between companies and academic institutions were reported in all countries, but they are particularly strong in Germany, France and Spain. The survey of universities indicated that at both the undergraduate and postgraduate levels, quantitative methods are extensively used on marketing research courses. However, it is only at postgraduate level that specific courses on quantitative techniques in marketing are generally offered.

Surprisingly, basic univariate and bivariate data analysis techniques are usually taught to marketing students by non-marketing staff. Multivariate techniques, however, tend to be taught by marketing staff. This may indicate the more specialized nature of these advanced methods or simply their more immediate application in marketing. Interestingly, respondents believed quantitative skills to be equally important to creative, general analytical, strategic planning and financial skills for successful future careers in marketing. They were considered less important, on the other hand, than the soft interpersonal and communication skills agreed as so necessary.

The most significant, but perhaps least surprising, finding was the extent to which, over the last ten years, the PC revolution had served to fuel an increase in both the volume and complexity of those quantitative methods applied to the solution of marketing problems. At a time when marketing academics are questioning the importance of quantitative skills relative to qualitative skills, and the traditional paradigms are coming under increasing attack by post-modernist perspectives, practitioners (both researchers and managers) are embracing quantitative methods to a far greater extent than previously.

References

Adler, L. (1967), Systems approach to marketing, *Harvard Business Review*, Vol 45, May–June 1967, p 166

Brown, S. Marketing as multiplex: screening postmodernism, *European Journal of Marketing* 28 (8/9) 1994 pp. 27–51

Hooley, G.J. and Hussey, M.K. (1994), *Quantitative Methods in Marketing* London: Academic Press

Lilien, G. and Kotler, P. (1983), *Marketing Decision Making: A Model Building Approach*, New York: Harper-Row

Lilien, G. (1994), Marketing models: past, present and future In: *Research Traditions in Marketing* Eds Laurent, G. , Lilien, G. and Pras, B. London: Kluwer

Little J.D.C. (1979), Decision support systems for marketing managers, *Journal of Marketing*, Vol 43, No. 3, pp. 9–27

Rivett, P.(1972), The twenty-first century: the mind of management, in *Quantitative Methods in Management*, Ed. R. Lim , pp. 3–8, London: BIM

Swetz, F.J. (1987), *Capitalism and Arithmetic*, Illinois: Open Court

Appendix

This short appendix gives brief details of the survey procedures employed in the four quantitative surveys.

Company survey

The quantitative phase of this research was conducted through the use of mailed surveys in six European countries and Japan. Japan was included in the study for comparison purposes. The questionnaires were developed after initial discussions with practitioners, academics and marketing researchers. Developed in English, the questionnaire was translated into Flemish, French, German and Spanish by students from those countries studying in the UK. Questionnaires were 'back translated' to ensure accuracy. In the Netherlands and Japan the UK version was used. Initial piloting of the translated questionnaire in each language resulted in minor modifications to the final versions. The questionnaires were addressed to the chief executive officer (CEO) of the top 600–700 companies in each country, ranked by turnover. Mailing lists were supplied by the business information service Dun and Bradstreet. Three weeks after despatch of questionnaires a total of 435 valid responses had been returned, a response rate of 11 per cent across Europe, and 5 per cent in Japan. Given the nature of the sample (top executives in the leading European and Japanese companies) the response rate was encouraging.

ESOMAR survey

As a result of preliminary interviews a questionnaire was developed, tested and mailed to a sample of members of ESOMAR, the European Society for Opinion and Market Research. Questionnaires were sent to 667 corporate members of ESOMAR in 24 countries. The questionnaires were addressed to named individuals. All questionnaires were printed in English and the limitations created by this are fully recognized. Three weeks after mailing 244 valid replies had been received from twenty-one European countries plus three from Japan. Not surprisingly, given the English language used in the questionnaires and the UK derivation of the study, the UK response was the greatest. An encouraging response was received, however, from other countries in addition to the UK. The final overall response rate was 37 per cent.

EMAC Survey

This part of the study was directed towards marketing academics in leading universities and business schools in Europe. A mailing list was obtained from the membership lists of the European Marketing Academy (EMAC). Screening was conducted to ensure that no more than one questionnaire was despatched to each institution. In total 180 questionnaires were despatched and 37 returned (a response rate of 21 per cent). Responses came from 14 different countries in total.

 3

Cluster Analysis

John Saunders

Cluster analysis is an interdependence technique which has been used most successfully with ratio or interval data. After reviewing some of the historical difficulties associated with this method, areas of crucial importance including problem selection, data preparation, process selection and cluster solutions are addressed. Alternative techniques including AID and Q-factor analysis are featured briefly by way of comparison and a final nine-point recipe for providing reliable and valid cluster solutions is included. Overall, the paper provides a clear guide to the range of cluster analysis tools available and discusses the potential difficulties involved in their application.

Introduction

Cluster analysis is a way of sorting items into a small number of homogenous groups. In marketing, the most common application is to cluster customers into segments (Wind, 1978) but it has also been used to group similar products (Srivastava, Leone and Shocker, 1981), in test market selection (Green, Frank and Robinson, 1967) and to identify companies pursuing similar strategies (Doyle, Saunders and Wong, 1989).

Cluster analysis, like factor analysis and multidimensional scaling, is an interdependence method where the relationships between objects and subjects are explored without a dependent variable being identified. Multi-dimensional scaling and cluster analysis are both terms used to refer to a wide range of related techniques. For cluster analysis users, the situation has been made more difficult than necessary by researchers often failing to disclose the approach they used, the use of several names to refer to essentially the same approach, and the lack of guidance into what methods to use and when. This diversity and uncertainty has led to a number of authors viewing the technique with some scepticism. Frank and Green (1968) were concerned about the difficulty of determining the appropriate measure of similarity and number of cluster, while Wells (1975) expressed reservations about using the approach unless very different homogeneous groups could be identified. However, it is worth noting that many of the problems associated with cluster analysis plague multivariate statistics in general, such as choice of an appropriate measure, selection of variables, cross validation, and external validation (Punj and Stewart, 1983).

The aim here is to provide a clear guide to the range of cluster analysis tools available, to discuss the potential difficulties in using the approach and suggest a process for its application. Cluster analysis does provide a great opportunity for confusion and misapplication but the aim here will be to provide an understanding of these difficulties and to suggest the best ways of overcoming them. These are studied by following the cluster analysis flow chart in Figure 3.1. The paper ends with a discussion of some old and some new alternatives to conventional cluster analysis and a set of recommendations for users of cluster analysis.

Problem selection

Cluster analysis has most successfully been applied to interval or ratio scales of the form shown in Table 3.1. Nominal or ordinal data is better analysed using non-metric multidimensional scaling or latent structure analysis (Kinnear and

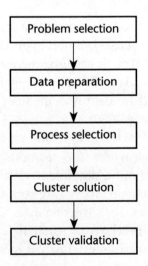

FIGURE 3.1 Cluster analysis flow chart

TABLE 3.1 Sample data

Economy	Ride	Speed	Acceleration	Handling	Reliability
1	3	5	5	3	1
1	2	3	3	2	1
2	2	1	1	2	2
5	1	3	4	4	5
5	3	2	2	2	4
4	4	3	2	3	4
4	2	5	5	5	3
4	3	4	3	3	2
4	1	2	2	2	3
2	1	4	3	4	5

Taylor, 1973). Algorithms for clustering non-metric data – or a mixture of metric and non metric data – exist, but these are rarely used in practice (Green, Tull and Albaum, 1988).

Like almost all multivariate methods, cluster analysis is quite capable of producing a solution, even if natural clusters (Everitt, 1980) do not exist. For this reason it is worth examining the data visually to see if any patterns are evident. This is almost impossible to do by eyeballing the data but various data presentation techniques allow very complex patterns to be identified (Tufte, 1990). Star plots are one way of doing this. Figure 3.2 shows an example based on the data in Table 3.1, where each star represents one of the observations and the axes show the magnitudes on each of the variables. In this case, observations 1 and 2 look as though they might form a cluster, as do observations 4, 7 and 10. Other ways of presenting data visually are sunray plots, Andrews plots and Chernoff faces (Everitt and Dunn, 1991). All these use a similar process of plotting a small sub-sample of the data and looking for patterns.

Another approach is to plot the whole database and look for patterns. Figure 3.3 shows a plot of three values across the whole of a database. In this, three possible clusters have been circled. It also suggests the presence of some outlayers: cars with much worse acceleration than the others. The isolation of these could be very important to later analysis.

A final approach for examining the data visually is to perform factor analysis on the observations and then plot the factor scores instead of the variables. If after doing this no clusters can be detected, it is likely that no natural clusters exist and that cluster analysis may be an unrewarding activity.

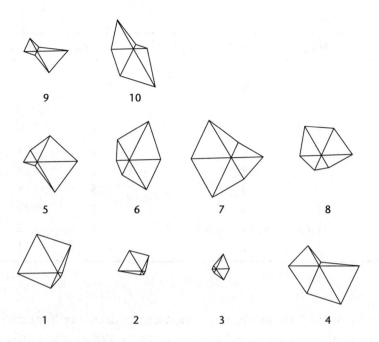

FIGURE 3.2 Star plot

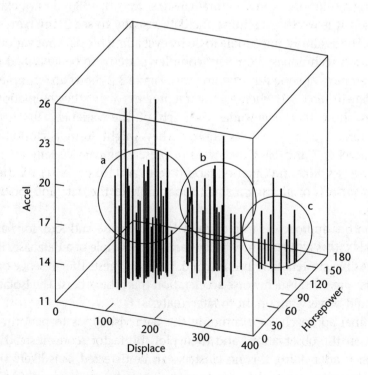

FIGURE 3.3 Three dimensional plot

Plotting the raw data also shows that, even if clusters are found, there is often great variability within them. The cluster average is just what it says and does not represent the actual profile of any set of observations.

Data preparation

Data are often manipulated in several ways prior to performing cluster analysis. Since some packages perform some sort of prior manipulation as a matter of course, or as a default, it is important to understand their impact.

Missing data is a common problem in multivariate analysis where a respondent has been asked to answer many questions or objective data on all observations are incomplete. If observations are missing in a database to be analysed using cluster analysis, the offending observations should be deleted rather than using some algorithm to estimate the missing case. The reason for this is that most routines estimate the value of missing data on the basis of average values of the variable. In cluster analysis such an assumption would bias results because each missing case would be assumed to have the same value and would therefore tend to cluster together. More sophisticated methods of data fusion (Coates, Doherty and French, Chapter 20) allow this process to be conducted more systematically, but this is best left until after clusters are formed rather than at the beginning of the process.

Cluster analysis software often requires users to specify whether their data are to be standardized or normalized. Normalization is often essential where the data are objective, as in Figure 3.3, and the dimensions used vary. If no adjustment is made, the dimensions with higher variance, e.g. displacement, will have a different influence from those with low variance, such as acceleration. However, where the data are subjective and gathered in the form of a set of uniform semantic scales, standardization appears to have little impact on the clusters formed (Green and Rao, 1969).

Factor analysis is often applied prior to cluster analysis. There are two benefits in doing this. First, it reduces the number of variables which have to be analysed by the cumbersome cluster analysis process. Second, the results from exploratory factor analysis can help the interpretation of the clusters.

The presence of one or more spurious attributes or dimensions in the analysis appears to have a marked detrimental effect on the performance of all clustering methods (Punj and Stewart, 1983). This suggests analysis should not use a shotgun approach in the selection of variables but only use those which prior hypotheses or visual inspection have indicated will have some bearing on the results. With larger databases it is quite likely that spurious variables would not be identified until after the clusters are formed. In this case the clustering process would have to be iterative and conducted again once the undesirable variables had been removed.

Both variables and observations are often partitioned prior to cluster analysis. A subgroup of observations is often removed to allow for validation; one set is used to form the clusters and the other to validate the results. The variables are sometimes split for similar reasons. The analysis variables are used to form the clusters and then a set of descriptive variables used to validate them. Usually the analysis and descriptive variables are of different types or from different sources, which makes them inappropriate for use in a single analysis in any case. For instance, Maier and Saunders (1990) used the prescribing habits of doctors as an analysis variable in identifying clusters of general practitioners. Demographic variables such as age, sex, etc. were then used to validate the solution. Even if there are no natural clusters, such is the power of cluster analysis that it will almost always find significant differences across the analysis variables, but if there are natural clusters, it would be surprising if there were not significant differences across the description variables as well.

Process selection

Once the data have been prepared, cluster analysis is just a matter of grouping together those observations which are alike. The problem is, what is alike and how should they be grouped? The data in Table 3.1 will be used to discuss the alternatives.

Figure 3.4 shows observations 1–3 plotted for ride against top speed. Two distance measures of alikeness are shown: Euclidean distance which is the shortest route between 1 and 2 and the city block measure which goes from 1 to 'a' to 2. Matrices for the two measures are presented in Table 3.2. This shows that whichever of the two distance measures used, 2 and 3 are most alike, 1 and 2 are the next most alike, and 1 and 3 are the least alike. This is consistent with findings generally, which have shown that, irrespective of what distance measure is chosen, cluster analysis results tend to be similar. This is not the case if other than distance measures are used. Table 3.3 shows the distance similarity and matching matrices for observations 1 to 3 across all six dimensions in Table 1. The distance matrix this time shows 1 and 2 and 2 and 3 equally alike and are therefore the first contenders to be clustered. In contrast, the matching matrix, representing the number of occasions on which observations have exactly the same score, shows all observations being equally alike.

Both the distance and matching matrix contrast with the similarity matrix, which is computed by correlating the observations against one another. As far as this is concerned, observations 1 and 2 are exactly alike (+1 being perfect correlation) while observations 1 and 2 are equally dissimilar from observation 3.

This difference is not a matter of one measure being wrong and the others right, but their dependence on measuring different things. When measuring medical records, it might be logical to look for patients who have been diagnosed in the same way and therefore matching may be a good tool to use. Distance measures seek for observations which are close together on all dimensions, whereas similarity measures examine the profile of the results, that is they recognize individuals as alike if they give their highest score to the same variables. The user of cluster analysis has to decide what measure of alikeness is most meaningful in their context, although few these days deviate from using Euclidean distance.

The most widely used form of cluster analysis is hierarchical. This starts with all the observations being separate and then looks at the two which are most alike. These two are then joined to form a new cluster. If this process is followed for the data in Table 3.1, 2 and 3 are found to be most alike and Figure 3.5 shows how their joining can be represented in the form of a dendrogram. The algorithm then searches among the remaining clusters, these being 1; 2 and 3 combined; and 4 to 10. This time 4 and 7 are found to be most alike and joined, shortly followed by 5 and 8. That leaves seven clusters (10, 1, 2 and 3, 4 and 7, 9, 5 and 8, 6). In the next stage, individuals

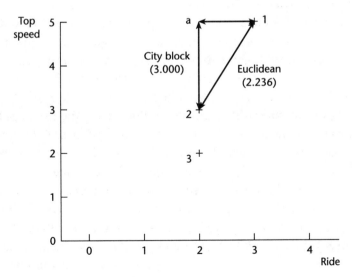

FIGURE 3.4 Distance measures

TABLE 3.2 Distance measures on two dimensions

		Euclidian distance Car			City block distance Car		
		1	2	3	1	2	3
	1	—			—		
Car	2	2.36	—		3.00	—	
	3	4.12	2.00		4.00	1.00	—

TABLE 3.3 Measures of alikeness on six dimensions

	Distance			Correlation			Matching		
	1	2	3	1	2	3	1	2	3
1	—			—			—		
2	2.83	—		1.00	—		0.33	—	
3	4.78	2.00	—	−0.87	−0.87	—	0.33	0.33	—

are not joined but the original cluster containing observations 2 and 3 is found to be closest to observation 1, so these now form into a larger cluster and this process continues until the appropriate level of clustering is found. In the dendrogram, the vertical axis represents the increasing magnitude of the distance measures, as clusters which are less and less alike are brought together. Originally there is little increase in error as they are joined but later the jumps become quite high.

In developing the hierarchy, a critical question soon arises. How does one measure the distance between two observations which have been joined and any other observations? The literature on cluster analysis has numerous names for ways of doing this. Unfortunately, most of these are aliases which could almost have been invented to confuse the researcher (Table 3.4).

The algorithm chosen has far more influence on the final results than does the measure of alikeness. The reasons for this can be seen by comparing single linkage with other algorithms. In this an observation is joined to a cluster, giving it a discerned level of alikeness to at least one member of that cluster. Connections between clusters are therefore based on links between single entities. As a consequence, the clusters formed tend to be a stringy series of overlapping groups. Complete linkage takes a totally different view and observation is joined to a cluster if this is closer to the furthest member of that cluster than the furthest member of any other cluster. This produces much more compact groupings but is very sensitive to outlayers.

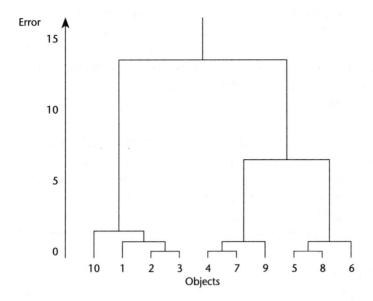

FIGURE 3.5 Dendrogram

TABLE 3.4 Cluster methods and aliases

Method	Aliases
Hierarchical methods	
Single linkage	Connectiveness method, linkage analysis, minimum method and nearest neighbour cluster analysis.
Complete linkage	Diameter method, furthest neighbour method, maximum method and rank order typal analysis.
Average linkage	Centroid method, median method, simple average linkage analysis and weighted average method.
Minimum variance	Error sum of squares method, minimum variance and Ward's method.
Partitioning method	
K-means	Density search
Hill climbing	—

In the average linkage approach, each time a cluster is formed its average score is computed. Clusters then join together if those average scores are close. Once again this method can be affected by outlayers as the centroid can be moved significantly if the cluster is joined by an observation with a deviant value. The final sets of minimum variance approaches are designed to minimize within cluster variance and so examine what would happen if individuals joined a cluster. This approach tends to produce robust, dense, spherical clusters with distinct characteristics (Everitt, 1980). Although widely recognized as the best approach, the formation of dense spherical clusters can be inappropriate if the natural clusters do not have that form. For instance, from a marketing point of view, the outlayers in Figure 3.3 are a group of low performance cars which do not form a spherical cluster at all.

Partitioning approaches to cluster analysis are quite different from the hierarchical methods. Here the number of clusters is decided at the start and observations are shuttled from cluster to cluster based on the proximity of their centroids. Hill climbing methods use a similar process of re-allocating observations and are able to use a variety of criteria for choosing the cluster to which an observation belongs. These partitioning approaches are less likely to produce degenerate and unstable solutions than hierarchical methods, but the hierarchical approach is superior to the partitioning in not demanding that the number of clusters has to be chosen *a priori*.

The best practice is to take advantage of the strengths of hierarchical clustering and partitioning, hierarchical clustering being used to form a reasonable number of clusters, say 12, at which point the process is stopped and the partitioning approach is used to re-allocate observations and clusters to find a best fit. This having been achieved, hierarchical clustering is then used to reduce the number of clusters to 11 and re-allocation is once again used to find the best solution. Fortunately, modern cluster analysis packages, such as CLUSTAN (Wishart, 1987), are able to follow this process automatically.

A complicating issue at the final stages of clustering is the powerful impact of outlayers. For this reason it is best to remove these before the cycle of hierarchical clustering and re-allocation is used.

Cluster solution

Both partitioning and hierarchical clustering approaches require the user to decide the number of groups in the final solution; is six, five or four the correct number? The most common approach is to observe the clustering process and note when the stress of bringing two clusters together becomes particularly large. The dendrogram (Figure 3.5) shows the results of hierarchical clustering using minimum variance where the pain in bringing two clusters together is measured in terms of the error sum of squares. Three clusters form with very little stress but when 4, 7 and 8 are joined with 5, 8 and 6, the error jumps up from just over one to six. This suggests the appropriate number of clusters is three and that by reducing the number to two, much information would be lost. A scree plot provides another way of presenting the change in stress (Figure 3.6). Once again using the same data, the scree plot shows the large jump in error sum of squares when the solution goes from three to two clusters. The appropriateness of this solution can be seen in Figure 3.7 where just two dimensions are plotted together and clearly show the groupings of A, B and C.

Scientific ways of choosing the number of clusters have been suggested. Wishart (1987) proposes a moving average rule, which monitors the scree plot and tracks the mean standard deviation of a window of data in order to recognize a significant jump in stress.

Operationally the stopping rule depends upon the utility of the solutions found. In their demographic databases CACI and CCN found it useful to break down the census population into over 30 groups but in many cases a company would find it quite impractical if more than half a dozen classes of customer were identified. Experience also indicates that it is rare to find a statistically significant solution with more than seven clusters.

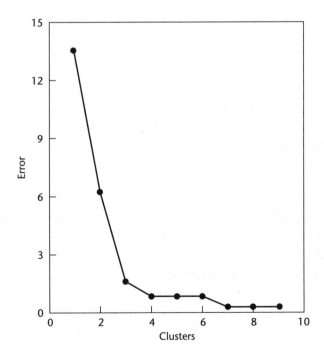

FIGURE 3.6 Scree plot

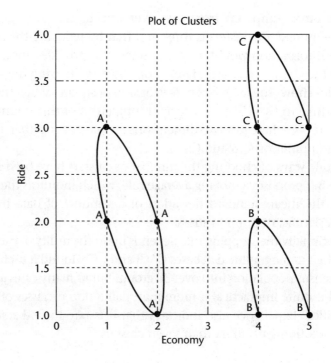

FIGURE 3.7 Three cluster solution

Cluster validation

The subjective nature of much of cluster analysis makes validation very important. Four layers are available and it would be wrong to omit any one and certainly wrong to depend upon the early ones.

Internal validity

The first test for validity examines the solutions looking at the analysis data. This can be done by conducting a series of cross tabulations of the clusters against variables. The significance of each contingency table can then be tested using a chi-square test. One snag here can occur if the clustering process is very effective and the chi-square test invalidated because of the number of cells with fewer than five observations. The normal practice of collapsing a table in this case is inappropriate since the whole aim is to examine clusters. A safer approach is to use multivariate analysis of variance looking at the change in the mean of observations across clusters.

Since analysis variables were used to perform the cluster analysis, it would be surprising if significant results were not found at this stage. So loaded are these internal tests of validity, it is customary to provide cluster counts or scores for the analysis variable without showing any significance tests.

External validity

When conducting cluster analysis it is usual to split the variables into two groups: one set used to form clusters and the other to describe the results. Quite often the descriptive data are nominal, rather than metric, so are in any case inappropriate for inclusion in the cluster analysis. With the variables split in this way it is quite reasonable to test to see if descriptive variables change significantly across the clusters. For example, do groups of customers identified using psychometric data also tend to have different genders, ages or income? Since these descriptive variables were not used in forming the clusters, it is quite acceptable to use statistical tests of this variability across clusters as a test of their validity.

Replicability

There is more agreement on the need to use a hold out sample to test for the stability and validity of cluster results than there is on how it should be done.

One of the simplest methods of cross-validation is to divide the original sample in half and then form separate cluster analyses on the two sets (Sherman and Sheth, 1977). Statistics on the analysis variables and descriptive variables can be used to compare the congruence of the two samples. By tabulating one solution against the other or comparing mean scores, it is possible to test for the consistency of many individual elements of the two solutions, but there is no objective measure of the overall reliability that has been obtained (Punj and Stewart, 1983).

A popular but cumbersome approach is to use discriminant analysis for cross-validation (Field and Schoenfeldt, 1975). In doing this, cluster analysis is performed separately on an analysis and hold out sample. Discriminant analysis is then applied using the groups from the analysis sample as a dependent variable. The discriminant function is then used to predict cluster membership of the hold out sample and the two sets of results for the hold out sample compared. A confusion matrix can be drawn, which shows correct and incorrect allocations using the two analyses and a coefficient agreement, such as a Kaffer, may be used to provide an objective measure of stability. An even more rigorous approach was adopted by Saunders and Jobber (1990), who adapted the U-method (Lachenbruch and Mickey, 1968) to test the robustness of solutions based on ten sub-sets of solutions.

The discriminant analysis approach appears to be rigorous but the use of discriminant analysis introduces its own problems. The discriminant coefficients may be a poor estimate of population values and need to be cross-validated themselves. This makes the whole procedure particularly cumbersome and demands a large sample from which hold out samples for both cross-validating cluster analysis and discriminant analysis can be drawn.

A relatively simple approach to cross-validation is proposed by McIntyre and Blashfield (1980). Once again, cluster analysis is performed on two sets of observations. Centroids describing the clusters of the analysis sample are then obtained and observations in the hold out sample allocated to clusters on the base of Euclidean distance measures. The degree of agreement between the nearest centroid assignments of the hold out sample and the results from the cluster analysis on the hold out sample is then taken as an indicator of the stability of the solution.

Operational validity

Statistically significant results are of no consequence if they are not usable or accepted by managers. This depends upon the extent to which the managers can believe in the clusters formed, recognize them, and see how they can be used. A problem here can be extending the use from the sample used to develop the cluster solution to the overall population. Descriptive variables such as geographical location, readership of magazines, age group, etc., can help in this. This stage can be difficult, so it is important that these variables are in the database from the start. Recent developments in database marketing (Hooley and Saunders, 1993) have made this grossing up easier. Typically the cluster analysis is performed on the subsample of the database available and the remainder of the sample allocated to the clusters formed.

Once cluster membership is known, it is quite easy to track their significance using natural experiments. In their analysis for general practitioner segments, Maier and Saunders (1990) tracked the results of a sales promotion sent to all doctors and found significant differences across the segments they had previously identified.

Early criticisms of cluster analysis have made its validation an important issue. It is very likely that a user will spend more time preparing the data and validating the results than actually conducting the cluster analysis and describing the groups found. But in this respect, cluster analysis is no different from other multivariate techniques, all of which make assumptions which have to be tested for their validity and for all of which some sort of cross-validation is essential. The users of cluster analysis are fortunate, in that the need for this validation has been long recognized and the necessary approaches well developed.

Alternative approaches to numerical taxonomy

There are many old and new alternatives to cluster analysis. Automatic interaction detection (AID) and Q-factor analysis have been used instead of cluster analysis for some time (Morgan and Sonquist, 1963). Q-factor analysis is sometimes called inverse factor analysis because it is performed on observations rather than on variables. The results show observations loaded on one factor or another. Although popular in the US (Saunders, 1980), the approach has many problems which have been forcefully argued by Cattell (1978) and Stewart (1981).

AID has its own problems of degeneracy (Fenwick and Doyle, 1975) but it is also very different from cluster analysis in requiring a dependent variable to be determined. This can be a great strength. Whereas AID can be used to deliberately search for groups who are particularly responsive to marketing variables such as direct mail, cluster analysis has no such focus.

Overlapping clustering

Methods for developing overlapping clusters have been available for some time (Arabie, 1977) but have been used far less than conventional cluster analysis. The rationale for using overlapping clustering is clear. In conventional cluster analysis observations are separated into mutually exclusive subsets which are then described. In reality, observations, such as customers, could belong to more than one group depending on the circumstances. For example, families, fast food junkies and office workers could all use a fast food chain and have different reasons for doing so. There is also evidence that within segments there is significant brand switching and that, depending on the time of day, people drift from segment to segment.

Although intuitively appealing, overlapping methods retain problems which detract from its use (Arabie et al., 1981). First, the methods tend to produce too many clusters with too much overlap. This means arbitrary constraints to prevent excessive confusion have to be used. The second drawback is that the clusters are often too inclusive. For instance, it is useful to know that individuals can migrate from one cluster to another, but unhelpful to know that one individual can be in each of several clusters. Third, the algorithms for overlapping clustering are even more computer intensive than cluster analysis and, because of this, are limited to very small numbers of observations; 30 in the case of MAPCLUS (Arabie and Carroll, 1980).

In a sense, overlapping clustering is an unnecessary confusion if clusters are interpreted intelligently. Descriptive statistics always show that the difference between groups is one of tendencies rather than absolutes. And when cluster analysis is used in conjunction with multidimensional scaling to show clusters, products and dimensions in multidimensional space (Hooley and Saunders, 1993), representation makes it clear that the clusters are not unique in sharing attributes or their proximity to brands.

Mixture models

This relatively new approach has the advantage of being able to handle continuous or binary variables and dispenses with the need to decide the measure of alikeness to be used (Everitt and Dunn, 1991). Like the partitioning approach to cluster analysis, mixture models require the number of clusters to be determined and so could be used in conjunction with hierarchical clustering to estimate a starting configuration. The means and variance of each group is then estimated and taken as a starting point for computing a distribution function representing, for example, the purchase rate of a particular product. The assumption is that the distribution of purchase across the whole population is the result of the distributions of several sub-populations. Maximum likelihood methods, as detailed in Everitt and Hand (1981), can then be used to find the best estimate of sub-group populations, their means, and variance. This approach is more computer intensive than conventional clustering but relaxes some of the assumptions and limitations that usually exist.

Normative cluster analysis

In the determination of market segments, cluster analysis appears almost casual in there being a hope that the clusters found will have an impact on the major dependent variable, for example, the ability of marketing mix elements to influence sales. Normative cluster analysis overcomes this by introducing a dependent variable, say sales across a range of product classes, and seeking a clustering solution which maximizes the variability. These approaches are massively computer intensive and use search procedures such as branch and bound or artificial annealing (see Chapter 20 by Coates, Doherty and French). However, when the returns are potentially high, such is the development of geodemographic databases that the use of normative clustering can be justified. Unfortunately, one problem still remains: although the segments were derived to isolate the variability on one dependent variable, there is no reason why the clusters found should be equally relevant to another. For example, one major retailer selling fast moving consumer goods, who had difficulty applying an off-the-shelf geodemographic database, found that it was actually optimized using the sales of a company selling consumer durables.

Conclusions

Cluster analysis is not one approach, but consists of many approaches, some of which are useful and some less so. In the past, its value in marketing has been limited by its ability to generate solutions where no natural clusters occur, confusion over the wide range of techniques available, and the frequent failure of analysts to validate their findings. Users are rightly concerned about the reliability of cluster analysis solutions but in that respect the method is no worse than other multivariate techniques.

Much uncertainty about cluster analysis has been caused by its users being vague about the approach they use and their choice of methods which have little record of success. With their current level of knowledge, there is little reason for these mistakes to be made. Several recommendations can help produce reliable and valid cluster solutions:

1. Use clean data, deleting cases with missing observations. These can later be allocated to clusters using data fusion.
2. Use graphical methods to visualize the existence of clusters and the potential relevance of variables. The inclusion of irrelevant variables can have a large influence on solutions, so be prepared to use an iterative process, starting the whole cluster analysis again, if some of the analysis variables are of insignificant variance across clusters.
3. Use the recommended procedures for using both hierarchical and partitioning approaches. Ward's (1963) method is widely recognized as producing reliable clusters and, when used in conjunction with K-means, is likely to avoid degenerate solutions.
4. Use stopping rules to see when it is appropriate to stop combining clusters. If there is no sudden increase in stress as the groups are gathered together, it is likely that there is something wrong with the data or that no clusters exist.
5. Prior to accepting a final cluster solution, search for, and eliminate, outlayers. These can influence the solution significantly and have to be removed.

6. Be aware that other than mixture models, assumptions are made about the distance measure used and the shape of the clusters found. These may be wrong and the graphical methods can sometimes allow this problem to be identified.

7. Validate cluster solutions using a hold out sample and descriptive data as well as the analysis data.

8. Where possible, validate the clusters using a natural experiment to see if the clusters have identified response differences which make them usable.

9. Consider implementation issues early on and ensure that descriptive variables are included which will allow the cluster results to be grossed up to the target population.

Cluster analysis is more statistically vague than many other multivariate methods and the alternatives within it means it is quite possible to produce a range of different results from the same data. Any solutions found should not be seen as absolute truths, but as only one of a set of possibilities. Cluster analysis is like a lens whose focal length can be changed to show completely different pictures of the same scene, or like a range of pictures taken using different wave lengths: x-ray, infra-red, and ultraviolet, as well as visible light. No one picture is correct but any one could give an insight which provides an opportunity.

References

Arabie, P. (1977), Clustering representations of group overlap, *Journal of Mathematical Sociology*, **5**, pp. 113–28

Arabie, P. and Carroll, J.D. (1980), MAPCLUS: a mathematical programming approach to fitting the ADCLUS model, *Psychometrika*, **45**, pp. 211–35

Arabie, P., Carroll, J.D., DeSarbo, W. and Wind, J. (1981), Overlapping clustering: a new method for product positioning, *Journal of Marketing Research*, **18** (August), pp. 310–17

Cattell, R.B. (1978), *The Scientific Use of Factor Analysis in the Behavioral and Life Sciences*, New York: Plenum Press

Doyle, P., Saunders, J. and Wong, V. (1989), International marketing strategies and organisation: a study of US, Japanese and British competitors, *American Marketing Association Educator's Proceedings*, Chicago, Il, pp. 100–105

Everitt, B.S. (1980), *Cluster Analysis* (2nd edition), London: Gower Publications

Everitt, B.S. and Dunn, G. (1991), *Applied Multivariate Analysis*, London: Edward Arnold

Everitt, B.S. and Hand, D.J. (1981), *Finite Mixture Distributions*, London: Chapman and Hall

Fenwick, I. and Doyle, P. (1975), The pitfalls of AID analysis, *Journal of Marketing Research* **12** (Nov), pp. 408–13

Field, H.S. and Schoenfeldt, L.F. (1975), Ward and Hook revisited: a two-part procedure for overcoming a deficiency in the grouping of two persons, *Educational and Psychological Measurement*, **35**, pp. 171–3

Frank, R.A. and Green, P.E. (1968), Numerical taxonomy in marketing analysis: a review article, *Journal of Marketing Research*, 5 (February), pp. 83–98

Green, P.E., Frank, R.A. and Robinson, P.J. (1967), Cluster analysis in test market selection", *Management Science*, 13, B-387–400

Green, P.E. and Rao, V.R. (1969), A note on proximity measures and cluster analysis, *Journal of Marketing Research*, 6 (August), pp. 359–64

Green, P.E., Tull, D.S. and Albaum, G. (1988), *Research for Marketing Decisions*, (fifth edition), Englewood Cliffs, NJ: Prentice-Hall

Hooley, G. and Saunders, J. (1993), *Competitive Positioning: the Key to Market Success*, London: Prentice-Hall

Kinnear, T.C. and Taylor, J.R. (1973), The effect of ecological concern on brand perceptions, *Journal of Marketing Research*, 10 pp. 191–97

Lachenbruch, P.A.. and Mickey, M.R. (1968), Estimation of error rates in discriminant analysis, *Technometrics*, 10 (Feb), pp. 1–10

Maier, J. and Saunders, J. (1990), The implementation process of segmentation in sales management, *Journal of Personal Selling and Sales Management*, X (Feb), pp. 39–48

McIntyre, R.M. and Blashfield, R.K. (1980), A nearest-centroid technique for evaluating the minimum-variance clustering procedure, *Multivariate Behavior Research*, 15, pp. 225–38

Morgan, J.N. and Sonquist, J.A. (1963), Problems in the analysis of survey data, and a proposal, *Journal of the American Statistical Association*, 58, pp. 87–93

Punj, G and Stewart, D.W. (1983), Cluster analysis in marketing research; a review and suggestions for application, *Journal of Market Research*, 20(2), pp. 111–129

Saunders, J. (1980), Cluster analysis for market segmentation, *European Journal of Marketing*, 14(7), pp. 422–435

Saunders, J. and Jobber, D. (1990), Product replacement strategies: occurrence and coincidences, Loughborough University Management Research Series paper number 1990:7

Sherman, L. and Sheth, J.N. (1977), Cluster analysis and its applications in marketing research, in *Multivariate Methods for Market and Survey Research*, (Ed) J.N. Sheth, Chicago, IL: American Marketing Association

Srivastava, R.K., Leone, R.P. and Shocker, A.D. (1981), Market structure analysis: hierarchical clustering of products based on substitution-in-use, *Journal of Marketing* 45 (Summer), pp. 38–48

Stewart, D.W. (1981), The application and misapplication of factor analysis in marketing research, *Journal of Marketing Research*, 18 (February), pp. 51–62

Tufte, E.R. (1990), *Envisioning Information*, Cheshire, KN: Graphics Press

Ward, J.H. (1963), Hierarchical grouping to optimize an objective function, *Journal of the American Statistical Association*, 58, pp. 236–44

Wells, W.D. (1975), Psychographics: A critical review, *Journal of Marketing Research*, 12 (May), pp. 196–213

Wind, Y. (1978), 'Issues and Advances in Segmentation Research', *Journal of Marketing Research*, 15 August, pp. 317–37

Wishart, D. (1987), *CLUSTAN User's Manual* (4th edition), St Andrews: University of St. Andrews

■ □ ■ ■ 4

Logit Model Analysis for Multivariate Categorical Data

David Jobber

Logit model analysis of dichotomous dependent and categorical independent variables has great potential in marketing research, supplementing other multivariate techniques such as regression and discriminant analysis. This paper describes the steps to be taken in its use and by means of a worked example shows how logic model analysis can be applied to a marketing research problem.

Introduction

Statistical analysis of research findings often takes the form of assessing the relationship between a dependent variable and a set of independent variables. For example, we may hypothesize that sales (dependent variable) is a function of relative prices, advertising spend, distribution coverage and product quality (independent variables). The relationship is estimated by generating a statistical model of the associations. A number of techniques are available to the researcher, each with its own set of assumptions which restrict its applicability. One key determinant of use is the way the dependent and independent variables have been measured. For example, when both dependent and independent variables are ratio or intervally-scaled then regression analysis may be an appropriate choice; discriminant analysis is often used when the dependent variable is categorical and the independent variables are ratio or intervally scaled and analysis of variance techniques are usually employed when the dependent variable is ratio or intervally scaled and the independent variables are categorical.

However, the nature of the variables to be measured may preclude the use of interval, ratio or even ordinal measures. Some variables may by their very nature be categorical, e.g. socio-economic group or gender. In some research situations, then, both dependent and independent variables may be categorical. It is here that logit model analysis can be used to determine associations (Fienberg, 1977).

Logit models are a special class of log-linear models which can be used to examine the relationship between a dichotomous dependent variable (e.g. having a bank account or not), and one or more independent categorical variables (e.g. male or female; AB, C or C2DE; living in the north, midlands or south of England).

In discriminant analysis the dependent variable is coded as having a value of 0 or 1, and calculations are based on these values. In a logit model, the value of the dependent variable is based upon the 'log odds'. It is the variation of this measure which is to be explained by the independent variables. An odds ratio is the ratio between the frequency of being in one category and the frequency of not being in that category. For example if 1000 people in a sample have a bank account and 500 do not, then estimated odds that a person has a bank account is 1000/500 = 2.00 or 2–1. In logit model analysis a log of the ratio of the two frequencies is taken (the 'logit'). Statistical analysis is then performed on this measure and the effects of the independent variables (Haberman, 1978).

Evaluating models fitted to data

The first step in model evaluation is to adopt a procedure that indicates which model specifications might prove reasonable to fit the data. One procedure is to examine the standardized values of the parameter estimates in the saturated model for the data (Everitt, 1977; Norusis, 1990). Saturated models contain all possible effect parameters, that is, all individual effects of the independent variables and all the interaction effects. A fully saturated model is therefore a perfect representation of the data (i.e. residuals equal zero). Effects with small estimated values can usually be deleted from the model.

The second step is to test various unsaturated models. An unsaturated model is formed by deleting some effects (independent variables and/or their interactions) from the saturated model. Those independent variables which have large estimated values in the saturated model are likely to form the basis of an unsaturated model that fits the data well. A number of alternative model specifications are tested to see which provides the best fit to the data. However, how do we decide which model provides the best fit?

Three criteria are normally applied (Knoke and Burke, 1980; Norusis, 1990):

- parsimony
- value of the likelihood ratio chi-squared statistic
- residual analysis.

Parsimony

A saturated model which contains all effects may represent the data well but it does not produce a parsimonious description of the relationship between variables. In general the researcher is looking for the smallest number of variables that gives a good representation of the data. Thus if two models differ only in the number of variables (i.e. both give similar levels of fit) the model with the fewer variables will be accepted.

The value of the likelihood ratio chi-squared statistic

The process of measuring model fit is to estimate the expected cell frequencies generated by the model and compare them to the observed frequencies using the likelihood ratio statistic (L^2) where

$$L^2 = 2 \sum_i \sum_j F_{ij} \, \ell n \frac{F_{ij}}{\hat{F}_{ij}}$$

where F_{ij} and $\hat{F}_{ij}$ are the observed and expected odds ratios respectively.

The larger the L^2 value in relation to the degrees of freedom, the more the expected frequencies differ from the observed frequencies. The value of degrees of freedom of a particular model is calculated by subtracting the number of independent variables in the model from the number of cells in the contingency table. In practice the calculation of the L^2 value and degrees of freedom is performed by the computer program. Thus for large values of L^2, the hypothesized model is rejected as being a good fit with the data and hence is not an acceptable representation of the relationships among the variables.

This procedure contrasts with that of traditional chi-square tests of association in two-way contingency tables and thus might be a source of confusion (Knoke and Burke, 1980). When conducting a traditional chi-square test we seek to reject the null hypothesis of independence between the variables. Consequently large values of chi-square relative to degrees of freedom are sought, and hence small p-values. However when searching for the best fitting logit model we hope to accept the hypothesized model and thus are looking for a low L^2 value relative to degrees of freedom (large p-values).

In order to compare models, the change in the L^2 statistic (L^2) is calculated so that the p-value of this difference can be determined. Significant p-values (P<0.05) show that the change in model specification has had a significant effect on model fit.

In summary the best fitting model is one which has a large p-value (>0.10) and yet contains as few independent variables as possible. However, care must be taken past p-values of 0.40 if the gain in fit is achieved by the inclusion of unnecessary variables (Bishop, Fienberg and Holland, 1975).

Residual analysis

The third method of assessing how well a model fits the data is to examine directly the discrepancies between the observed and expected cell frequencies based on the model. For an acceptable model, these discrepancies or residual values should be small in value and have no discernible pattern. The procedure is to calculate standardized residuals by dividing the difference between the observed and expected frequencies by the square root of the expected frequency (standard error). The SPSS software program performs this calculation and prints a plot of standardized residuals against observed cell frequencies. No standardized residuals should be greater than +1.96 or less than −1.96 for adequate model fit (Norusis, 1990). If the model is a good fit to the data the standardized residuals should be normally distributed with a mean of zero and a standard deviation of one. By observing the residual/observed cell frequencies plot it may be possible to assess normality but to confirm this judgement the SPSS program performs a plot of standardized residuals against 'expected residuals' from a normal distribution. If the standardized residuals are normally distributed, this plot should be approximately linear.

To summarize, the best fitting model has a large p-value for the likelihood-ratio statistic with as few variables as possible, and has standardized residuals within ±1.96 that are normally distributed.

A worked example

In order to show the application of the logit modelling approach a real life example will be used. The research problem was to assess the effect of four categorically scaled variables on response rate to an international mail survey (Jobber, Mirza and Wee (1991)). Since the dependent variable (response rate) was dichotomous (respond or do not respond) logit analysis was used to model the effects of the independent variables. An experiment was designed to measure the effects of the following variables on response rate:

1. a non-monetary incentive (bookmark v no bookmark)
2. offer of survey results (offer v no offer)
3. country of destination (Singapore v Malaysia v Thailand)
4. nationality of parent company (Japanese v American).

Thus all variables were categorically scaled. The results of the experiment are given in Table 4.1. The data were subjected to logit model analysis to identify the variables (and their interactions) that best fitted the data. In so doing the significant effects on response rate could be identified.

Step one involved the computation of the saturated model which included all main and interaction effects and thus fitted the data perfectly. Table 4.2 presents the results. Inspection of the z-values indicated that the main effects of bookmark and nationality of the parent company were significantly related to response rate. Thus both of these variables should be important variables to include in unsaturated model specifications.

Step two involved the specification and testing of a number of unsaturated models (see Table 4.3). Since bookmark (B) and nationality of parent company (P) were significantly related to response rate, models 1 and 2 were tested showing the individual effects of each of these variables. As a confirmatory check on the main effects of report (R) and country destination (C) models 3 and 4 were specified. Model 5 contained the main effects of both bookmark (B) and nationality of parent (P) to check if each variable affected response rate, net of the effects of each other.

TABLE 4.1 Response by independent variable

	% Response
No bookmark	9.1
Bookmark	22.8
No offer of results	12.6
Offer of results	19.4
American	23.6
Japanese	10.1
Singapore	14.8
Malaysia	16.7
Thailand	17.2
Overall Response Rate = 16.0	

$n = 332$.

TABLE 4.2 Parameter estimates for the saturated logit model

Variables (response by)	Coefficient	Standard error	Z-value
Main effects			
Bookmark (B)	0.24	0.08	2.84*
Report (R)	0.09	0.08	1.13
Nationality of parent (P)	0.24	0.08	2.89*
Country (C)	0.44	0.11	0.41
	0.41	0.13	0.32
First order interaction effects			
B by R	−0.02	0.08	−0.27
B by P	0.03	0.08	0.36
B by C	0.06	0.11	0.51
	0.10	0.13	0.77
R by P	−0.05	0.08	−0.58
R by C	0.03	0.11	−0.25
	0.09	0.13	0.73
P by C	−0.02	0.11	−0.15
	0.03	0.13	0.25
Second order interaction effects			
B by R by P	−0.02	0.08	−0.29
B by R by C	−0.02	0.11	−0.15
	−0.11	0.13	−0.87
B by P by C	−0.07	0.11	−0.67
	0.10	0.12	0.74
R by P by C	−0.04	0.11	−0.32
	0.03	0.13	0.20
Third order interaction effect			
B by R by P by C	0.02	0.11	0.22
	−0.03	0.13	−0.22

*Significant at 0.05 level.

Model 6 specified the main effect of bookmark (B) and the interaction effect of bookmark and country destination (B by C) to check if the effect of the bookmark depended on the country to which it was sent. Similarly model 7 (B and B by R) checked whether the effect of the bookmark depended on whether an offer of survey results was made.

Model 8 specified the main effect of nationality of parent (P) and the interaction effect of nationality and country destination (P by C) to check if the

TABLE 4.3 Comparison of unsaturated logit models

Model	Variables (response by)	L^2	d.f.	P
1.	Bookmark (B)	23.0	22	0.42
2.	Nationality of Parent (P)	21.6	22	0.48
3.	Report (R)	31.0	22	0.10
4.	Country (C)	32.9	21	0.04
5.	B and P	10.4	21	0.97
6.	B and B by C	21.0	20	0.40
7.	B and B by R	22.4	21	0.38
8.	P and P by C	21.6	20	0.36
9.	P and P by R	20.35	21	0.50

Note: L^2 is the Likelihood-ratio Chi-squared statistic which is calculated as:

$$L^2 = 2 \sum_i \sum_j F_{ij} \, \ell n \frac{F_{ij}}{\hat{F}_{ij}}$$

where F_{ij} and $\hat{F}_{ij}$ are the observed and expected odds ratios respectively.

impact of nationality depended on country destination. Finally Model 9 (P and P by R) assessed if the effect of nationality depended on whether an offer of survey results was made.

The specifications thus formed a logical sequence based upon the initial findings from the saturated model. However, with the flexibility of the SPSS PC programs now available a large range of alternative specifications can be assessed very quickly if the researcher requires. Obviously a great deal of judgement is required during this stage.

Table 4.3 shows the comparison between the nine unsaturated logit models. Assessing main effects (models 1 to 4), the results confirm the saturated model findings that bookmark (model 1) and nationality of parent (model 2) provide better model fit than the offer of the survey report (model 3) and country destination (model 4). This conclusion is based on the L^2 values which are smaller for bookmark and nationality (p-value larger) and hence the difference between expected and observed cell frequencies is smaller.

However, by including the main effects of both bookmark and nationality in one model (model 5) the L^2 value falls still further and is associated with a very large p-value (p = 0.97) indicating very good fit. A test on whether this specification improves fit over models 1 and 2 was performed by calculating the change in the L^2 statistic (and the degrees of freedom) so that a p-value of this difference was determined. Since we are assessing differences, we are looking for significant p-values. In this case the change from model 1 to model 5 resulted in $\Delta L^2 = 12.6$, d.f. = 1, p<0.01, and the change from model 2 to model 5 resulted in $\Delta Lp^2 = 11.2$, d.f. = 1, p<0.01). This model 5 provided an improvement in model fit over both models 1 and 2. If a large number of variables was included in the model the p-value associated with model 5 might indicate too good a fit (Knoke and Burke, 1980). However in this case only two variables are present and so this specification has the dual virtues of parsimony and very good model fit.

An inspection of the L^2 and p-values of models 6–9 show that they produced no improvement over main effects (models 1 and 2). Consequently we can be confident that the effects of the bookmark and nationality of the parent company are neither dependent on country destination nor on the offer of results.

The final criterion for checking model adequacy is residual analysis. The standardized residuals were calculated for model 5 and plotted against observed cell frequencies. The plot is shown in Figure 4.1. It indicates that all residuals are comfortably within ±1.96 and that the distribution appears normal with no discernible trend.

A check on normality is provided by a plot of standardized residuals against expected residuals from a normal distribution. Figure 4.2 shows an almost perfect linear trend confirming that the standardized residuals are normally distributed.

Thus model 5 is accepted as the best fit to the data. It has the highest p-value and is parsimonious; also residual analysis indicates low residual values that are normally distributed. Clearly the inclusion of a bookmark and the nationality of the parent company have significant effects on response to this international mail survey.

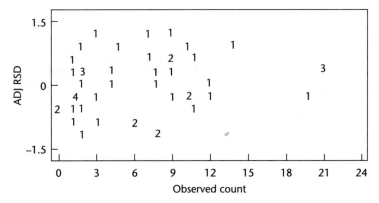

FIGURE 4.1 Plots of observed and expected cell counts against adjusted standardized residuals

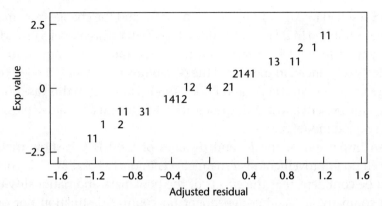

FIGURE 4.2 Plots of adjusted standardized residuals against expected residuals (normal plot)

Summary

Logit model analysis is a useful technique when the dependent variable is dichotomous and the independent variables are categorically scaled. In such circumstances techniques like regression analysis and analysis of variance are not appropriate for such categorical data where observations are not from populations that are normally distributed with constant variance. The use of the SPSS PC statistical package provides an efficient tool for applying logit model analysis. This paper has provided a step-by-step guide to its application.

References

Bishop, Y.M.M., Fienberg, S.E. and Holland, P.W. (1975), *Discrete Multivariate Analysis*, Cambridge MA: MIT Press

Everitt, B.S. (1977), *The Analysis of Contingency Tables*, London: Chapman and Hall

Fienberg, S.E. (1977), *The Analysis of Cross-classified Categorical Data*, Cambridge MA: MIT Press

Haberman, S.J. (1978), *Analysis of Qualitative Data*, New York: Academic Press.

Jobber, D., Mirza, H. and Wee, K.H. (1991), Incentives and response rates to cross-national business surveys: a logit model analysis, *Journal of International Business Studies*, **22**, 4, pp. 711–722

Knoke, D. and Burke, P.J. (1980), *Log-Linear Models*, Beverly Hills: Sage Publications

Norusis, M.J. (1990), SPSS/PC + advanced statistics 4.0, Chicago: SPSS Inc.

■ □ ■ ■ 5

Solving Marketing Problems with Conjoint Analysis

Marco Vriens

Conjoint analysis has become a popular research tool after its introduction in marketing in 1977 by Green and Rao. Both the academic as well as the commercial community have shown a strong interest in the conjoint methodology. In the academic literature attention is either directed at methodological issues or is aimed at application issues. A considerable amount of academic research is now available, both in the field of marketing as well as in other disciplines. The methodological developments have been reviewed extensively, as well as the commercial use of conjoint analysis. In the academic literature no systematic evaluation of the developments in the area of applications has been given. In this article we aim to fill this gap in the literature. After a brief discussion of the basic concepts of conjoint analysis we discuss the range of marketing problems which can be addressed by conjoint analysis. Issues to which attention is addressed include among others (1) strategic issues, (2) segmentation issues, (3) product related issues (including market simulations), (4) pricing issues, (5) distribution issues and (6) promotion and advertising issues. For each kind of issue the applicability of conjoint analysis is systematically reviewed. By classifying the applications according to the research purpose (i.e. the marketing problem) we obtain insight into the areas in which conjoint analysis may be successfully applied. In addition, a brief discussion of the types of products (e.g. consumer durables, fast moving consumer goods, industrial goods, etc.) to which conjoint analysis may be applied is provided. Finally, we also comment on the limitations of the methodology with respect to its applicability.

Introduction

The starting point for the marketing discipline lies in an adequate analysis of consumers' preferences for specific products or services. Organizations underscoring the marketing conception will be eager to match their products (or services) as closely as possible to these consumer preferences. To be able to do this, the marketing manager needs to know exactly to what extent the various characteristics of a product contribute to its overall attractiveness, or better yet to its overall profitability. This need not only concern the characteristics of the tangible product (e.g. features, brand name, packaging), but may also concern elements of the augmented product (e.g. after sales service, warranty, etc.; see Kotler, 1988).

A general model for the analysis of consumer preferences is the conjoint measurement model, developed originally by Luce and Tukey (1964), for which Green and Srinivasan adopted the name conjoint analysis. In the academic literature on conjoint analysis attention is either directed at methodological issues (e.g. estimation methods, preference elicitation procedures, improving predictive validity, etc.) or is aimed at application issues (cf. Vriens, 1992). Sometimes, the methodological angle cannot be separated from the specific application at hand. For example, several developments concerned with improving the predictive validity of conjoint analysis combined this issue with the issue of segmentation (e.g. Hagerty, 1985; Kamakura, 1988). Currently, a considerable amount of academic research is available both in the field of marketing as well as in other disciplines, such as psychology, transportation research, medical decision making.

During the development of the technique, several review articles have been written (Rao 1977; Green and Srinivasan, 1978; Timmermans, 1984; Louviere, 1988; Green and Srinivasan, 1990). These review articles are mainly concerned with the methodological and statistical developments, and little attention is given to applications. In addition, the commercial use of conjoint analysis has been documented extensively (Cattin and Wittink, 1982; Wittink and Cattin, 1989; and Wittink, Vriens and Burhenne, 1993). Wittink and Cattin have studied the commercial use of conjoint analysis in the US and Wittink, Vriens and Burhenne have replicated their study in Europe. These studies report the incidence of conjoint analysis applications by market research suppliers during a prespecified period of time. In addition, these studies report the percentages of applications which were designed for specific study purposes. For example, Wittink, Vriens and Burhenne (1993) found that pricing was the single most frequently identified purpose in Europe, whereas in the U.S. it was third in frequency. In Europe, new product/concept identification was ranked second and market segmentation was ranked third. Other purposes specified in these studies include competitive analyses, repositioning and distribution. The 'commercial use' studies demonstrate the increasing popularity of conjoint analysis. However, the commercial use studies remain incomplete for two reasons. First, several of the identified study purposes may in fact represent a rather broad class of marketing problems. For example, new product/concept identification probably represents marketing problems like product modification, redesigning of product lines and new product development (i.e. developing innovations). It is important to review the possibilities of conjoint analysis in each of these areas. Second, for some of the marketing problems, such as market segmentation, several approaches have been proposed in the literature to deal with the problem at hand. It is important to consider these approaches in some detail and to identify the pros and cons (which may even depend upon the specific application at hand).

Thus, to conclude, although in the academic literature much attention is directed at the way in which conjoint analysis may be applied to all kinds of marketing problems, no systematic evaluation of these developments has been given. In this article we aim to fill this gap in the literature. We begin with a brief discussion of the basic concepts of conjoint analysis. As in the commercial use papers we will also classify conjoint applications on the basis of the purpose for which it is used (e.g. segmentation, product modification, pricing etc.) and the type of product to which the conjoint methodology is applied (e.g. consumer durables, industrial goods, fast moving consumer goods, services, etc.). These classifications may serve as a useful framework for the practitioners who are currently using the technique or who are planning to use the technique in the near future. The purpose based classification is discussed in the next section followed by discussion of the product type based classification. These considerations show the powerful possibilities conjoint analysis has to offer for quite a large number of marketing problems. We conclude our paper with some considerations regarding the limitations of the technique with respect to its applicability to certain application areas.

Basic concepts

Conjoint analysis is a technique used by marketing managers to gain an insight into consumers' preferences for products and services. Products and services are hereby defined on a limited number of relevant characteristics. These characteristics are called **attributes**. These attributes can be defined on a number of levels. An example will make this clear. Coffeemakers can, among other things, be defined on the following attributes: price, brand name, capacity, colour and the presence/absence of a flavourcap. Subsequently, these attributes are defined by the values that they can adopt. An example of this is given in Table 5.1.

The (hypothetical) coffeemakers can be specified on the basis of these five attributes and corresponding levels. In the example mentioned above, 512 ($4 \times 4 \times 4 \times 4 \times 2$) coffeemakers can be constructed by varying the levels within the attributes. Full product descriptions of this kind are called 'full profiles'. An example of a full profile is given in Table 5.2.

Next in a conjoint analysis experiment respondents are asked to evaluate a limited collection out of the complete set of 512 in terms of preference or attraction (e.g. ordering or rating). The overall appreciations for the profiles can be related to the different levels of the attributes. To every level of each attribute a number is attached in such a way, that given a certain model, the rating or ordering can be reconstructed as well as possible. The numbers attached to these levels are called **partworth utilities**. Summing the partworth utilities, which belong to a certain profile, yields the overall utility if the additive model is used. It should be noted that the levels of the different attributes are quantified on one common scale: the utility scale. In this way we can see how the different characteristics are balanced against each other. This analysis takes place, in first instance, at the individual level. This means that we have a set of partworth utilities for each respondent and for each attribute. Such results enable us to answer the following questions:

TABLE 5.1 Attributes of coffeemakers

Capacity	max. 6 cups;	max. 8 cups;	max. 10 cups;	max. 14 cups
Price	$20	$30	$40	$50
Brand	Philips	Moulinex	Rowenta	Ismet
Colour	White	Black	Brown	Red
Flavour cap	Present/Absent			

TABLE 5.2 An example of a full profile

Brand:	Philips
Capacity:	Max. 10 cups
Price:	$50
Colour:	White
Flavour Cap:	Present

- What is the importance or utility of a certain level within a certain attribute?
- What is the importance of the attributes? This is usually defined as the difference between the utility of the most attractive level (within that attribute) and the utility of the least attractive level (as indicated by the partworth utilities).
- How are the attributes balanced against each other?
- Can we identify sharp increases or decreases of partworth utilities within an attribute (the critical transitions or barriers)?
- What is the overall utility of the profiles not involved in our research? We cannot only make statements about the overall utility of the alternatives used in our experiment, but we can also compute the overall utility for the remaining possible alternatives.
- Are there any individual differences? Because each respondent gives a number of evaluations about a set of different profiles, enough degrees of freedom are available to perform analyses at an individual level. By making a comparison of the estimated partworth utilities at the individual level between respondents, one can investigate the existence of individual differences. Combining these analyses with a cluster analysis procedure may yield respondents which are homogeneous with respect to their preference structure. Such segments are referred to as benefit segments.
- Finally, conjoint results enable us to perform market simulations in which we can ask 'what if' type of questions.

In most conjoint applications, questions like those above are answered. In the remaining part of this paper the discussion will centre around which specific marketing problems may be solved by the conjoint analysis approach described above.

A purpose based classification of conjoint analysis

Conjoint analysis studies can be classified according to the purpose they were meant to serve. Based on a survey among commercial users in the U.S. Cattin and Wittink (1982) identified five different purposes (new product/concept identification, pricing, market segmentation, advertising, distribution). In their 'update' study Wittink and Cattin (1989) added to this list competitive analysis and repositioning. Adapting the classifications found in the commercial use papers we arrived at a purpose based classification (see Table 5.3) which will be used in this paper to discuss the various possibilities. It should be stressed that these categories are not mutually exclusive. In fact Wittink and Cattin (1989) observed that on average more than two purposes were served by a given study, whereas Wittink, Vriens and Burhenne (1992) observed that on average approximately 1.5 purposes were served by a given study. In this section the various marketing problems mentioned are discussed according with their appearance in Table 5.3. We believe this to be the best way to convey valuable information to the practitioner.

Segmentation purposes

Modern marketing in industrialized countries cannot do without segmentation of the market. The implementation of the segmentation concept can take a variety of forms depending mainly on which type of segmentation base is used. Constructing segments on the basis of partworth utilities certainly assures that the responsiveness criterion is satisfied. Other criteria which should be satisfied for target segments include (1) substantiality and (2) accessibility and actionability. From the literature it is evident that the use of benefits outperforms the other segmentation bases, because this base is the only one which can (potentially) satisfy all of the aforementioned criteria (Wedel, 1990). The most common approach to operationalize the concept of benefits is through the use of conjoint analysis. The partworth utilities obtained via conjoint analysis may serve as the numerical representations of the benefits. In practice, the construction of benefit segments usually takes place in two stages. At the first stage partworths are estimated at the individual level. At the second stage individuals are clustered on the basis of similarity of benefits using some clustering algorithm. Examples can be found in Antilla, van den Heuvel and Möller (1981) and Sands and Warwick (1981). Before we discuss some drawbacks of the two-stage approach the results in these studies and others will be discussed.

In Antilla *et al.* (1981) conjoint analysis is applied to the market of colour television sets. The choice of colour television sets is considered to be dependent on six attributes namely: (1) size, (2) brand name, (3) price,

TABLE 5.3 A purpose-based classification

1.	Market segmentation
2.	Product decisions
3.	Competitive analyses
4.	Pricing decisions
5.	Promotional decisions
6.	Distribution purposes
7.	Remaining marketing problems

(4) guarantee, (5) colour reproduction and (6) design. The full profile method was chosen for data collection, using a fractional factorial design of 26 profiles. The sample consisted of 200 respondents. After individual analyses of the preferences a cluster analysis was performed to identify meaningful segments. These segments (clusters) are constructed in such a way that respondents within a segment have similar partworth utilities while there exist important differences between the identified segments. The authors were able to identify a quality-prone segment, a price-conscious segment and a segment in which modern design and small-tube television sets were highly valued. These results were compared with the existing product line. It turned out that the current product line of the company did not cover the third segment. These results initiated some further research and this resulted in the introduction of a new model specially designed for the third segment. Sands and Warwick's study (1981) concerned the optimal specification of a new table radio, which still had to be designed at the time of the study. Using the above described two-stage procedure, these authors found four benefit segments.

Knowing the attribute importances for every segment can also support the formulation of an appropriate communication message. For this purpose we may also want to link these segments to socio-economic data and media coverage for the respondents. Wind, Grashof & Goldhar (1978) for example, studied preferences for a system to obtain scientific and technical information (the STI system) and they found five benefit segments. To obtain more detailed information about the nature of the five segments the authors performed a series of multiple discriminant analyses in which segments were linked to several background characteristics.

However, the traditional two-stage approach to consumer benefit segmentation has a number of important methodological limitations. First, estimating conjoint models at the individual level results in unreliable partworth estimates which may cause misclassifications (Kamakura, 1988). An alternative two-stage procedure may overcome this limitation. In the alternative two-stage procedure subjects are clustered, at the first stage, on the basis of their stated preferences. At the second stage, partworths are estimated across respondents within each of the resulting segments (Green and Srinivasan, 1978). A second shortcoming, which concerns both two-stage procedures, is related to the criterion being optimized in clustering algorithms. Such algorithms are generally not directed at optimizing some measure of predictive fit (e.g. R^2) of the conjoint models within the segments or the expected mean square error of prediction (Hagerty, 1986). Fortunately, a number of procedures have been developed specifically to alleviate one or both of the aforementioned disadvantages. They have been proposed by, among others, Hagerty (1985), Kamakura (1988), DeSarbo et al. (1992), Wedel and Steenkamp (1989a,b) and

Wedel, Vriens and DeSarbo (1991). It is beyond the scope of this article to discuss this issue fully (see for an overview Vriens, Wedel and Wilms, 1992).

Another important development in which the segmentation concept is linked to conjoint analysis is the componential segmentation procedure developed by Green and DeSarbo (1979). Componential segmentation involves an extension of conjoint analysis (Green, 1977; Green and DeSarbo, 1979). The principle behind componential segmentation is the acknowledgement that background characteristics or characteristics of the situation may interact with product attributes. This interaction between respondent background characteristics and product attributes is assumed to influence the respondents' overall preferences with respect to a set of multi-attribute alternatives. In componential segmentation we are interested to what extent the interaction between respondents' background characteristics and product attributes contribute over and above the variance accounted for by the product attributes. It is important to see that we are not interested in the main effects due to respondents' background variables because these main effects only represent response biases, such as the tendency of some respondents to give higher evaluative ratings (Green and DeSarbo, 1979). The procedure discussed in Green and DeSarbo (1979), called the COSEG II approach, utilizes multiple regression model comparisons tests. The product attributes are entered first and unconditionally in the regression equation. In the next step, the interactions between product attributes and respondent or situation characteristics are systematically entered in the regression equation and tested by means of a model comparison test. The procedure is extended in a recent paper by Green, Krieger and Zelnio (1989). In their article they discuss how optimal products can be found for segments and vice versa. However, the implementation of the componential segmentation procedure involves the availability of a large database from which the sample of respondents can be drawn according to the chosen fractional factorial design. In addition, model misspecification arises because the parameters are estimated across respondents. Furthermore, it is not clear to what extent the componential segmentation procedure shows superior performance. Moore (1980) found no difference in the empirical performance of both the traditional two-stage procedure and the componentential segmentation procedure.

Product related purposes and competitive analyses

Product related marketing problems, especially those concerned with new product development, require a considerable amount of information. Part of these decisions are currently made by intuition, sometimes supported by small scale qualitative research findings or simulated purchase testing procedures. In this section we discuss the possibilities conjoint analysis has to offer to several product related issues. Among the product related issues we consider in this paragraph are those applications which are designed to assist possible product modifications, optimal product design, the redesigning of product lines, and the development and evaluation of new product concepts (see Table 5.4). The product related purposes in Table 5.4 may concern both consumer goods as well as industrial products. The principles discussed in this section may also apply, to a certain extent, to services. Each of the possibilities depicted in Table 5.4 can be combined with competitive analyses by using market simulation models.

The possibilities depicted in Table 5.4 are more or less hierarchically related. Product modifications usually refer to modifications or changes on one or two attributes. Also, adding a new feature to the product may be characterized as a product modification. Decisions with respect to optimal product design take into account all the attributes on which the product is defined. The redesigning of product lines not only considers all relevant product attributes but is also concerned with what happens to the other products in the product line. At the highest level in the hierarchy we consider those decisions which are concerned with new product concepts.

The introduction of the flavour cap on coffeemakers by Braun can be considered as an example of a product modification. Questions typically asked by management are:

1. Would consumers be interested in the modification?
2. What is the trade-off between this new feature and the other attributes?
3. How much is one willing to pay for this modification?

Sometimes management is completely unsure about the ideal specification of the product attributes. For example, in the study reported by Sands and Warwick (1981) the client was interested in introducing a new table radio and was completely unsure about what features to build into it. The conjoint results were used to identify a number of benefit segments, and the question was which combination of characteristics will lead to the highest utility within a given market segment. This problem is, in principle, easy to solve because

TABLE 5.4 Possible product decisions

1.	Product modifications
2.	Optimal product design
3.	Redesigning of product lines
4.	Evaluation of new product concepts

one just has to choose the most preferred level of each attribute. In reality, such problems are somewhat more complicated for a number of reasons. First, the costs to implement the different levels of the attributes must be calculated. Second, one should take into account the way in which other marketing mix variables are specified (e.g. distribution and promotion). Thirdly, it will be clear that product decisions can hardly ever be made in isolation. For example, when we consider the whole product line the problem becomes more complex. We speak of a product line when we are dealing with a group of closely related products. The individual models in the product line are more or less related. Decisions to add or eliminate models may influence the cost structure as well as the demand for different models in the product line. Changes in demand may have two important effects: (1) cannibalization effects and (2) competition effects. Naturally cannibalization effects should be kept to a minimum. In addition, competition effects should seriously be taken into account as well and their deteriorating effects should also be minimized. When a market share is taken away from one or more competitors, it is important to know where it comes from.

Page and Rosenbaum (1987) describe the way in which conjoint analysis can support redesigning decisions. The authors describe this in view of the Sunbeam case, in which the preferences for food processors were investigated. Sunbeam, the client for this research, thought it necessary to redesign the product line for food processors. Based on the results of conjoint analysis a segmentation analysis was executed. This analysis produced a clearer insight into a number of likely product modifications. Next, an estimation was made of the preference shares of all brands and models currently on the market, based on the results of conjoint analysis. For each respondent, the overall utility was estimated for every brand and model. Further, the position of the preference shares (or estimated market shares) for the different brands and models were calculated. The correlation with the actual market shares appeared to be no less than 0.96. This situation is called 'base case' and it will be clear that a reliable market simulation can be based on it. A market simulation examines the way in which market shares will move when the current product line is changing. For example by (1) adding a model in the product line; (2) adding two or more models in the product line; (3) adding one model and eliminate another, etc. These simulations will help us understand to what extent the proposed changes lead to an increase (or even decrease) of the organization's market share in the market concerned.

Based on a simulation such as those described above the Sunbeam organization has added three completely new models to the product line. However, it is possible to go even one step further. The simulations also show from which competitors the market share is taken away and to what extent this has been done. In a case study reviewed by Clarke (1987), similar research is described to the one by Page and Rosenbaum. This case centres around the product line of forklift trucks. The set-up of this study is basically similar to the study by Page and Rosenbaum. In this study, however, a Japanese firm was expected to enter the market in the short term with a cheap, but good quality model. The organization's management thought Japan capable of producing cheaper models for the low price segment against lower costs. A second problem concerned the existence of a strong competitor on the market. Every increase in market share made at that specific competitor's expense might cause strong and undesirable reactions. Therefore a scenario was chosen that did not lead to an optimal improvement in market share. Instead a scenario was chosen that led to an improvement in market share, which was taken away from weaker competitors, who probably lacked the power to strike back.

The results of the product simulator approach, described above, have been used to provide an estimate of the probable market share of some possible product modification or product line modification. According to Zufryden (1988), who refers to product modifications as new products, this approach disregards two critical aspects of the so-called new product performance, namely: (1) the prediction of cumulative trial, and (2) the prediction of repeated purchase patterns of the new product over time. Zufryden's approach consists of a stochastic model that utilizes the outputs of a market simulation, based on conjoint results, to estimate the distribution of purchase probability for a new product over a population of potential consumers. That is, the actual predicted choice probabilities are used to fit a beta distribution. These results then, describe the consumer brand-choice behaviour given the occurence of a product-category purchase occasion. This fitted distribution is then combined with a model of product-class purchase incidence. The brand-choice model and the product-category purchase incidence model are now integrated in a brand-choice purchase incidence model and enable us to estimate the cumulative purchase pattern of the simulated brands.

The development of new products probably is the most risky endeavour among product related marketing problems. Conjoint analysis has often been identified as a relevant method in the new product development process. Among the 24 methods and models to deal with new product development problems, Mahajan and Wind (1991) found conjoint analysis the sixth frequently used. Moreover, Mahajan and Wind (1991) found conjoint analysis to be the most satisfactory method. Among commercial conjoint applications Wittink, Vriens and Burhenne (1992) demonstrate that new product development was mentioned as one of the most frequent application areas. In the process of new product development, product evaluation takes place after generating new ideas. The aim of this is to eliminate ideas that do not correspond with the organization's long term objectives. Next, as a transition to the business economical analysis following, it could be investigated what the specification of the new product should look like to attract as many buyers as possible, also with the help of conjoint analysis.

Pricing related purposes

In most applications price is considered equally important as other attributes. In those cases where the effect of pricing is not the main course of interest, the definition of a number of realistic price levels will do. It is not advisable simply to omit the attribute from the study, because in that way non-realistic profiles develop and respondents will label prices to those profiles themselves. An example of such a price application can be found in Currim, Weinberg and Wittink (1981). This study centres around the potential features of a subscription to a number of theatre shows. The management was interested in the level of discount the subscribers should get. Such reductions are usually based on the manager's intuition and/or experience. With the help of conjoint analysis this can be investigated systematically. The study by Currim *et al.* (1981) showed that pricing is relatively less important than some other attributes. The results of this study enabled the management to decide on the right marketing mix for subscriptions.

It could be imagined that the fixing of an optimal price is so important that we cannot treat it as just another attribute in the conjoint analysis research. In the literature a number of methods are suggested to approach pricing problems with the help of conjoint analysis. Besides, it is well recognized that management should have information about the price elasticity of demand. Market planners, for example, do want to forecast brand demand at various alternative price levels in order to develop pricing strategies and in order to set sales goals (Wyner, Benedetti and Trapp (1984). In some cases demand curves can easily be estimated for existing brands by multiple regression, using historical data. In other cases, for example, for new products, there are no historical data available to correlate quantities demanded at various price levels. Therefore other procedures have been proposed for dealing with these kinds of pricing problems. The traditional conjoint approach may be less attractive for these kinds of problems because of one of the following reasons. First, in the traditional conjoint approach it is assumed that each price can appear at each level of the other attributes, including brand name. This means that all brands are subject to identical variations in the price levels. Second, it is assumed that no interaction exists between price and brand name. Although it is possible to adapt the traditional conjoint approach, in order to relax these assumptions, a number of authors have proposed a series of alternative approaches which circumvent the above assumptions and which also exhibit some additional advantages.

A first alternative conjoint approach was proposed by Mahajan, Green and Goldberg (1982). By adapting the data collection procedure used by Jones (1975) they were able to determine own-product and cross-product price demand relationships. The main features of the procedure are discussed below. Let us assume that we only consider brand name and price. As opposed to traditional conjoint analysis each brand is seen as a single attribute. For these so-called brand-attributes a number of price levels are defined: the specific price levels belonging to that specific brand. If we have, for example, four brand names, each defined on five price levels then a full factorial design would consist of $5^4 = 625$ combinations. The next step is to select some fractional factorial design to construct a manageable stimulus set for the respondents. A stimulus of the type described above could look like:

    brand A $150
    brand B $165
    brand C $220
    brand D $125

In traditional conjoint analysis a stimulus would represent one product profile which can be evaluated by the respondent. In this approach one stimulus in fact represents four product profiles where each profile is defined on two attributes. In the procedure of Mahajan, Green and Goldberg the respondent is not asked to rate each product profile separately but the respondent is asked to allocate 100 points across the four alternatives so as to reflect the likelihood of choosing each brand–price combinations. Note that for each brand a set of brand-specific price levels is or can be defined. Subsequently, the data are transformed in order to be able to estimate a conditional logit model using generalized least squares for parameter estimation at the segment level (see Theil, 1969). Because the model also includes the prices of competitive brands, the results yield price elasticities as well as cross-price elasticities.

The procedure proposed by Mahajan, Green and Goldberg (1982) was extended by Wyner, Benedetti and Trapp (1984). Their procedure not only models the choice for a specific brand but also models the quantity bought. In addition it allows for the possibility that more than one type of product is chosen by an individual. Their procedure extends the procedure proposed by Mahajan, Green and Goldberg (1982) in at least two important ways. First, instead of considering only price and brand name other attributes are included. Second, their procedure not only models the choice for a specific brand but also the quantity bought. A similar procedure was proposed by Louviere (1986).

An important disadvantage of procedures like the one proposed by Mahajan, Green and Goldberg (1982), Wyner, Benedetti and Trapp (1984) and Louviere (1986) is the fact that these choice-like data cannot be estimated at the individual level. Therefore, as an alternative Goldberg, Green and Wind (1984) and Green and Krieger (1990) propose to use a hybrid conjoint modelling approach in which it is possible to estimate price–demand relationships while maintaining individual differences. An extensive discussion of this approach is beyond the scope of this article.

Promotion and distribution problems

A smaller number of applications of conjoint analysis focusing on promotional and distribution problems has appeared in the literature. Nevertheless, conjoint analysis can also be applied succesfully in these areas, as the following discussion will illustrate. An example of how conjoint analysis may be applied to the design of optimal trade promotions can be found in Levy, Webster and Kerin (1983). They discuss how conjoint analysis can contribute to gain an insight in the way push strategies should be formulated. It is often clear which action variables are important to the distributors, but it is not always certain how high these variables should be. It is for instance known that distributors appreciate corporate advertising, but the level of the available budget is to be discussed. Consequently, it may be wondered to what extent actions directed at increasing the distributor's preference for the product will have effect on the profits. This problem was solved by

1. identifying relevant action variables (in this case corporate advertising, use of coupons, financial payment conditions and service level);
2. determining the preference of possible combinations (the conjoint analysis part);
3. creating a sales response function, a cost function and finally the profit function.

In this way the push strategy leading to an optimal profit can be selected. An example of the way in which sales quota are determined can be found in the study by Darmon (1979). In determining sales quotas profits, among other things, a balance must be found between risk and reward. An example of a promotional/distribution decision can be found in a study by Akaah and Korgaonkar (1988). In this study the best way to style a direct mail offer is discussed. The applications mentioned above can be characterized by a combination of promotion and distribution decisions.

Although the concept of distribution represents a complex set of variables it is possible to include elements of distribution in a conjoint study. For example, suppose we assume that the demand for a product is negatively related to the implicit costs. Implicit costs may include transportation costs as well as opportunity costs. Such aspects could be incorporated in a conjoint study by using attributes like 'travelling time' or 'availability'. Another problem in this area may simply focus on the extent to which general attributes of a store, such as location and architectural characteristics, affect store patronage. For example, Verhallen and DeNooij (1982) investigated to what extent characteristics of the store positively influence consumers' shopping behaviour. The characteristics involved were price level, distance to the shops, the assortment and the quality of the offered goods.

For some specialized retailers, adding new products to their product line may constitute an important source of revenue. In such cases it is vital to assess the likely number of consumers who will try a particular new product. Louviere (1984) presents an approach for solving such problems. Louviere's approach attempts to forecast the likely number of consumers who can be expected to try new products offered at competing fast food restaurants.

The study of Verhallen and DeNooij (1981) models store choice and not choice of shopping centre. However, assessing the impact of changes in retail facilities, for example the opening of a new shopping centre, or the distribution of consumer expenditures among shopping centres appears to be another important retail marketing problem. Modelling the choice of a shopping centre provides incremental information to retailers and planners for two reasons. First, the prediction of sales levels of total shopping centres from store choice models is practically impossible. Second, it seems important to include relevant attributes of shopping centres that emerge at the shopping centre only (e.g. routing and furnishings, physical layout and atmosphere). A study where this retail marketing problem is tackled can be found in Oppewal and Timmermans (1991). These authors use the conjoint choice approach to tackle this retail marketing problem. Other studies where this type of marketing problem is tackled include the studies of Timmermans (1982); Timmermans, Van der Heyden and Westerveld (1984).

A product-type based classification

In reviewing the literature on conjoint analysis (both the methodological parts as well as the applications part) we encountered a broad range of products to which conjoint analysis has been applied. We can assign these products to a number of distinct product types. These product types are depicted in Table 5.5, along with some selected examples. The list of examples is probably not complete, but it provides the (prospective) user an overview of the possibilities.

TABLE 5.5 A product type based classification

Product types	Examples
Fast moving consumer goods	Hair shampoos, potatoes, detergents, meat, yoghurt, cakes
Frequently bought consumer goods	Shoes, carpet cleaners, sweaters
Consumer durables	Typewriting machines, automobiles, refrigerators, cameras, food processors, colour television sets, cooking equipment, pick up trucks
Industrial products	Scientific technological information system, fork lift trucks
Services	
Financial services	Checking accounts, subscriptions to performing art series
Entertainment services	Menus
Transportation services	Airplane travelling
Health care services	Clinical laboratories, primary rural health care organizations, health maintenance organizations, medication drugs, treatment strategies

A number of these examples were found in papers where the application of conjoint analysis on some product was meant to illustrate some methodological or statistical argument. For example, in Wedel, Vriens and DeSarbo (1991) data obtained from a commercial study, which was concerned with preference for cakes, were used to demonstrate the potential of their maximum likelihood procedure for simultaneous segmentation and estimation. In other cases examples were found in papers which were fully application oriented. For example, Page and Rosenbaum (1987) devote a full paper to the application of conjoint analysis on food processors. All steps taken in a conjoint study are discussed extensively, from the data collection phase to the market simulation phase.

Sometimes special problems are encountered in the application of conjoint analysis, which are related to the particular product category. For example, many high-tech products such as cameras or car stereos are so complex (i.e. attributes are perhaps unknown to the prospective buyer) and have so many possible relevant attributes that this becomes a problem in itself, because differences may then occur between respondents with respect to the set of relevant attributes. To accommodate this type of heterogeneity between consumers, we either have to include a large number of relevant attributes, for which we then have to use special data collection methods, or we can individualize the conjoint tasks. For example in their study on price premiums for hotel amenities Goldberg, Green and Wind (1984) use 43 attributes. In order to keep respondents task manageable they use the hybrid modelling approach (Green, Carroll and Goldberg, 1981). In an alternative approach, which individualizes the conjoint task, proposed by Böcker and Schweikl (1988), respondents have to indicate, before they are confronted with the actual conjoint task, the set of relevant attributes via either direct questioning, or working through a computer assisted information display matrix.

Finally, we want to mention that a number of previous studies have demonstrated the utility of conjoint analysis to solve health care marketing problems. Wind (1974), as one of the first to apply conjoint analysis in a health care related context, studied physicians, selection of a clinical laboratory. A more general approach of how conjoint analysis may support marketing decisions in health care organizations was provided by Wind and Spitz (1976) in a pilot study (N = 56) in which they use conjoint analysis to model the hospital selection decision of individuals. In addition, these authors distinguish basically between two health care problem areas which can be tackled with the help of conjoint analysis.

A first problem area is concerned with the determination of the objectives, criteria and decision rules for various health care decisions. An example of such a problem is 'How should we allocate resources among competing objectives?' (e.g. profits, expansions, etc.). A second problem area is concerned with the selection of target markets for a given health care organization. Problems in this area could be (1) what target markets should a health maintenance organization (HMO) appeal to; (2) what product/service mix should be charged, and where should the HMO be located. Parker, Barnett and Srinivasan (1976), for example, propose the conjoint methodology for the location problem of the rural primary health care facility. The problem in their study was to determine the number, location and physical characteristics of those additional facilities that would, with respect to the existing system, yield the greatest incremental benefit to the regional population given a capital constraint. Other studies also demonstrated the usefulness of conjoint analysis for health care marketing (e.g. Malhotra and Jain, 1982; Rosko and McKenna, 1983; Akaah and Becherer, 1983; Rosko *et al.* 1985). All these studies have used conjoint analysis to measure consumers' preference structure for health care services. The study of Rosko *et al.* (1985) provides, in addition to the other examples, a demonstration of how market responses can be simulated as a result of changes in the providers' marketing mix. For example, the study assessed the price elasticity for some new products.

A final health care problem area to be mentioned here in which conjoint analysis may be applied successfully is found in a number of papers published by Maas (1992). These papers dealt with ways in which conjoint analysis can be used to improve and support the medical decision making of patients. For example, how should patients choose among alternative treatments strategies. The basic idea is to identify the treatment with the highest utility (using pair comparisons data obtained from the patient) among outcomes that vary in quality and quantity of life.

Conclusions and discussion

Conjoint analysis has received quite a lot of attention in the literature, ever since its introduction in marketing by Green and Rao (1977). Developments were either directed at methodological issues or at application issues. Knowledge of the methodological state of affairs is of extreme importance and therefore several authors have reviewed these methodological developments. In these reviews the various ways in which conjoint analysis may be able to solve marketing problems are only scarcely covered. However, both the marketing manager and the market researcher would like to know first why they should use conjoint analysis in the first place. Therefore, it is important to know for which types of marketing problems conjoint analysis may be used and to which types of products it may be applied. Reviewing the literature with respect to this matter shows that conjoint applications can be classified according to the marketing problem they were meant to solve. This purpose-based classification illustrates the value conjoint analysis has to offer for dealing with various marketing problems. Issues like market segmentation, product development and pricing have been the subject of much research which has resulted in sound knowledge regarding the way to deal with these problems. Given the fact that these areas are also the most popular areas in commercial practice, this knowledge seems especially relevant for both commercial users and their clients.

Although promotion and distribution seem less popular in commercial practice, the academic developments in these areas have clearly shown that there is much potential here especially in the area of consumers' retail choices. To provide a comprehensive discussion of conjoint applications we also investigated for which types of products and services conjoint analysis has been used. We found conjoint analysis to be applicable to practically all sorts of products such as fast moving consumer goods, consumer durables, industrial goods and various types of services. We also identified some characteristics of products which may have implications for the way conjoint analysis is applied.

For example, products which need to be defined on a large number of attributes need some adaptation to make the task of the respondent manageable. For products in which the design-attribute may be expected to play an important role one has to adapt the stimulus (profile) presentation method. Instead of using verbal description, one should use pictorial representation (see for example Page and Rosenbaum, 1987) or even better computer assisted design techniques to make realistic representations of the set of hypothetical products, (see Vriens, Looschilder, Rosbergen and Wittink, 1992).

Thus, although we demonstrated that conjoint analysis may be useful in a broad range of situations, there are also circumstances under which the application of conjoint analysis may either be difficult or not advisable. One limitation of conjoint analysis mentioned by Mahajan and Wind (1991) includes the method's 'inability to capture the complexity of the market'. Furthermore it may be difficult to apply conjoint analysis in situations in which a product's preference is predominantly determined by image characteristics. Product categories like cigarettes and jeans are examples of these kinds of products. In situations where the research budget is very low or where the time to conduct the study is rather limited we probably would also not advise use of the conjoint approach, because a proper execution of a conjoint study requires a considerable amount of both time and money. The adoption of advanced method and techniques in marketing research is strongly influenced by the extent in which these advanced techniques are able to solve marketing problems. We hope to have demonstrated the potential of conjoint analysis and as a result to have contributed to its adoption by marketing managers and market researchers.

References

Acito, F. and Hustad, T.P. (1981), Industrial product concept testing, *Industrial Management Review*, Vol. **10**, pp. 157–164

Addelman, S. (1962), Orthogonal main-effect plans for asymmetrical factorial experiments, *Technometrics*, Vol. 4, pp. 21–46

Akaah, Ishmael and Becherer, R. (1983), Integrating a consumer orientation into the planning of HMO programs: an application of conjoint segmentation, *Journal of Health Care Marketing*, Vol. **3** (Spring), pp. 9–18

Akaah, I.P. and Korgaonkar, P.K. (1988), A conjoint investigation of the relative importance of risk relievers in direct marketing, *Journal of Advertising Research*, (Aug./Sept.), 38–44

Antilla, M., van den Heuvel, R.R. and Möller, K. (1981), Conjoint measurement for marketing management, *European Journal of Marketing*, Vol. **14**, No. 7, pp. 397–409

Böcker, F. and Schweikl, H. (1988), 'Better preference prediction with individualized sets of relevant attributes, *International Journal of Research in Marketing*, Vol. 5, 15–24

Cattin, P., and Wittink, D.R. (1982), Commercial use of conjoint analysis: a survey, *Journal of Marketing*, **46** (Summer), 44–53

Clarke, D.G. (1987), *Marketing Analysis and Decision Making*, Redwood City CA: The Scientific Press

Currim, I.S., Weinberg C.B. and Wittink D.R. (1981), Design of subscription programs for a performing art series, *Journal of Consumer Research*, **8** (June), 67–75

Darmon, R.Y. (1979), Setting sales quotas with conjoint analysis, *Journal of Marketing Research*, Vol. **XVI**, 133–140

DeSarbo, W.S., Wedel, M., Vriens, M. and Ramaswamy, V. (1992), Latent class metric conjoint analysis, *Marketing Letters*, 3:3, 273–288

Elrod, T., Louviere, J.J. and Davey, K.S. (1992), An empirical comparison of ratings-based and choice-based conjoint models, *Journal of Marketing Research*, Vol. **XXIX** (August), pp. 368–377

Fishbein, M. (1966), The relationship between beliefs, attitudes and behavior, in S. Feldman (Ed.), *Cognitive Consistency*, New York: Academic Press

Goldberg, S.M, Green, P.E. and Wind, Y. (1984), Conjoint analysis of price premiums for hotel amenities, *Journal of Business*, Vol. **57**, no. 1, pp. s111–s147

Green, P.E. (1977), A new approach to market segmentation, *Business Horizons*, Vol. **20** (February), pp. 61–73

Green, P.E., Carroll, J.D. and Goldberg, S.M. (1981), A general approach to product design optimalization via conjoint analysis, *Journal of Marketing*, **45** (Summer), 103–123

Green, P.E. and DeSarbo, W.S. (1979), Componential segmentation in the analysis of consumer tradeoffs, *Journal of Marketing*, Vol. **43** (Fall), pp. 83–79

Green, P.E. and Krieger, A.M. (1990), A hybrid conjoint model for price demand estimation, *European Journal of Operations Research*, **44**, 28–38

Green, P.E., and Krieger, A.M. (1991), Segmenting markets with conjoint analysis, *Journal of Marketing*, Vol. **55**, No. 4, pp. 20–31

Green, P.E., Krieger, A.M. and Zelnio, R.N. (1989), A componential segmentation model with optimal product design features, *Decision Sciences*, Vol. **20**, pp. 221–238

Green, P.E. and Srinivasan, V. (1978), Conjoint analysis in consumer research: issues and outlook, *Journal of Consumer Research*, Vol. **5** (September), pp. 103–123

Green, P.E., and Srinivasan, V. (1990), Conjoint analysis in marketing research: new developments and directions, *Journal of Marketing*, Vol. **54**, No. 4, pp. 3–19

Hagerty, M. (1985), Improving the predictive power of conjoint analysis: the use of factor analysis and cluster analysis, *Journal of Marketing Research*, Vol. **22** (May), pp. 168–184

Hagerty, M. (1986), The cost of simplifying preference models, *Marketing Science*, Vol. **5**, No. 4, pp. 298–319

Jones, D.F. (1975), A survey technique to measure demand under various pricing strategies, *Journal of Marketing*, Vol. **39** (July), pp. 75–77

Kamakura, W.A. (1988), A least squares procedure for benefit segmentation with conjoint experiments, *Journal of Marketing Research*, Vol. **25** (May), pp. 157–67

Keeney, R.L. and Lilien, G.L. (1987), New industrial product design and evaluation using multiattribute value analysis, *Journal of Product Innovation Management*, Vol. **4**, pp. 185–198

Kotler, P. (1988), *Marketing management*, Englewood Cliffs, NJ. Prentice-Hall.

Leeflang, Peter S.H. and Beukenkamp, P.A. (1987), *Probleemgebied Marketin, een Management Benadering (Problem Area Marketing, A Management Approach)*, deel 1b, Leiden/Antwerpen, Stenfert Kroese.

Levy, M., Webster, J. and Kerin, R.A. (1983), Formulating push marketing strategies: a method and application, *Journal of Marketing*, Vol. **47** (Winter 1983), 25–34

Louviere, J.J. (1984), Using discrete choice experiments and multinomial logit choice models to forecast trial in a competitive retail environment: a fast food restaurant illustration, *Journal of Retailing*, Vol. **60**, No. 4, pp. 81–107

Louviere, J.J. (1986), A conjoint model for analyzing new product positions in a differentiated market with price competition, *Advances in Consumer Research*, 375–380

Louviere, J.J. (1988), Conjoint analysis modeling of stated preferences: a review of theory, methods, recent developments and external validity, *Journal of Transport Economics and Policy*, Vol. **22** (January), pp. 93–119

Louviere, J.J. and Johnson, R.D. (1991), Using conjoint analysis to measure retail image, In: *New Developments in Retail Location Analysis*. (Eds.) E. Ghosh and C. Ingene, Lexington Books

Louviere, J. and Woodworth, G.G. (1983), 'Design and analysis of simulated consumer choice or allocation experiments: an approach based on aggregated data, *Journal of Marketing Research*, Vol. **20** (November), pp. 350–367

Luce, R.D. and Tukey, J.W. (1964), Simultaneous conjoint measurement: a new type of fundamental measurement, *Journal of Mathematical Psychology*, Vol. **1**, pp. 1–27

Maas, A. (1992), The use of conjoint measurement in medical decision making, a theoretical and practical contribution, Dissertation, University of Nijmegen, The Netherlands

Mahajan, V., Green, P.E. and Goldberg, S.M. (1982), A conjoint model for measuring self- and cross-price/demand relationships, *Journal of Marketing Research*, **XIX**, 334–342

Mahajan, V. and Wind, W. (1991), 'New product models: practice, shortcomings and desired improvements', Report No. 91–125, Marketing Science Institute, Cambridge, MA.

Malhotra, Naresh and Arun Jain (1982), A conjoint analysis approach to health care marketing and planning, *Journal of Health Care Marketing*, Vol. **2** (Spring), pp. 35–44

Messier, W.F. and Emery, D.R. (1980), Some cautionary notes on the use of conjoint measurement for human judgment modeling, *Decision Sciences*, Vol. **11**, pp. 678–690

Moore, W.L. (1980), Levels of aggregation in conjoint analysis: an empirical comparison, *Journal of Marketing Research*, Vol. **XVII** (November), pp. 516–523

Oppewal, H. and Timmermans, H.J.P. (1991), 'A conjoint choice approach to model consumer choice of shopping centre', Paper presented for the Meeting of the SISWO Working Group onMathematical Geography and Urban Planning, Utrecht, 29 November 1991

Page, A.L. and Rosenbaum, H.F. (1987), Redesigning product lines with conjoint analysis: how sunbeam does it, *Journal of Product Innovation Management*, (June) **4**, 120–137

Parker, B. and Srinivasan, V. (1976), A consumer preference approach to the planning of rural primary health care facilities, *Operations Research*, Vol. **24** (September/October), pp. 991–1025

Rao, Vithala (1977), Conjoint measurement in marketing analysis', In: *Multivariate Methods in Market and Survey Research*. (Eds) J.N. Sheth, Chicago: American Marketing Association, pp. 257–86

Rosko, M.D., and McKenna, W. (1983), Modeling consumer choices of health plans: a comparison of two techniques, *Social Science and Medicine*, Vol. **17** (July), pp. 421–29

Rosko, M.D., DeVita, M., McKenna, W.F. and Walker, L.R. (1985), Strategic marketing applications of conjoint analysis: an HMO perspective, *Journal of Health Care Marketing*, Vol. **5**, no. 4, pp. 27–38

Sands, S. and Warwick, K. (1981), What product benefits to offer to whom: an application of conjoint segmentation, *California Management Review*, Vol. **XXIV**, No. 1, pp. 69–74

Steenkamp, J-B. E.M. and Wedel, M. (1991), Segmenting retail markets on store image using a consumer-based methodology, *Journal of Retailing*, Vol. **67** (Fall), No. 3, pp. 300–20.

Theil, H. (1969), A multinominal extension of the linear logit model, *International Economics Review*, Vol. **10** (October), pp. 251–59

Timmermans, H.J.P. (1982), Consumer choice of shopping centre: an information integration approach, *Regional Studies*, Vol. **16**, pp. 171–82

Timmermans, H.J.P. (1984), Decompositional multiattribute preference models in spatial choice analysis: a review of some recent developments, *Progress in Human Geography*, Vol. **8**, pp. 189–221

Timmermans, H.J.P., van der Heijden, R.E.C.M. and Westerveld, H. (1984), Decision-making between multiattribute choice alternatives: a model of spatial shopping behaviour using conjoint measurement, *Environment and Planning A*, Vol. **16**, pp. 377–87

Verhallen, T.M.M. and de Nooij, G.J. (1982), Retail attribute and shopping patronage, *Journal of Economic Psychology*, **2**, 39–455

Vriens, Marco (1992), Strengths and weaknessess of various conjoint analysis techniques and suggestions for improvement, In: Proceedings of the 2nd SKIM Seminar *Market Opportunities with Advanced Research Techniques*.

Vriens, M., Loosschilder, G., Rosbergen, E. and Wittink, D.R. (1992), Using computer-aided designing techniques in conjoint analysis, Research Proposal

Vriens, M., Wedel, M. and Wilms, T. (1992), Segmentation for metric conjoint analysis: a Monte Carlo comparison, Working Paper

Wedel, M. (1990), Clusterwise regression and market segmentation, developments and applications, Doctoral dissertation, Wlacenincen

Wedel, M. and Kistemaker, C. (1989), Consumer benefit segmentation using clusterwise linear regression, *International Journal of Research in Marketing*, Vol. **6**, pp. 45–59

Wedel, M. and Steenkamp, J-B. E.M. (1989), Fuzzy clusterwise regression approach to benefit segmentation, *International Journal of Research in Marketing*, Vol. **6**, pp. 241–258

Wedel, M., Vriens, M. and DeSarbo, W. (1991), 'A maximum likelihood methodology for segmentation in conjoint models', Research Memorandum, Institute of Economic Research, Faculty of Economics, University of Gröningen

Wind, Y. (1974), Recent approaches to the study of organizational buying behaviour, In: T.V. Green (Ed.), *Combined Proceedings of the 1973 American Marketing Association Conferences*, pp. 203–206, Chicago

Wind, Y., Grashof, J.F. and Goldhar, K.D. (1978), Market-based guidelines for design of industrial products, *Journal of Marketing*, (July), 27–37

Wind, Y. and Spitz, L. (1976), Analytical approach to marketing decisions in health-care organizations, *Operations Research*, Vol. **24**, No. 5 (September/October), pp. 973–90

Wittink, D.R. and Cattin, P. (1989), Commercial use of conjoint analysis: an update, *Journal of Marketing*, Vol. **53** (July 1989), 91–6

Wittink, D.R., Vriens, M. and Burhenne, W. (1994), Commercial use of conjoint analysis in Europe: results and critical reflections, *International Journal of Research in Marketing*, **11**, 41–52

Wyner, G.A., Benedetti, L.H. and Trapp, B.M. (1984), Measuring the quantity and mix of product demand, *Journal of Marketing*, Vol. **48** (Winter), 101–109

Zufryden, F.S. (1988), Using conjoint analysis to predict trial and repeat-purchase patterns of new frequently purchased products, *Decision Sciences*, Vol. **19**, pp. 55–71

■ □ ■ ■ 6

Forecasting for Marketing

J. Scott Armstrong and Roderick J. Brodie

Research on forecasting is extensive and includes many studies that have tested alternative methods in order to determine which ones are most effective. We review this evidence in order to provide guidelines for forecasting for marketing. The coverage includes intentions, Delphi, role playing, conjoint analysis, judgemental bootstrapping, analogies, extrapolation, rule-based forecasting, expert systems, and econometric methods. We discuss research about which methods are most appropriate to forecast market size, actions of decision makers, market share, sales, and financial outcomes. In general, there is a need for statistical methods that incorporate the manager's domain knowledge. This includes rule-based forecasting, expert systems, and econometric methods. We describe how to choose a forecasting method and provide guidelines for the effective use of forecasts including such procedures as scenarios.

Introduction

Forecasting has long been important to marketing practitioners. For example, Dalrymple (1987), in his survey of 134 U.S. companies, found that 99 per cent prepared formal forecasts when they used formal marketing plans. In Dalrymple (1975), 93 per cent of the companies sampled indicated that sales forecasting was 'one of the most critical' aspects, or a 'very important' aspect of their company's success. Jobber, Hooley and Sanderson (1985), in a survey of 353 marketing directors from British textile firms, found that sales forecasting was the most common of nine activities on which they reported.

Managers' forecasting needs vary considerably. They may need to forecast the size and growth of a market or product category. When strategic issues are being considered, they need to forecast the actions and reactions of key decision makers such as competitors, suppliers, distributors, governments, their own actions, and complementors' (organizations with whom they cooperate) actions. These actions can help to forecast market share. The resulting forecasts allow one to calculate a sales forecast. If strategic issues are not important, one can extrapolate sales directly. Finally, by forecasting costs and using the sales forecast, one can forecast profits and other financial outcomes. These forecasting needs and their relationships are illustrated in Figure 6.1.

The purpose of this chapter is to provide guidance to managers about the use of formal forecasting methods in marketing. In developing the guidelines, it is recognized that managers may have negative attitudes towards the usefulness of formal forecasting. This may have occurred because they have used poor forecasts in the past, because they had unrealistic expectations about forecasting accuracy, or because they do not like it when forecasts conflict with their beliefs about the future.

The guidelines draw on the evidence collected in the Forecasting Principles Project, which is described on the website http://www-marketing. wharton.upenn.edu/forecast. The evidence is provided in *Principles of*

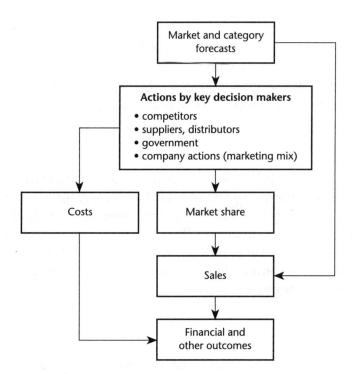

FIGURE 6.1 Needs for marketing forecasts

Forecasting: A Handbook for Researchers and Practitioners (2000) edited by Scott Armstrong.

Forecasting methods

Forecasting involves methods that derive from judgemental sources and from statistical sources. These methods and the relationships between them are shown in the flowchart in Figure 6.2. Going down the flowchart, there is an increasing amount of integration between judgemental and statistical data and procedures. This integration, which has been studied by researchers in the last decade, can improve forecast accuracy (Armstrong and Collopy, 1998).

   We provide only a brief description of the methods and their application. More detailed descriptions are provided in forecasting textbooks such as Makridakis, Wheelwright and Hyndman (1998).

Methods based on judgement

Intentions

With intentions surveys, people are asked to predict how they would behave in various situations. Intentions surveys are widely used when sales data are not available, such as for new product forecasts. There is much empirical research about the best way to assess intentions and Morwitz (2000) draws upon this to develop principles for using intentions in forecasting.

Role playing

A person's role may be a dominant factor in some situations, such as in predicting how someone in a firm would behave in negotiations. Role playing is useful for making forecasts of the behaviour of individuals who are interacting with others, and especially when the situation involves conflict. The key principle here is to provide a realistic simulation of the interactions. It is a method that has considerable potential for forecasting although, currently, it is seldom used (Armstrong, 2000b).

Expert opinions

Expert opinion studies differ substantially from intentions surveys. When an expert is asked to predict the behaviour of a market, there is no need to claim

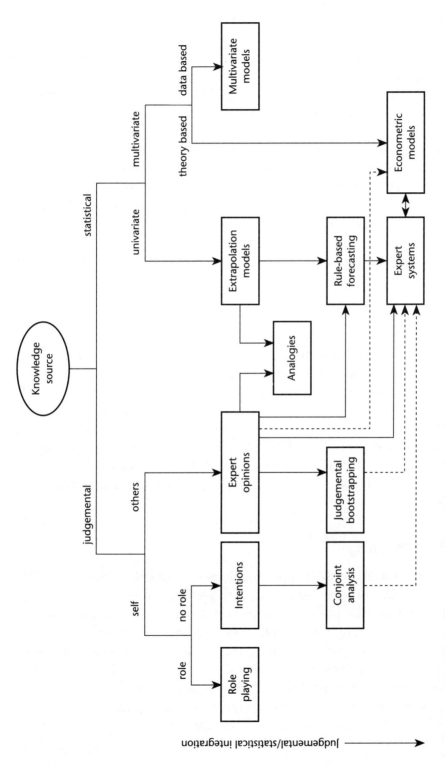

FIGURE 6.2 Characteristics of forecasting methods and their relationships (dotted lines represent possible relationships)

that this is a representative expert. Quite the contrary, the expert may be exceptional.

One principle is to combine independent forecasts from a group of experts, typically 5 to 20 (Ashton and Ashton, 1985). The required level of expertise is surprisingly low (Armstrong 1985). The preferred procedure is to weight each expert's forecast equally.

The accuracy of expert forecasts can be improved through the use of structured methods, such as the Delphi procedure. Delphi is an iterative survey procedure in which experts make forecasts for a problem, receive anonymous summary feedback on the forecasts made by other experts, and then make a further forecast. For a summary of the evidence on the accuracy of Delphi versus unstructured judgement, see Rowe and Wright (2000). One principle is that experts' forecasts should generally be independent of one another. Focus groups *always* violate this principle; as a result, they should not be used in forecasting.

Conjoint analysis

Intentions can be explained by relating consumers' intentions to various factors that describe the situation. For example, by asking consumers to state their intentions to purchase for a variety of different product offerings, it is possible to infer how the factors relate to intended sales. This can be done by regressing intentions against the factors, a procedure which is known as 'conjoint analysis'. It is a method that is used in many areas of marketing, but particularly for new product decisions. It is based on sound principles, such as using experimental design to create situations and soliciting independent intentions from a sample of potential customers (Wittink and Bergesteun, 2000).

Judgemental bootstrapping

As with conjoint analysis, one can develop a model of the expert. This approach, known as judgemental bootstrapping, converts subjective judgements into objective procedures. Experts are first asked to make predictions for a series of conditions. For example, they could make forecasts for next year's sales in various geographical regions. This process is then converted to a set of rules by regressing the forecasts against the information used by the forecaster. Once developed, judgemental bootstrapping models offer a low-cost procedure for making forecasts. They almost always provide an improvement in accuracy in comparison to judgemental forecasts, although these improvements are typically modest (Armstrong, 2000a).

Methods based on statistical sources

Extrapolation

Extrapolation methods use historical data on the series of interest. Exponential smoothing is the most popular and cost effective of the extrapolation methods. It implements the principle that more recent data should be weighted more heavily and also seeks to 'smooth' out seasonal and/or cyclical fluctuations to predict the direction in which the trend is moving.

Alternatively, one may simply make judgemental extrapolations of historical data. Judgemental extrapolations are preferable to quantitative extrapolations when there have been large recent changes in the sales level and where there is relevant knowledge about the item to be forecast (Armstrong and Collopy, 1998).

An important principle for extrapolation is to use long time series when developing a forecasting model. Yet Focus Forecasting, one of the most widely used time series forecasting software packages, does not do this; as a result, its forecasts are less accurate than alternative procedures (Gardner and Anderson, 1997).

Another principle for extrapolation is to use reliable data. The existence of retail scanner data means that reliable data can be obtained for existing products. Scanner data is detailed, accurate, timely, and inexpensive. As a result, forecast accuracy should improve, especially because of the reduction in the error of assessing the current status. Not knowing where you are starting from has often been a major source of error in predicting future values. Scanner data may also be used for early identification of trends.

Empirical studies have led to the conclusion that relatively simple extrapolation methods perform as well as more complex methods. For example, the Box–Jenkins procedure, one of the more complex approaches, has produced no measurable gains in forecast accuracy relative to simpler procedures (Makridakis, *et al.*, 1984; Armstrong, 1985). More recently forecasters have extensively examined another complex procedure, neural networks. Neural networks are computer intensive methods that use decision processes analogous to that of the human brain. Like the brain, they have the capability of learning and updating their parameter estimates as experience is acquired. Neural networks have not produced more accurate forecasts than other methods (Chatfield, 1993). Some promising work has been done in the study of market share forecasting (Agrawal and Schorling, 1996) and in predicting consumer's choice (West *et al.*, 1997), but our advice at present is to ignore neural nets.

Rule based forecasting

Quantitative extrapolation methods make no use of managers' knowledge of the time series. The basic assumption is that the causal forces that have affected a historical series will continue over the forecast horizon. This assumption is sometimes false. Rule based forecasting is a type of expert system that allows one to integrate managers' knowledge about the domain with time series data in a structured and inexpensive way. For example, in many cases a useful guideline is that trends should be extrapolated only when they agree with managers' prior expectations. When the causal forces are contrary to the trend in the historical series, forecast errors tend to be large (Armstrong and Collopy, 1993). While such problems may occur only in a small percentage of cases, their effects can be disastrous.

Analogies

Experts can identify analogous situations. Extrapolation of results from these situations can be used to predict the situation of interest (Duncan, Gore and Szczypula, 2000). For example, to assess the loss in sales when the patent protection for a drug is removed, one might examine results for previous cases, especially if the drugs are similar.

Expert systems

As the name implies, expert systems use the rules of experts. These rules are typically created from protocols, whereby the forecaster talks about what he is doing while making forecasts. The real promise, however, is for expert systems to draw upon empirical results of relationships that come from econometric studies. In fact, this is a common way to construct expert systems. Expert opinion, conjoint analysis and bootstrapping can also aid in the development of expert systems.

Multivariate time series methods

Despite much research effort, there is little evidence that multivariate time series provide benefits for forecasting. As a result, these methods are not discussed here.

Econometric methods

Econometric methods use prior knowledge (theory) to construct a model. This involves selecting causal variables, identifying the expected directions of the relationships, imposing constraints on the relationships to ensure that they are sensible, and selecting functional forms. In most marketing problems, one can also make reasonable prior estimates for the magnitude of the relationships, such as for price or advertising elasticities. Data from the situation can then be used to update the estimates, especially if one has sufficient amounts of relevant and reliable data.

Econometric models have the advantage that they can relate directly to planning and decision making. They can provide a framework to examine the effects of marketing activity as well as key aspects of the market and the environment, thus providing information for contingency planning. While some causal variables can be forecast with a reasonable level of accuracy (e.g. demographic changes), others are more difficult to forecast (e.g. changes in fashion and competitors' actions).

Econometric methods are most useful when:

- strong causal relationships with sales or other entities are expected;
- these causal relationships are known or they can be estimated;
- large changes are expected to occur in the causal variables over the forecast horizon; and
- these changes in the causal variables can be accurately forecast or controlled, especially with respect to their direction.

If any of these conditions does not hold (which is typical for short-range forecasts), econometric methods are less likely to contribute to accuracy.

Forecasting market size

Market size is influenced by environmental factors such as economic conditions, population, ability to purchase, social trends, technological change, or government legislation. For example, demographic factors such as the size and age distribution of the population, distribution of disposable income, culture, and religious factors influence the market for alcoholic beverages.

Econometric methods have been used for environmental forecasting. Econometric researchers have devoted much effort to short-term forecasting, an area that has yielded unimpressive results. Econometric methods would be expected to be more useful for long-range forecasting because the changes in the causal variables are not swamped by random variations, as in the short run. Armstrong (1985, Chapter 15) reported seven empirical comparisons of methods used in long-range forecasting. In all comparisons, econometric methods were more accurate than extrapolations. Fildes (1985) located 20 studies on long-range forecasting; he found 15 where econometric methods were more accurate than other methods, 3 ties, and 2 showing econometric forecasts to be less accurate.

Improved environmental forecasts should lead to more accurate market forecasts. Surprisingly, research in this area indicates that forecasting errors are not particularly sensitive to the accuracy of environmental forecasts. Measurement error in the causal variables (e.g. the environmental inputs to a market forecasting model) had little impact on the accuracy of an econometric model in the few studies done on this topic (Armstrong, 1985). Moreover, conditional econometric forecasts (those made with actual data on the causal variables) have generally been found to be no more accurate than unconditional forecasts (where the causal variables themselves must be forecasted). Of 18 studies found, only 3 have shown conditional forecasts to be more accurate, 5 showed no difference, and 10 showed them to be less accurate (Armstrong, 1985; Rosenstone, 1983; and four studies from Fildes, 1985). A possible explanation for these strange findings is that the unconditional forecasts may have included subjective revisions that might have reduced the error in estimating starting values (current levels).

Methods based on judgement

Market forecasts are often based on judgement, especially, it seems, for relatively new or rapidly changing markets. This carries some risk, as research since the 1960s has identified biases that occur in judgemental forecasting. Among these biases are optimism, conservatism, anchoring, and availability.

The Delphi technique offers a useful way to implement many of the basic principles for expert forecasting. It uses (1) more than one expert, (2) unbiased experts, (3) structured questions, and (4) equal weights for each expert's forecast. It could be used to answer questions about market size such as: 'By what percentage will the New Zealand wine market grow over the next 10 years?' But it is especially appropriate when one has scant relevant prior data. Thus, one might ask: 'What proportion of U.S. households will subscribe to movies on demand over telephone or cable lines?'

Surprisingly, research indicates that high expertise in the subject area is not important for judgemental forecasts of change (Armstrong, 1985). The conclusion, then, is not to spend heavily to obtain the best experts to forecast change. On the other hand, one should avoid people who clearly have no expertise. Also, experts are helpful for assessing current levels.

Methods based on statistical sources

When considering forecasts of market size, one can use either time series extrapolation methods or econometric methods. Time series extrapolation is inexpensive. Econometric methods, while more expensive, are expected to be more accurate than judgemental methods and extrapolation.

Organizations should use systematic procedures for scanning the environment to be sure that they do not overlook variables that may have a large impact on their market. Periodic brainstorming with a group of experts should be sufficient to identify which variables to track, especially if the experts represent diverse areas. The key is to identify important variables and the direction of their effects. Once identified, crude estimates of the coefficients of these environmental variables are often sufficient in order to obtain useful forecasts.

When forecasting environmental factors related to market prices, it is important to remember what might be called Adam Smith's rule for forecasters: 'Forecasters cannot beat the market'. (Some people refer to this as the rule of efficient markets.) In other words, when an active market of buyers and sellers is at work (such as in stocks, bonds, money, commodities and land), forecasters have not had much success at finding methods that can improve upon the market's forecast. This rule assumes that the forecaster lacks inside information, so the market price is a reflection of available information. Judging from research since the 1930s, the market can forecast prices as effectively as can be done by any alternative forecasting procedure.

Decision makers' actions

The development of a successful marketing strategy sometimes depends upon having a good forecast of the actions and reactions of competitors. A variety of judgemental and statistical methods can be used to forecast competitive actions. These include:

- expert opinion (using experts who know about this and similar markets);
- intentions (ask the competitors how they would respond in a variety of situations);
- role playing (formal acting out of the interactions among decision makers for the firm and its competitors); and
- experimentation (trying the strategy on a small scale and monitoring the results). For example, if you lower your price, will competitors follow?

After forecasting their actions, the next step is to forecast their impact upon market size and market share.

It may also be important to forecast the actions of suppliers, distributors, complementors, government, and people within one's firm in order to develop a successful marketing strategy. Sometimes one may need to forecast the actions of other interest groups, such as 'concerned minorities'. For example, how would an environmental group react to the introduction of plastic packaging by a large fast food restaurant chain? A range of techniques similar to those for forecasting competitors' actions appears useful.

Role playing is well suited to predicting how decision makers will act. It provides substantially more accurate forecasts than can be obtained from expert opinion (Armstrong, 2000). In one study, role playing was used to forecast interaction between suppliers and distributors. Philco (called the Ace Company in the role play), a producer of home appliances, was trying to improve its share of a depressed market. They had developed a plan to sell appliances in supermarkets using a cash register tape discount plan. Secrecy was important because Philco wanted to be first to use this strategy. Implementation of such a plan depended upon the supermarket managers. Would the plan be acceptable to them? In this case, a simple role playing procedure produced substantially more accurate forecasts of the supermarket managers' decisions (8 of 10 groups were correct) than did unaided opinions (1 of 34 groups was correct). In the actual situation, the supermarket managers did accept the plan proposed by Philco. The superior accuracy of role playing relative to opinions seems to be due to its ability to provide a more realistic portrayal of the interactions.

Company plans typically require the cooperation of many people. For example, if the organization decides to implement a given marketing strategy, will it be able to carry out the plan? Sometimes an organization fails to do what it intends to do because of a lack of resources, misunderstanding, opposition by key stakeholders, or a lack of commitment to the plan by key people. The need to forecast organizational behaviour is sometimes overlooked. Better forecasting here might lead to more realistic plans and to plans that are easier to implement.

Surveys of key decision makers in an organization may help to assess the likelihood that a given strategy can be implemented. Because those who are not committed to a plan may be reluctant to admit it, projective questions may be useful when asking about intentions to implement plans.

It is also important to predict the effects of the various actions. For example, in the Philco situation, the change in distribution channels led to substantial losses for all involved. One can make such forecasts by using expert judgement, judgemental bootstrapping, or econometric methods.

Forecasting market share

The primary approaches to forecasting market share are:

- expert opinion;
- judgemental bootstrapping;
- extrapolation (statistical analysis of the market or of analogous markets);
- econometric methods (using relative prices, advertising, and product features).

In many cases, markets have reached a rough state of equilibrium. That is, the future is expected to consist of an extension of the same causal forces and the same types of actions. Under such conditions, a simple extrapolation of market share, such as the naïve 'no change' model, is usually sufficient.

When large changes are expected, one should draw upon methods that incorporate causal reasoning. If the changes are unusual, judgemental methods such as Delphi would be appropriate. If the changes are expected to be large, the causes are well understood, and if one lacks historical data, then judgemental bootstrapping is relevant.

In some cases, econometric models are relevant. They should be based on theory. Bell, Keeney and Little (1975) provide a start with their market share theorem, which states that market share changes depend upon the marketing effort for the brand (price, advertising, product, etc.) divided by the sum of marketing effort for all the brands in the market. There are many ways to formulate this model (Brodie *et al.*, 2000) and much prior research exists to help specify these models. For example, a meta-analysis by Tellis (1988) of 367 brand price elasticities, estimated using econometric models, reports a mean value of -2.5. Hamilton *et al.*'s (1997) analysis of 406 price brand elasticities also reported a value of -2.5. Generalizations can also be made about other measures of market activity, such as advertising elasticity.

In addition to being useful for policy issues, econometric models are sometimes more accurate forecasts than time–series extrapolations. Brodie *et al.*'s (2000) review of empirical evidence on market share forecasting concludes that econometric methods are most accurate when

1. there are strong causal relationships between the marketing mix variables and market share;
2. ample historical data exhibit sufficient variation to allow one to improve the estimates;
3. the causal variables can be forecast or controlled, especially with respect to their direction;

4. causal variables are expected to change substantially.

This implies that there is the need to be able to forecast large changes in competitors' actions.

Sales forecasts

Our assumption above was that one would prepare a market forecast and a market share forecast and then forecast sales by multiplying these components. Alternatively, sales can be forecasted directly. The direct approach seems most appropriate for short-range sales forecasting in situations where one is not concerned about assessing the effects of alternative strategies.

Methods based on judgement

One popular belief is that to improve forecasts, one should survey consumers about their desires, needs, plans, or expectations. The benefit of asking consumers depends on the situation. In particular, if sales (behavioural) data already exist, then it is obviously less important to seek information from consumers. However, intentions data can be used to improve the accuracy of sales extrapolation.

Focus groups are often used to forecast behaviour. But this, procedure conflicts with certain principles. First, focus groups are seldom representative of the population. Second, the responses of each participant are influenced because they hear opinions stated by others. Third, the sample sizes are small. And fourth, questions for the participants are generally not well structured. As a result, focus groups should not be used in forecasting. In addition, no evidence exists to show that focus groups lead to improved forecasts.

Another approach is to solicit expert opinions. Expert opinion studies are widely used for forecasting of marketing problems. For example, forecasts are often obtained from the sales force. It is important to learn more about how to pose the questions, how to adjust for biases in these forecasts, and how to aggregate the responses.

Judgemental bootstrapping is likely to improve upon expert's sales forecasts. This is due largely to improved consistency.

Methods based on statistical sources

When a large number of sales forecasts are needed, the preferred method has been extrapolation. Here, relatively simple methods suffice. Sophistication beyond a modest level does not improve accuracy, but it does increase costs and reduce understanding. Marketers need a consistent set of forecasts for their products. If you are selling for computer parts, the forecasts for hard drives, disk drives and disks may be related to one another. On one forecast the aggregate (e.g. number of computer parts), then allocate percentages to the components ('top–down'). Alternatively, one could forecast for each part and then sum up the whole ('bottom–up'). Arguments can be made for each approach. The bottom–up seems best when one has reasonably good information on the parts. Empirical tests on the two approaches indicate that, in general, the bottom–up approach is more accurate (MacGregor, 2000)

Probably the most important principle when forecasting sales using data from intervals of less than a year (e.g. monthly data) is to adjust the data for seasonality. Dalrymple's (1987) survey results are consistent with this principle. Substantial improvements were also found in the large-scale study of time series by Makridakis *et al.* (1984). We believe that seasonal factors should be dampened, but no direct tests have yet been made.

Schnaars (1986) examined which extrapolation models are most accurate for annual sales forecasts for various consumer products. Two principles that helped were to dampen the trend and combine alternative forecasts. These principles improved accuracy in comparison with the rule 'pick the model that provides the best fit to the historical sales'.

Some controversy exists as to whether mechanical extrapolations will do better than judgemental extrapolations. A study by Lawrence *et al.* (1985) concluded in favour of judgemental or 'eyeball' extrapolations, but Carbone and Gorr (1985) concluded the opposite. Of course, mechanical extrapolation methods are less expensive when many forecasts must be made, such as for inventory control.

New product sales

Sales forecasting for new products is a particularly important area, especially in view of the substantial investments and the likelihood of large forecasting errors. Forecasts are required at the different stages of product development to assist managers with the go/no-go decisions and then in planning the introduction of the new product.

Large errors are typical for new product forecasts. Tull (1967) estimated the mean absolute percentage error for new product sales to be about 65 per cent. It is not surprising then, that pre-test market models have gained wide acceptance among business firms. Shocker and Hall (1986) provide an evaluation of some of these models. Because of the lack of systematic and unbiased forecast validation studies, they conclude it is difficult to draw conclusions about which approach is best.

The choice of a forecasting model to estimate customer response depends on the stage of the product life cycle. As one moves from the concept phase to prototype, test market, introductory, growth, maturation, and declining stages, the relative value of the alternative forecasting methods changes. In general, the movement is from purely judgemental approaches to quantitative models. For example, intentions and expert opinions are vital in the concept and prototype stages. Later, expert judgement is useful as an input to quantitative models. Extrapolation methods may be useful in the early stages if it is possible to find analogous products (Claycamp and Liddy, 1969). In later stages, quantitative methods become more useful as less expensive sales and cost data become available.

When a new product is in the concept phase, a heavy reliance is usually placed on intentions surveys. Intentions to purchase new products are complicated because potential customers may not be sufficiently familiar with the proposed product and because the various features of the product affect one another (e.g. price, quality and distribution channel). This suggests the need to prepare a good description of the proposed product. The description may involve prototypes, visual aids, product clinics, or laboratory tests. However, brief descriptions are sometimes sufficient, as found in Armstrong and Overton's (1970) study of a new form of urban mass transportation.

In a typical intentions study, potential consumers are provided with a description of the product and the conditions of sale, and then are asked about their intentions to purchase. Rating scales of eleven points (0–10) are recommended. The scale should have verbal designations such as 0 = 'No chance, almost no chance (1 in 100)' to 10 = 'Certain, practically certain (99 in 100)'. It is best to state the question broadly about one's 'expectations' or 'probabilities' of purchase, rather than the narrower question of intentions. This distinction was proposed and tested by Juster (1966) and its importance has been shown in other empirical studies (Day et al., 1991).

Intentions surveys are useful when all of the following conditions hold: (1) the event is important; (2) the respondent (at least the intenders do); (3) the respondent can fulfil the plan; (4) events are unlikely to change the plan; (5) responses can be obtained; and (6) the respondent reports correctly. These conditions imply that intentions are more useful for short-term forecasts and business-to-business sales.

Intentions survey methodology has improved since the 1950s. Useful methods have been developed for selecting samples, compensating for nonresponse bias, and reducing response error. Dillman (1978) provides advice for designing intentions surveys. Improvements in this technology have been demonstrated by studies on voter intentions (Perry, 1979). Response error is probably the most important component of total error (Sudman and Bradburn, 1982). Despite the improvements, the correspondence between intentions and sales is often not close, as shown in Morwitz (2000).

As an alternative to asking potential customers about their intentions to purchase, one can ask experts to predict how consumers will respond. For example, Wotruba and Thurlow (1976) discuss how opinions from members of the sales force can be used to forecast sales. One could also ask distributors or marketing executives to make forecasts. Experts may be able to make better forecasts if the problem is decomposed so that the parts are better known to them than the whole. Thus, if the task was to forecast the sales of high-definition television sets, rather than making a direct forecast one could break the problem into parts such as ' How many households will there be in the U.S. in the forecast year?' 'Of these households, what percentage will make more than $30,000 per year?' 'Of these households, how many have not purchased a large screen TV in the past year?' and so on. The forecasts are obtained by multiplying the components. Decomposition is more accurate where there is much uncertainty about the direct or 'global' forecast (MacGregor, 2000). It turns out that much uncertainty is induced because people have difficulty in comprehending large numbers (operationalized as numbers over a million).

Unfortunately, experts are often subject to biases in new product forecasting (Tyebjee 1987). Sales people may try to forecast on the low side if the forecasts will be used to set quotas. Marketing executives may forecast high in their belief that this will gain approval for the project or motivate the sales force. If possible, avoid experts who would have obvious reasons to be biased. Another strategy is to use a heterogeneous group of experts in the hopes that their differing biases may cancel one another.

Producers often consider several alternative designs for a new product. In such cases, potential customers may be presented with a series of perhaps 20 or so alternative offerings. For example, various features of a personal computer, such as price, weight, battery life, screen clarity and memory might vary according to rules for experimental design (the basic ideas being that each feature should vary substantially and the variations among the features should not correlate with one another). The customer is forced to make trade-offs among various features. This is called 'conjoint analysis' because the consumers *consider* the product features *jointly*. This procedure is widely used by firms (Wittink and Bergestuen, 1999). An example of a successful application is the design of a new Marriott hotel chain (Wind *et al.*, 1989). The use of conjoint analysis to forecast new product demand can be expensive because it requires large samples of potential buyers, the potential buyers may be difficult to locate, and the questionnaires are not easy to complete. Respondents must, of course, understand the concepts that they are being asked to evaluate. Although conjoint analysis rests on good theoretical foundations, little validation research exists in which its accuracy is compared with the accuracy of alternative techniques such as Delphi or judgemental forecasting procedures (Wittink and Bergestuen, 2000).

Expert judgements can be used in a manner analogous to conjoint analysis. That is, experts would make predictions about situations involving alternative product designs and alternative marketing plans. These predictions would then be related to the situations by regression analysis. (Following the philosophy for naming conjoint analysis, this could be called **exjoint analysis**.) It has advantages as compared to conjoint analysis in that few experts are needed (probably between five and ten). In addition, it can incorporate policy variables, such as advertising, that are difficult for consumers to assess.

Once a new product is on the market, it is possible to use extrapolation methods. Much attention has been given to the selection of the proper functional form to extrapolate early sales. The diffusion literature uses an S-shaped curve to predict new product sales. That is, growth builds up slowly at first, becomes rapid if word of mouth is good and if people see the product being used by others. Then it slows as it approaches a saturation level. A substantial literature exists on diffusion models. Despite this, the number of comparative validation studies is small and the benefits of choosing the best functional form are modest (Meade, 2000).

Forecasting profits and other outcomes

Forecasts can be used to examine how each of the stakeholders will be affected. It may be useful to start the forecasting process with the analysis of stakeholders to ensure that the forecasts are relevant to decisions. For example, we might want to forecast whether a proposed plan will benefit consumers, how it might affect the local community, or how it might affect the long-term relationship with one of your complementors.

Forecasts of marketing costs can affect the marketing plan. Costs may be so high as to render a proposed plan unprofitable. Extrapolations are often used to forecast costs. Typically, unit costs decrease, but at a decreasing rate. Thus, a learning curve is often appropriate. This concept originated in educational psychology and was adopted by industrial engineering in the early 1900s. In simple terms, one estimates the percentage annual decrease in variable costs.

Sudden changes in costs can be forecasted by expert judgement, such as engineering estimates. Another approach is to use econometric models. Given the availability of relevant historical data, econometric models are especially useful for large changes in costs, such as those created by government actions. For example, costs of electricity vary substantially by geographic region due to the level of regulation. Econometric models might help to forecast prices given planned changes in regulation.

Assessing uncertainty

In addition to improving accuracy, forecasting is concerned with assessing uncertainty. This can help in managing risk.

Statisticians have given much attention to assessing uncertainty. They have relied heavily on tests of statistical significance. However, statistical significance is inappropriate for assessing uncertainty in forecasting. Furthermore, its use has been attacked as being misleading (e.g., see Cohen, 1994). It is difficult to find studies in marketing forecasting where statistical significance has made an important contribution.

Instead of statistical significance, the focus should be on prediction intervals. Chatfield (2000) summarizes research on prediction intervals. Unfortunately, prediction intervals are not widely used in practice. Rush and Page (1979) found a decreasing use of measures of uncertainty for metals forecasts from 22 per cent of forecasts during the period 1910–1939 to only 8 per cent during 1940–1964. Tull's (1967) survey noted that only 25 per cent of 16 respondent companies said they provided confidence intervals with their forecasts. Dalrymple (1987) found that 48 per cent did not use confidence intervals, and only 10 per cent 'usually' used them.

The fit of a model to historical data is a poor way to estimate prediction intervals. It typically results in confidence intervals that are too narrow. It is best to simulate the actual forecasting procedure as closely as possible, and use the distribution of the resulting *ex ante* forecasts to assess uncertainty. For example, if you need to make forecasts for two years ahead, withhold enough data to be able to have a number of two-year ahead *ex ante* forecasts.

Methods based on judgement

Much work has been done on judgemental estimates of uncertainty. One of the key findings is that judges are typically overconfident (Arkes, 2000). This occurs even when subjects are warned in advance about this overconfidence phenomenon. Fortunately, there are procedures to improve the calibration of judges. Where possible, judges should be provided with frequent and well summarized feedback of the outcomes of their predictions along with reasons why they were right or wrong. Arkes (2000) shows that when feedback is good, judges' estimates of confidence are well calibrated. For example, when weather forecasters say that there is about 60 per cent chance of rain, it rains 60 per cent of the time. This suggests that marketing forecasters should ensure that they receive feedback on the accuracy of their forecasts. The feedback should be frequent and it should summarize accuracy in a meaningful fashion.

In cases where good feedback is not possible, certain procedures can be used to improve estimates of confidence. One is to have experts write all the reasons why their forecasts might be wrong (Arkes, 2000). Another is the devil's advocate procedure, where someone is assigned for a short time to raise arguments about why the forecast might be wrong.

Still another way to assess uncertainty is to examine the agreement among judgemental forecasts. For example, Ashton (1985), in a study of forecasts of annual advertising sales for *Time* magazine, found that the agreement among the individual judgemental forecasts was a proxy for accuracy. Little evidence exists on this topic and it is not clear how to translate such information into prediction intervals. For example, in McNees' (1992) examination of economic forecasts from 22 economists over 11 years, the actual values fell outside the range of their individual forecasts about 43 per cent of the time.

Methods based on statistical data

Prediction intervals from quantitative forecasts tend to be too narrow even when based on *ex ante* n-ahead forecasts. Some empirical studies have shown that the percentage of actual values that fall outside the 95 per cent prediction intervals is substantially greater than 5 per cent, and sometimes greater than 50 per cent (Makridakis *et al.*, 1987). This occurs because the estimates ignore various sources of uncertainty. For example, discontinuities might occur over the forecast horizon. In addition, forecast errors in time series are often asymmetric, so this makes it difficult to estimate prediction intervals. This is likely to occur when the forecasting model uses an additive trend. The most sensible procedure is to transform the forecast and actual values to logs, then calculate the prediction intervals using logged differences. Interestingly, researchers and practitioners do not follow this advice (except where the original forecasting model has been formulated in logs). This procedure does not solve the situation where the trend extrapolation is contrary to the managers' expectations. Such errors are asymmetrical in logs. Evidence on the issue of asymmetrical errors is provided in Armstrong and Collopy (1999).

Loss functions can also be asymmetric. For example, the cost of a forecast that is too low by 50 units may differ from the cost if it is too high by 50 units. But this is a problem for the planner, not the forecaster.

Selecting, evaluating and using forecasting methods

At a minimum, the use of new forecasting methods depends upon knowledge about them. While the acceptance of the new forecasting methods has been slow in the past, this is changing. The traditional methods of gaining acceptance, such as attending courses, reading textbooks and using consultants, are being augmented by the Internet. The latest methods can be fully disclosed on web sites and they can be incorporated into expert systems and software packages. For example, the complete set of rules for rule based forecasting is kept available and up to date and can be accessed through the forecasting principles site (hops.wharton.upenn.edu/forecast). Expert systems and software packages have the ability, then, to incorporate the cumulative wisdom about forecasting software. Users would apply the latest findings unless they chose to override the system to avoid them.

Rationally, one would expect that it helps to base the selection of the proper method upon previous research. So we describe how generalizations from prior research can aid in the selection of a forecasting method. Typically, however, one also needs to evaluate the performance of methods in the given situation.

Choosing a method based on prior research

The choice of the best forecasting method for any particular situation is not a simple task and sometimes more than one method may be appropriate. To provide guidance, Armstrong (2000c) used the findings from the Forecasting Principles Project to develop a flow chart to aid the selection of the most appropriate forecasting method for any particular situation.

The first issue that the analyst needs to address is whether many data points are available. If not, judgemental procedures are called for.

For judgemental procedures, the next issues are whether the situation involves interaction among decision makers and whether large changes are involved. For large changes, is policy analysis involved, and if it is, what is the best source of evidence?

If one has a large quantity of data, does this consist of time series data? The next issue is whether there is knowledge about the expected empirical relationships. For example, meta-analyses have been done so that, in most situations, excellent prior knowledge exists about price elasticities (Tellis, 1988). If empirical knowledge of relationships is available, use econometric models. In addition, one should consider domain knowledge, such as a manager's knowledge about the situation.

For time series situations where one lacks causal knowledge, extrapolation is appropriate. If there is no prior knowledge about relationships, but domain knowledge exists (such as if a manager knows that sales will increase), use rule based forecasting.

In situations where one does not have times series data and also has no prior knowledge about relationships, analogies are appropriate if domain knowledge is lacking. But given domain knowledge, expert systems should be used.

Figure 6.3 summarizes the above guidelines. While these represent the major considerations, the list is not comprehensive. Furthermore, the conditions may not always be clear. In such cases, one should use different approaches to the problem. The forecasts from these approaches can then be combined. To illustrate the use of the flow chart, we provide some examples.

Market size

Consider a case where the New Zealand Wine Institute wishes to forecast the market size for white wine in New Zealand for the next five years. Ample time series data are available for wine consumption and the environmental factors influencing the demand. These include demographic and economic variables such as the size and distribution of the population, the changing age composition, and disposable income. Data are available about the price of white wine and the substitute products such as red wine and other alcoholic beverages. Also there is substantial empirical knowledge about the relationships from studies on the alcoholic beverage market conducted in New Zealand and other countries. These studies allow for generalizations to be made about price and income elasticities. Thus, an econometric modelling approach is recommended.

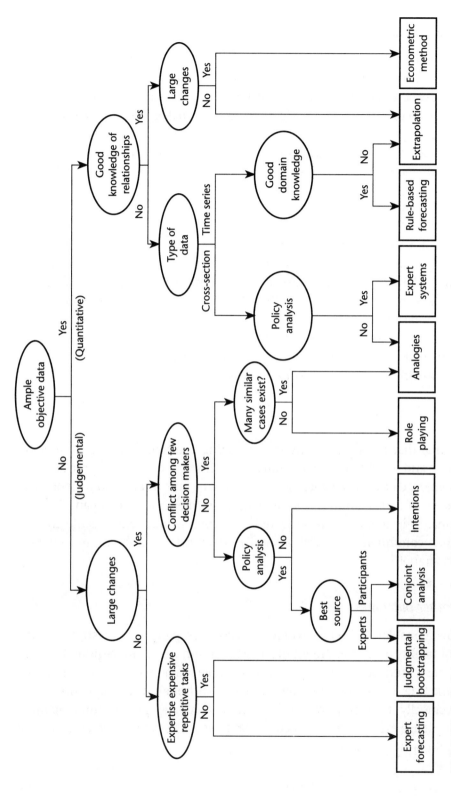

FIGURE 6.3 Selection tree for forecasting methods

Decision makers' actions

Assume that the New Zealand Wine Institute is trying to assess likely effects of government protection and subsidies for local production in some of the newer export markets. In this case, little objective data are available, there is the possibility of interaction amongst the decision makers (i.e. New Zealand and foreign government trade officials), and the effects of the outcomes of these negotiations could be large. In this case, role playing or the use of experts is recommended.

Market share

What if a wine company wants to assess the effects that a new marketing strategy might have on its market? Here, scanner data are available, including market share data for the competing brands in the various product categories and data about the marketing activity for the competing brands. Also, there is substantial empirical knowledge about the relationships between the relevant variables from the response elasticities of the various marketing variables (e.g. price, point of sale promotion, advertising, and retail availability). Thus, econometric methods are recommended.

Sales

Assume that a wine company is considering planting a premium variety of grapes and the market is not familiar with this type of wine. Assume also that not many data are available, there is likely to be little interaction with decision makers, and the plantings require a large investment for the company. Hence a formal judgemental method would be recommended which could involve either consumers (conjoint analysis) or experts (Delphi or judgemental bootstrapping).

Profits and other outcomes

Now consider the case where a wine company is investigating the profitability of an investment in a new premium wine. This requires forecasts of costs and sales revenues. Considerable data about production and marketing costs are typically available, although they may not relate specifically to this new venture. Thus analogies are recommended. If knowledge exists about the factors that affect costs, an econometric analysis would be appropriate.

Evaluating forecasts for specific applications

Statisticians have relied upon sophisticated procedures for analysing how well models fit historical data. They then select the model with the best fit. Typically, this has been of little value for the selection of forecasting methods. Forecasters should not use measures of fit (such as R^2 or the standard error of the estimate of the model) because they have little relationship to forecast accuracy. This conclusion is based on a series of studies that go back at least to Ferber (1956). For a summary see Armstrong (2000c).

Ex ante forecasts from realistic simulations of the actual situation faced by the forecaster are likely to provide useful information about the expected accuracy of a forecasting model. By *ex ante,* we mean that the analyst uses only information that would be available at the time of an actual forecast.

Traditional error measures, such as the mean square error (MSE), do not provide a reliable basis for comparison of forecasting methods (Armstrong and Collopy, 1992). The median absolute percentage error (MdAPE) is more appropriate because it is invariant to scale and is not influenced by outliers. For comparisons using a small set of series, it is desirable to also control for degree of difficulty in forecasting. One measure that does this is the median relative absolute error (MdRAE), which compares the error for a given model against errors for the naïve, no change forecast (Armstrong and Collopy, 1992).

In situations where uncertainty exists as to the best method, one should use two or more relevant methods, then combine the forecasts. Considerable research suggests that, lacking well structured domain knowledge, equally weighted averages are typically as accurate as other weighting schemes (Armstrong, 2000d). Equal weights combined forecasts produce consistent, though modest, improvements in accuracy and they reduce the likelihood of large errors. They are especially useful when the component methods differ substantially from one another. For example, Blattberg and Hoch (1990) obtained improved sales forecast by equally weighting managers' judgemental forecasts and forecasts from a quantitative model.

There is an exception to the equal weights principle. The selection and weighting of forecasting methods can be improved by using domain knowledge (about the item to be forecast), as shown in research on rule based forecasting (Collopy and Armstrong, 1992). Domain knowledge can be structured, especially with respect to trend expectations. These expectations, along with a consideration of the features of the data (e.g. discontinuities), enable improvements in the weightings assigned to various extrapolations.

Rule based forecasting is just one of a number of procedures for integrating various methods. In particular, we have been stressing the need to integrate judgemental and statistical methods. Much research has been done on this topic in the past decade (Armstrong and Collopy, 1998). This integration is more effective because the judgements are collected in a systematic manner and then used as inputs to the quantitative models, rather than simply as adjustments the outputs. Unfortunately, the latter procedure is commonly used.

Using forecasts effectively

Forecasts that contradict management's expectations have much potential value. However, they are often ignored (Griffith and Wellman, 1979). One way to avoid this problem is to gain agreement on what forecasting procedures to use prior to presenting the forecasts. This may involve making adjustments to the forecasting method in order to develop forecasts that will be used.

Another way to gain acceptance of forecasts is to ask decision makers to decide in advance what decisions they will make given different possible forecasts. Are the decisions affected by the forecasts?

Prior agreements on process and on decisions can greatly enhance the value of forecasts, but they are difficult to achieve in many organizations. The use of scenarios offers an aid to this process. Scenarios involve writing detailed stories of how decision makers would handle alternative possibilities for the future. Decision makers project themselves into the situation and they write the stories about what they did in that situation. They should be written in the past tense. Detailed instructions for writing scenarios are summarised in Gregory (2000). Scenarios are effective in getting forecasters to accept the possibility that certain events might occur. They should not be used to make forecasts, however, because they distort subjective probability estimates.

Conclusions

Significant gains have been made in forecasting for marketing, especially since the 1960. Advances have occurred in the development of methods based on judgement, such as Delphi, role playing, intentions studies, opinions surveys, and bootstrapping. They have also occurred for methods based on statistical data, such as extrapolation, rule based forecasting, and econometric methods. In the 1990s, gains have come from the integration of statistical and judgemental forecasts.

Some of the more important principles for forecasting methods for marketing can be summarized as follows.

General principles

- Domain knowledge should be used.
- When making forecasts in highly uncertain situations, be conservative. For example, the trend should be dampened over the forecast horizon.
- When making forecasts in highly uncertain situations, use more than one method and combine the forecasts using equal weights.
- Complex methods have not proven to be more accurate than relatively simple methods. Given their added cost and the reduced understanding among users, highly complex procedures cannot presently be justified.
- When possible, forecasting methods should use data on actual behaviour, rather than judgements or intentions, to predict behaviour.
- Methods that integrate judgemental and statistical data and procedures (e.g. rule based forecasting) can improve forecast accuracy in many situations.
- Overconfidence occurs with quantitative and judgemental methods.

Methods based on judgement

- When using judgement, a heavy reliance should be placed on structured procedures such as Delphi, role playing, and conjoint analysis.
- Role playing is useful to predict the decisions or variations in practice involved in conflict situations, such as in negotiation.
- In addition to seeking good feedback, forecasters should explicitly list all the things that might be wrong about their forecast. This will produce better calibrated prediction intervals.

Methods based on statistical data

- With the increased availability of data, econometric models play an increasingly important role in forecasting market size, market share and sales.
- Methods should be developed primarily on the basis of theory, not data.

Finally, efforts should be made to ensure forecasts are free of political considerations in a firm. To help with this, emphasis should be on gaining agreement about the forecasting methods, rather than the forecasts. Also, for important forecasts, decisions on their use should be made before the forecasts are provided. Scenarios are helpful in guiding this process.

References

Agrawal, D. and Schorling, C. (1996), Market share forecasting: an empirical comparison of artificial networks and multinomial logit model,' *Journal of Retailing*, **72**(4): 383–407

Armstrong, J.S. (1985), *Long-range Forecasting: From Crystal Ball to Computer*, (second ed.) New York: John Wiley

Armstrong, J.S. (2000a), Judgmental bootstrapping: inferring experts' rules for forecasting, in J.S. Armstrong (Ed.) *Principles of Forecasting: Handbook for Researchers and Practitioners*, Norwell MA: Kluwer Academic Publishers

Armstrong, J.S. (2000b), Role playing: a method to forecast decisions, in J.S. Armstrong (Ed.), *Principles of Forecasting: Handbook for Researchers and Practitioners*, Norwell MA: Kluwer Academic Publishers

Armstrong, J.S. (2000c), Evaluating forecasting methods, in J.S. Armstrong (Ed.), *Principles of Forecasting: Handbook for Researchers and Practitioners*, Norwell MA: Kluwer Academic Publishers

Armstrong, J.S. (2000d), Combining forecasts, in J.S. Armstrong (Ed.) *Principles of Forecasting: Handbook for Researchers and Practitioners*, Norwell MA: Kluwer Academic Publishers

Armstrong, J.S. and Collopy, F. (1992), Error measures for generalizing about forecasting methods: empirical comparisons, *International Journal of Forecasting*, **8**: 69–80

Armstrong, J.S. and Collopy, F. (1993), Causal forces: structuring knowledge for time series extrapolation, *Journal of Forecasting*, **12**: 103–115

Armstrong, J.S. and Collopy, F. (1999), 'Identification or asymmetric prediction intervals through causal forces', Working Paper

Armstrong, J.S. and Collopy, F. (1998), Integration of statistical methods and judgment for time series forecasting: principles from empirical research, in G. Wright and P. Goodwin (Eds.), *Forecasting with Judgment*, Chichester: John Wiley

Armstrong, J.S. and Overton, T. (1970), Brief vs. comprehensive descriptions in measuring intentions to purchase, *Journal of Marketing Research*, **8**, 114–117

Ashton, A.H. (1985), Does consensus imply accuracy in accounting studies of decision making? *Accounting Review*, **60**, 173–185

Ashton, A.H. and Ashton, R.H. (1985), Aggregating subjective forecasts: some empirical results, *Management Science*, **31**, 1499–1508

Bell, D.E., Keeney, R.L. and Little, J.D.C. (1975), A market share theorem, *Journal of Marketing Research*, **12**, 136–141

Blattberg, R.C. and Hoch, S.J. (1990), Database models and managerial intuition: 50 per cent model + 50 per cent manager, *Management Science* **36**, 887–899

Brodie, R.J., Danaher, P., Kumar, V. and Leeflang, P. (2000), Econometric models for forecasting market share, in J.S. Armstrong (Ed.) *Principles of Forecasting: Handbook for Researchers and Practitioners*, Norwell MA: Kluwer Academic Publishers

Carbone, R. and Gorr, W. (1985), Accuracy of judgmental forecasting of time series, *Decision Sciences*, **16**, 153–160

Chatfield, C. (1993), Neural networks: forecasting breakthrough or passing fad? *International Journal of Forecasting*, **9**, 1–3

Chatfield, C. (2000), Prediction intervals, in J.S. Armstrong (Ed.) *Principles of Forecasting: Handbook for Researchers and Practitioners*, Norwell MA: Kluwer Academic Publishers

Claycamp, H.J. and Liddy, L.E. (1969), Prediction of new product performance: An analytical approach, *Journal of Marketing Research*, **6**, 414–20

Cohen, J. (1994), The earth is round (p< .05), *American Psychologist,* **49**, 997–1003

Collopy, F. and Armstrong, J.S. (1992), Rule-based forecasting: development and validation of an expert systems approach to combining time series extrapolations, *Management Science,* **38**, 1394–1414

Dalrymple, D.J. (1975), Sales forecasting: methods and accuracy, *Business Horizons* **18**, 69–73

Dalrymple, D.J. (1987), Sales forecasting practices: results from a U.S. survey, *International Journal of Forecasting,* **3**, 379–391

Day, D.B., Gan, B., Gendall, P. and Esslemont, D. (1991), Predicting purchase behavior, *Marketing Bulletin,* **2**, 18–30 (Full text available at http://marketing-bulletin. massey.ac.nz/)

Dillman, D.A. (1978), *Mail and Telephone Surveys,* New York : John Wiley

Duncan, G., Gore, W. and Szczypula, J. (2000), Forecasting analogous time series, in J.S. Armstrong (Ed.) *Principles of Forecasting: Handbook for Researchers and Practitioners,* Norwell MA: Kluwer Academic Publishers

Ferber, R. (1956), Are correlations any guide to predictive value? *Applied Statistics,* **5** (June): 113–22

Fildes, R. (1985), Quantitative forecasting – the state of the art: econometric models, *Journal of the Operational Research Society,* **36**, 549–80

Gregory, L. (2000), Scenarios as a strategy for the presentation of forecasts, in J.S. Armstrong (Ed.) *Principles of Forecasting: Handbook for Researchers and Practitioners,* Norwell MA: Kluwer Academic Publishers

Griffith, J.R. and Wellman, B.T. (1979), Forecasting bed needs and recommending facilities plans for community hospitals: a review of past performance, *Medical Care* **17**, 293–303

Hamilton, W., East, R. and Kalafatis, S. (1997), The measurement and utility of brand price elasticities, *Journal of Marketing Management,* **13**, 285–98

Jobber, D., Hooley, G. and Sanderson, S. (1985), Marketing in a hostile environment: the British textile industry, *Industrial Marketing Management,* **14**, 35–41

Juster, T. (1966), Consumer buying intentions and purchase probability: an experiment in survey design, *Journal of the American Statistical Association,* **61**, 658–96

Lawrence, M.J., Edmundson, R.H. and O'Connor, M.J. (1985), An examination of the accuracy of judgmental extrapolation of time series, *International Journal of Forecasting* **1**, 25–35

MacGregor, D. (2000), Decomposition for judgmental forecasting and estimation, in J.S. Armstrong (Ed.) *Principles of Forecasting: Handbook for Researchers and Practitioners,* Norwell, MA: Kluwer Academic Publishers

Makridakis, S., *et al.* (1984), *The Forecasting Accuracy of Major Time Series Methods,* New York: John Wiley

Makridakis, S., Hibon, M., Lusk, E, and Belhadjali, M. (1987), Confidence intervals: an empirical investigation of the series in the M-competition, *International Journal of Forecasting,* **3**, 489–508

Makridakis, S., Wheelwright, S.C., and Hyndman, R.J. (1998), *Forecasting Methods for Management.* Third edition. New York: John Wiley

McCloskey, D.N. and Ziliak, S.T. (1996), The standard error of regressions, *Journal of Economic Literature,* **34**, 97–114

McNees, S.K. (1992), The uses and abuses of 'consensus' forecasts, *Journal of Forecasting,* **11**, 703–10

Meade, N. (2000), Forecasting the diffusion of innovations: Implications for time series extrapolation, in J.S. Armstrong (Ed.) *Principles of Forecasting: Handbook for Researchers and Practitioners,* Norwell MA: Kluwer Academic Publishers

Morwitz, V. (2000), Methods for forecasting from intentions and probability data, in J.S. Armstrong (Ed.) *Principles of Forecasting: Handbook for Researchers and Practitioners*. Norwell, MA: Kluwer Academic Publishers

Perry, P. (1979), Certain problems in election survey methodology, *Public Opinion Quarterly*, **43**, 312–25

Rosenstone, S.J. (1983), *Forecasting Presidential Elections*, New Haven CT: Yale University Press

Rowe, G. and Wright, G. (2000), The Delphi technique as a forecasting tool, in J.S. Armstrong (Ed.) *Principles of Forecasting: Handbook for Researchers and Practitioners*, Norwell MA: Kluwer Academic Publishers

Rush, H. and Page, W. (1979), Long-term metals forecasting: The track record, *Futures*, **11**, 321–37

Schnaars, S.P. (1986), An evaluation of rules for selecting an extrapolation model on yearly sales forecasts, *Interfaces* **16** (Nov–Dec.): 100–7

Shocker, A.D. and Hall, W.G. (1986), Pretest market models: A critical evaluation, *Journal of Product Innovation Management*, **3**, 86–107

Sudman, S. and Bradburn, N.R. (1982), *Asking Questions: A Practical Guide to Questionnaire Design*, San Francisco: Jossey-Bass

Tellis, G.J. (1988), The price elasticity of selected demand, *Journal of Marketing Research*, **25**, 331–341

Tull, D.S. (1967), The relationship of actual and predicted sales and profits in new-product introductions, *Journal of Business*, **40**, 233–250

Tyebjee, T.T. (1987), Behavioral biases in new product forecasting, *International Journal of Forecasting*, **3**, 393–404

West, P.M., Brockett, P.L. and Golden, L.L. (1997), A comparative analysis of neural networks and statistical methods for predicting consumer choice, *Marketing Science*, **16**, 370–391

Wind, J., Green, P.E., Shifflet, D. and Scarbrough, M. (1989), Courtyard by Marriott: designing a hotel facility with consumer-based marketing, *Interfaces*, **19**,1, 25–47

Wittink, D.R., and Bergestuen T. (1999), Forecasting with conjoint analysis, in J.S. Armstrong (Ed.) *Principles of Forecasting: Handbook for Researchers and Practitioners*, Norwell MA: Kluwer Academic Publishers

Wotruba, Thomas R. and Thurlow, M.L. (1976), Sales force participation in quota setting and sales forecasting, *Journal of Consumer Research*, **8**, 162–71

■ □ ▨ ■ 7

The AHP: Structuring Marketing Information for Decision Support

Mark A.P. Davies

Many marketing planning and evaluation tasks involve making multicriterion decisions, sometimes involving groups. The analytic hierarchy process, by building a customized hierarchy to represent each problem, leads to the likely identification of all key components affecting decision making, which contrasts with 'seat of the pants' decisions. The most important objectives and alternatives at each hierarchical level are determined through trading off preferences. This can also help reconcile group conflict.

The AHP methodology requires each decision maker to determine their relative intensity of preferences by uniquely combining quantitative and qualitative data on to a single scale. To reduce tedium, appropriate software can significantly speed up results. Furthermore, the ability to calculate and present results at each decision level can be used to support, persuade and justify proposed outcomes to top management. This is important for marketing managers who need to optimize the allocation of scarce resources.

Introduction

The prime skill in marketing management is arguably about making bold decisions with limited resources in an uncertain environment to help reach the organizational goals. The rapid improvements in information technology in the 1990s has increased the demands on marketing management, with a continuous increase in exposure to market information at their disposal. Consequently, accountability and justification of decision making is becoming a firmer requirement of the function. Marketing management is also exposed to unprecedented events which frequently arise, such as new market trends.

Such a complex environment calls for a premium on reliable, intuitive decision making (Agor, 1991).

This is achieved by combining appropriate objective and subjective information in a systematic way that relates to a given problem. Executive decision support systems can help guide marketing managers to set appropriate objectives and alternative courses of action.

The AHP (or analytic hierarchy process), developed by Saaty (1977; 1980), fulfils the requirements of an executive decision support system. According to Forman (1985), it offers decision makers an opportunity to set priorities and make choices on the basis of corporate objectives and executive knowledge and experience consistent with intuitive thought processes.

This is achieved by representing the problem hierarchically by at least two levels or sets of criteria: objectives for evaluation, and activities or alternative courses of action. Marketing management is frequently faced with such multicriterion problems in planning and evaluation, requiring trade-off decisions between conflicting objectives competing for scarce resources. A characteristic of the AHP is the opportunity for those who are closest to the problem (the decision makers directly involved, hereafter referred to as the DMs) to identify and structure a customized hierarchy representing their multicriterion problem, from which a trade-off of relative preferences takes place (Saaty and Wind, 1980). The AHP rests on the assumption that behaviour is explained, in part, through subjective judgements as well as objective reasoning. There are two ways of customizing the decision hierarchy.

Forward process

Any attempt at planning what is likely to happen in the future is referred to as a forward process. For example, the DM may wish to examine which from a range of new products is most likely to succeed, given the objectives, capabilities and policies of the firm.

Backward process

Alternatively, management may evaluate what can or should be done to achieve a desired or ideal outcome. This is called a backward process. For example, a typical goal facing a high street bank is to seek the best marketing strategy (price, place, product and promotion) to fulfil the satisfaction of the majority of its stakeholders. Recognizing that different stakeholders will want different services, a trade-off model is a sensible way of satisfying as many as possible. If it is assumed that the mode of selling operation drives this ultimate strategy, it is necessary to consider deciding the optimum selection in modes of sales operation, or service environments. For the purposes of this illustration, assume these are choices between alternative branches, interactive television, telephone banking, interactive computers and video kiosks to name a few. For example, employees may prefer traditional branches (since there are fewer jobs at threat), whilst consumers may prefer the convenience of new technological developments such as telephone banking and video kiosks, with perhaps corporate customers requiring something else. Clearly this is a multi-level, multicriterion problem because the bank needs to consider not only the importance of each stakeholder in contributing towards the top goal, but also the priorities or preferences between each stakeholder in terms of sales modes required. This problem can be represented by three levels: the top goal or objective (such as rate of return to the bank, or corporate reputation), the second level beneath this, representing the alternative stakeholders, and finally the third level representing the alternative modes of selling. Marketing management is frequently faced with making complex decisions involving both forward and backward processes (refer to Saaty and Alexander, 1989 for more details).

Since 1980, there have been a number of marketing applications using AHP. These include consumer purchase choice determination, (Bahmani, Javalgi and Blumberg, 1986; Bahmani and Blumberg, 1987; Javalgi, Armacost and Hosseini, 1989), industrial buyer behaviour (Vargas and Saaty, 1981), forecasting (Cook, Falchi and Mariano, 1984), marketing mix strategy and new product development (Wind and Saaty, 1980), site location (Tone and Yanagisawa, 1989), advertising budgeting (Mazanec, 1986), media scheduling (Dyer *et al.*, 1992) and advertising creativity (Davies and Saunders, 1990; Davies, 1994). The last of these cases illustrates the power of executive decision support systems when the problem is complex (consisting of four levels: market segments, advertising objectives, creative strategies and finally executions). Insight is offered into decision making at each level. At level one, the decision makers determine which segments are most likely to achieve greatest market penetration (i.e. the top goal of the hierarchy in this example). The exact combination of creative strategies and executions is then dependent and determined by the segmentation strategy by comparing the outcomes under a concentrated segmentation strategy with a multisegment approach.

Although the method is becoming more established, many of the benefits of AHP are not widely appreciated. First, this paper aims to show how AHP can be used to resolve many of the special, complex problems that confront marketing management. These complex problems addressed include:

1. how to reconcile a range of conflicting objectives, under scarce resources;
2. managing a plethora of data;
3. dealing with subjective and objective data to make a decision; and
4. managing to resolve conflict amongst multidisciplinary teams (referred to as multiperson problems).

Second, the basic method is outlined. Third, some marketing applications, benefits and limitations are presented for discussion. Finally, potential avenues for further research are discussed.

Addressing marketing problems

Using AHP to resolve complex problems requires the building of an initial hierarchy. Consider a strategic planning problem facing marketing management. The relative importance of *criteria* (the collective name given to the components at each level of the hierarchy) for making future decisions will depend upon uncertain conditions. The aim, in achieving the overall well-being of the firm, is to produce the correct product mix for a new car line faced with an uncertain future. This will be guided by positioning and marketing mix strategies. Simplified, this might be represented in Figure 7.1. This includes making decisions on the likelihood of each environmental scenario arising, and the relative importance of:

• each objective, relative to the alternative scenarios;
• each customer group or market segment alternative, (in this case, using benefits segmentation of safety, performance and looks (i.e. aesthetics), relative to each objective;
• each price/quality positioning alternative, relative to each segment; and
• each aspect of the marketing mix in terms of achieving the intended positioning alternatives.

Trading off conflicting objectives

Upon examining the components or elements at each hierarchical level, management must base resource allocation upon trading off conflicting criteria. For example, referring to the hierarchy in Figure 7.1, although sales and profits might contribute toward the well-being of the company, segment 1 might best serve sales whereas segment 2 might best serve profits. The relative importance of each segment would then be influenced by the importance attached to each of the objectives, in terms of serving the well-being of the

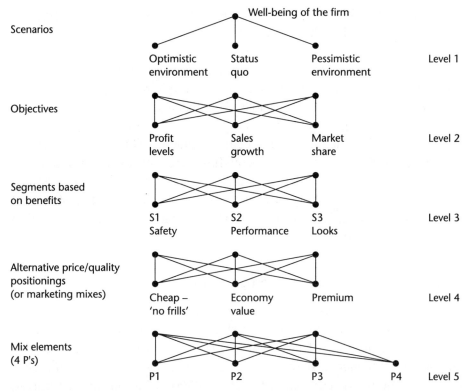

FIGURE 7.1 Hierarchy for developing the best positioning for a new car line for the well-being of the firm

company. This is achieved by weighting the criteria by their parents (i.e. those elements in the immediate level above) in the hierarchy. It is then possible to determine, in terms of corporate well-being, the most important segment overall, as well as the overall aspects of the marketing mix overall, as well as the overall aspects of the marketing mix, should mass marketing be adopted. If a multisegment approach is required, the best mix for each segment can also be evaluated.

This framework enables marketing management to make decisions at any level of the hierarchy, which is of considerable benefit if future courses of action require changes arising from a turbulent environment.

Facing complexity with a plethora of data

The strategic planning example (Figure 7.1) shows that marketing management trades off multicriteria to make a number of choice decisions from alternative elements (the components at each criterion). Consider all the elements of the hierarchy at each level from the top goal, through to positioning alternatives (level 4). If it is assumed only one element at each level can be chosen, the number of alternatives facing the marketing manager is $3^4 = 81$ outcomes. In practice, the notion of mutual exclusivity is unlikely, since options can be chosen in bundles at most levels, resulting in a plethora of data. With so many options available, if the manager wished to offer a single product positioning to all segments, akin to compromising between the individual needs of each segment, (a common practice if financial resources are scarce), it would be necessary to trade off the different needs of each segment to reach the best solution. Since the number of units of information recalled simultaneously in the short-term memory is 7 ± 2, according to studies of chess players, (Miller, 1956), heuristic decision choice, faced with information overload, is evidently prone to error.

Managing complexity with pairwise comparisons

AHP simplifies the above process by making the simultaneity of decision making more manageable. This is achieved by restricting judgements to pairwise comparisons (Saaty, 1977; 1980) for evaluating the relative importance of hierarchical elements. Without AHP, such complexity may lead to seat of the pants decisions (Dyer *et al.*, 1988), using our limited human cognitive capabilities (Harker and Vargas,1990).

Integrating subjective and objective data on to a single scale

An important feature of AHP is its ability to integrate both objective and subjective data, and both qualitative and quantitative data on to a single ratio scale. Without this, there is a danger that subjective data may be overlooked, or worse still, decisions rest only on subjectivity and intuition, ignoring hard data because they cannot easily be integrated with soft data (Dyer *et al.*, 1988).

Saaty (1990a) discusses in detail why it is possible to misinterpret numerical data taken from standard scales. One explanation is that values depend upon reference points. For example, the arithmetic value of a pound is assumed to be the same, whether a person earns a few thousand pounds or a million pounds a year. But the value of an extra thousand pounds may be considered far more significant to the bearer in the former example compared to the latter. The implication is that standard scales force us into a line of thinking which is not in complete harmony with how we really feel and act. The AHP uses a method of relative measurement which is useful for properties for which there is no standard scale of measurement. The number of such intangible properties in marketing is large. For instance, consider difficulties in evaluating the political clout between distributors and manufacturers, the trustworthiness required of advertising agencies, and the empathy of customers, to name a few.

A further advantage of relative scales is that they can incorporate information from standard scales, when necessary. The AHP transforms standard ratio scale measurements to relative ratio scale measurements by normalizing them. This determines the priority values of decision elements at each level of the hierarchy. Consequently, AHP allows the decision maker both intuitive insight and flexibility in prioritizing the order of hierarchical elements, based on marketing context.

Dealing with conflicting judgements involving multidisciplinary team decisions

Even when information is complete, there is the likelihood of disagreement amongst key decision makers, particularly when evaluating the importance of various criteria. For example, one DM might favour financial criteria as a means of choosing between alternative new products, another might consider market share to be more important. AHP can help to resolve conflicting judgements across different DMs.

Managing multiperson problems through AHP

Harker and Vargas (1990) suggest that if DMs (who hold equal power or influence in decision making) cannot agree on their judgements to reach a combined consensus, the decision hierarchy can be simply extended at the first level, by allocating individual hierarchies to each DM who then arrives at an individual judgement. These judgements are aggregated to give a combined outcome, which represents the importance of each group outcome. In other circumstances, if the DMs hold divergent judgements and hold unequal weight in decision making, then this should be recognized. One method for resolving such a dispute is called 'combined group judgements' (Aczel and Saaty, 1983). This is explained under Application later in this chapter.

Method

The methodology consists of four main stages. These are (1) building the multicriterion decision model (or MCDM); (2) making judgements; (3) computing algorithms; and (4) interpreting the data and making decisions. Stage (4) is explained by an application.

Building the MCDM

Since the output is only as good as the decision inputs, building the hierarchical structure representing the problem, comprising criteria and objectives, is an important stage of the method.

Who Builds the Model?

The role of the researcher is to explain how the method operates, and how it might help solve a problem. In order to facilitate this process, there may be occasions when it is necessary for the researcher to build the model, using background literature. But it is generally considered that, where feasible, those DMs who are directly involved or responsible for the outcome of such decision problems should structure the model because they are closest to it, and so should be able to provide the best input (Checkland, 1983). Nevertheless, the interpersonal skills of the researcher are often warranted.

It is generally considered that DMs should be interviewed separately to reduce the initial problems of group-think (Jelassi and Beauclair, 1987). Semistructured interviewing is used to identify the problem, if it is not already clear, along the lines of: 'Why do you believe you have a problem?' 'What is the main focus of the problem?' 'How will this problem affect you?'

Such questions should help to focus on the root problem, rather than a mere symptom. If there is widespread disagreement amongst a group, it is essential to determine the root consensus of the problem through probing. After confirming the central objective, or focus of the problem, the next stage is first to identify the elements contributing to the central objective, and then ascertain their relative levels within the hierarchical structure. This involves further questioning, such as 'What are the important elements that affect the central objective?' This might be followed by 'How are these objectives to be evaluated?' Objectives may be refined, through probing, into subobjectives.

The Axiom of Homogeneity

It is necessary to classify and discriminate between elements in order to identify separate criteria that constitute different levels of the hierarchy. Elements can be discriminated on the basis of homogeneity. Homogeneity is a basic axiom of AHP, which requires that elements must be mutually exclusive and ideally exhaustive in order to qualify on the same level of a hierarchy. Each DM is interviewed to identify the elements considered relevant to the problem, and the results transcribed and content analysed.

Once the elements at each level have been identified, it is usually easier to decide on the criteria that represent them, and what they should be called. Any remaining differences of opinion regarding the structure can often be decided by holding group meetings, through probing and semantical exploration.

Making judgements

The approach described here is using a single DM. The approach for a multiperson problem is explained later. The DM makes pairwise comparisons of elements for each level of the hierarchy in relation to how each contributes toward achieving each goal in the immediate level of the hierarchy above. For example, if the second level of the hierarchy in Figure 1 is examined, the researcher would ask: 'To what extent is profit level more or less important than sales growth with respect to each scenario?' or 'How important is profit relative to sales as a factor under each scenario?'

For each scenario, pairwise judgements would then be made between profit levels and sales growth, then between profit levels and market share, and also between sales growth and market share. The pairwise judgements are based on a ratio scale ranging from 1 to 9, graduating from equal importance to extreme importance respectively. This scale for measuring the intensity of preferences is represented in Figure 7.2, which has proved to be reliable (Saaty, 1977). It contrasts with data collection for conjoint analysis, which uses a simple ranking scale (Anttila *et al.*, 1980).

Intensity of importance	Definition	Definition, based on experience and judgement
1	Equal importance	Two activities considered equally important
3	Moderate importance of one over another	One activity is marginally favoured over another
5	Essential or strong importance	One activity is strongly favoured over another
7	Very strong importance	One activity is very strongly favoured and its dominance is demonstrated in practice
9	Extreme importance	The evidence favouring one activity over another is of the highest possible order
2, 4, 6, 8		Intermediate values between two adjacent judgements

FIGURE 7.2 The meaning of the 9-point ratio scale devised by Saaty

Comparison Matrices

Preference judgements are completed in the form of comparison matrices. The number of elements, n, at a given hierarchical level determines the matrix structure (of n columns and n rows). The number of comparison matrices required at a particular level is equivalent to the number of elements at the preceding level, from which pairwise judgements are based. This is continued throughout the hierarchy. For example, for a hierarchy of five levels represented in Figure 7.1, the number of comparison matrices required would be three 4×4 matrices at level 5, three 3×3 matrices at each of the levels 2–4 inclusive, and one 3×3 matrix at level 1.

The axiom of reciprocal comparison

An important aspect of AHP is that the intensity of these preferences must satisfy the reciprocal condition (Saaty, 1980), e.g. if profits are x times more preferred than sales, then sales are $1/x$ times more preferred than profits. Therefore, if the hierarchy includes n factors or elements at each level, then only $n(n-1)/2$ pairwise comparisons are required for each $n \times n$ matrix. In other words, only half of the potential cells of each matrix require completing because the other half will be the reciprocals. Using Figure 7.1, level 4, if a decision maker considered economy value position moderately more important than a cheap, 'no frills' version in achieving the goal of safety, then a scale of 3 might be assigned to the appropriate cell of the comparison matrix. A 'no frills' position relative to an economy value position is then allocated the reciprocal or 1/3. Similarly, if a high performance position was judged to compromise on safety in its preoccupation for speed and acceleration, this might be considered to be marginally less safe than an economy value version, and so ranked as 1/2. The cells are completed and the process is repeated for each matrix. Figure 7.3 shows a completed comparison matrix with these entries.

Manual calculations

Calculating algorithms: (i) local priorities

Several methods have been used for estimating the relative weights derived from the preferences above. Indeed, there is no consensus as to the best method to adopt. See Zahedi, (1986) for a summary of methods, beyond the realm of this paper. The procedure adopted here uses the geometric mean, which is simple to understand (Saaty and Kearns, 1985), and which is considered to provide a better estimate of underlying ratio scales than other popular methods (Crawford and Williams, 1985).

Safety	No Frills	Economy Value	Premium	Geometric		Normalisation		Local Priorities
No Frills	– 1 –	1/3	1/2	$\sqrt[3]{1 \times 1/3 \times 1/2}$	= 0.55	$\dfrac{0.55}{3.367}$	=	0.163
Economy Value	3	– 1 –	2	$\sqrt[3]{3 \times 1 \times 2}$	+ = 1.817	$\dfrac{1.817}{3.367}$	=	0.540
Premium	2	1/2	– 1 –	$\sqrt[3]{2 \times 1/2 \times 1}$	+ = 1.00	$\dfrac{1.00}{3.367}$	=	0.297
					3.367			1.000

FIGURE 7.3 A comparison matrix of ratio judgement with calculated priorities measuring alternative benefits segments with respect to safety

First, the geometric mean of each row of scores for each comparison matrix is calculated. The resulting column vector of scores for each matrix is then normalized to unity to represent the *local priorities*, illustrated by the ratio scores in Figure 7.3. These resultant local priorities assigned to each element represent their relative value with respect to each particular objective in the immediate hierarchical level above. For example, the local priority value of 'no frills' with respect to the 'safety' segment is considered far less important, at 0.163, compared to economy value, at 0.540. Calculations are continued for each level of the hierarchy.

Global priorities

The decision maker also needs to know the impact of each element with respect to the main focus or top goal of the hierarchy. These are referred to as *global priorities*. By definition, the top hierarchical goal or objective is allocated a global priority of 1.0, which is also its local priority (Saaty, 1980). Global priorities for any hierarchical elements are calculated by weighting their local priorities by the global priorities allocated to the elements they emanate from, (i.e. at the preceding hierarchical level), called their parents. Therefore, for a vector of local priority values $x_1 - x_3$, representing the first level of the hierarchy, their global priorities remain unaltered, as follows:

$$\text{Elements at first level} \begin{pmatrix} x_1 \\ x_2 \\ x_3 \end{pmatrix} \rightarrow \Sigma(X_n . 1.00) = \begin{pmatrix} x_1.(1.00) \\ x_2.(1.00) \\ x_3.(1.00) \end{pmatrix} = \begin{pmatrix} x_1 \\ x_2 \\ x_3 \end{pmatrix}$$

Local priorities   Global priorities
of first level   of first level

However, for subsequent levels, the priorities will be weighted by the global priorities of their parents, in which the local and global priorities will *not* be equal.

Alternative computer calculations

Whilst it is useful to understand how to calculate local and global priorities manually, it can be tedious. Computer software called Expert Choice (Forman and Saaty, 1983) has been designed to calculate these priority values quickly and accurately. The hierarchy describing the model is drawn on the computer screen, using the package, not unlike a decision tree, using labels at each node. The next stage is to enter the ratio scores describing the pairwise preferences. These may already be available from prior interviews with the decision makers. With subsequent practice, it is possible to procure judgements directly from the computer screen, which saves valuable time. By moving to each element using the drawing of the hierarchical problem, and moving to the numerical mode, comparison matrices are automatically presented. By entering the appropriate pairwise judgements for each comparison matrix, the package can calculate local and global priorities for any chosen level of the hierarchy within seconds, by switching to their respective modes.

Application

Using the decision model of Figure 7.1, pairwise comparisons were developed by the author. These judgements aim to demonstrate the process rather than to necessarily reflect the authenticity to a real problem. The comparison matrices a and b–d of Figure 7.4 represent the ratio judgements for levels 1 and 2 respectively. The remaining matrices are not shown to avoid unnecessary detail.

Managerial benefits in presentation and interpretation of information

Expert Choice can calculate local priorities for each element, as each comparison matrix is completed. Figure 7.4 shows the computed vectors of local priorities for each comparison matrix. Also, Expert Choice can produce an elaborate breakdown of global priorities at each hierarchical level, once all the data from the matrices have been entered. Table 7.1 shows part of such a spreadsheet of results. Frequently, marketing managers need to be able to justify their ideas, objectives and recommendations clearly and succinctly. These spreadsheets provide useful evidence to support a decision, in order to

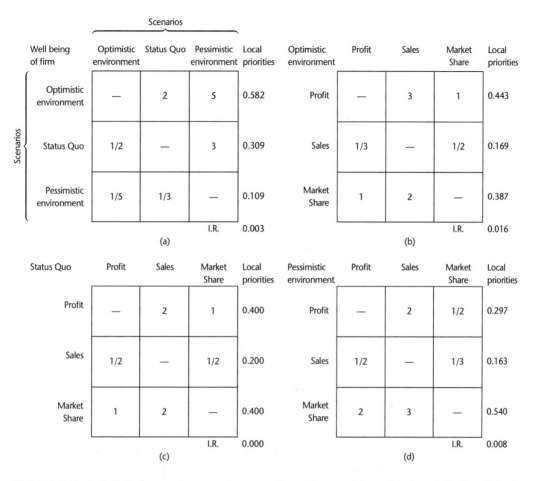

Well being of firm	Optimistic environment	Status Quo	Pessimistic environment	Local priorities
Optimistic environment	—	2	5	0.582
Status Quo	1/2	—	3	0.309
Pessimistic environment	1/5	1/3	—	0.109
			I.R.	0.003

(a)

Optimistic environment	Profit	Sales	Market Share	Local priorities
Profit	—	3	1	0.443
Sales	1/3	—	1/2	0.169
Market Share	1	2	—	0.387
			I.R.	0.016

(b)

Status Quo	Profit	Sales	Market Share	Local priorities
Profit	—	2	1	0.400
Sales	1/2	—	1/2	0.200
Market Share	1	2	—	0.400
			I.R.	0.000

(c)

Pessimistic environment	Profit	Sales	Market Share	Local priorities
Profit	—	2	1/2	0.297
Sales	1/2	—	1/3	0.163
Market Share	2	3	—	0.540
			I.R.	0.008

(d)

FIGURE 7.4 Ratio judgements comparing scenarios with respect to well-being of the firm (Matrix a) and objectives with respect to scenarios (Matrices b–d)

gain approval for scarce resources from senior management (Dyer *et al.*, 1988). Indeed, frequently analysis is required as a persuading device to legitimatize policy decisions (Eden, 1982).

To aid interpretation for executive action, the vectors of local priorities derived from each comparison matrix, along with the global priorities from the spreadsheet analysis, can be reconstructed for each particular level of the hierarchy (See Tables 7.2–7.5). From the spreadsheet, the composite global priorities can be calculated. For example, to construct Table 7.3, the global priorities of objectives (level 2), taken from the spreadsheet, are added under each scenario to derive their composite global priorities with respect to the top goal, or well-being of the firm. The figures for profit, sales and market share respectively are

profit: $0.258 + 0.124 + 0.032 = 0.414$
sales: $0.098 + 0.062 + 0.018 = 0.178$
market shares: $0.225 + 0.124 + 0.059 = 0.408$

Alternatively, the global priorities can be derived manually by weighting the local priorities at each level, (derived from the comparison matrices) by the global priorities of their parents. The total composite global priorities are then aggregated. For instance, the global priority of profit (Table 7.3) is:

$$(0.443 \times 0.582) + (0.400 \times 0.309) + (0.297 \times 0.109) =$$
$$0.258 + 0.124 + 0.032 = 0.414$$

This procedure is continued throughout the hierarchy.

The final column of composite global priorities (Tables 2–5) indicate the most important elements at each level with respect to the well-being of the firm, which are:

1. an optimistic scenario, (at 0.582, Table 7.2), because this is considered the most likely;
2. profits and market share, (at 0.414 and 0.408 respectively, Table 7.3);
3. any benefits segments, since there is little to choose between them (at around 0.300 each, Table 7.4); and
4. the premium version of product positioning (at 0.533, followed by economy value, at 0.351, Table 7.5).

Therefore, the best courses of action to be taken at each level for the firm appear to be to choose profits and/or market share as the main objectives, consider seriously all the benefits segments, and focus more effort in developing a premium positioning.

The remaining figures in each Table help to explain how the composite global priorities are derived, useful for selling the idea to senior management. For example, the overall importance of profits and market share as objectives can be explained by their local priorities under both an optimistic and status quo scenario (at around 0.400 each, Table 7.3). Also, the high rating of a premium version is probably accounted for by its significant importance with respect to both performance and looks benefits (at 0.692 and 0.643 respectively, Table 7.5).

Finally, the inconsistency ratio produced by Expert Choice measures the likelihood of the scores relative to a set of random responses and provides a measure of their concentration in making judgements, reflecting transitivity. An inconsistency ratio, (IR) of <0.1 is acceptable, otherwise DMs are encouraged to revise their judgements. Many multiattribute techniques such as conjoint analysis do not provide such checks.

TABLE 7.1 Spread sheet analysis showing global priorities under an optimistic scenario

Level 1		Level 2		Level 3		Level 4	
Optimistic	0.582	Profit levels	0.258	Safety	0.028	Cheap	0.005
						Economy	0.015
						Premium	0.008
				Performance	0.080	Cheap	0.006
						Economy	0.018
						Premium	0.055
				Looks	0.150	Cheap	0.015
						Economy	0.038
						Premium	0.096
		Sales growth	0.098	Safety	0.053	Cheap	0.009
						Economy	0.029
						Premium	0.016
				Performance	0.029	Cheap	0.002
						Economy	0.007
						Premium	0.020
				Looks	0.016	Cheap	0.002
						Economy	0.004
						Premium	0.010
		Market share	0.226	Safety	0.122	Cheap	0.020
						Economy	0.066
						Premium	0.036
				Performance	0.067	Cheap	0.005
						Economy	0.015
						Premium	0.046
				Looks	0.037	Cheap	0.004
						Economy	0.009
						Premium	0.024
Status quo	0.309	Profit levels	0.124	Safety	0.014	Cheap	0.002
						Economy	0.007
						Premium	0.004
Data used for Tables:	2		3		4		5

TABLE 7.2 Local and global priorities at level 1 (representing the likelihood) of each scenario with respect to the overall objective of the firm

Environmental scenarios	Local priorities	Global priorities
Optimistic	0.582	0.582
Status quo	0.309	0.309
Pessimistic	0.109	0.109
Inconsistency ratio	0.003	

TABLE 7.3 Local priorities at level 2 for each objective according to each scenario (and global priorities with respect to well-being of the firm in parentheses)

| Objectives | Scenarios | | | |
	Optimistic (0.582)*	Status quo (0.309)*	Pessimistic (0.109)*	Total composite global priorities
Profit levels	0.443 (0.258)	0.400 (0.124)	0.297 (0.032)	(0.414)
Sales growth	0.169 (0.098)	0.200 (0.062)	0.163 (0.018)	(0.178)
Market share	0.387 (0.225)	0.400 (0.124)	0.540 (0.059)	(0.408)
Inconsistency ratio	0.016	0.000	0.008	

* Global priorities for prior level.

TABLE 7.4 Local priorities at level 3 for each benefits segment with respect to each objective (and global priorities with respect to the well-being of the firm in parentheses)

| | Objectives | | | |
	Profit levels (0.414)*	Sales growth (0.178)*	Market share (0.408)*	Total composite global priorities
Safety	0.109 (0.045)	0.540 (0.096)	0.540 (0.220)	(0.361)
Performance	0.309 (0.128)	0.297 (0.053)	0.297 (0.121)	(0.302)
Looks	0.582 (0.241)	0.163 (0.029)	0.163 (0.067)	(0.337)
Inconsistency ratio	0.003	0.008	0.008	

* Global priorities from prior synthesis.

TABLE 7.5 Local priorities at level 4 for each positioning alternative with respect to each benefits segment (and global priorities with respect to the well-being of the firm in parentheses)

| Price/quality positioning | Segments | | | |
	Safety (0.361)*	Performance (0.302)*	Looks (0.337)*	Total composite global priorities
No frills	0.163† (0.059)	0.077 (0.023)	0.101 (0.034)	(0.116)
Economy value	0.540† (0.195)	0.231 (0.070)	0.255 (0.086)	(0.351)
Premium	0.297† (0.107)	0.692 (0.209)	0.643 (0.217)	(0.533)
Inconsistency ratio	0.008	0.000	0.046	

* Global priorities from prior synthesis.
†Also illustrated in Figure 3.

Further benefits in using AHP: dealing with group decision making

Marketing decision making frequently involves multidisciplinary teams, (e.g. finance, marketing) whose members are drawn from different levels of the organizational hierarchy (e.g. directors in discourse with middle management). Consequently, their varied backgrounds are likely to release divergent viewpoints. Govoni *et al.* (1986) argue there is a necessity to integrate individual objectives to work towards the good of the company as a whole. But consensus may be difficult if some perceive others to hold too much influence in overall decision making. To overcome this problem, the method of combined group judgements, (CGJ) can be used to provide a group outcome, providing that the participants agree to the outcome arising from the process. This is conducted by simply averaging the group's judgements using the geometric mean. If a_{ij}^1, a_{ij}^2, . . . ,aa_{ij}^M represent different pairwise judgements of M members of the group, the composite judgement is given by:

$$CGJ = [a_{ij}^1 \times a_{ij}^2 \times ,\ldots, \times a_{ij}^M]^{(1/M)}$$

Davies (1991, 1994) has used the 'combined group judgements' method to develop weights representing the relative influence or power expected of multiple decision makers holding divergent judgements confronted with an advertising agency selection problem. Each DM makes pairwise judgements about each other's relative importance as decision makers, whose scores are averaged. The resulting comparison matrix of CGJ scores is then treated in the usual way to derive priority values for each DM. Each DM then makes separate judgements at subsequent levels of a common hierarchy. By using the spreadsheet analysis derived from Expert Choice, it is possible to identify how well an individual's set of judgements about criteria compare to the group judgements. This can be used to emphasize voting power, or can help individuals revise their judgements for the good of the group.

Other Benefits in Using Expert Choice

Sensitivity analysis can be used with Expert Choice to show the impact of a change in judgements upon the subsequent outcome. For example, market dynamics may dictate that the judgements given to environmental scenarios should change, and this will have an impact upon the importance given to subsequent objectives and alternatives of the decision hierarchy. In particular, Expert Choice provides graphics which enable the decision maker to identify whether, and to what extent, a change in values of an element will affect subsequent priority values on another hierarchical level and, by implication, ultimate decision choices. For decisions involving big budgets, such as in strategic planning, identifying the impact of changes can be significant.

By combining sensitivity analysis with the CGJ application, Davies (1994) demonstrated how potentially dominant decision makers are able to reflect on their influence in the process of how overall decisions are reached, with the opportunity for restraint. By restraining their level of dominance, a decision can be reached which is acceptable to the whole group. Whatever the recommended choice, the process leading to it must be acceptable to the participants, otherwise commitment in carrying it forward will be dampened.

Criticisms of AHP

Difficulties in making judgements

It has been suggested that DMs may have difficulty in using the ratio scale for estimating the relative importance of different factors. If this is due to unfamiliarity of the scale, a series of pilot runs can be used to fine tune judgements. The IR, developed by Saaty, also keeps a check on the concentration of judgements made. But the IR alone does not necessitate that the preferences made reflect the true preferences of the DM, and is therefore not a sufficient condition for determining how good a set of judgements are (Saaty, 1977). For some marketing decisions involving creative input, the DM may not have formed a strong enough opinion on a particular issue. In these circumstances, the skill of the researcher may be required to identify any hesitation which might lead to tentative judgements. Where uncertainty is identified, the underlying preference structure can still be evaluated by using a range of scale values, rather than forcing precise values (Arbel, 1989). This involves expressing a range of preferences as a set of double-sided inequalities (characterizing upper and lower bounds), and solving as a linear programming problem.

The controversy over rank reversal

Under changing conditions, rankings are sometimes reversed, which has produced criticisms about the arbitrary way the judgements are ranked (Dyer, 1990). Saaty, in defence, suggests that normalization is used to apportion the priority of a criterion to each alternative, according to the relative dominance of that alternative. Normalization can be used to differentiate alternatives according to scarcity or abundance of criteria. Saaty (1990b) uses this argument to explain why rank reversal can be a healthy phenomenon, an apparent paradox of utility theory. The presence of copies of alternatives reduces the relative dominance of every alternative, including the original of the copies. The changes in relative dominance explain any reversal in rankings and can reflect real consumer behaviour, e.g. Saaty uses an example of a woman buying a hat. At one store, A is preferred to B slightly, but B is eventually purchased upon subsequent abundance of A at another store.

An alternative viewpoint, offered by Belton and Gear, (1983) is that preference order can only be preserved by renormalizing the priority vector weights. This is achieved by allocating unity to the highest ranked option, rather than to the sum of the options.

Thresholds must be monitored

Both conjoint analysis and AHP need to ascertain if decision choice is ruled by threshold requirements. If all alternative combinations of elements need to satisfy a minimal requirement of a particular objective, then such a threshold needs to be reached before any trade-off can take place.

Pragmatism and model building

Implicitly, the fusion or synthesis of multilevel judgements assumes that integration is achievable between a range of business functions or departments with divergent political agendas. Critics might therefore suggest that structuring problems in this way is technically acceptable or even altruistic, but not pragmatic. The author acknowledges this obstacle and suggests that commitment towards integration must arise from top management offering a leadership role by example. Various techniques, such as cross functional teams, can also help understanding between different business divisions. Further research is required into group decision support systems to help resolve organizational tasks in strategic planning.

Future avenues for research

Content issues

Although published marketing applications have been diverse since 1980, international marketing appears to have been neglected. Accordingly, a rudimentary structure for screening markets and making entry decisions is demonstrated in Figure 7.5. This represents making decision preferences upon market entry objectives, environmental factors and markets

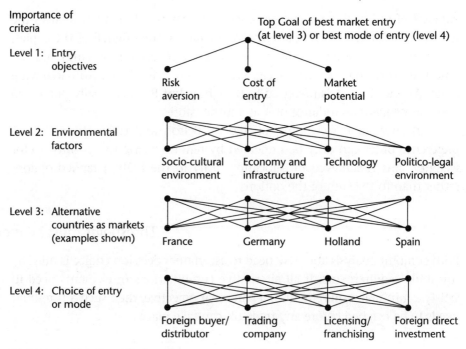

FIGURE 7.5 Simplified, exploratory model of international marketing plan

(countries). The choice of entry, in turn, will be determined by the markets considered. There are many other applications which might be considered or refined.

Process issues

According to Eom *et al.* (1990), one or more of the following factors induces conflict: limited resources, multiple decision makers, multiple decision criteria or multiple alternatives. Since these factors are common to marketing, another potential area for development is to explore alternative processes for reducing conflict amongst group decision makers. For instance, Expert Choice could be applied to decision conferencing (Phillips, 1986). In this case, outcomes from Expert Choice, based on individual judgements, would be projected on to a large screen, visible to everyone, to encourage feedback and revision of judgements until a satisfactory group outcome is reached.

Finally, more sophisticated methods must be developed for assessing the overall effectiveness of marketing decision making arising from AHP, compared to conventional methods. In the absence of control experiments, DM satisfaction and questionnaires could be two approaches to adopt.

Summary

Many marketing planning and evaluation tasks involve making multicriterion decisions, sometimes within a group context. The AHP technique, by systematically structuring the problem as a customized hierarchy, can lead to the likely identification of all key components affecting decision making, which is less likely if making 'seat of the pants' decisions. The most important objectives or alternatives at each decision level are derived from a trade-off analysis, which can also help reconcile group conflict. Data collection uses relative intensities of preferences, in which both qualitative and quantitative data are uniquely combined on a single ratio scale of measurement, very useful for marketing management. Although the technique can appear tedious, Expert Choice allows data to be transferred directly on to the screen, from which results can be obtained speedily. Furthermore, the ability to calculate and present results at each decision level can be used to support, persuade and justify proposed outcomes to top management. This is important for marketing managers fighting for scarce resources. Despite the criticisms of AHP, the process of model building sharpens and refines managerial thinking concerning objectives and alternative courses of action, thus providing much insight into areas of potential conflict.

References

Aczel, J. and Saaty, T.L. (1983), Procedures for synthesizing ratio judgments, *Journal of Mathematical Psychology*, **27**, No.1, pp. 93–102

Agor, W.H. (1991), How Intuition Can be Used to Enhance Creativity in Organizations, *Journal of Creative Behavior*, **1**, First Quarter, pp. 11–19

Anttila, M., Van den Heuvel, R.R. and Moller, K. (1980), Conjoint Measurement for Marketing Management, *European Journal of Marketing*, **14**, No.7, pp. 397–408

Arbel, A. (1989), Approximate articulation of preference and priority derivation, *European Journal of Operational Research*, **43**, pp. 317–326

Bahmani, N. and Blumberg, H. (1987), Consumer preference and reactive adaption to a corporate solution of the OTC medication dilemma – an analytic hierarchy process, *Mathematical Modelling*, **9**, pp. 293–298

Bahmani, N., Javalgi, G. and Blumberg, H. (1986), An application of the analytical hierarchy process for a consumer choice problem, *Developments in Marketing Science*, **9**, pp. 402–6

Belton, V. and Gear, T. (1983), On a short-coming of Saaty's method of analytic hierarchies, *Omega*, **11**, 3, pp. 228–230

Checkland, P. (1983), O.R. and the systems movement: mappings and conflicts, *Journal of the Operational Research Society*, **34**, No.8, pp. 661–75

Cook, T., Falchi, P. and Mariano, R. (1984), An urban model combining time series and analytic hierarchy methods, *Management Science*, **30**, No.2, pp. 198–208

Crawford, G. and Williams, C. (1985), A note on the analysis of subjective judgment matrices, *Journal of Mathematical Psychology*, **29**, pp. 387–405

Davies, M.A.P., (1991), 'A decision support system for advertising agency selection, *Proceedings of the 24th Marketing Education Group Conference*, Cardiff Business School, **1**, pp. 271–90

Davies, M.A.P. (1994), A multicriterion decision model for managing group decisions, *Journal of the Operational Research Society*, 45, **1**, pp. 47–58

Davies, M.A.P. (1994), Managing the complexity of advertising strategy using an analytic hierarchy process, *Proceedings of the 23rd Annual Conference of the European Marketing Academy*, Maastricht, May, pp. 151–65

Davies, M.A.P. and Saunders, J. (1990), 'Multicriteria advertising decision making: a decision support system using an analytic hierarchy process', *Proceedings of the 23rd Marketing Education Group Conference*, Oxford Polytechnic, **1**, pp. 276–308

Dyer, J.S. (1990), Remarks on the analytic hierarchy process, *Management Science*, **36**, No.3, pp. 249–58

Dyer, R.F., Forman, E.A., Forman E.H. and Jouflas, G. (1988), *Marketing Decisions Using Expert Choice*, Pittsburgh PA Decision Support Software Inc.

Dyer, R.F., Forman, E.H. and Mustafa, M.A. (1992), Decision support for media selection using the analytic hierarchy process, *Journal of Advertising*, Vol **XXI**, 1, March, pp. 59–72

Eden, C. (1982), Problem construction and the influence of O.R., *Interfaces*, **12**, No.2, pp. 50–60

Eom, H.B., Lee, S.M. and Suh, E-H. (1990), Group decision support systems: an essential tool for resolving organizational conflicts, *International Journal of Information Management*, **10**, pp. 215–27

Forman, E., (1985), Decision support for executive decision makers, *Information Strategy: The Executive's Journal*, Summer, pp. 4–14

Forman, E. and Saaty, T.L. (1983), *Expert Choice*, McLean VA, Decision Support Software

Govoni, N., Eng, R. and Galper, M. (1986), *Promotion Management*, Englewood Cliffs NJ Prentice-Hall International

Harker, P.T. and Vargas, L.G. (1990), Reply to 'Remarks on the analytic hierarchy process' by J. S. Dyer, *Management Science*, **36**, No.3. pp. 269–73

Javalgi, R.G., Armacost, R.L. and Hosseini, J.C. (1989), Using the analytic hierarchy process for bank management: analysis of consumer bank selection decisions, *Journal of Business Research*, **19**, No.1, pp. 33–49

Jelassi, Tawfik, M. and Beauclair, R.A. (1987), An integrated framework for group decision support systems design, *Information and Management*, **13**, No.3, pp. 143–53

Mazanec, J.A. (1986), A decision support system for optimizing advertising policy of a national tourist office model outline and case study, *International Journal of Research in Marketing*, **3**, pp. 63–77

Miller, G.A. (1956), The magical number seven, plus or minus two: some limits on our capacity for processing information, *The Psychological Review*, **63**, No.2, pp. 81–97

Phillips, L.D. (1986), Computing for consensus, *Datamation*, October, 68-2–68-6

Saaty, T.L. (1977), A scaling method for priorities in hierarchical structures, *Journal of Mathematical Psychology*, **15**, pp. 234–81

Saaty, T.L. (1980), *The Analytic Hierarchy Process*, New York: McGraw Hill

Saaty, T.L. (1990a), How to make a decision: the analytic hierarchy process, *European Journal of Operational Research*, **48**, No.1, pp. 9–26

Saaty, T.L. (1990b), An exposition of the AHP in reply to the paper 'Remarks on the analytic hierarchy process', *Management Science*, **36**, No.3, pp. 259–68

Saaty, T.L. and Alexander, J.M. (1989), *Conflict Resolution: The Analytic Hierarchy Approach*, New York: Praeger

Saaty, T.L. and Kearns, K.P. (1985), *Analytical Planning*, Oxford: Pergamon Press

Tone, K. and Yanagisawa, S. (1989), 'Site selection for a large scale integrated circuits factory', in: *Applications of the Analytic Hierarchy Process*. B.L. Golden, E.A. Wasil, and P.T. Harker, (Eds.) New York: Springer-Verlag

Vargas, L.G. and Saaty, T.L. (1981), Financial and intangible factors in fleet lease or buy decisions, *Industrial Marketing Management,* **10**, No.1, pp. 1–10

Wind, Y. and Saaty, T.L. (1980), Marketing applications of the analytic hierarchy process, *Management Science*, **26**, No.7, pp. 641–58

Zahedi, F. (1986), The analytic hierarchy process – a survey of the method and its applications, *Interfaces*, **16**, No 4, pp. 96–108

■ □ ▨ ■ 8

The Structure of Consumers' Place Evaluations

Paul M.W. Hackett and Gordon R. Foxall

A model for place evaluation is developed through a facet theoretical study of a convention centre. A questionnaire viewing user satisfaction with the centre was given to 86 respondents. Similarity structure analysis (SSA) produced a three facet solution, with facets of: **referent** (life area) with elements of social, service, spatial and aesthetic, **focus** (centrality) with elements of central and peripheral, and **level** with elements of internal physical, external and internal atmosphere. Partial order analysis with base coordinates (POSAC) identified individuals in terms of their responses to these facets of place evaluations. These analyses allowed respondents to be classified as either structuring their principal evaluations in terms of either social and service aspects of the location or in terms of features relating to spatial, aesthetic, physical qualities and elements which were central to the subject's location specific purpose. The results are compared with previous facet studies which have enabled a generic model of place evaluation to be developed.

Introduction

A multiattribute conception of consumer location and consumer motivation is a framework which has been employed in attempting to understand situated consumer behaviour (e.g. Monroe and Guiltinan, 1975; Tauber, 1972). In attempting this many specific attributes of the location of consumer behaviour may be listed. However, no systematic classification system has emerged with the ability to integrate these disparate elements.

Assuming that the decision and appraisal aspects which initiate consumer behaviour are separable components of behaviour and that these have been gone through, the first purposive aspect of consumer behaviour is the choice of purchase location. The selection of this will be based upon the likelihood of a place (store/mall) stocking the requisite item, and then the nearest of such locations will probably be chosen (Hackett *et al.*, 1993). Having chosen the broad retail area the consumer then visits the selected place. This will probably not be an experiential appraisal ranging from 'satisfactory place', to 'unsatisfactory place', rather it will embody several different criteria for evaluation.

When attempting to assess levels of satisfaction, the question must therefore be asked 'satisfactory for what?' Consumer behaviour will be facilitated or inhibited, and made more or less pleasurable by a variety of factors, each of which will have several specific effects. For example, the spatial qualities of a location determine distances which must be walked; shop assistants help or hinder purchasing; and general aesthetics and the range of product choice all affect consumers'/users' responses to places. Successful formal place evaluation must therefore encompass multiple dimensions in appraisal. Individuals within a convention centre can be seen to be directed in their behaviours by the fact that they are all consumers of the facilities of this setting.

Consumer locations have been seen to attract users or customers largely on the basis of location convenience and the range of the goods or services they offer. Thus purposiveness within consumer locations may be satisfied by the attainment of such goals. Little attention is paid to the integration of these features with other aspects of service location such as the already mentioned friendliness of staff, locational atmosphere, etc.

Several post occupation evaluation studies have been carried out which have been designed within the facet meta-theoretical framework (Donald, 1985) and it is to this approach that we will turn in order to guide the present research. (For a detailed description of facet metatheory or the facet metatheoretical approach see Borg, 1977, 1981; Borg and Lingoes, 1987; Canter, 1985; Donald, 1987; Hackett, 1989; Levy, 1985; Morrison *et al.*, 1991; Shye, 1986.) A newly opened international convention centre is a construction on a scale which is of local, national and regional importance. The present study extends facet research into another form of public building.

Facet theory approach to design appraisal

Facet theory (Canter, 1985; Shye, 1978) is an approach to applied social research which has been employed in order to gauge user–place satisfaction by using a mapping sentence to coordinate research design (Borg, 1977; Canter, 1983b). A mapping sentence is a formal specification of a research area in terms of the features pertinent to the research content, the range over which data will be gathered, the respondents for the study and any relevant background variables. The inclusion of several content variables (facets) concurrently within a design affords inspection of the relationship between content facets and allows their specific combined effects upon responses (range) to be observed.

Arising out of the findings of facet research into place evaluation (Donald, 1985) a non-context specific 'general mapping sentence for the evaluation of the built environment' has been developed. 'The model [mapping sentence of place evaluation] has been applied in a number of settings and has revealed a consistent empirical structure to evaluations.' (Donald, 1985). The mapping is a theoretical statement which lists a series of hypotheses regarding the structure of evaluations within specific environments. This specifies three content facets to be common to location evaluations:

1. a referent facet, drawing upon the purposive nature of place experience and reflecting the multiple references a person makes within any situation;
2. these will be modified in accordance with the value, centrality or importance of these behaviours within this context;
3. a level of interaction facet is stated which differentiates place by physical scale or by levels of user contact.

This structure has provided a consistent template for the design of user/place evaluation studies within airports (Hackett, 1985; Hackett and Foxall, 1992) public housing (Canter and Rees, 1982), hospitals (Canter and Kenny, 1982; Kenny and Canter, 1981; Kenny, 1983) and offices (Donald; 1983, 1987). The mapping sentence for place evaluation has thus allowed for an accumulation of research findings. A model with a common structure (known as a cylindrex (see Appendix 8.1)) has been found with a similar structure across studies, (Canter, 1983a; Donald, 1985; Hackett, 1985., Hackett and Foxall, 1992). Donald (1985) provides a review of research in this area.

To permit additional statements to be made regarding the validity of the cylindrex structure, and more importantly, to allow the identification of individuals in terms of their responses as they are classified by the elements of the cylindrex, further analyses will be performed using partial order structural analysis with base coordinates (POSAC). (For a further discussion of POSAC, see Appendix 8.2.) This will significantly extend understanding regarding evaluation of the built environment.

Person (x) evaluates the extent to which being in place (p) facilitates

Focus
  (1) the overall essence
  (2) the general qualities   of his/her
  (3) specific aspects

Referent
  (1) social
  (2) spatial   objectives at the
  (3) service

Level
  (1) local
  (2) intermediate   levels of interaction, at the
  (3) greater

Scale
  (1) immediate
  (2) intermediate   level by stating that it
  (3) global

(greatly facilitates)
      (to)   his/her objectives
(interferes with)

where (p) is a place of which person (x) has direct experience.

FIGURE 8.1 General mapping sentence for place evaluation
(Donald, 1985)

Person (x), being a   (conference delegate)
                                  (visitor)
                                  (staff member)

assess the:
Referent
  social
  spatial
  service
  aesthetic
qualities of the:
Level
  conference hall
  conference centre
  locality
which are of:
Focus
  direct relevance
  indirect relevance
to their purpose as being:
Range   very satisfactory (1) to very unsatisfactory (5)
in terms of their purposes within the centre.

FIGURE 8.2 Mapping sentence for convention centre evaluation study

Design

In the design of the present research tool the general mapping sentence for place evaluation (Figure 8.1) was adapted to the convention centre location. The process of adaptation was achieved through reference to official publications from the convention centre and through personal visits to the development. A mapping sentence for the evaluation of the convention centre was therefore formulated (see Figure 8.2). From this a questionnaire was compiled which was subject to a short pilot study. The final questionnaire was essentially the same as the one piloted as only minor modifications were made to the instrument (see Figure 8.3). Respondents were required to assess 17 features of the convention centre development along a five point scale ranging from very unsatisfactory to very satisfactory.

Sample

In the survey, 86 users of the centre were approached and asked to complete the questionnaire. Respondents were of different user types (a list of

---

Please answer each question by giving a number from 1 to 5, where

      1 = Bad   (very unsatisfactory)
      2 = Poor   (unsatisfactory)
      3 = Neutral (neither satisfactory nor unsatisfactory)
      4 = Fair   (satisfactory)
      5 = Good   (very satisfactory)

In terms of your purposes within the International Convention Centre (ICC) to what extent do you find the following features satisfactory ?

(1)   The location of the ICC within the city.
(2)   Staying in Birmingham as a delegate.
(3)   The appearance of the ICC.
(4)   The design of the halls.
(5)   Acoustics within the halls.
(6)   The friendliness of people in the centre.
(7)   Lighting levels within the halls.
(8)   Hotel facilities around the ICC.
(9)   Temperature levels within the halls.
(10)   The overall design of the centre.
(11)   Acoustics within the centre.
(12)   Lighting levels within the centre.
(13)   Temperature levels within the centre.
(14)   Sign posting within the centre.
(15)   The helpfulness of staff at the ICC.
(16)   The ease of finding your way around the ICC.
(17)   The friendliness of people in the surrounding area.

FIGURE 8.3 Questionnaire

respondents and respondent characteristics is provided in Table 8.1). Potential participants were approached in the streets near to the convention centre. Those agreeing were then asked to complete the questionnaire *in situ*.

Results: similarity structure analysis

Similarity structure analysis (SSA) (Guttman, 1968; Schlessinger and Guttman, 1969) was performed on the questionnaire data producing a solution with three content facets of referent, focus and level, with a Guttman–Lingoes coefficient of alienation of 0.11 (this being at an acceptable level, Lingoes, 1973). Table 8.2 lists facets and facet elements.

TABLE 8.1 Sample composition

Gender	male	60
	female	26
Age	mean	39
	S.D.	15
	range	14–77
Normal domicile	within city	60
	within U.K.	23
	outside U.K.	3
Experience	delegate	18
	visitor	48
	employee	14
	concert goer	6

TABLE 8.2 Facets and facet elements

Referent facet of life area	social
	service
	spatial
	aesthetic
Focus facet of centrality	central
	peripheral
Level of interaction facet	internal physical
	external
	internal atmosphere

A referent facet of life area was discovered which played a role characteristic of a polarizing facet (Borg and Lingoes, 1987; Levy 1985) and the resulting configuration had a *circumplex* structure (one represented in a spatial arrangement as a circle of points or items) with elements of 'social', 'service', 'spatial' and 'aesthetic' qualitatively arranged in this circular configuration (i.e. no element was first or last, lesser or greater, see Figure 8.4). Also present in the same two dimensional plot of multidimensional space was a focus facet of centrality in a modular role (Borg and Lingoes, 1987), modulating assessments present in the life area referent facet. The elements of this facet were of 'central' and 'peripheral'. Thus, the two facets of life area and focus formed an interacting two by four classification system in the configuration known as a *radex* (Guttman, 1954). The third facet present was a level facet. This had three elements of 'internal physical', 'external' and 'internal atmosphere' levels of interaction with the development arranged in a Simplex structure (see Appendix 8.1) (Figure 8.5). The internal physical level element contained items which were internal to the convention centre and with which individuals had direct contact, whereas the internal atmosphere element contained features internal to the centre but with which individuals

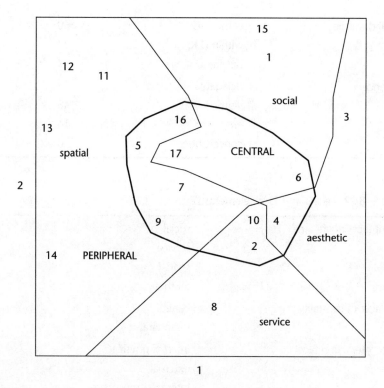

FIGURE 8.4 Projection of SSA showing life area and focus facet

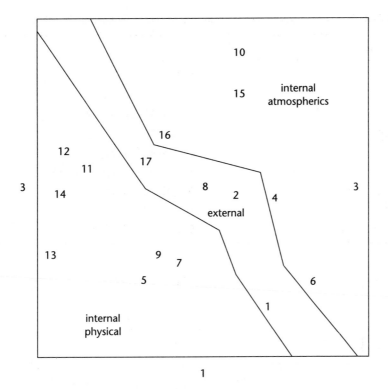

FIGURE 8.5 Projection of SSA showing level facet
Note: Guttman–Lingues coefficient of alienation = 0.11

had a more indirect level of contact. This facet was present in a separate plot to the referent and focus facets and can be seen to structure evaluations in a relatively independent manner (independent relative to the structure implied in the referent and focus facets).

To enable further analyses through POSAC to be performed, composite scores were calculated for each of the facet elements. The element items comprising each of these are listed in Table 8.3. The procedure and rationale for undertaking partial order structural analysis is given in Appendix 8.2 and may also be found in Shye and Amar (1985); details of the present analyses are given below.

Results: Partial order structural analysis with base coordinates (POSAC)

The first element which may be identified as defining the first qualitative pole of an axis which differentiates between respondents (and thus structures the POSAC) can be seen in Figure 8.6. Here the plot for the social life area facet element is shown to partition in a vertical manner. Figure 8.7 shows similar

TABLE 8.3 Element item: composition, mean scores, standard deviations

Element name	Items
social	6, 15 17
service	2, 8
spatial	5, 7, 9, 11, 12, 13, 14, 16
aesthetic	1, 3, 4, 10
central	2, 4, 5, 6, 7, 9, 10, 16, 17
peripheral	1, 3, 4, 8, 11, 12, 13, 14, 15
internal atmosphere	3, 4, 6, 10, 15, 16
external	1, 2, 8, 17
internal physical	5, 7, 9, 11, 12, 13, 14

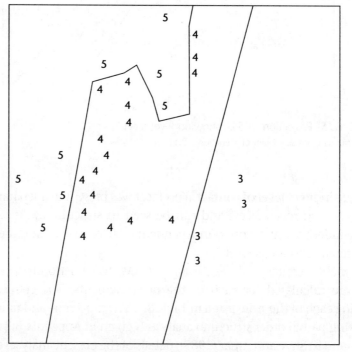

FIGURE 8.6 POSAC item diagram for social item

direction partitioning to be present for the service life area element and consequently this element forms the second component of the first qualitative pole of differentiation. As partitioning of the service life area element was achieved through the use of vertical lines which were less straight than those of the social life area element; the latter of these plays a

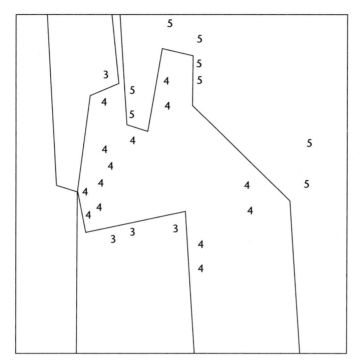

FIGURE 8.7 POSAC item diagram for service item

clearer role in structuring judgements. These two elements are the only elements to partition vertically and the two elements may be identified as the first axis.

The first component of the second axis is formed by the central focus element (Figure 8.8). Partitioning can here be seen to be horizontal and straight. A second major component of this axis can be seen in Figure 8.9 where the spatial life area element can be seen to divide horizontally. Two further elements were found to partition horizontally, these being aesthetic life area and internal physical level (Figures 8.10 and 8.11 respectively): the second qualitative axis of assessments is formed by spatial life area, aesthetic life area, internal physical level and central focus elements.

Figures 8.12 and 8.13 show analyses of external level element and peripheral focus element features. Both of these caused partitions characteristic of the relatively minor role of a moderator. This means that high scores upon these features were associated with mid-range values of lateral scores. Finally, Figure 8.14 shows divisions of items comprising the internal atmosphere level element did not clearly partition and this did not play a significant part in structuring assessments.

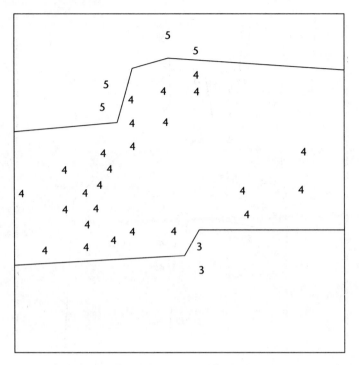

FIGURE 8.8 POSAC item diagram for central item

Discussion

Within the convention centre the three facets of the general mapping sentence for place evaluation were discovered to structure evaluations of locational satisfaction (see Table 8.2). The referent life area facet had elements of social, service, spatial and aesthetic; differentiating respondents' interactions with the centre by these criteria. The structure of this facet has been found to be largely consistent across studies. However, the aesthetic element has only occasionally been reported (Donald, 1983; Hackett, 1985; Hackett and Foxall, 1992). Donald explained the presence of this element in evaluations as being due to the poor aesthetic qualities of the location used in his investigation (offices). However, this was not the case in either the present study, nor that of Hackett, 1985 (a new air terminal) and Hackett and Foxall, 1992 (a new convention centre). In all of these the aesthetic qualities of the setting were extremely good. Therefore it would appear that an aesthetic element is relevant to evaluations when aesthetics are both prominent and pertinent locational features, this prominence being due to their qualities being either extremely poor or extremely good or simply being a major component of users' place experience.

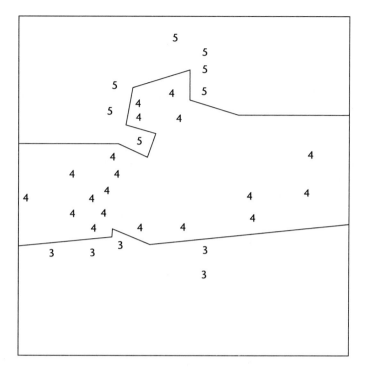

FIGURE 8.9 POSAC item diagram for spatial item

As in all previous studies, judgements implicit within the referent facet were differentiated (or modified) by a focus facet according to the centrality of these to the attainment of place specific goals. Consequently, what constitutes an item of central focus is place specific, but that some items will be evaluated as being more central than others, is not. This facet 'focuses' the assessment categories of the referent facet in accordance with the notion that references may be identified as of more or less importance in purpose fulfilment.

Canter (1983a) stated that evaluations will be focused within informal settings in terms of the generality or the specificity of the object of the evaluation, whilst in formal locations (such as a convention centre) differentiation will be in terms of central (direct)/peripheral (indirect) in respect to formal goal attainment. The present results were supportive of this hypothesis.

The level facet differentiated locational features (internal atmosphere, external, internal physical) each requiring a different type and level of user contact. Previous research has found two forms of level facet; physical location scales, or a hierarchy of place/person interaction level. The former of these types produces facet elements of different physical scale features (for example,

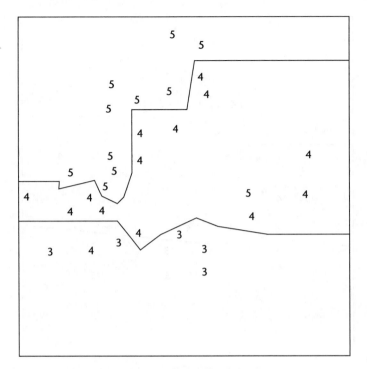

FIGURE 8.10 POSAC item diagram for aesthetic item

conference halls, conference centre, centre surroundings), whilst the latter would produce elements of direct contact, indirect contact with the centre. Donald (1985) claims that the feature determining which of these facet structures is apposite is the presence of a single respondent goal, or specifying a single goal in research design. In these cases differentiations will be on the basis of level of contact, otherwise physical scale becomes pertinent. It is interesting to note that in the present study neither one single goal existed or was identified and that multiple location related scales were also present. Consequently, analyses revealed the level facet to be somewhat of a combination of the two forms of this facet: the elements differentiated scales of the location (internal v. external) and also caused a sub-division of the internal element into 'physical' (items with which users had more direct contact levels) and 'atmosphere' (lower direct contact level items).

The novel occurrence of an aesthetic referent facet element within an aesthetically good environment and the structure of the level facet, implying a combination of scale and levels of evaluation to be present, represent extensions of the general mapping sentence model. The facet structure discovered supports the multiattribute hypothesis regarding consumers' purposive evaluations within consumer service location.

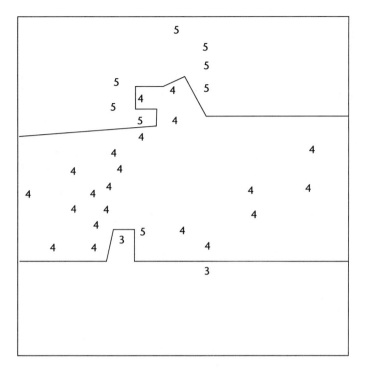

FIGURE 8.11 POSAC item diagram for internal–physical item

POSAC of the three elements of the facet model identified the common manner in which individuals in the sample structured their place evaluations. The social life area and service life area elements formed one pole of a criteria set for evaluations which formed an opposing pole to the spatial life area element and the central focus element. Thus, respondents may be classified as 'either' structuring their evaluations in terms of the centre's social, service and features which were peripheral to user purpose, or in terms of its spatial, aesthetic, physical qualities and those qualities central to respondents purpose at the convention centre. POSAC enables individual respondents' evaluations to be 'systematically' differentiated by two criteria. First, it is possible to state that some respondents will report being more or less satisfied with the conference centre overall. Secondly, some respondents will differentially report satisfaction with centre features represented by the one pole of the lateral axis (high scores on social, service) whilst others will be differentially satisfied with the centre's features characterized by the opposing pole of the lateral axis (high scores on spatial, aesthetic, physical, central).

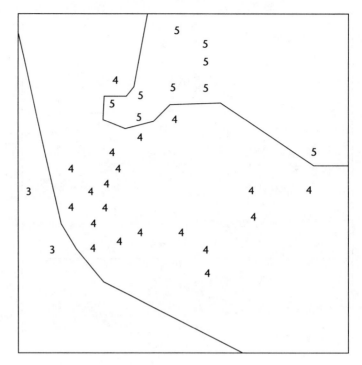

FIGURE 8.12 POSAC item diagram for external item

Generic place evaluation

Canter (1983a) in stating the need for a theory of place evaluation made several recommendations in terms of such a theory and what this should achieve. Among these he stated that a theory for place evaluation should facilitate hypotheses regarding intralocational consistencies in environmental evaluation, and provide a general template (allowing comparison between studies) for the design of evaluation instruments (instruments which are adaptable to location). Furthermore, he claimed: 'human experiences of places are consistent across people and places, it is the content of these processes and their emphasis that will vary in important and identifiable ways . . . from one place to another'; and that the purposive model of place evaluation based within the facet metatheory approach provides 'a structure to the evaluation of places that may be generalized across most settings'.

The present research has presented the results from an evaluation study of a conference centre which employed a purposive facet model in its design. The findings from this study provide further support for the model as a general template for the design of evaluation research. Moreover, the results further illustrate consistencies in the structure of evaluations between locations.

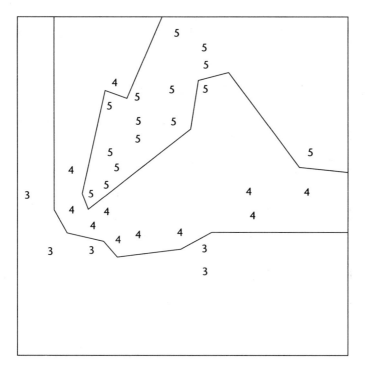

FIGURE 8.13 POSAC item diagram for peripheral item

Within this research a cylindrex model was found to best represent place evaluative structure. This geometric was first posited by Canter (1983a) and later supported by Donald (1985). Canter (1983a) reviewed research which considered the structure of evaluation within public housing (Canter and Rees, 1982) and hospital wards (Kenny and Canter, 1981) and found these to produce consistent results in line with the cylindrex hypothesis. He suggested that it would be remarkable if a similar structure was discovered in other locations. Donald (1983, 1985, 1987) and Hackett (1985) Hackett and Foxall (1992) reported the findings of research supportive of the cylindrex structure within airports and offices.

The present findings support a cylindrical structure as being appropriate for the conceptualization of place experience and for the design of place evaluation research within a conference centre location. This finding is not only of interest to those who would wish to assess the behaviour and satisfaction of consumers within this type of setting, but the cumulative nature of the research findings is of great import to all who wish to examine human behaviour within the situation of its occurrence.

The three content facets of centre evaluation may be combined to form a model. The life area and focus facets were found to interact in the same plane

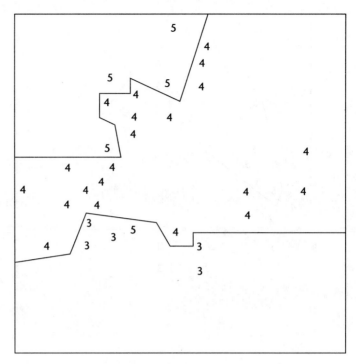

FIGURE 8.14 POSAC item diagram for internal–atmosphere item

of multidimensional space (i.e. they are related assessment criteria) whilst the level facet appeared in a separate plot (it is an independent criterion). A holistic model must thus preserve these facets and their interrelationships. In Figure 8.15 this is achieved in a cylindrex of convention centre evaluation.

The cylindrex presents the three level facets' elements of internal atmosphere, external, internal physical as tiers in the cylinder (the vertical dimension in Figure 8.15). At each of these levels may be found the qualitatively arranged (circular) wedges of the life area facet each of which is modified by the focus facet causing individual items to be positioned either centrally or peripherally within the circular arrangement.

The roles played by the facet elements in systematically structuring place evaluations is presented in the Hasse diagram in Figure 8.16. The Hasse diagram is formed through the superimposition of all item diagrams, with the resulting diagram being rotated 45 degrees anticlockwise. Thus, persons located at point J1 are those with the highest levels of overall satisfaction with the development. Those at point J2 are those with the lowest. At position L1 reported high levels of satisfaction with social life area, service life area and central focus aspects of the centre, but low levels of satisfaction with spatial life area, aesthetic life area, internal physical level and peripheral focus features. At

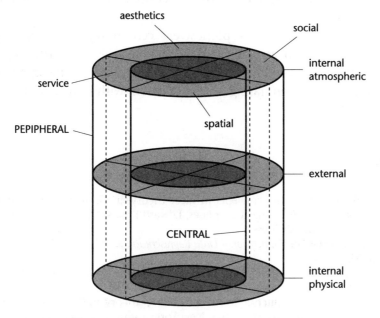

FIGURE 8.15 Cylindrex of place evaluation: a convention centre

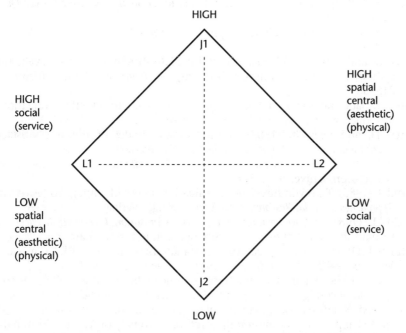

FIGURE 8.16 Hasse diagram of place evaluation: a convention centre

point L2 are located respondents with opposite high–low scores upon these facet elements.

To summarize, features purposively central to, and social, spatial, aesthetic, service life areas, along with interaction levels with different physical features of the convention centre have been found to be important in discriminating between ratings of satisfaction within this form of built environment:

References

Borg, I. (1977), Some basic concepts in facet theory, in *Geometric Representations of Relational Data*, Ed. James C. Lingoes, Edward E. Roskam and Ingwer Borg, Ann Arbor MI: Mathesis Press

Borg, I. (Ed.) (1981), *Multidimensional Data Representations: When and Why*, Ann Arbour MI: Mathesis Press

Borg, I. and Lingoes, J.C. (1987), *Multidimensional Similarity Structure Analysis*, New York: Springer Verlag

Brown, J. (1985), An introduction to the uses of facet theory, in *Facet Theory: Approaches to Social Research*, (Ed.) D. Canter, New York: Springer Verlag

Canter, D. (1977), *The Psychology of Place*, London: Architectural Press

Canter, D. (1983a), The purposive evaluation of place: a facet approach,' *Environment and Behavior*, November 1983, 659–99

Canter, D. (1983b), The potential of facet theory for applied social psychology, *Quantity and Quality*, **17**, 35–67

Canter, D. (1985), (Ed.) *Facet Theory: Approaches to Social Research*, New York: Springer Verlag

Canter, D. and Kenny, C. (1981), The multivariate structure of design evaluation: a cylindrex of nurses' conceptualisations,' *Multivariate Behaviour Research*, **16**, 215–35

Canter, D. and Kenny, C. (1982), Approaches to environmental evaluation: an introduction,' *International Review of Applied Psychology*, **31**, 145–151

Canter, D. and Rees, K. (1982), A multivariate model of housing satisfaction, *International Review of Applied Psychology*, **31**, 185–208

Donald, I. (1983), '*The multivariate structure of office evaluation*', Unpublished Master's Dissertation, University of Surrey

Donald, I. (1985), The cylindrex of place evaluation, in David Canter, (Ed.) *Facet Theory: Approaches to Social Research*, New York: Springer Verlag

Donald, I. (1987), '*Office evaluation and its organisational context: a facet study*', Unpublished Ph.D. thesis, University of Aston in Birmingham

Guttman, L. (1954), A new approach to factor analysis: the radex, in P.F. Lazarsfeld, (Ed.) *Mathematical Thinking in the Social Sciences*, New York: Free Press

Guttman, L. (1968), A general nonmetric technique for finding the smallest co-ordinate space for a configuration of points, *Psychometrika*, **33**, 469–506

Hackett, P.M.W. (1985), 'Birmingham International Airport user evaluation study: a faceted appraisal', *Unpublished Dissertation*, University of Aston in Birmingham

Hackett, P.M.W. (1989), 'Environmental and nature conservation: a facet study of concern for the quality of the natural environment', Unpublished Ph.D. Thesis, University of Aston in Birmingham

Hackett, P.M.W. (in press), *Conservation and the Consumer: Understanding Environmental Concern*, London: Routledge

Hackett, P.M.W. and Foxall, G.R. (1992), 'How consumers structure evaluations of satisfaction within complex service and retail locations: a mapping sentence design study of a modern international airport development', University of Birmingham, Working Papers in Consumer Research

Hackett, P.M.W., Foxall. G.R. and Van Raiij, W.F. (1993), Consumers in retail environments, in *Behavior and Environment: Psychological and Geographical Approaches*, R.G. Garling and T. Golledge (Eds.), Amsterdam: Elsevier

Kenny, C. (1983), '*A multivariate model of hospital ward evaluation*', Unpublished Ph.D. Thesis, University of Surrey

Kenny, C. and Canter, D. (1981), A facet structure for nurses' evaluation of ward design, *Journal of Occupational Psychology*, **54**, 93–105

Levy, S. (1985), Lawful roles of facets in social theories, in D. Canter (Ed.) *Facet Theory: Approaches to Social Research*. New York: Springer Verlag

Levy, S. (1986), *The Structure of Social Values*, Tel Aviv: The Israel Institute of Applied Social Research

Lingoes, J.C. (1973), *The Guttman–Lingoes Non-Parametric Program Series*, Ann Arbor MI: Mathesis Press

Monroe, K.B. and Guiltinan, J.P. (1975), A path-analytic exploration of retail patronage influences, *Journal of Consumer Research*, June, 19–28

Morrison, P., Burnard, P. and Hackett, P.M.W. (1991), A smallest space analysis of nurses' perceptions of their interpersonal skills, *Counselling Psychology Quarterly*, **4**, 1/3, 119–25

Runkel, P.J. and McGrath, J.E. (1972), *Research on Human Behavior: a Systematic Guide to Method*, New York: Holt, Rinehart and Winston

Schlesinger, I.M. and Guttman, L. (1969), Smallest space analysis of intelligence and achievement tests, *Psychological Bulletin*, **71**, 95–100

Shye, S. (Ed.) (1978), *Theory Construction and Data Analysis in the Behavioral Sciences*, London: Jossey Bass

Shye, S. (1986), *Multiple Scaling: the Theory and Application of Partial Order Scalogram Analysis*, Amsterdam: North Holland

Shye, S. and Reuven Amar (1985), Partial-order scalogram analysis by base co-ordinates and lattice mapping of the items by their scalogram roles, in D. Canter, (Ed.) *Facet Theory: Approaches to Social Research*, New York: Springer Verlag

Tauber, E.M. (1972), Why do people shop? *Journal of Marketing*, **36**, 46–59

Appendix 8.1

1. A cylindrex is a triple-role (or triple facet) structure. It is formed through the combination of a series of radexes (see (4), below) stacked one above the other. Thus, a polarizing facet (see (2), below) causes items to be qualitatively arranged as wedges within a circle. A modular facet (see (3) below) interacts with the polarizing facet to cause items to be nearer or further from the centre of the circle. Finally, an axial facet (see (5) below) may be seen to structure items into planar slices. However, the radex structure implicit within the modular and polar facets may be seen to operate at each level (or within each planar slice)

of the axial facet. The geometric array formed by the combination of the three facets is a cylinder and the facet configuration a cylindrex (Levy, 1986).

2. Borg and Lingoes (1987) define a polarizing facet as a facet which 'defines different directions in space' and which is represented as 'wedge-like regions emanating from a common origin' (Levy, 1985).

3. A modular facet (one playing a modulating role) causes the organization of 'points into regions with different distances from the centre' (Borg and Lingoes, 1987). This is displayed in the form of points being arranged as circular bands around a common origin.

4. A radex structure is formed by the combination of a polarizing and modulating facet in two-dimension space (Guttman, 1954).

5. A simplex is the simplest structure that an array of variables may take. In a simplex objects may be arranged in terms of their similarity to each other and the resulting configuration approximates a line along which each item is more similar to its neighbour than items further down the array (Runkel and McGrath, 1972; Brown, 1985). An axial facet is a simply ordered facet (see simplex, above) whose notion of order is not related to the notions present in other ordered or unordered facets in an analysis (Levy, 1985).

Appendix 8.2

The qualitative and quantitative ways in which facets affect place evaluation may be analysed through partial order structure analysis. POSA is a broad term of analysis procedures which analyse scores representative of respondents facet profiles. Individuals may be identified as differing in two basic ways in terms of their place evaluations. The first of these differences is purely quantitative (an individual's total score on all evaluation questions). A second way in which individual responses may differ is qualitative. At each quantitative level of evaluation qualitative differences may exist between respondents, however these totals may differ in terms of the individual scores comprising them. POSAC provides two types of information: (1) total scores for individuals' responses; (2) differentiation is made between responses which are similar in their totals but which differ in the items which compose them, allowing observation of differences in the composite scores and the identification of the qualitative dimensions of differentiation. Nine element item scores were calculated representing each facet element(see Table 8.2 for items comprising each element) and analysed using POSAC.

The location of individual respondents in a space diagram is thus derived from each complete data profile, qualitative and the quantitative variations in the data are both taken into account in locating an individual response profile. The distance apart of two profiles in a space diagram being dependent upon the summation of the profile and an attempt to locate all similar scores for each profile item in adjacent two-dimensional space.

POSAC provides a space diagram for each item (element scale) within an investigation (known as item diagrams) with respondents who have similar profiles being represented by a single value in the two-dimensional Euclidean space item diagram. In the study described in Chapter 8 there are nine element scales and thus nine item diagrams.

To interpret item diagrams, lines (which should be as straight as possible) are drawn to partition regions and attempting to ensure that each region contains a single score for an item. The direction of lines reveals how the items structure the POSA with different shapes produced in partitioning regions showing the role the item plays in structuring responses. The partitioning lines reveal the role of elements in determining the qualitative (lateral) dimensions of evaluations; the joint (quantitative) axis is simply the sum of a profile score.

The more that lines partitioning regions deviate from being straight, or the more element items that are excluded from a region by the fitting of straight lines, the less 'important' the element item is in structuring evaluations. Minor roles may however be identified. These form polarizing roles and moderating roles which produce L and inverted L shape partitioning. The association between these minor roles and the orientation of the L shaped partitioning is dependent upon the direction of the response range (e.g. which category of the range is representative of a 'psychologically greater' response (Shye and Amar, 1985)).

In the present study, a score of '1' is indicative of a low level of satisfaction with the development and thus L and inverted L shaped partitioning are associated with items playing moderating and polarizing roles respectively. With polarizing elements, high values on this are associated with extreme values upon the lateral axis, whilst moderators, tends to have high scores upon its axis associated with mid value scores upon the lateral axis.

■ □ ■ ■ 9

An Introduction to Hierarchical Moderated Regression Analysis

Gordon E. Greenley

There are many situations in marketing research where there is a requirement to investigate whether the relationship between two variables differs with respect to the value of a third variable. In these situations the effect of the third variable is said to moderate the relationship between the other two variables. The statistical technique for investigating such effects is hierarchical moderated regression analysis. Unfortunately, books on multivariate data analysis give little, if any, attention to this technique, while there is confusion in the statistics literature about its application. This chapter explains the nature of moderator effects, the use of hierarchical moderated regression analysis, and the procedure for investigating monotonicity in identified moderator effects. Attention is also given to a range of issues that are pertinent to the application of hierarchical moderated regression analysis.

Introduction

Readers of this book will no doubt be familiar with the standard treatment given to regression analysis in books on multivariate data analysis, for example by Hair *et al.* (1995) and Sharma (1996). Here the aim is to investigate whether a number of independent variables exert main effects on a dependent variable. When main effects from independent variables are expected they are often labelled predictor variables, while the dependent variable is labelled the criterion variable. However, it is often the case that the relationship between a predictor variable, x, and a criterion variable, y, is influenced by a third variable, z, which is said to specify the relationship between x and y. Jaccard *et al.* (1990) have identified three general situations in which this happens, as illustrated in Figure 9.1. An **indirect relationship** is where one variable, x, exerts an

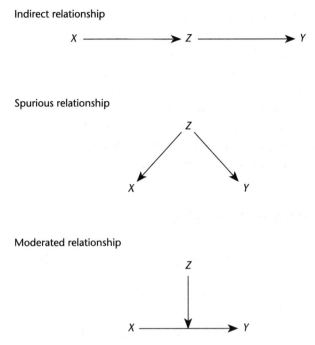

FIGURE 9.1 Three types of general relationship

influence on another variable, *y*, but only through its impact on a third variable, *z*. A **spurious relationship** is where variables *x* and *y* are related, but only because each has a common relationship with another variable, *z*. A **moderated relationship** is where the relationship between *x* and *y* differs with respect to the value of *z*.

The focus of this chapter is on moderator effects, as much marketing theory includes relationships that differ, or potentially differ, with respect to change in another variable, for example, the influence of marketing tactics on performance being moderated by corporate mission (Covin *et al.*, 1994), and the influence of market orientation on performance being moderated by the market environment (Slater and Narver, 1994; Greenley, 1995). Given the complexity of theories throughout marketing, it is likely that most relationships between variables will exhibit some moderator effects from other variables. However, as Jaccard *et al.* (1990) point out, there is a great deal of confusion about how to carry out analysis for identifying moderator effects. Indeed, books on multivariate data analysis that are commonly used by marketing researchers, such as Hair *et al.* (1995) and Sharma (1996), give little attention to the multivariate technique for investigating moderator effects, which is hierarchical moderated regression analysis (HMRA).

The aim of this chapter is to introduce HMRA and to explain its use. However, this explanation comes with an important health warning. Not only is there confusion in the statistics literature about the identification of moderator effects, there is also controversy surrounding a number of issues pertaining to the application of HMRA. These issues are dealt with in two sections. First, **major application issues**, which are particularly relevant to HMRA, the treatment of which is quite controversial in the statistics literature. Second, **general application issues**, which, although general with respect to regression analysis, are also important when using HMRA.

Investigating moderator effects

Although hierarchical moderated regression analysis (HMRA) has been little used in marketing literature, several books on multiple regression give considerable attention to the technique, for example Aiken and West (1991), Blalock (1971), Cohen and Cohen (1975 and 1983), Jaccard *et al.* (1990), Kerlinger and Pedhazur (1973), and Pedhazur (1982). In the marketing literature the principles of HMRA have been explained by Sharma *et al.* (1981), who also recommend a technique for investigating the presence of moderator effects. Sharma *et al.* (1981) present a typology of variables that specify or influence the relationship between a predictor variable and a criterion variable, which includes moderator variables, as shown in Figure 9.2. This is based on whether or not a specification variable is related to the criterion variable, on the horizontal axis in Figure 9.2, and whether the specification variable interacts with the predictor variable, given on the vertical axis in Figure 9.2.

Variables falling into cell 1 are related to the predictor or criterion variables, but do not interact significantly with the predictor variable. As there is no interaction these variables are not moderators, but are classified as intervening, exogenous, antecedent, suppressor or predictor variables. Therefore, this cell is not relevant to HMRA.

Variables located in cell 2 (homologizer) are not related to the predictor or criterion variables, and do not feature a significant interaction with a predictor variable. As there is no interaction they are not strictly moderators but are homologizers, although Sharma *et al.* (1981) label them as a type of moderator. Homologizers influence the strength of the relationship between a predictor and criterion variable across homogeneous groups of cases defined by the homologizer. Here the error term of the relationship between the predictor and criterion variable is a function of the homologizer variable.

Variables in cell 3 (quasi moderator) significantly interact with a predictor variable, but are also related to either the predictor or criterion variables.

	Related to criterion and/or predictor variables	Not related to criterion or predictor variables
No significant interaction with predictor variable	**Cell 1** Intervening, exogenous, antecedent, suppressor or predictor variable	**Cell 2** *Moderator:* Homologizer
Significant interaction with predictor variable	**Cell 3** *Moderator:* Quasi moderator	**Cell 4** *Moderator:* Pure moderator

Adapted from Sharma *et al.* (1981).

FIGURE 9.2 Typology of moderator variables

Although such a variable moderates the form of the relationship between a predictor and criterion variable through its interaction with the predictor, it also affects the relationship through a main effect. As it creates two effects the moderator effect is not pure, hence the label quasi moderator. Consider the following equation:

$$y = a + b_1 x + b_2 z + b_3 xz$$

where x is the predictor, z is a potential moderator, and xz is the interaction between the predictor and the potential moderator. If b_3 is significant then z moderates the relationship between y and x. If b_2 is also significant then z is also directly related to y, and therefore z is a quasi moderator.

A variable in cell 4 (pure moderator) moderates the form of the relationship between a predictor and criterion variable, through its interaction with the predictor. However, as it is not related to either the predictor or criterion variables it does not feature a main effect, and therefore it is a pure moderator as this is the only effect that it generates. Consider the following equation:

$$Y = a + b_1 x + b_2 z + b_3 xz$$

where x is the predictor, z is a potential moderator, and xz is the interaction between the predictor and the potential moderator. If b_3 is significant then z moderates the relationship between y and x. Also, if b_2 is not significant then the influence of z is restricted to a moderator effect, and therefore z is a pure moderator. In this equation the interaction between x and z is specified as a multiplicative function. Smith and Sasaki (1979) and Southwood (1978) explain that there are many other forms that the interaction between a predictor variable and a potential moderator can take. However, throughout this chapter the multiplicative interaction term is used, as it is the most common form that has been used in the business administration literature.

Investigation technique

The HMRA procedure has been documented by several writers, such as Arnold (1982), Cohen and Cohen (1983), Evans (1991), Jaccard *et al.* (1990), and Sharma *et al.* (1981). The aim of the analysis is to investigate the presence of pure or quasi moderator effects (cells 3 and 4 of Figure 9.2), on the form of the relationship between a predictor and a criterion variable. The analysis specifies three levels of regression analysis, giving three different equations, as follows:

(1) $$Y = a + b_1 x$$

(2) $$Y = a + b_1 x + b_2 z$$

(3) $$Y = a + b_1 x + b_2 z + b_3 xz$$

where x is the predictor variable, z is the potential moderator, and xz is the multiplicative interaction term. In equation (1) the hypothesized predictor variables are entered simultaneously, in order to investigate main effects on the criterion variable. In equation (2) the hypothesized moderator variables are simultaneously or stepwise entered, in order to investigate whether or not these variables feature main effects. (In the statistics literature there is controversy about the use of stepwise versus simultaneous variable entry. Some of the issues are discussed below, but readers are urged to refer to a relevant text.) In equation (3) the interaction terms are entered, in order to investigate hypothesized moderator effects. At each stage of the analysis the significance of the regression coefficients are examined, along with the change in R^2 from equations (1) to (2), and from (2) to (3).

A **pure moderator effect** (cell 4, Figure 9.2) is identified when equations (1) and (2) are not different, but are different to equation (3); where b_2 is not significant, but where b_3 is significant, so that ΔR^2 is accounted for by the interaction term. This fulfils the conditions for a pure moderator, which interacts with a predictor to produce a moderator effect on the predictor's relationship with the criterion variable, but does not feature a main effect, and therefore is not also a predictor.

A **quasi moderator effect** (cell 3, Figure 9.2) is identified when equations (1), (2) and (3) are different; where b_2 is significant, indicating a main effect from z, and where b_3 is significant, indicating a moderator effect on the predictor's relationship with the criterion variable. The magnitude of the main effect is given by ΔR^2 from equation (1) to equation (2), while the magnitude of the moderator effect is given by ΔR^2 from equation (2) to equation (3).

If equations (2) and (3) are not different then z is not a moderator. For this result b_3 must be insignificant, indicating that the interaction term does not generate a moderator effect, coinciding with no change in R^2. If b_2 is significant in equation (2) then there is a main effect, and z is a predictor variable. If b_2 is not significant z could be a homologizer, although this effect cannot be detected using HMRA, but by the procedure outlined in the final step of Figure 9.3.

Sharma et al. (1981) summarize the above in the procedure illustrated in Figure 9.3.

Step 1: Using the three HMRA equations, determine whether or not there is a significant interaction between a hypothesized moderator variable and a predictor variable.
If a significant interaction is identified go to Step 2.
If there is no significant interaction then go to Step 3.

Step 2. Identify whether or not the moderator is related to the criterion variable.
If it is not related then a pure moderator has been identified (cell 4 in Figure 9.2).
If the moderator is related to the criterion variable then a quasi moderator has been identified (cell 3 in Figure 9.2)

Step 3: Identify whether or not the hypothesized moderator is related to the predictor or criterion variable.
If it is then it is not a moderator but an intervening, exogenous, antecedent, suppressor, or predictor variable.
If it is not related to either the predictor or criterion variable then go to step 4.

Step 4: Split the sample into subgroups based on the hypothesized moderator, using a median, quartile or other justifiable split. Complete a test of significance for differences in predictive validity across the subgroups.
If significant differences are found the hypothesized moderator is a homologizer variable, operating through the error term (cell 2 in Figure 9.2).
If there are no significant differences the variable is not a moderator, and the analysis is terminated.

Adapted from Sharma *et al.* (1981).

FIGURE 9.3 Framework for identifying moderator variables

Nature of the moderator effect

Having identified the presence of a moderator effect, further analysis can reveal information about its nature. In particular further analysis can investigate monotonicity in the form of the relationship between the predictor and criterion variable, over the range of the moderator (Jaccard *et al.*, 1990; Schoonhoven, 1981; Southwood, 1978). This analysis has been developed by Schoonhoven (1981), who demonstrates that the sign of the regression coefficient is insufficient to identify whether or not the moderator effect is monotonic; that is, in the same direction throughout the range of the moderator variable, or nonmonotonic; that is, positive over part of the range of the moderator and negative over the other part of its range. The analysis requires the calculation of a partial derivative of equation (3), using simple differential calculus, as follows:

(4) $$\frac{dy}{dx} = b_1 + b_3 z$$

where b_1 and b_3 are unstandardized regression coefficients. This equation indicates that the effect of x on y is a function of z and the values of b_1 and b_3.

There are six possible outcomes of examining the rate of change of the criterion variable with respect to the rate of change of the predictor variable, over the range of the moderator, which are illustrated in Figure 9.4. In graph 1 the nature of the relationship is such that change in the criterion variable with respect to change in the predictor is negative throughout the range of the moderator, and is therefore monotonic. In graph 2 there is a nonmonotonic pattern, as dy/dx is positive over the lower range of the moderator, and negative over the higher moderator range. Graph 3 also illustrates a nonmonotonic relationship, as dy/dx is negative over the lower range of the moderator, and positive over the higher range of the moderator. For the patterns in graphs 2 and 3, there is a point on the axis of the moderator variable where the relationship changes direction. This is the point of inflection, where the dy/dx relationship changes direction. Graphs 4, 5 and 6 all show monotonic relationships, as dy/dx is either totally positive or totally negative over the full range of the moderator. The identification of monotonicity is through equation (4), the partial derivative equation, which is set to zero, as follows:

(5) $$\frac{dy}{dx} = b_1 + b_3 z = 0$$

The values of the unstandardized regression coefficients are substituted into equation (5) and the value of z is calculated. Examples of such calculations are

Graph 1: Monotonic pattern

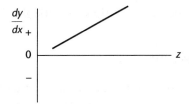

Graph 4: Monotonic pattern

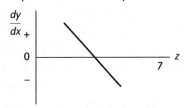

Graph 2: Nonmonotonic pattern

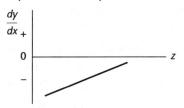

Graph 5: Monotonic pattern

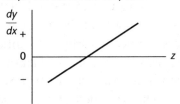

Graph 3: Nonmonotonic pattern

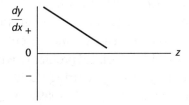

Graph 6: Monotonic pattern

FIGURE 9.4 Investigating monotonicity

given in the article, *External moderation of associations among stakeholder orientations and company performance,* (Greenley and Foxall, 1998), which is reproduced in Chapter 19 of this book. If, for example, the moderator was measured on a 7 point scale, then a value for z from equation (5) of, say, 3.1, will give an inflection point. Values above and below 3.1 are then substituted into equation (5), and the signs of the answers will indicate the direction of the dy/dx relationship above and below the inflection point of 3.1.

Major application issues

As mentioned in the Introduction, there are several major issues of application that need to be considered when using HMRA. In the literature a number of major issues are addressed. These are: multicollinearity, form and degree of relationships, order of variable entry, and the basis for the search for moderators. Of these, multicollinearity has received the most attention.

Multicollinearity

Because an interaction term entered into equation (3) is formed as the sum of two independent variables that are also in the equation, it is likely that the interaction term will be highly correlated with these independent variables. Therefore, it is argued that the introduction of multicollinearity, through an interaction term, creates problems in the interpretation of equations (Althauser, 1971; Aiken and West, 1991; Blalock, 1979; Jaccard *et al.*, 1990). The recommended method for avoiding multicollinearity is transformation of the variables, with most authors recommending mean centring (for example, Allison, 1977; Cronbach, 1987; Smith, and Sasaki, 1979; Yi, 1989). (Marquardt (1980) and Marquardt and Snee (1975) recommend transformation to standardized scores with a mean of zero and a standard deviation of one, while Tate (1984) explains other types of transformations.) In this approach x and z are transformed to deviations from their means, and these deviation scores are entered into the regression equation, rather than the raw scores. It has been shown that mean centring reduces multicollinearity substantially, and avoids associated problems, while the predictive power of the equation, R^2, is not affected by centring (Cohen and Cohen, 1983; Marquardt, 1980; Smith and Sasaki, 1979; Yi, 1989). A general procedure for performing variable transformation is given by Marquardt (1980).

Discussions in the literature about whether or not multicollinearity in HMRA is of any consequence, and whether or not mean centring should be adopted, are controversial. Evans (1991) says that multicollinearity is of no consequence, as the aim is to identify whether the interaction adds unique variance, and not to estimate the parameters for each component of the equation. Friedrich (1982) discusses the changes that occur to coefficients b_1 and b_2 when an interaction term is added to equation (2) to form equation (3). In an additive equation (one without interaction terms), as in equation (2), b_1 and b_2 estimate the general trends of change in y with changes in x and z across all levels of z and x respectively. In an interactive equation, as in equation (3), b_1 and b_2 estimate the particular trends of change in y with changes in x and z, when z and x, respectively, equal zero. Therefore, Friedrich (1982) argues that changes in b_1 and b_2 that often result when an interaction term is added to a regression equation occur not because multicollinearity has made the results unstable, but because b_1 and b_2 estimate particular conditional relationships rather than general relationships. Both Tate (1984) and Katrichis (1993) argue that transformation changes the conceptual meaning of the variables.

Typically in marketing research a five or seven point scale will be used to collect data, and subtracting the mean of a variable from each case is likely to result in forcing some negative values, where such variables could not naturally take on negative values. As Katrichis (1993) says: 'This brings the simple rules of multiplying positive and negative numbers together in the formation of interaction terms and obscures the effects that either the main or interaction terms have on the dependent variable. In effect we have changed the conceptual meaning of the interaction term from what it was intended to represent.' Tate (1984) also argues that, as centring is likely to change the correlations between variables, such changes also change the conceptual meaning of the variables, as (1) the meaning of a variable is partly dependent on its relationship with other variables, (2) the convergent validity of a variable is determined by comparing correlations of the measures of that variable with other conceptually different variables.

The above arguments clearly beg the question, is there a need to transform variables to address multicollinearity when investigating moderator effects? Many scholars have demonstrated that mean centring does not change the unstandardized regression coefficient and the t-statistic of the interaction term, while the coefficient of determination, R^2, does not change (Aiken and West, 1991; Allison, 1977; Cohen and Cohen, 1983; Schoonhoven, 1981; Yi, 1989). Also, HMRA is designed to investigate main and moderator effects separately. As interaction terms are not included in equation (2), no multicollinearity will be introduced, so that main effects from predictors and potential moderators can be determined (assuming that the general rules for assessing multicollinearity among independent variables are followed). As explained in the previous section, moderator effects are then investigated in equation (3), by inspecting the unstandardized regression coefficients, the t-statistics and ΔR^2, while main effects are not investigated. Therefore, a hierarchical approach should be taken when investigating moderator effects (Allison, 1977; Cohen and Cohen, 1983; Sharma *et al.*, 1981; Smith and Sasaki, 1979; Tate, 1984; Yi, 1989), with or without variable transformation. Given the above arguments, the final decision on transformation is the responsibility of the researcher.

Form and degree of relationships

The second major issue concerns the appropriateness of using HMRA for investigating a relationship. Arnold (1982) explains that there are two aspects of a relationship between a dependent variable, y, and an independent variable, x. First, the degree of the relationship between the two variables, which is indicated by the correlation coefficient, with the square of the coefficient giving the percentage of variance in y accounted for by x. Second, the form of the relationship, which is indicated by the regression coefficient, which represents the amount of score difference in y associated with a unit score change in x. With respect to a third variable z, the degree, or form, or both, may vary across different values of z, or they may remain constant.

Degree of relationship

Arnold (1982) explains change in the degree of the relationship with respect to change in z with an illustration, in which a sample is simply split into two groups, E and F, based on variable z. In order to determine whether the degree of the relationship of y with x differs with respect to z, it is necessary to determine whether or not the correlation of y and x in group E is significantly different to that in group F. If it is then the degree of the relationship varies with z, and differential validity is said to obtain.

Form of relationship

In order to determine whether the form of the relationship of y with x differs with respect to z, it is necessary to compare regression coefficients, to determine whether or not the rate of change of y associated with a given change in x is a constant function of x, or whether it varies with change in the value of z. (Using calculus terminology, the first partial derivative of y with respect to x is not constant, but is a function of z. Hence, the use of calculus in equation (4) in the HMRA technique.) Arnold (1982) recommends using HMRA to investigate these changes. If the form of the relationship varies with z, then x and z are said to interact in determining y, and the form is conditioned by z.

Stone and Hollenbeck (1984) disagree with the propositions of Arnold (1982). They assert that the above is only valid if one accepts the unduly restrictive assumption that the degree of a relationship must be indexed by the product–moment correlation. They state that the slope of the regression line also reflects the degree of a relationship between two variables, citing writers such as Cohen and Cohen (1975), Ghiselli *et al.* (1981), and Neter and Wasserman (1974) as their authority. They also say that the degree of the relationship, as measured by the slope of the regression line, may be conditioned by a moderator variable. Therefore, Stone and Hollenbeck (1984) claim that HMRA generates information about the degree as well as the form of the relationship. They also argue that forming subgroups of a sample, based on a moderator variable, in order to compare correlations to investigate the degree of association is arbitrary and problematic, because (1) there is degradation of information following categorization of a variable; (2) statistical power is lost when comparing only subsets of cases from a larger sample; (3) information about subgroups of cases whose data is not considered in the analysis is wasted.

However, Arnold (1984) challenges the propositions of Stone and Hollenbeck (1984). He claims that correlation and regression coefficients carry different information regarding the relationship between two variables, citing Cohen and Cohen (1975) as the authority. He says that comparisons of correlation coefficients, among subgroups give information about how the amount of variance in a dependent variable, explained by an independent variable, varies with the value of a moderator variable. He says that HMRA does not give this information, as it tells us nothing whatsoever regarding whether correlations coefficients differ significantly for different values of the moderator. Arnold (1984) goes on to say that HMRA gives different information, by addressing the hypothesis that a dependent variable is jointly determined by the interaction of an independent variable and a moderator variable.

The above arguments clearly indicate that researchers should give careful consideration in setting appropriate research questions and hypotheses, and in selecting the appropriate analytical techniques for testing these hypotheses.

Order of variable entry

Another major issue is the order in which the predictor variables, potential moderator variables, and interaction terms are entered into equation (3). The alternatives are to enter the independent variables first, followed by the interaction terms, or to enter the interaction terms first, followed by the independent variables. Blood and Mullet (1977) have argued that entering interaction terms last is an overly conservative technique that is generally incapable of detecting the true effects of moderator variables, even in data bases generated from theory that predicts strong moderator effects. The justification that they give for this approach is twofold:

- if the independent variables are entered first, virtually all the variance will be accounted for by the main effects of these variables, leaving little capacity for the interaction term to explain some of the variance (the main effects 'steal' variance from the interaction term);
- as there is a small proportion of variance left to be explained by the interaction term, a Type II statistical error prevents true moderator effects from being detected.

Therefore, Blood and Mullet (1977) recommend that interaction terms should be entered first, followed by the predictors and potential moderators.

Stone and Hollenbeck (1984) argue against this recommendation. They assert that, in order to determine the presence of a moderator effect through an interaction term, it is necessary to partial out all of the variance associated with the main effects of the variables that are used to form the interaction term, quoting Cohen (1978) and Pedhazur (1982) as their authority. They go on to say: 'Only when the main effects of terms that are part of an interaction are partialed from the cross-product term is it possible to assess whether or not there is a true interaction.' Stone and Hollenbeck (1984) used a Monte Carlo simulation to test their arguments, the results of which supported the argument that entering the interaction term last, in order to partial out main effects, provides more reliable identification of moderator effects. Indeed, they argue that following the Blood and Mullet (1977) recommendation of entering the interaction term first exacerbates the problem of not identifying true moderator effects, rather than solving the problem.

Therefore, in constructing equation (3) in HMRA it is important that researchers understand the ramifications of different orders of variable entry.

Basis for the search for moderators

All the above discussions are based on the assumption that there is a requirement to search for moderator effects within a particular research project. However, writers have warned against the gratuitous search for moderator effects among a set of variables (Arnold, 1982 and 1984; Cohen and Cohen, 1983; Jaccard et al., 1990; Zedeck, 1971). Like all other statistical techniques, HMRA is a tool to aid the interpretation of data, when testing specific hypotheses or propositions, and when addressing particular research questions and objectives. The technique is only appropriate if there has been a systematic synthesis of the literature relevant to the research domain, which itself has been based on an exhaustive literature search. The synthesis needs to be carefully completed to ensure that formulated theory is consistent with previous and current theory, and that this formulated theory can be logically defended. The setting of specific hypotheses also needs to be consistent with empirical results of testing similar hypotheses, and formulated with the expectation that the results of their testing will contribute to advancing knowledge. In marketing a problem is, of course, that often the theoretical domain extends into other literatures, such as strategic management and psychology.

A random search for significant moderator effects, without a sound theoretical basis, is no more justifiable than a random search for significantly different means or proportions, or for significant correlation coefficients. A random search for moderator effects, especially in a large data base composed of several variables, is likely to produce some random significant regression coefficients, based on the general rule that the larger the number of variables the greater the chance of finding significant coefficients. The problem will be, of course, that such random effects are unlikely to have any theoretical basis and justification, and will, therefore, be unlikely to be enlightening, and indeed may lead to inappropriate and misleading conclusions. The same arguments apply when the research is led by a desire on the part of researchers to utilize a particular technique of statistical analysis, such as HMRA. Indeed, Hooley and Hussey in Chapter 1 warn against such an approach, citing Young (1973), who says: 'The danger we must avoid is becoming pedlars of techniques in search of problems, rather than problem solvers in search of techniques.' A technique led approach is also likely to generate random effects, as the researchers strive to find significant regression coefficients to fit their technique, which again violates the principles of theory driven research.

Once the theory has been developed, the hypotheses have been set, and the need for an investigation of moderator effects has been established, the use of HMRA can proceed. However, Hair *et al.* (1995) recommend a structured approach for the use of any multivariate technique, incorporating the following stages:

Stage 1:   Define the research objectives and hypotheses.
Stage 2:   Develop an analysis plan of issues such as sample size, range and type of variables, and the operationalization of variables.
Stage 3:   Evaluate the assumptions that underlie the application of the technique.
Stage 4:   Complete the analysis and determine whether the results achieve acceptable levels of appropriate statistical criteria, such as level of statistical significance.
Stage 5:   Interpret the results in relation to the hypothesized relationships.
Stage 6:   Validate the results, to test their applicability to wider populations, or to further theoretical propositions.

Therefore, HMRA should only be used after an exhaustive review of the literature, development of theory, and the establishment of hypotheses in which potential moderator effects can be justified on logical and theoretical grounds. Researchers are also advised to follow a structured approach in using HMRA, of the type advocated by Hair *et al.* (1995).

General application issues

As mentioned in the Introduction, there are several general issues of application, which although general to regression analysis, are also pertinent to HMRA. These are violation of assumptions in regression analysis, measurement accuracy, and response artifacts effects.

Violation of assumptions

The treatment given to the assumptions underlying multiple regression analysis is fairly standard throughout the statistics literature, which refers to the individual variables and to the relationship as a whole. Sources such as Hair *et al.* (1995) recommend assessment of violation of the assumptions after the regression model has been estimated, which examines the collective effect of the independent variables on the dependent variable. This assessment is based on error resulting from the prediction of the combined effects of the independent variables on the dependent variable in the sample, and is determined by measurement of the residuals of the equation. The standard treatment in the statistics literature gives considerable attention to this assessment, which is not included in the scope of this chapter. The recommendation of Hair *et al.* (1995) is that there are four major assumptions in regression analysis, the possible violation of which needs to be examined:

- the linearity of the variables measured;
- the constant variance of the error terms;
- the dependence of the error terms;
- the normality of the error distribution.

To assess violation of each of the above the residuals are plotted against the appropriate criterion, and the plots are interpreted as detailed in the statistics literature. The outcome of this analysis gives an appraisal of the appropriateness of the equation, and researchers are urged to complete this analysis. However, in most surveys there will be some violation, although perhaps minor, but such violations are a matter of degree, and must be interpreted by the researcher. Indeed, Hair *et al.* (1995) say that we assume that random error will occur, but we also assume that this error is an estimate of true random error in the population and not just in the prediction from our sample. However, this practical reality does not discharge the responsibility of researchers for addressing violation of these assumptions.

Measurement accuracy

Here the concern is with the measurement of the independent and dependent variables in the sample survey, rather than with the behaviour of these variables in the regression analysis. Measurement accuracy is the extent to which the measured variables are free from error (Churchill, 1979; Tull and Hawkins, 1984). Validity is the extent to which a measured variable accurately reflects the construct that it is meant to represent, being the extent to which a measurement is free from systematic error. Although there are several ways of addressing validity, convergent and discriminant validity are of central importance. Reliability is the extent to which the measurement can be repeated, such as in different places, by different people, and at different times, while still yielding similar results. It is the extent to which a measurement is free from variable or random error. Detailed attention is given to validity and reliability in the statistics literature, and is therefore not included in the scope of this chapter. Researchers should be able to demonstrate both validity and reliability in the measurement of their variables before tackling HMRA.

Artifact effects

In this section the issue is concerned with the method that was used to gather the data for measuring the independent and dependent variables. In marketing the method typically is, of course, the sample survey, probably using a self-report questionnaire, that is completed by either the respondents, or by a researcher who records the oral self-reports of the respondents. With this type of method the general problems are that it is likely to be difficult to control bias from the data gathering method (Salancik and Pfeffer, 1977; Podsakoff and Organ, 1986), and to verify the responses of respondents (Podsakoff and Organ, 1986).

There are several ways in which the data gathering method can bias answers and hence the data collected, the outcome of which is referred to as artifact bias in the data (Salancik and Pfeffer, 1977). Consistency effects may occur as people tend to answer a series of questions in a way that they regard as being a consistent pattern of response. Answers to earlier questions may influence answers to later questions, so that the later answers do not accurately measure the true views of the respondents. Priming effects are where the wording or form of the questions, or the way in which they are asked, leads the respondents toward answers that do not reflect the true answers. Similarly, the orientation of respondents to particular information associated with the questions may also lead to inaccurate answers, resulting in a priming effect. Overestimation or justification effects are where respondents overstate the magnitude or importance of certain answers, or where they have personal theories about what the answers ought to be, which they report rather than the true answers. Artifact effects result in difficulty in verifying the responses given by respondents, especially when both the independent and dependent variables are measured with the same questionnaire, through the same people (Podsakoff and Organ, 1986). This can lead to the problem of common method variance (Campbell and Fiske, 1959; Fiske, 1982; Podsakoff and Organ, 1986), where, given that the measures come from the same source, any defect in that source is likely to contaminate all measures, with any artifact effects likely to apply similarly to the independent and dependent variables.

Although in practice it is highly unlikely that artifact effects can be totally eliminated, and that the responses can be fully verified, there are several pre and post survey remedies that are advocated in the literature (see Churchill, 1979 and Podsakoff and Organ, 1986 for a practical, comprehensive guide). The standard textbook treatment is that the research method should incorporate multiple measures, from multiple sources, using multiple methods, based on the approach recommended by Campbell and Fiske (1959). This includes measuring the independent and dependent variables from different sources, or from different respondents. After data collection attention should be given to assessing convergent and discriminant validity, especially if it is not possible to measure the independent and dependent variables through different respondents. Convergent validity is an assessment of the extent to which several measures of a particular theoretical construct actually converge onto that specified construct, which reflects the extent of agreement among the respondents that the measures actually represent the specified theoretical construct. Discriminant validity is an assessment of the extent to which measures that are meant to measure different constructs represent their respective and differing theoretical constructs, which reflects the extent to which the respondents are able to differentiate among the range of constructs being measured.

Therefore, it is important that researchers take steps to control for artifact effects when measuring the variables that are to be used in HMRA, and to demonstrate evidence of convergent and discriminant validity in these measures.

Concluding remarks

There are clearly many situations in marketing research where the association of two variables is likely to differ with respect to the value of a third variable. An example of the application of HMRA is reproduced in Chapter 19 of this book,

TABLE 9.1 Examples of the application of HMRA

Covin *et al.* (1994)
 Implementing strategic mission: effective strategic, structural and tactical choices

Golden (1992)
 SBU strategy and performance: the moderating effects of the corporate–SBU relationship

Govindarajan (1986)
 Impact of participation in the budgetary process on managerial attitudes and performance: universalistic and contingency perspectives

Govindarajan and Fisher (1990)
 Strategy, control systems, and resource sharing: effects on business unit performance

Greenley (1995)
 Market orientation and company performance: empirical evidence from UK companies

Gupta and Govindarajan (1984)
 Business unit strategy, managerial characteristics, and business unit effectiveness at strategy implementation

Hitt and Ireland (1986)
 Relationships among corporate level distinctive competencies, diversification strategy, corporate structure and performance

Hitt *et al.* (1982)
 Functional importance and company performance: moderating effects of grand strategy and industry type

Jauch *et al.* (1980)
 Short term financial success in large business organizations: the environment–strategy connection

Laroche and Howard (1980)
 Nonlinear relations in a complex model of buyer behaviour

McArthur and Nystrom (1991)
 Environmental dynamism, complexity, and munificence as moderators of strategy-performance relationships

Prescott (1986)
 Environments as moderators of the relationship between strategy and performance

Schoonhoven (1981)
 Problems with contingency theory: testing decisions hidden within the language of contingency 'theory'

Slater and Narver (1994)
 Does competitive environment moderate the market orientation–performance relationship?

Szymanski *et al.* (1993)
 Standardization versus adaptation of international marketing strategy: an empirical investigation

in the article, *External moderation of associations among stakeholder orientations and company performance* by Greenley and Foxall, while other examples in the literature are listed in Table 9.1. However, a recommendation to use HMRA should come with an important health warning, given the confusion in the literature about its use, and the controversy surrounding a number of issues pertaining to its application. Readers are advised to take care in using HMRA in their research.

As the technique is designed for investigating a particular type of relationship among variables, it is essential that moderator effects can be justifiably predicted in the theoretical modelling of the research project. Indeed, it is essential that hypotheses predicting moderator effects can be fully justified by a comprehensive literature synthesis and subsequent theory development. Consideration should also be given to whether it is the form or the degree of the relationship that is central to the research questions, and consequently whether regression or correlation analysis is appropriate. When designing the methodology for measuring the variables to be used in the HMRA equations it is important to control for artifact effects, while recognizing that these effects are unlikely to be totally eliminated. After the data is collected an assessment of the accuracy of the measurements should be made, by estimating their validity and reliability.

The analysis for moderator effects can then proceed, using the three HMRA equations, and the framework given in Figure 9.3. Within the analysis it is necessary to check for violation of the assumptions that underlie multiple regression analysis, and in particular to check for multicollinearity, taking any necessary remedial action. However, the only moderator effects that should be investigated are those that were theoretically predicted, and there should be no gratuitous, random search for effects among the set of variables. Finally, monotonicity in identified relationships can be investigated, by using the simple differential calculus technique.

References

Aiken, L.S and West, S.G. (1991), *Multiple Regression: Testing and Interpreting Interactions*, Newbury Park: Sage

Allison, P.D. (1977), Interaction in multiple regression, *American Journal of Sociology*, **83**, 1, pp. 144–53

Althauser, R.P. (1971), Multicollinearity and non-additive regression models, In H.M. Blalock (Ed.), *Causal Models in the Social Sciences*, London: Macmillan

Arnold, H.J. (1982), Moderator variables: a clarification of conceptual, analytic, and psychometric issues, *Organizational Behavior and Human Performance*, **29**, pp. 143–74

Arnold, H.J. (1984), Testing moderator variable hypotheses: a reply to Stone and Hollenbeck, *Organizational Behavior and Human Performance*, **34**, pp. 214–24

Blalock, H.M. (1971), *Causal Models in the Social Sciences*, London: Macmillan

Blood, M.R., and Mullett, G.M. (1977), 'Where have all the moderators gone?: the perils of type II error', Technical Report No. 11, College of Industrial Management, Georgia Institute of Technology

Campbell, D.T. and Fiske, D.W. (1959), Convergent and discriminant validation by the multitrait–multimethod matrix, *Psychological Bulletin*, **56**, pp. 81–105

Churchill, G.A. (1979), A paradigm for developing better measures of marketing constructs, *Journal of Marketing Research*, **XVI**, pp. 64–73

Cohen, J. (1978), Partialed products are interactions: partialed powers are curve components, *Psychological Bulletin*, **85**, pp. 858–66

Cohen, J. and Cohen, P. (1975), *Applied Multiple Regression/Correlation Analysis for the Behavioral Sciences*, Hillside NJ:, Lawrence Erlbaum

Cohen, J. and Cohen, P. (1983), *Applied Multiple Regression/Correlation Analysis for the Behavioral Sciences*, Hillside NJ: Lawrence Erlbaum

Covin, J. G., Slevin, D.P. and Schultz, R.L. (1994), Implementing strategic mission: effective strategic,structural and tactical choices, *Journal of Management Studies*, **31**, 4, pp.481–505

Cronbach, L.J. (1987), Statistical tests for moderator variables: flaws in analyses recently proposed, *Psychological Bulletin*, **102**, 3, pp. 414–17

Evans, M.G. (1991), The problem of analyzing multiplicative composites, *American Psychologist*, **46**, 1, pp. 6–15

Fiske, D.W. (1982), Convergent-discriminant validation in measurements and research strategies, in D. Brinberg and L. Kidder (Eds.), *New Directions for Methodology of Social and Behavioral Science: Forms of Validity in Research*, San Francisco: Jossey-Bass

Friedrich, R.J. (1982), In defence of multiplicative terms in multiple regression equations, *American Journal of Political Science*, **26**, 4, pp. 797–833

Ghiselli, E.E., Campbell, J.P. and Zedeck, S. (1982), *Measurement Theory for the Behavioral Sciences*, San Francisco: Freeman

Golden, B.R. (1992), SBU stratgey and performance: the moderating effects of the corporate-SBU relationship, *Strategic Management Journal*, **13**, pp. 145–58

Govindarajan, V. (1986), Impact of participation in the budgetary process on managerial attitudes and performance: universalistic and contingency perspectives, *Decision Sciences*, **17**, pp. 496–516

Govindarajan, V. and Fisher, J. (1990), Strategy, control systems, and resource sharing: effects on business-unit performance, *Academy of Management Journal*, **33**, 2, 259–85

Greenley, G.E. (1995), Market orientation and company performance: empirical evidence from UK companies, *British Journal of Management*, **6**, 1, pp. 1–13

Gupta, A.K. and V. Govindarajan (1984), Business unit strategy, managerial characteristics, and business unit effectiveness at strategy implementation, *Academy of Management Journal*, **27**, 1, pp. 25–41

Hair, J.F., Anderson, R.E., Tatham, R.L. and Black, W.C. (1995), *Multivariate Data Analysis*, 4th ed., Englewood Cliffs, NJ: Prentice-Hall

Hitt, M.A. and Ireland, R.D. (1986), Relationships among corporate level distinctive competencies, diversification strategy, corporate structure and performance, *Journal of Management Studies*, **23**, 4, pp. 401–16

Hitt, M.A., Ireland, R.D. and Stadter, G. (1982), Functional importance and company performance: moderating effects of grand strategy and industry type, *Strategic Management Journal*, **3**, pp. 315–30

Jaccard, J., Turrisi, R. and Wan, C.K. (1990), *Interaction Effects in Multiple Regression*, Newbury Park: Sage

Jauch, L.R., Osborn. R.N. and Glueck, W.F. (1980), Short term financial success in large business organizations: the environment-strategy connection, *Strategic Management Journal*, 1, pp. 49–63

Katrichis, J.M. (1993), The conceptual implications of data centering in interactive regression models, *Journal of the Market Research Society*, 35, 2, pp. 183–92

Kerlinger, F.N. and Pedhazur, E.J. (1973), *Multiple Regression in Behavioral Research*, New York: Holt, Rinehart and Winston

Laroche, M. and Howard, J.A. (1980), Nonlinear relations in a complex model of buyer behaviour, *Journal of Consumer Research*, 6, pp. 377–88

Marquardt, D.W. (1980), A critique of some ridge regression methods, *Journal of the American Statistical Association*, 75, pp. 87–91

Marquardt, D.W., and Snee, R.D. (1975), Ridge regression in practice, *The American Statistician*, 29, pp. 3–20

McArthur, A.W. and Nystrom, P.C. (1991), Environmental dynamism, complexity, and munificence as moderators of strategy-performance relationships, *Journal of Business Research*, 23, pp. 349–61

Neter, J. and Wasserman, W. (1974), *Applied Linear Statistical Models*, Homewood: Irwin

Pedhazur, E.J. (1982), *Multiple Regression in Behavioral Research*, New York: Holt, Rinehart and Winston

Podsakoff, P.M. and Organ, D.W. (1986), Self-reports in organizational research: problems and prospects, *Journal of Management*, 12, 4, pp. 531–44

Prescott, J.E. (1986), Environments as moderators of the relationship between strategy and performance, *Academy of Management Journal*, 29, 2, pp. 329–46

Salancik, J.R. and Pfeffer, J. (1977), Examination of need-satisfaction models of job attitudes, *Administrative Science Quarterly*, 22, pp. 427–56

Schoonhoven, C.B. (1981), Problems with contingency theory: testing decisions hidden within the language of contingency 'theory', *Administrative Science Quarterly*, 26, pp. 349–77

Sharma, S. (1996), *Applied Multivariate Techniques*, New York: Wiley

Sharma, S., Durand, R.M. and Gur-Arie, O. (1981), Identification and analysis of moderator variables, *Journal of Marketing Research*, XVII, pp. 291–300

Slater, S.F. and Narver, J.C. (1994), Does competitive environment moderate the market orientation–performance relationship?, *Journal of Marketing*, 58, pp. 46–55

Smith, K.W. and Sasaki, M.S. (1979), Decreasing multicollinearity: a method for models with multiplicative functions, *Sociological Methods and Research*, 8, 1, pp. 35–56

Southwood, K.E. (1978), Substantive theory and statistical interaction: five models, *American Journal of Psychology*, 83, pp. 1154–203

Stone, E.F., and Hollenbeck, J.R. (1984), Some issues associated with the use of moderated regression analysis, *Organizational Behavior and Human Performance*, 34, pp. 195–213

Szymanski, D.M., Bharadwaj, S.G. and Varadarajan, P.R. (1993), Standardization versus adaptation of international marketing strategy: an empirical investigation, *Journal of Marketing*, 57, pp. 1–17

Tate, R.L. (1984), Limitations of centering for interactive models, *Sociological Methods and Research*, 13, 2, pp. 251–71

Tull, D.S. and Hawkins, D.I. (1984), *Marketing Research*, New York: Macmillan

Yi, Y. (1989), On the evaluation of main effects in multiplicative regression models, *Journal of the Market Research Society*, 31, 1, pp. 133–38

Young, S. (1973), Pitfalls down the primrose path of attitude segmentation, *European Research*, November, pp. 157–73

Zedeck, S. (1971), Problems with the use of moderator variables, *Psychological Bulletin*, 76, 4, pp. 295–310

■ □ ▨ ■ 10

Attitude Survey Data Reduction Using CHAID: An Example in Shopping Centre Market Research

Steve Baron and Dianne Phillips

For response modelling, chi-square automatic interaction detection (CHAID), it is claimed, is 'easy to use, produces intuitively appealing results, and is statistically valid' (Babinec, 1990). A market research project concerned with a proposed redevelopment of a 100 000 sq.ft. area of the largest city centre shopping centre in Europe afforded an ideal opportunity for assessing the practical value of CHAID. A survey of samples of existing shopping centre users sought responses on attractiveness and usage of various leisure facilities. Once the popular facilities had been identified, some appropriate segmentation of respondents showing a high level of interest in a particular facility was required. Initially, this was achieved by standard cross-tabulation analysis with age, gender, frequency of visit, etc. and testing for significance. Subsequently, the same data was analysed using CHAID. The paper reports on the similarities and differences between results from the two approaches and focuses on the intuitive appeal and value of CHAID results to the shopping centre owner/ managers.

Introduction

Sonquist and Morgan (1964) developed the technique AID (Automatic Interaction Detection) because, according to Holmes (1981), they were 'dissatisfied with standard cross-tabulation analyses, and their inability to reveal complex interactions in survey data'. AID provides analysts with the means to explore interactions in the data in a systematic manner. In a marketing context, such explorations may lead to identification of suitable market segments to target. For example, AID can help the direct marketer to identify the characteristics of customers who have responded to a mailshot, or it can help the marketing department of a car manufacturer to identify the characteristics of purchasers of a particular model over the past six months.

AID has a number of limitations (Bishop, Fienberg and Holland, 1975; Holmes, 1981; MacLachlan and Johansson, 1981). It is assumed that the dependent, or behavioural criterion, variable is measured at interval level (although often in practice it is converted to a dichotomous variable, e.g. those who own/do not own a particular model of car (Perreault and Barksdale, 1980)). The categorical predictors, the explanatory variables, can only be split in a dichotomous fashion. For a predictor variable such as gender, where there are only two categories, this is not a problem, but for other potential predictor variables, such as educational background, socio-economic group or age, a premature collapsing into a dichotomous split could obscure real differences in responses between categories. The AID search procedure tends to favour splits on predictor variables with a large number of original categories. If, for example, the predictor variable 'household income' was categorized into ten groups, AID would automatically favour a (dichotomous) split on this variable, simply because of the large number of categories. This may render the segmentation procedure invalid.

Despite these limitations, AID does satisfy a need in providing analysts with a systematic approach to studying and identifying interactions between categorical predictor variables. According to MacLachlan and Johansson (1981), some of the limitations 'can be overcome with cautious analysis, large samples and replication subsamples'.

Chi-square automatic interaction detection (CHAID) is a development of AID which addresses the limitations of AID without sacrificing the benefits (Kass,1980). An overview of CHAID is given in the next section. When AID and CHAID have been compared with regard to meeting the needs of the analyst (Perreault and Barksdale, 1980; Magidson 1982, 1990) it has been concluded that CHAID is more appropriate and more flexible than AID. Furthermore it is claimed that CHAID, is 'easy to use, produces intuitively appealing results, and is statistically valid' (Babinec,1990). If this is so, CHAID could also satisfy the needs of the client who commissions the work, as well as the analyst who undertakes the work.

There are few references to CHAID in the marketing literature considering its apparent potential, and CHAID is not mentioned in recent marketing research texts (e.g. Parasuraman, 1991; Baker, 1991; Chisnall, 1992; Aaker and Day, 1990). One possible explanation is that the software was not readily available. This obstacle to use may now have been overcome as a version of CHAID is available for purchase to use with SPSS.

Recent marketing examples of the use of CHAID are mainly concentrated in direct marketing (Magidson, 1990). In such applications, very large samples of potential purchasers of a product are mailed, and response rates are generally low. Any increase in response rate, through the identification of important market segments, can result in large financial benefits. CHAID has also been employed by geographers to model mobility and housing choice (Clark, Duerloo and Dieleman, 1988, 1990). There is potential, however, for CHAID to be used in other areas of application. In particular, CHAID could be an appropriate technique for segmenting attitude survey respondents according to their responses on key questions.

An attitude survey was recently undertaken with a sample of 903 visitors to a large UK covered shopping centre. An analysis of the findings, including a number of standard cross-tabulations, had already been completed and presented to the shopping centre management. The survey and interpretation of the results provided a good opportunity for retro-spectively testing CHAID and for comparing CHAID output with the output which had resulted from the standard cross-tabulation analyses. Such a comparison is of particular relevance to consultants interpreting survey data for clients.

This paper outlines the main features of CHAID, provides a description of the attitude survey and its objectives, and compares CHAID findings with the earlier findings. Finally, the value of CHAID in this type of application is discussed from the viewpoints of both the client and analyst, and suggestions for further research are made.

CHAID: an overview

CHAID uses a semihierarchical sequential procedure for partitioning a contingency table. The program first selects the smallest number of splits of the categories of a predictor using pairwise merging and splitting of the response levels of each predictor variable. Once the new categories have been determined, the original sample response is split using the most significant predictor. Each of the subgroups is then regarded as a new 'parent' subgroup and is split in a similar fashion. The analysis proceeds down additional levels until the size of the group becomes too small or there are no further significant splits. The particular version we have been using is SPSS CHAID, developed by Statistical Innovations Inc. (Belmont, Massachusetts) and marketed as an 'add-on' to SPSS.

The program is very much exploratory in purpose. It allows the analyst to produce a tree diagram showing the most important predictor variables and interactions associated with the dependent variable. Hence it facilitates the identification of meaningful groups in terms of the predictor variables and screens out extraneous predictors.

The three components of CHAID consist of the following:

- Chi-square statistic;
- Bonferroni adjustment;
- algorithm for the combination of categories.

The chi-square significance test is very familiar. It is an appropriate statistic in those situations where both the dependent and independent variables are categorical. The procedure relies on few assumptions about the data and provides an identification of the 'most significant' predictor. This contrasts with the identification of 'the most explanatory predictor' as in AID.

The significance of a chi-square test for independence is of course affected by the number of degrees of freedom. The Bonferroni correction to the p-value is used to provide for the problem which can arise when the number of degrees of freedom for the chi-square test becomes too small. This could lead to the spurious identification of significant predictors.

The algorithm for the combination of categories provides a means of reducing the number of categories of the predictor variables to a more parsimonious grouping. The permissible combinations are determined by the types of variables. A free variable, i.e. a variable measured at nominal level, assumes no ordering; hence any combination of categories can be combined. For a monotonic variable, i.e. measured at ordinal level, and above, only adjacent categories can be merged. A 'floating' variable is as a monotonic variable except for the last category (an appropriate way of dealing with 'don't knows').

At the first stage CHAID forms full two-way tables with the dependent variable for each predictor. The latter can have between 2 and 15 categories. All eligible pairs of categories of the predictor variables are compared and similar pairs merged into a single category. For a given number of response categories, the largest number of possible combinations occurs when predictor variables are measured on the nominal scale because there is no restriction on grouping. For a monotonic predictor, with a floating response, the number of possible combinations will be smaller. It will be smallest for a monotonic predictor. Pairs of the new categories are compared and adjusted p-values calculated. The sample is split using the predictor that has the lowest adjusted p-value. The new categories of the predictor are used to subdivide the sample into segments. The process is then repeated on the segments until no additional significant split is possible or until the segment size becomes too small. All stages of this process are outlined and explained in the Appendix. (For a useful discussion of the partitioning and merging procedures see especially Perreault and Barksdale, 1980.)

The survey of shopping centre users

An opportunity for introducing leisure activities/amenities into the shopping centre had arisen because a proposed re-routing of city transport would free an area of 100,000 square feet hitherto used as a bus station in the centre. The sample of 903 shopping centre users was interviewed, by trained fieldworkers, over a three day period in order to establish the centre users' level of interest in five named leisure activities/amenities. The shopping centre management were only concerned at this stage with very broad categories of leisure activities/amenities.

The five categories of leisure activity/amenity were 'live entertainment', 'exhibition centre', 'cinema', 'craft market' and 'children's fun park'. A key question on the survey was: 'Here are some activities/amenities which could be part of the redeveloped bus station area. Please state your personal level of interest in the ideas according to the scale on the card.'

The scale on the card was as follows.

Very low	Low	Neither low nor high	High	Very high
1	2	3	4	5

Centre users were also asked questions about their age, the occupation of the chief wage earner, (as a means of establishing socio-economic group (SEG)), and their frequency of visit to the centre. Gender was recorded as part of the classification data.

The shopping centre management wished to rank the activities/amenities in terms of level of centre user interest and to further identify interested and highly interested respondents in terms of age, gender, socio-economic group and frequency of visit. Such information, in turn, can be made available to leisure group organizations who express interest in locating in the shopping centre.

Survey findings without CHAID

The summaries and analysis of the survey were produced in two stages.

1. a 'hole count' for each question and, where appropriate, the calculation of mean values
2. cross-tabulations of level of interest in each activity/amenity against age, gender, socio-economic group and frequency of visit – a total of 20 separate two-way tables.

The identification of exceptions and differences apparent in the cross-tabulations together with the combining of categories of a given predictor variable was made using standard cross-tabulation commands supported by chi-square tests for independence. Each predictor variable was treated in isolation from the others in order to simplify and understand the data. Groups of categories within each predictor variable which produced an interest response significantly higher than the sample as a whole were highlighted. Table 10.1 shows an extract of the results presented to the shopping centre management.

Interactions between predictor variables had not been considered as three, four, and five-way nested cross tabulations tend to hide more information than they reveal and the time involved in undertaking such a task was considered to be too great. However, this was of concern to the analysts as they may have inadvertently missed some important segment through their inability to process speedily the interaction data. To say, as with 'exhibition centre', that those aged 45+ are likely to be interested or that those in SEGs ABC1 are likely to be interested is useful, but not as useful as being able to say something about both those aged 45+ and SEG's ABC1. It was for this reason that the use of CHAID appeared attractive.

TABLE 10.1 Extract from summary of survey results

Activity/Amenity	Mean rating by total sample	% choosing 4 or 5	Comments
Cinema	2.91	40.0	Popular with ages 16–34; for this group mean rating is 3.60, and 66.4% chose 4 or 5.
Children's fun park	2.68	33.4	Popular with ages 25–44 & 65+; for this group mean rating is 2.88 and 40.9% chose 4 or 5.
Exhibition centre	3.00	33.9	Popular with ages 45+; for this group mean rating is 3.15 and 45.7% chose 4 or 5.
			Popular with SEGs A,B,C1: for this group, mean rating is 3.11, and 40.0% chose 4 or 5.

Survey findings with CHAID

The CHAID analysis of level of interest in the three activities/amenities, 'cinema', 'children's fun park', and 'exhibition centre' is shown in Figures 10.1–10.3. The order in which it is presented is determined by the relative complexity of the CHAID output. In each case, for the dependent variable, centre users answering 4 or 5 (high or very high level of interest)were regarded as giving a positive response.

In Figures 10.1–10.3, the boxes contain four pieces of information which are (reading from the top): the abbreviated name of the variable, the list of initial categories which have been combined (e.g. 4567 means a combination of categories 4,5,6 and 7), the percentage of positive responses from the combined group or segment, and the number of respondents in the combined group.

Cinema

The CHAID classification tree for this is shown in Fig 10.1. Age is the most important, and only, predictor of positive response of the four predictor variables considered. Three distinct and significantly different age segments have been identified: 16–24 years (categories 1,2) with 66.7 per cent positive response, 25–34 years (category 3) with 42.9 per cent positive response and 35+ years (categories 4,5,6,7) with 18.6 per cent positive response.

The CHAID results are not markedly different from those in Table 10.1, where centre users aged 16–24 years were highlighted by the analysts. CHAID has however shown that those aged 25+ years are split into two distinct groups those aged 25–34 years with a (slightly) higher positive response rate than for

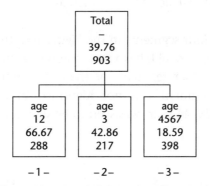

FIGURE 10.1 CHAID classification tree – the dependent variable is positive response to level of interest in a cinema

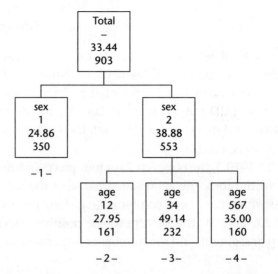

FIGURE 10.2 CHAID classification tree – the dependent variable is positive response to level of interest in a children's fun park

the total sample (43.9 per cent c.f. 39.8 per cent), and those aged 35+ who have a very much lower positive response rate than for the total sample (18.6 per cent cf 38.8 per cent).

Children's fun park

The CHAID classification tree is shown in Figure 10.2. In this case, the gender of the respondent is the best predictor, with females (category 2) showing a 38.9 per cent positive response, in contrast with males (category 1) 24.9 per cent. The age factor, originally identified by the analysts, only has an interaction effect with females. Males of each age respond in an homogeneous way.

Looking at the four segments in the Figure 10.2 tree, it is apparent that segment 3, females aged 25–44, has a much higher positive response rate, 49.1 per cent, than any other segment, or than the sample as a whole. This important specific segment was not identified in the original analysis, although age range 25–44 years was seen to be significant.

Exhibition centre

The CHAID classification tree is shown in Figure 10.3. Age is the best predictor, with those aged 45+ years (categories 5,6,7) giving the highest positive

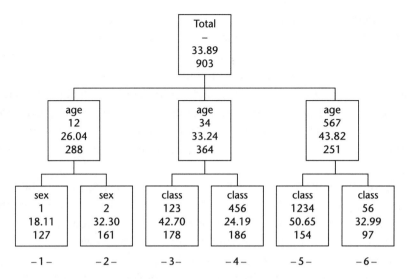

FIGURE 10.3 CHAID classification tree – the dependent variable is positive response to level of interest in an exhibition centre

response (43.8 per cent). However, CHAID has shown that, for those aged 25+ years, 'class', i.e. SEG, is also an important interactive predictor with age. In particular, segments 5 and 3, those aged 45+ years in SEGs ABC1C2 and those aged 25–44 in SEGs ABC1, are the groups with much higher positive response rates, 50.7 per cent and 42.7 per cent, than the sample as a whole. The original analysis failed to identify segment 3, although socio-economic grouping ABC1 was seen to be significant.

Of interest to the statistician is the feature that for those aged 16–24 years (categories 1,2) the interacting variable is gender, rather than class. Of those aged 16–24 years, females show a significantly higher positive response rate than males (although still below the positive response rate for the sample as a whole).

Using CHAID – the analyst's perspective

CHAID presents a very useful development of AID (automatic interaction detection) type analyses. Despite well known criticisms of its limitations (e.g. Bishop, Fienberg and Holland, 1975, Perreault and Barksdale, 1980) AID's promise as an appropriate statistical tool for analysing contingency tables has continued to attract interest. One useful extension is MAID (Multivariate AID) (Maclachlan and Johanssen (1981). This is an AID based technique for use with multiple dependent variables as opposed to a single dependent variable. CHAID owes much to AID but does not have the constraints of the binary splits. CHAID also presents an improvement in 'model' building. For example, Bishop *et al.* pointed out '(AID) never really takes into account the sampling variability inherent in the data. Thus . . . the models generated by AIDs tend to be too elaborate' (Bishop, Fienberg and Holland, 1975). In CHAID the degree of elaboration of the model is strictly controlled by the analyst's setting of the numbers of levels of analysis, significance criteria and desired minimum size of segment.

There are still few alternative exploratory techniques suitable for handling the problem of data reduction for variables measured on categorical scales. After the most relevant predictors have been identified, then of course procedures such as log linear modelling come into their own.

The most obvious advantage of CHAID over the more usual process of working through successive cross-tabulations is its very speedy identification of which categories can be combined and which are potentially the best target groups.

The program is very easy to use, although the current manual does assume you are familiar with the technique (SPSS/PC+ CHAID, Magidson, 1989). For the examples in this paper we had no problems in importing existing SPSS/PC+ system files. CHAID provides a useful message and warning system to enable you to check the quality of the data before you proceed with the analysis. (Free format, fixed format and SPSS export files are also file organizations recognised by CHAID.)

Documentation can be as extensive (e.g. full before-merging and after-merging tables) or as brief as needed (e.g. the tree diagram). The tree diagrams were drawn using default values; there are some additional procedures which allow, for example, solid lines instead of dashed lines to be used in the diagram. These can improve the standard of presentation.

The procedure can be run either in automatic or interactive mode. Even in the automatic mode the analyst has a great deal of control over such matters as default values, the number of levels of analysis, types of variables and the form of the documentation. Stopping rules can be set by the analyst. These instruct the program to cease segmentation when the subgroup falls below an acceptable size. Similarly, the chi-squared significance levels can be changed by the researcher. Whilst the 5 per cent level of significance is regarded in many contexts as acceptable, there can be circumstances where higher levels are desirable. CHAID's flexibility in this is useful.

In the interactive mode the analyst can, in addition, inspect the procedure at any stage, override CHAID's suggested next step, back up paths, etc. All of these are welcome facilities.

There are some minor grumbles about how the program runs. In comparison to many current statistical programs, CHAID seems somewhat cumbersome. The operator is constantly moving from menu to submenu to window and back and the functions of the space and enter keys for selecting options are confusing for the novice. The results can be printed out from DOS but they are more easily edited in a word processing package, such as WordPerfect.

As in AID, clean datasets (i.e. without coding errors and numerous missing values) and large samples are prerequisites for CHAID to operate effectively. Recommendations for an acceptable sample size vary in the literature. MacLachlan and Johansson (1981) recommend 33 times as many observations as predictor variables. Sonquist, Baker and Morgan (1964) suggest a minimum sample size of 1000. Holmes (1981) suggests that first and second order predictors can be successfully identified on samples of 200 to 300. Perreault and Barksdale (1971) suggest a 'reasonable' minimum group size to be 40 and a sample size of 200 times the number of predictor variables. Such factors are well known considerations in market research but explorations in using CHAID with other datasets have reinforced their importance. The initial design of the survey and the questionnaire/interview schedule are crucial to ensure a satisfactory response rate and reliable data.

Using CHAID: the shopping centre management's perspective

Whilst the analysts found value in the tree diagram, that particular form of display was only of passing interest to the shopping centre management. A large amount of verbal explanation is required (by the analysts) to make the tree comprehensible, principally because the concise presentation of the figures in each box requires constant reference to other sources for meaning to emerge.

The management expressed a preference for a method of presentation which clearly highlights the important market segments (i.e. those yielding the highest positive response). With the classification tree, each segment appears to have equal importance. The style of presentation shown in Table 10.2 was appreciated more than the tree.

Clearly, the uses to which CHAID output are subsequently put will determine the preferred form of presentation. In this application, the shopping centre management will need to present information on target market segments, together with other relevant information such as catchment area population, transport and car parking availability and mean dwell times of

TABLE 10.2 Children's fun park – level of interest and estimated size of different centre user segments

Segment	Percentage showing interest	Percentage of sample in segment	Estimated weekly No. showing interest*	Degree of importance
1. Female, 25–44 years	49.1	25.6	100 600	**Very high**
2. Female, 45+ years	35.0	17.7	49 600	**High**
3. Female, 16–24 years	28.0	17.8	39 800	**Low**
4. All males	24.9	38.7	77 100	**Low**
Total			267 100 (33.4 per cent of weekly throughput)	

* Based on an average figure of 800,000 shopping centre visits per week.

centre users, to interested leisure group organizations. As many leisure group organizations will expect the shopping centre management to provide such information, clarity of presentation is paramount. With regard to the important centre user segments, the leisure group can compare them with their own consumer profiles to identify synergies.

The CHAID output in the form of a classification tree is a welcome variant to analysts who are used to tabular presentations. However, the needs of the analysts to have a logical, visual display of the complete set of distinct segments are likely to conflict with the needs of the various decision makers who require clear prioritizing and descriptions of the segments.

Conclusions and suggestions for further research

CHAID offers the experienced market research analyst a very useful tool for the rapid and effective identification of population segments, and of key predictor variables for more sophisticated modelling procedures. It does, however, need to be used with care; its automatic mode may well turn out to be a source of misinformation for the unwary, particularly if the data are of poor quality with the problem of many missing values for some variables. Despite its appeal to the analyst, CHAID output, even with the enhanced print options, is likely to be inappropriate for client ready reports.

Our work suggests that CHAID's 'promise of parsimony' might fruitfully be extended to questionnaire design. If the model suggests, for example, that there are only three significant groupings for the variable age, why provide for more than three categories on the questionnaire itself? Different topics and samples with different profiles may not of course produce similar results. However, research on questionnaire design has suggested that data quality can be affected by the number and character of response categories (Sudman, 1982). CHAID provides an efficient tool for exploring this further.

Further study could look at the effects on data collection and analysis of using the reduced number of specified categories suggested by CHAID for common explanatory variables such as age or level of education. For example, in the CHAID runs for the shopping centre survey, the age categories 5,6, and 7 (i.e. 45–54 years, 55–64 years, 65+ years) were always grouped together, suggesting that in this context these three initial age groups can be treated as homogenous. Overall three age categories – less than 25 years, 25–44 years and 45+ years – would have sufficed, rather than the seven originally chosen. Similarly, from the example in the Appendix, a reduced list of only three levels of educational background may prove appropriate in future surveys of social attitude.

An initial choice of a relatively large number of categories for a predictor variable is probably made for prudential reasons so that potential information and serendipity is not inadvertently lost. However, if confidence in these reduced response categories could be built up, substantial benefits could accrue. Questionnaires could be short, easier and simpler for the respondent to complete. Coding, data entry and analysis time could be considerably reduced. In brief, questionnaires could become more efficient without loss of key information and resources would not have to be allocated to cover the processing of irrelevant or redundant data.

Finally the effectiveness of the tool must be judged by users in different contexts. Is the use of CHAID best restricted to direct marketing? Can it contribute to the measurement and modelling of social attitudes? Could it be useful to planners and decision makers in other fields?

References

Aaker, D.A. and Day, G.S. (1990), *Marketing Research*, Fourth edition, New York; John Wiley & Sons

Babinec, T. (1990), CHAID response modelling and segmentation, *Quirk's Marketing Research Review,* June/July 1990, pp. 12–15

Baker, M.J. (1991), *Research for Marketing,* Basingstoke: Macmillan

Bishop, Y.M., Fienberg, S.E. and Holland P.W. (1975), *Discrete Multivariate Analysis,* Cambridge MA: MIT Press

Chisnall, P.M. (1992), *Marketing Research*, 4th Edition, London: McGraw-Hill

Clark, W.A.V., Duerloo, M.C. and Dieleman, F.M. (1988), Modeling strategies for categorical data: examples from housing and tenure choice, *Geographical Analysis*, Vol **20**, July pp. 198–219

Clark, W.A.V., Duerloo, M.C. and Dieleman, F.M. (1991), Modeling categoric data with chi square automatic interaction detection and correspondence analysis, *Geographical Analysis*, Vol **23**, October, pp. 332–345

Holmes, C. (1981), AID Comes to the aid of marketing management, *European Journal of Marketing*, Vol **14**, No 7, pp. 409–13

Kass, G. (1980), An exploratory technique for investigating large quantities of categorical data, *Applied Statistics*, 1980 **29** pp. 129–27

MacLachlan, D.L. and Johannson, J.K. (1981), Market segmentation with multivariate AID, *Journal of Marketing*, Vol **45**, Winter, pp. 74–84

Magidson, J. (1982), Some common pitfalls in causal analysis of categorical data, *Journal of Marketing Research*, Vol **19**, pp. 461–71

Magidson, J. (1990), CHAID, LOGIT and log-linear modeling, *Marketing Information Systems*, Datapro Report IM11–130 pp. 101–15. Delran NJ: Datapro Research Corporation

Parasuraman, A. (1991), *Marketing Research*, 2nd edition, Wokingham: Addison-Wesley

Perreault, W.D. and Barksdale, H.C. (1980), A model-free approach for analysis of complex contingency data in survey research, *Journal of Marketing Research*, Vol **17**, November, pp. 503–15

Sonquist, J.A and Morgan, J.N. (1964), The detection of interaction effects. Ann Arbor, MI: Institute for Social Research, University of Michigan

Sudman, S. and Bradburn, N. M. (1982), *Asking Questions: A Practical Guide to Questionnaire Design*. San Francisco: Jossey Bass

Appendix: An example of CHAID applied to Social Attitudes

One question in the 1985 British Social Attitudes survey was whether the respondent was of the opinion that the UK should continue to be a member of the European Community (EC). There were four response categories – continue, withdraw, don't know and not applicable. In the analysis outlined below, the relationship, if any, between these responses and a selection of predictor variables, education, political party affiliation, age and tenure, was explored.

To illustrate the process of merging categories, Table 10.3 below shows how CHAID grouped the categories of level of education into three groups. Educational level was defined as 'highest educational qualification' and had seven categories in the original coding. These were as follows:

1. Degree
2. Professional qualifications
3. A Level

TABLE 10.3 Details of the analysis of the predictor 'level of education' on the sample

(a) *Predictor hedqual (before merging): Frequency counts*

hedqual	CONTINUE	WITHDRAW	DK	NA	Total
1	104	16	2	0	122
2	161	37	7	1	206
3	110	38	9	1	158
4	200	97	16	2	315
5	90	63	13	1	167
6	19	6	1	0	26
7	328	425	56	1	810
Total	1012	682	104	6	1804

Chi-square: 194.3 (df = 18 ; $p <\ =$ 1.4e–31)

(b) *Predictor hedqual (after merging): Frequency counts*

hedqual	CONTINUE	WITHDRAW	DK	NA	Total
12	265	53	9	1	328
3456	419	204	39	4	666
7	328	425	56	1	810
Total	1012	682	104	6	1804

Chi-square: 181.7 (df = 6 ; p $<\ =$ 2.2e–35)

4. O level
5. CSE
6. Foreign and Other
7. None

(Note that the analyst could regard 'highest educational qualification' (hedqual) as either a free variable or a monotonic variable. In the latter case, CHAID would be restricted to combining only adjacent categories, e.g. 1,2 and 3, whereas in the former combinations such as 1,2 and 5 would be considered. In this analysis it was treated as a free variable).

Table 10.3 a is the starting point: a cross tabulation of the opinion on EC membership against 'Highest educational qualification'. This gives a chi-square of 194.3, which is highly significant, with 18 degrees of freedom.

After all possible mergers have been tested, CHAID regroups the categories of the predictor variable (highest educational qualification), into three as in Table 10.3b. The chi-square value of 181.7 is still highly significant, with now 6 degrees of freedom. The new categories are:

TABLE 10.4 The significance of the predictor variables

Predictor	p-value
Level of education	2.2e–35
Political party	3.3e–21
Type of tenure	3.4e–20
Age category	0.008

1. Degree, Professional, etc. qualifications (originally categories 1,2).
2. A level, O level, CSE, Foreign and other qualifications (originally categories 3,4,5,6).
3. No qualifications (originally category 7).

An examination of each of the predictor variables in turn, i.e. political party affiliation, type of housing tenure, and age category, suggested that the highest educational qualification was the most significant (i.e. had the smallest *p*-value).

Next CHAID gave the percentage of respondents in favour of continuing in the EC in each of the new combined categories of the predictor variable, level of education. (See Table 10.5).

Having carried out a three-way split on 'hedqual', CHAID examined the first subgroup, those respondents with degrees or other professional qualifications and repeated the analysis. It found that, for those respondents who had degrees or professional qualifications, the best predictor was political party (recategorized from the original six categories into two) The procedure revealed that in this segment, those respondents who identified with the Conservative and Alliance parties were more likely to favour staying in the EC (86 per cent) than those who identified with the Labour party (66 per cent).

The next subgroup to be examined in this example run was those with A and O level educational qualifications, and again a split along party affiliation

TABLE 10.5 Percentage in favour of continuing in the EC by level of education

Level of education	%
New category 1	81
New category 2	63
New category 3	41

lines was identified. The examination of each level of each subgroup will continue until the best predictor does not meet the significance criteria set. This would normally be when $P < 0.05$. When this happens, such a segment is not partitioned any further.

The analysis can also be terminated when the size of the subgroup has become too small (Perreault and Barksdale, 1971). Both types of criteria – the significance level and the size of the subgroup are determined by the analyst.

CHAID provides ample documentation of the analysis both in the forms of tables before and after merging, as in Tables 10.3a and 10.3b, and in the form of tree diagrams (see output on shopping centre survey).

■ □ ▨ ■ 11

Regression Type Techniques and Small Samples: A Guide to Good Practice

Richard Speed

Marketing researchers frequently face constraints on the size of the sample they can assemble, and may feel that quantitative analysis cannot be undertaken. This article seeks to illustrate approaches that improve the performance of regression type techniques with small samples. The article focuses on areas where small samples can lead to problems, particularly test power, violation of assumptions, collinearity and validation. Sample reuse validation techniques such as jackknife and bootstrap are explained, and some general guidelines are given.

Introduction

This paper addresses the impact of small sample size on the use of quantitative methods, in particular regression and related techniques, and what researchers can do to minimize problems. It is not intended as a definitive guide to the area, rather as a source of ideas and references that will act as a starting point for researchers trying to cope with sample size problems.

It is important to realize the limitations of quantitative methods. Researchers using any quantitative techniques must bear in mind that quantitative methods have a dual role (Cowan, 1990). The first role is to describe a relationship in a way that makes understanding easier (the modelling role). The second is to assess the strength and validity of any relationship defined (the testing role). To qualify as 'excellent' research, quantitative research must show both excellent modelling and excellent testing, but neither alone is sufficient.

In the modelling role, good research will produce a model that says something interesting and useful about the world we see around us. Models can vary from the very simple, e.g. associations between two measurable variables, to the startlingly complex, e.g. causal models with unobservable variables, but the basic approach is the same. Regardless of complexity, most researchers in marketing seek to define a model in such a way that if it proves to be valid, managers can use it to help determine actions. However, marketing effects are undoubtedly complex. Leeflang (1974) proposed that a good description of a relationship will reflect how marketing phenomena operate, and so avoid unreasonable assumptions or simplifications. A counter argument (Armstrong, 1975) is that, because of the level of complexity, the maximum amount of simplicity and parsimony are also desirable. In the modelling role, the researcher therefore engages in a trade-off between realism and simplicity.

In the testing role, good research examines proposed relationships to the maximum level of rigour that is both appropriate and possible. When models are tested, many issues emerge to influence the quality of the testing and therefore the overall quality of the research. Many of these are sample size related, but other issues will also influence testing such as data type (categoric, ordinal, interval, ratio), data structure (orthogonal or intercorrelated) and data source (sample structure, respondent choice, etc). For reasons of space this paper concentrates on problems relating directly to sample size, but researchers can find overviews of testing problems in most basic research methodology texts (e.g. Green, Tull and Albaum, 1983, Moser and Kalton, 1975).

As the above discussion has illustrated, in good research good quantitative analysis has a relatively limited role. It cannot salvage research with poor modelling or poor quality sampling, for instance. A poor model rigorously tested is still a poor model. What good quantitative analysis can do is increase the validity of the research, and so improve its overall quality. Sample size does not affect the modelling role at all, so the first thing that researchers dealing with small samples must do is to get that right first.

This paper concentrates on the testing role of the group of quantitative methods most popular amongst marketing researchers, regression and the regression family of techniques. The paper addresses the issues of using these techniques with small samples by looking first at some general issues relating to small samples and how small samples influence test power. How small samples impact on the assumptions underlying these techniques are examined, and some approaches to minimize violation of these assumptions are discussed. Since it is not always possible to avoid the violation of underlying assumptions, the paper draws on recent research to examine the robustness of regression when such problems occur. The final section of the paper examines the issues of validation in quantitative analysis, and outlines some techniques particularly appropriate for small samples. Finally, some guidelines are given to assist the researcher in using these techniques.

What do we mean by 'small sample'?

A small sample does not mean a sample of a very small part of the population under examination. Researchers should note that the relationship between sample size and population size is essentially unimportant in quantitative analysis. Opinion polls in the UK drawing conclusions about the entire population (55 million people) regularly use samples of 1500, or a sample of 0.0027 per cent of the population. It is the quality of the sample, how well it represents the population as a whole, not the proportion of the population represented by the sample, that is important in establishing validity.

So in defining whether a sample is small or not, the size of the population does not matter, since sample size is not measured relative to the population. However, the nature of the population is important in assessing sample quality. For instance, consider the difference between these two studies:

1. 'This research investigates the relationship between advertising budgets and performance of UK manufacturing industry.'
2. 'This research investigates the relationship between advertising budgets and performance of UK building societies operating a national branch network.'

Imagine that both studies gathered data on a total of 15 companies. In the former case we are talking about a population of many thousands of companies. In the latter case, we are talking about a total population of about 15 companies. Although both studies have sample sizes of 15 the implications of this are very different. The quality of the sample depends on the relationship between sample and population. The strongest defence of a small sample is to have captured 100 per cent of a small population. However, the technical problems in applying quantitative techniques are the same.

Sample size and test power

Researchers should note that the overwhelming case is that reduction in sample size is far more likely to reduce the likelihood of finding any significant relationships than to increase it. This is due to the way that sample size affects test power. The researcher sets the level of type I error (the probability of accepting a hypothesis when false in reality) in any test, normally at 0.05, and

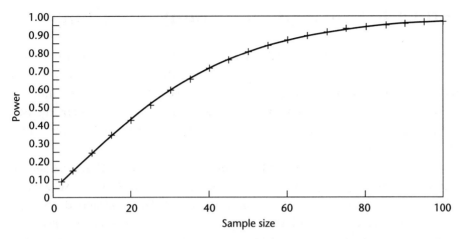

FIGURE 11.1 Power distribution. H1: Mean = 1. Normal distribution (0, 6.25)

critical values calculated for the given size of sample. Small sample sizes are no more likely to result in wrongfully claiming a relationship exists than is the case for larger samples. However, the sample size does affect type II error (the probability of rejecting a hypothesis when true in reality) and hence the power of the test (power being 1 – type II error). The power of a test climbs as sample size increases, reducing the likelihood of type II error. Figure 11.1 provides an illustration of this effect. The test under consideration is that the mean of a sample equals one. In this case the sample is drawn from a normally distributed population with mean equal to zero, variance = 6.25. When the sample size is 10, power = .25, which means that there is a 75 per cent chance that type II error will occur. As the sample size increases, the probability of type II error occurring falls (to 10 per cent when sample size is 66 and to 5 per cent when the sample size is 82). Because the probability of type II error is higher at small sample sizes, the results are likely to be unreasonably conservative.

What this implies is that the size of observed differences required to identify significant differences increases as sample size falls. Thus any significant differences observed with a small sample size will be repeated in larger samples, so long as the sample is representative. A smaller sample size is going to make it harder to find a significant relationship.

The implications of this general relationship between sample size and test power are important for the discussion in the following sections. Small samples increase the conservatism of statistical tests. Since the likelihood of rejecting a relationship is inflated by the influence of a small sample, the problem faced by users of small samples is validating the relationship, rather than identifying spurious ones.

General rules for the regression family of techniques

Regression and the family of related techniques are amongst the most popular multivariate techniques in marketing research. Accordingly this paper pays particular attention to these quantitative methods. The regression family of techniques can be categorized on the basis of the nature of the data being used (metric and nonmetric) and by the number of dependent variables. Table 11.1 shows one such classification.

Common to all these techniques are a set of problems that arise due to sample effects including sample size. Generally, these problems arise because with a small sample size greater importance is being attached to each individual observation. This level of importance might not be justifiable by the quality of the data. We can illustrate this by imagining that each observation (i) on each variable (j) consists of the sum of two terms.

$$X_{ij} = R_{ij} + e_{ij}$$

Where X_{ij} = the value of the jth variable for the ith observation.

The first term (R_{ij}) reflects information that is general to the population, the second term reflects error (e_{ij}), error being information that is unique to that observation and is randomly distributed throughout the population. If we collect data from the whole population, the total error would be zero. Increasing the sample size leads the sum of errors to tend to zero. However the greater the importance of the individual observation, the greater the impact of each particular element of error. This model of the structure of information in regression will be used to illustrate some of the points in the remainder of the article.

TABLE 11.1 The regression family of techniques

Multiple regression analysis
  $Y = k_1 X_1 + k_2 X_2 + \ldots + k_n X_n$
Y is metric, $X_{1,\ldots n}$ are metric or nonmetric
Multiple discriminant analysis
  $Y = k_1 X_1 + k_2 X_2 + \ldots + k_n X_n$
Y is nonmetric, $X_{1,\ldots n}$ are metric
Canonical correlation analysis
  $j_1 Y_1 + j_2 Y_2 + \ldots + j_n Y_n = k_1 X_1 + k_2 X_2 + \ldots + k_n X_n$
$Y_{1,\ldots n}$ are metric or nonmetric, $X_{1,\ldots n}$ are metric or nonmetric
Principal components analysis
  $Y = k_1 X_1 + k_2 X_2 + \ldots + k_n X_n$
Y is metric but unknown, $X_{1,\ldots n}$ are metric or nonmetric

---

Based on Cowan (1991)

There are a range of assumptions underpinning all multivariate techniques, including the regression family of techniques. Violation of the assumptions means that the technique is performing in a situation where it is not meant to be used, and the validity of the findings is therefore affected. Sample size does adversely affect some of these assumptions and therefore it is necessary for researchers to be aware of the problem. Others are not directly affected by sample size but failure to recognize them will produce problems that compound sample size problems.

Assumptions directly affected by sample size

Multivariate normality

All regression based techniques make the same basic assumptions about the data being used. Firstly they assume a multivariate normal distribution for all data. This assumption is necessary in order to allow significance testing using the t and F statistics. Multivariate normality means that not only are the distributions of individual variables normal, but also the distributions of combinations of variables are normal.

Equality of variance

The second assumption is that for any value of a dependent (predictor) variable, the values of the independent (criterion) variables have the same pattern of dispersion (variance). Equality of variance is called homoscedascity, and inequality of variance is called heteroscedascity. The variation in independent variable variance will mean that the ability of the resulting function to predict its value will vary with the different levels of the dependent variable. Failure of this assumption affects discriminant analysis in particular (Morrison, 1969).

Increasing sample size improves the reasonableness of both these assumptions. It is more difficult to accept the assumption of normality if we only have a few cases to examine. Also with a small sample each observation has a greater effect on variance, so heteroscedascity is a greater problem. In small samples it is very hard to tell what is a 'reasonable' observation, i.e. one that shows a reasonable relationship between the actual value of the dependent variable and the predicted. 'Unreasonable' observations are termed 'outliers', and their identification and elimination are essential to avoid distortion in the analysis. In a small sample, the outliers are hard to identify and their distorting effect is greater because of the smaller number of cases used to calculate mean and variance (Barnett and Lewis, 1984).

Data can be transformed to better fit both of these assumptions without losing quality (e.g. taking logs). Reducing the extent to which data violates assumptions underlying techniques is the best way to reduce the demands being made on the robustness of the technique. Data transformation for regression type techniques is discussed in Mosteller and Tukey (1977), a more detailed treatment is Box and Cox (1964).

More general assumptions

Several further assumptions are necessary in regression type techniques, mostly relating to relationships within the data. The first is that errors in prediction are uncorrelated. This is an assumption that the data used capture all variables that are relevant in prediction. If this is not the case an unexplained systematic relationship exists and we cannot be confident about our predicted values. Correlation of errors will not be affected specifically by sample size.

A second assumption is that no independent variables used either interact or are correlated. The most important of these two assumptions is correlations. Two uncorrelated variables (i.e. with a correlation coefficient of 0) bring twice as much information into any analysis as two perfectly correlated variables (i.e. with a correlation coefficient of 1). The inclusion of two perfectly correlated variables, where one variable perfectly predicts the other, introduces considerable instability into the coefficients. The same information is shared between two variables, so it becomes a matter of luck how these variables are included in any function. One variable might receive a very high coefficient and the other a low one, or alternatively both may have a moderate coefficient. This effect, termed collinearity, is a major problem for researchers using regression techniques (see Belsley, Kuh and Welsh, 1980; Krishnamurthi and Rangaswamy, 1987; Mason and Perreault, 1991). The fundamental problem of collinearity is that the variance of regression coefficients is inflated (Stewart, 1987). Coping with the problem requires the researcher to examine the relationships within the data set carefully, identifying any independent variables that are correlated, and including in the analysis only those variables from each correlated set that are the best predictors of the dependent variable. As will be explained in the next section, it is always likely that small samples will require that a subset of variables be selected for inclusion, so removing collinearity is usually possible.

Careful selection of which variables to include can reduce the problems of error correlation and collinearity. However, with a small sample the first two assumptions (normality and homoscedascity) are almost certain to be violated, and transformations may not be sufficient to correct the problems. What is important to researchers therefore is the robustness of the techniques, their performance when the assumptions are violated. The robustness of the techniques is a matter of much debate amongst statisticians, and the debate is largely impenetrable by the lay person.

Some general agreements in this dispute can be identified. Several authors have pointed out that multiple discriminant analysis is particularly sensitive to violation of assumptions, because it requires homoscedascity across the groupings being investigated (Huberty, 1984; Johnson and Wichern, 1982), although others dispute this (Lachenbruch, 1975). Researchers facing problems with discriminant analysis are recommended to examine a form of regression analysis, logistic regression, which uses a dichotomous dependent variable. However the robustness of a technique in statistical terms may not affect its performance in practical terms. Remember that the effect of sample size on tests tends to make them more conservative. Even with a technique regarded as amongst the most sensitive of the regression family, the impact of violations of assumptions has been questioned.

> For the researcher whose main interest is in a mathematical model which can predict well or serve as a reasonable description of the real world, the best guide (*to the impact of the violation of assumptions on discriminant analysis performance*) is the percentage of correct classifications. If this percentage is high, the violation of assumptions was not very harmful. Efforts to improve the data or use alternative formulas can only give marginal improvements. When the percentage of correct classifications is low, however, we cannot tell whether this is due to violating the assumptions or using weak discriminant variables.
>
> (Klecka, 1980)

Effects of sample size on regression

There are no hard and fast rules about the absolute minimum number of observations required to utilize the regression family of techniques. Absolute sample size affects the validity of the assumptions behind the techniques, and so indirectly affects validity. Of more direct importance is the ratio of cases to variables.

The relative sample size is the number of cases being predicted or being used in prediction. With a fixed sample size, the more variables we are using in an analysis, the more importance is being placed on each observation. As was stated earlier, small samples attach greater importance to each individual observation of any given variable. If we have a sample size of 30, and use this sample to identify the principal components of three variables, we are effectively using data from ten cases for each variable. If we use the same sample to identify the principal components of 15 variables, we are effectively using data from two cases for each variable, and the importance attached to each case rises substantially. Hence the error element in each observation has a greater impact on the analysis. In the first case we have ten error elements to include in each variable, in the second case we have two. The likelihood that these error terms cancel out to zero is far greater in the first case than the second.

Because of the importance of relative sample size, most regression type techniques have lower limits for the ratio of the number of cases to the number of variables. These are normally given in the range of three to five cases per variable, but there are variations across techniques (See Huberty, Wisenbaker and Smith, 1987 – discriminant analysis; Gorsuch, 1983 – principal components/factor analysis).

Ratio effects are the most important area of concern in carrying out small sample based regression type analysis. A researcher should limit the variables included so that there is a reasonable ratio of cases to variables. The selection of variables should also seek to minimize collinearity. Essentially the maximum number of variables, justified by the ratio and the number of cases, should be included, provided that correlations amongst these variables are minimal.

Conclusions about sample size and regression techniques

This discussion has identified a range of areas where deviations from the ideal conditions for using regression techniques may occur. In several of these cases, small sample size increases the likelihood that these deviations do occur. It is possible to draw some general conclusions from this discussion. Recent research (Mason and Perreault, 1991) used simulations to examine the impact of collinearity in regression. The conclusions of this research have important implications for marketing researchers confronted by small samples. Mason and Perreault found that as test power declines (i.e. sample size falls) or true strength of the relationship under investigation declines, so the problems caused by collinearity increase. By varying such design factors in simulations as sample size, 'true' strength of relationships, bivariate correlations amongst independent variables and data structure, the researchers identified that it is the combination of these variations that create problems, and individual variations can have no effect if they occur in isolation. For instance, the researchers found that with a strong 'true' relationship, (i.e. $R^2 = 0.75$), even if sample size was as low as 30, correlation between independent variables of 0.65

increased type II error to about 10 per cent. However, with a weaker 'true' relationship ($R^2 = 0.50$), type II error rose to nearly 50 per cent.

The first important finding from this research is that the impact of small sample size, high collinearity and low 'true' relationship strength is to increase test conservatism. The likelihood is that high correlations or low sample size will mean that researchers do not have significant findings, rather than that they will have findings that are significant but wrong. If small samples do lead to significant findings, these findings are likely to be repeated with larger samples, rather than overturned. The effects are the same as the simple normal distribution example used earlier. For researchers with small samples, this implies that regression is worth doing, since if you do find something, it is far more likely to be true than not.

The second key finding relates to interaction amongst variations. The research shows that collinearity and weak 'true' relationships exacerbate problems due to small sample size, and suggests that type II error is much lower, even with small samples, when collinearity is low and relationships are strong. For researchers with small samples, the advice must be first to eliminate as much collinearity as possible through variable selection, meaning that careful investigation of the data is important. Second, research that only has access to small samples should concentrate on relationships that the researcher has reason to believe are strong. This is a research design problem, and highlights once again the link between good analysis and good design.

Validation with small samples

Identification of relationships is not generally considered sufficient for research to be considered 'excellent'. Suggesting from quantitative investigation of a single sample that a relationship exists within a population generally means that the researcher is making assumptions about the validity of the analysis and research. However, it is possible for researchers to provide further evidence to support the case for the research being considered valid. Due to aspects of the techniques, the majority of multivariate techniques require validation before there is a case for generalizing beyond that sample, and an unvalidated study has minimal value.

The results of using multivariate techniques are unreasonably accurate (upwards bias) when their construction and their validation use the same data set. This occurs because the data set contains not only information that reflects features and trends of the underlying population, but also the error terms, information that reflects the peculiarities of the cases sampled. Using the same sample for validation as for construction means that the function reflects the peculiarities of these particular cases. Because of this accuracy is abnormally high when validating the function. This is a particular problem in discriminant analysis when classification accuracy is inflated (Montgomery, 1969; Frank, Massy and Morrison, 1965) and canonical correlation analysis when canonical weights are inflated (Lambert and Durand, 1975). Mosier (1951) pioneered the split-half, cross-validation approach that is now conventional. With this approach, cross-validation occurs by holding out half the sample (the validation sample), and running the analysis on the first half (construction sample). The resulting multivariate function is used to predict values (or categories) for the dependent variable using the validation sample. Such an approach allows an assessment of the extent to which the result achieved using the construction sample was due to features specific to that sample rather than features common to the construction and validation samples (and, by implication, the population as a whole). An important issue in cross-validation is the splitting of the sample to avoid creating split halves with different statistical properties (see Dorans and Drasgow (1980) for a discussion). Researchers have discussed the cross-validation method in relation to non-regression multivariate techniques, such as covariance structure modelling (Homburg, 1991) and cluster analysis (Calantone and Sawyer, 1978), with similar reasoning.

Such an approach is obviously problematic when the sample size is small to start with. Halving the sample only compounds the problem. A set of alternative methods, which have been used successfully with small samples, are sample reuse approaches (Hartigan, 1969). These approaches have the advantage that they do actually use all the data available, considered a major virtue in statistics (Cooil, Winer and Rados, 1987). The major techniques in this set are jackknifing, bootstrapping and the U-method. Their increased popularity is due to the decreasing cost of computer time, allowing these computer intensive methods to be more widely accessible.

The basic philosophy of both jackknifing and bootstrapping is to assign a standard error to any coefficients generated, so that stability of the coefficient can be assessed. Possession of a standard error allows assessment of confidence about the coefficient's value, for instance using simple t tests.

The jackknife

The jackknife is a bias-reduction technique that provides estimates of the parameters in the function and measures their stability with respect to changes in the sample (Fenwick, 1979; Crask and Perreault, 1977; for a technical discussion of more general applications of jackknife see Shao and Wu, 1989). It gives researchers an indication of the extent to which values for the parameters vary as the sample changes and hence how much validity their inclusion in the function has. Jackknifing is carried out by omitting one case or more from the analysis in turn and running the analysis to construct the relevant function. From each run of the analysis different values for each of the parameters are obtained and based on these an estimate of the parameter value, and the standard error of this estimate, can be made, allowing stability to be assessed. The construction of the jackknife estimator for investigating a statistic Θ, which can represent any coefficient, (regression coefficient, correlation coefficient and so on) is as follows (Crask and Perreault, 1977):

The observed sample is of size n with an observed value x for each of the n sampling units ($\mathbf{y} = (x_1, x_2, \ldots, x_n)$). Let the sample be partitioned into k subsets of size $n-m$. The optimum value of m depends on the nature of the statistic under investigation (Shao and Wu, 1989). In the case of regression 1 is appropriate but in more general cases, e.g. investigation of the median, a larger value of m might be appropriate. Let Θ' be the observed value of the statistic under investigation based on all the observations and Θ'_i be the observed value when subgroup i is removed. Pseudo observations are computed for each of the resulting subgroups. These measure the difference between the full sample observation Θ' and each subgroup observation Θ'_i

e.g. $$J_i = k\Theta' - (k-1)\Theta'_i \quad i = 1, 2, \ldots, k$$

The jackknife estimator of the coefficient is then:

$$J = [\sum_{i=1}^{k} J_i/k].$$

The jackknife process generates a jackknife estimator, the mean of the pseudo observations, and a standard error for the sample of pseudo observations can easily be measured. The value of these statistics is twofold. Firstly the pseudo values can be treated as independent, identically distributed random variables and used to obtain a confidence interval for J, which can then be tested using Student's t test ($k-1$ degrees of freedom). In addition the bias of the jackknife estimator is less than the bias of the individual estimate. The jackknife provides a valuable tool to analyse the stability of coefficients. It is discussed in more detail by Diaconis and Efron (1983).

The bootstrap

Bootstrapping (Efron and Gong, 1983; Efron and Tibshirani, 1986) is a related procedure, which also provides an estimation of parameter values and standard errors associated with them. The following discussion is based on Efron and Tibshirani (1986).

The basic bootstrapping technique relies on the Monte Carlo algorithm. The Monte Carlo algorithm is a mechanism for generating a set of numbers at random. In the bootstrap process, this algorithm is used to generate a set of n numbers at random ($\mathbf{y}^* = (x_1^*, x_2^*, \ldots, x_n^*)$), based on the observed distribution of data ($\mathbf{y} = (x_1, x_2, \ldots, x_n)$), where n is the original sample size. This is termed a 'bootstrap sample'. Since the Monte Carlo algorithm is being applied to the observed data set, the bootstrap sample generated is equivalent to a random sample drawn with replacement from the actual sample.

Let Θ be the statistic we are interested in (and let the observed value be Θ'). Once again, it can represent any coefficient. Carrying out bootstrapping is a three stage process. Firstly, using the mechanism described above, a large number (B) of bootstrap samples are constructed, which we can label $\mathbf{y}^*(1)$, $\mathbf{y}^*(2), \ldots, \mathbf{y}^*(B)$. The symbol * is used to indicate data arising from a bootstrap sample. Secondly, for each bootstrap sample, $\mathbf{y}^*(b)$, the statistic of interest is evaluated, and we will label it $\Theta'^*(b) = \Theta'(\mathbf{y}^*(b))$

Finally, the sample standard deviation is calculated for the bootstrap values of the statistic of interest. The calculation is outlined below:

$$\hat{\sigma}_B = \left(\frac{\overset{B}{\Sigma} \{\Theta'^*(b) - \Theta'^*(\cdot)\}^2}{[B-1]} \right)^{1/2}$$

Where:

$$\Theta'^*(\cdot) = \overset{B}{\underset{b=1}{\Sigma}} [\Theta'^*(b)]/B$$

It can be seen that the bootstrap approach involves a similar process to jackknife, using the change in the statistic of interest with changes in the bootstrap sample to construct the standard error estimate. Because B tends to be relatively large, from 50 to 200, bootstrapping is more expensive in terms of computational effort, but is considered by statisticians to be a superior method.

The U method

Another method of sample reuse is the U method, which is particularly used with discriminant analysis (Lachenbruch and Mickey, 1968). It uses the same holdout approach as jackknifing, but concentrates on assessing unbiased classification accuracy. From a sample of k cases one case is omitted and the remaining $k-1$ cases used to construct a discriminant function. The omitted case is classified on the basis of that discriminant function, and the overall unbiased classification accuracy is assessed by summing across all *k* cases.

The importance attached to classification accuracy in discriminant analysis means that the U method is a valuable technique for those with small samples. The well documented bias in classification accuracy means that validation of any discriminant analysis is an important step, and the use of the U method avoids the sample reducing effects of sample splitting.

Comparison of jackknife and bootstrap

Comparing the bootstrap and jackknife, we can see that both focus on re-using data to provide an estimate of how the observed value of the statistic changes with changing sample. Both examine the variation in values as the sample changes; however the jackknife generates a new coefficient (the jackknife estimate), which has a standard error associated with it. The bootstrap, by contrast, directly calculates a standard error associated with the full sample estimate.

Although ideal for small sample work, note that both techniques are sensitive to the ratio of sample size to variable numbers (guidelines for minimum ratios are normally given as 3 to 5). Given the issues discussed earlier in the paper, this is understandable. By re-using the sample, both techniques place emphasis on how well individual cases represent the sample as a whole. Outliers will inflate the standard error estimates, and low ratios of cases to variables mean that we are trying to predict coefficients from relatively little information, which is also likely to inflate standard error. The problem is therefore the same as was outlined in the general discussion of regression type techniques. This sensitivity means that researchers should not use the bootstrap or the jackknife to carry out or validate a regression using large numbers of variables for the size of the sample.

Given the greater complexity of the bootstrap, a question must be 'is it better than the jackknife?'. Statisticians seem to be largely in favour of the bootstrap as the better techniques (see Efron, 1981), but acknowledge the need for substantially greater computing power. Both techniques are a major improvement on conventional cross-validation techniques, and are powerful tools for validating small sample data that would otherwise prove impossible to validate. One drawback is that the major computing packages for quantitative analysis do not currently have bootstrap and jackknife as program options (the exception is Dixon, 1990). Using these techniques therefore requires some effort on the part of the researcher, e.g. exporting data into spreadsheets, which makes the simpler jackknife more attractive than bootstrap.

A final point is that researchers cannot use sample re-use validation in conjunction with stepwise variable selection. The comparison between estimates of parameters is only valid when the same function is being estimated. Hence, for regression or for regression type analysis, variable entry must be direct, and so researchers must select the variables to include prior to running the analysis. However, since coefficient stability is not known before validation is carried out, it is not possible to predict accurately the best set of variables to include. The process of variable selection is therefore likely to involve some experiment (see Speed and Smith, 1991 for an example of such an approach).

Conclusions

This paper has sought to identify the major problems confronting researchers working with small samples. It has focused on the most popular techniques amongst marketing researchers, the regression type techniques. The paper has concentrated on the two areas where small sample size can have a major impact, factors affecting the effectiveness of the techniques and techniques for validating models. Figure 11.2 summarizes the main points raised in the paper.

The paper has pointed out that the main danger encountered using small samples is over-conservative testing. Researchers should therefore expect low levels of significance in relationships under examination, rather than spurious significance in relationships. It is the conclusion of this paper that steps can be taken to minimize this impact of small sample size. Transformation of data, selection of variables and monitoring cases to variable ratios are all useful tools in ensuring the effectiveness of regression type techniques. The sample reuse validation techniques, although demanding in terms of computational power, are ideal for validation when split half samples are not practical. Judicious use of these techniques can ensure the maximum effectiveness of regression type techniques.

It should be noted that using these techniques makes the analysis process considerably more subjective. The researcher must exercise judgement in variable selection and deletion, for instance, and alternative combinations should always be tried. The investigation of relationships becomes more experimental than in standard quantitative analysis, with different combinations of variables being included. The researcher must seek out the method of analysis that yields the best results. The ability to defend the results of such experimentation come from a thorough understanding of the issues and processes involved, and readers are encouraged further to investigate issues affecting their work.

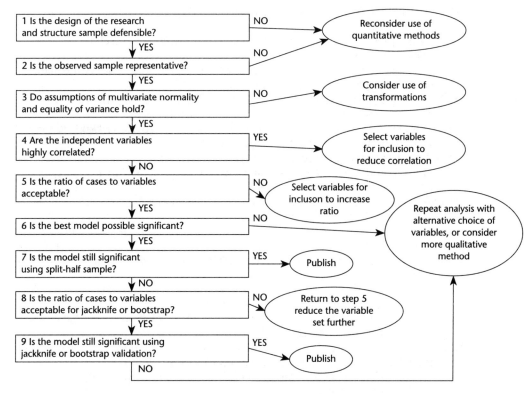

FIGURE 11.2 Guidelines for using small samples

References

Armstrong, J.S. (1975), Monetary incentives in mail surveys, *Public Opinion Quarterly* **39** pp. 111–16

Barnett, V. and Lewis, T. (1984), *Outliers in Statistical Data*, Second edition, New York: Wiley

Belsley, D.A., Kuh, E. and Welsh, R.E. (1980), *Regression Diagnostics – Identifying Influential Data and Sources of Collinearity*, New York: John Wiley and Sons

Box, G.E.P. and Cox, D.R. (1964), An analysis of transformations, *Journal of the Royal Statistical Society* B (**26**) pp. 211–43

Calantone, R. and Sawyer, A.G. (1978), The stability of benefit segments, *Journal of Marketing Research* **XV** pp. 395–404

Cooil, B., Winer, R.S. and Rados, D.L. (1987), Cross validation for prediction, *Journal of Marketing Research*, **XXIV** pp. 271–9

Cowan, C.D. (1990), Why statisticians need their probabilities – getting into regression, *Marketing Research*, December pp. 65–8

Cowan, C.D. (1991), Extensions to regression theory: parallel developments and other techniques, *Marketing Research* March pp. 67–71

Crask, M.R. and Perreault, W.D. (1977), Validation of discriminant analysis in marketing research, *Journal of Marketing Research* **XIV** pp. 60–8

Diaconis, P. and Efron, B. (1983), Computer intensive methods, *Scientific American*, **248**, pp. 116–130

Dixon, W.J. (1990), *BMDP – Biomedical Computer Programs*, Los Angeles: University of California Press

Dorans, N.J. and Drasgow, F. (1980), A note on cross-validating prediction equations, *Journal of Applied Psychology* **65** pp. 728–9

Efron, B. (1981), Non-parametric estimates of standard error: the jackknife, the bootstrap and other resampling methods *Biometrika* **68** pp. 589–99

Efron, B. and Gong, G. (1983), A leisurely look at the bootstrap, the jackknife and cross-validation, *American Statistician* **9** pp. 586–96

Efron, B. and Tibshirani, R. (1986), Bootstrap methods for standard errors, confidence intervals and other measures of statistical accuracy, *Statistical Science* 1/1 pp. 54–77

Fenwick, I. (1979), Techniques in marketing management: the jackknife, *Journal of Marketing Research*, **XXVI** pp. 410–14

Frank, R.A., Massy, W.F. and Morrison, D.G. (1965), Bias in multiple discriminant analysis, *Journal of Marketing Research* **II** pp. 250–8

Gorsuch R.L. (1983), *Factor Analysis* Second edition, Lawrence Erlbaum Associates Ltd: USA

Green, P.E., Tull, D.S. and Albaum, G. (1988), *Research for Marketing Decisions*, Fifth edition, Hemel Hempstead: Prentice-Hall International

Hartigan, J.A. (1969), Using subsample values as typical values *Journal of the American Statistical Association* **64** pp. 1303–17

Homburg, Christian (1991), Cross-validation and information criteria in causal modeling, *Journal of Marketing Research* **XXVIII** pp. 137–44

Huberty, C.J. (1984), Issues in the use and interpretation of discriminant analysis, *Psychological Bulletin* **95** pp. 156–71

Huberty, C.J., Wisenbaker, J.W. and Smith. J.C. (1987), Issues in the use and interpretation of discriminant analysis, *Multivariate s Behavioural Research*, July 1987, **22** pp. 307–29

Johnson, N. and Wichern, D. (1982), *Applied Multivariate Statistical Analysis*, Englewood Cliffs NJ: Prentice-Hall

Klecka, W.R. (1980), 'Discriminant analysis' Sage University Paper Series on Quantitative Applications in the Social Sciences no. 07–019 Beverly Hills and London: Sage Publications

Krishnamurthi, L. and Rangaswamy, A. (1987), The equity estimator for marketing research, *Marketing Science* **6** (Fall) pp. 226–57

Lachenbruch, P.A. (1975), *Discriminant Analysis*, New York: Hafner

Lachenbruch, P.A. and Mickey, M.R. (1968), Estimation of error rates in discriminant analysis, *Technometrics* **10** pp. 1–11

Lambert, Z.V. and Durand, R.M. (1975), Some precautions in using canonical analysis, *Journal of Marketing Research* **XII** pp. 468–75

Leeflang, P.S.H. (1974), *Mathematical Models in Marketing, A Survey, the Stage of Development, some Extensions and Applications*, Leiden: HE Steufert Kroese BV

Mason, C.H. and Perreault, W.D. (1991), Collinearity, power and interpretation of multiple regression analysis, *Journal of Marketing Research* **XXVIII** pp. 268–80

Montgomery, D.B. (1975), New product distribution: an analysis of supermarket buyer decisions, *Journal of Marketing Research* **XII** pp. 255–64

Morrison, D.G. (1969), On the interpretation of discriminant analysis, *Journal of Marketing Research* **VI** pp. 156–63

Moser, C.A. and Kalton, G. (1975), *Survey Methods in Social Investigation*, Second edition, London: Heineman Education Books

Mosier, C.I. (1951), Problems and designs of cross validation, *Education and Psychological Measurement* **11** Spring pp. 5–11

Mosteller, F., and Tukey, J.W. (1977), *Data Analysis and Regression*, Reading, MA: Addison-Wesley

Shao, J., and Wu, C.F.J. (1989), A general theory for jackknife variance estimation, *Annals of Statistics* 17/3 pp. 1176–97

Speed, R.J., and Smith, I.G. (1991), Performance measurement by expert assessment in the UK retail financial services industry, *Proceedings of the 20th European Marketing Academy Conference*, Michael Smurfit Graduate School of Business, University College Dublin pp. 1526–44

Stewart, G. (1987), Collinearity and least squares regression, *Statistical Science* pp. 68–100

Tukey, J.W. (1958), Bias and confidence in not-quite large samples, *Annals of Mathematical Statistics* **29** p. 614

Wu, C.F.J. (1986), Jackknife, bootstrap and other resampling methods for regression, *Annals of Statistics* 14/4 pp. 1261–94

■ ☐ ▨ ■ 12

Modelling with LISREL: A Guide for the Uninitiated

A. Diamantopoulos

During the last decade, structural equation models with unobservable variables and measurement error have been increasingly applied in the marketing discipline. By far, the most widely used approach has been the covariance structure modelling framework implemented through the LISREL computer program. However, for many marketing academics LISREL modelling is still something of a mystery. This appears to be partly due to the mathematical complexity of most methodological articles dealing with the LISREL model and partly due to the not particularly user friendly documentation accompanying the program. Against this background, the present paper provides a non-technical introduction into the basic concepts and issues of LISREL modelling, bearing the needs of a potential user in mind. To this end, an eight-step procedure is followed, encompassing all stages associated with the formulation and testing of a set of hypotheses using the LISREL approach. An illustrative model is used as an example throughout the discussion and an effort is made to draw attention to the potential limitations/problems associated with the approach.

Introduction

LISREL stands for LInear Structural RELationships and, strictly speaking, is a computer program for covariance structure analysis. However, originally introduced in 1972 (Jöreskog and van Thillo, 1972) and now in its 8th release, the LISREL program 'has played such a vital role in the acceptance and application of the covariance structure model that such models are often referred to as 'LISREL models' (Long, 1983a). Although LISREL is undoubtedly the market leader in the field, a number of competing software packages have become available in recent years, such as MILS (Schoenberg, 1982), COSAN (Fraser, 1980), EQS (Bentler, 1985), EzPATH (Steiger, 1989) and LISCOMP (Muthén, 1987). In addition, the use of the partial least squares (PLS) modelling approach, as implemented by the LVPLS program (Lohmöller, 1984), has also been increasing.

Covariance structure analysis (and, thus, LISREL modelling) is a 'second generation' multivariate technique (Fornell, 1987) combining methodological contributions from two disciplines: the (confirmatory) factor analysis model from psychometric theory and the structural equations model typically associated with econometrics (Goldberger, 1971). Its aim is to explain the structure or pattern among a set of latent (i.e. unobserved or theoretical) variables, each measured by one or more manifest (i.e. observed or empirical) and typically fallible indicators. Thus there are two parts to a covariance structure model: the measurement part describes how each of the latent variables is operationalized via the manifest variables and provides information about the validities and reliabilities of the latter. The structural part specifies the relationships between the latent variables themselves (reflecting substantive hypotheses based on theoretical considerations) and the amount of unexplained variance. The analysis is predominantly confirmatory in nature, that is, it seeks to determine the extent to which the postulated structure (as described by the linkages among the latent variables and among the latter and their indicators) is actually consistent with the empirical data at hand. This is done by computing the covariance matrix implied by the specified model and comparing it to the (actual) covariance matrix based on the empirical data.

In the literature, covariance structure analysis is also commonly referred to as 'structural modelling with unobservables', 'linear structural relations', 'latent variable equation systems', 'moments structure models', 'latent variable structural equation modelling', 'linear structural equation modelling' and, perhaps most often, as 'causal modelling with unobservables'. Differences in terminology notwithstanding, structural equation models have been used extensively in a variety of disciplines, including psychology, sociology, economics and marketing (for respective literature reviews see Bentler, 1980; Bielby and Hauser, 1977; Goldberger, 1972; and Förster *et al.*, 1984) and applied to both survey and experimental data based on cross-sectional as well as longitudinal research designs.

Within the marketing discipline, LISREL models can be found in a wide variety of contexts, including consumer behaviour (e.g. Oliver and Swan, 1989), organizational buying behaviour (e.g. Michaels *et al.*, 1987), channel management (e.g. Schul and Babakus, 1988), product policy (e.g. DeBrentani and Droge, 1988), pricing strategy (e.g. Walters and MacKenzie, 1988), advertising (e.g. MacKenzie and Lutz, 1989), salesforce management (e.g. Dubinski *et al.*, 1986), retailing (e.g. Good *et al.*, 1988), international marketing (e.g. Han, 1988) and services marketing (e.g. Arora and Cavusgil, 1985). Bagozzi (1977) pioneered the use of structural equations models with LISREL in marketing in his classic JMR article.

In contrast to the US where the use of LISREL modelling is widespread, in the UK it seems to have found very little acceptance among researchers. Given the somewhat weaker mathematical/statistical training of UK marketing academics, for many, LISREL related papers seem to range from 'heavy-going' to 'completely incomprehensible', a situation which is not helped by the LISREL manual itself. As anyone who has read it (and lived to tell about it) will readily testify, the authors' claim that it was '*not* written for mathematical statisticians' (Jöreskog and Sörbom, 1989a) is not the most accurate of statements, also reflected in the fact that entire books have been written in recent years on how to use LISREL (Hayduk, 1987; Pfeifer and Schmidt, 1987). A second (not entirely unrelated) reason appears to be the reluctance of researchers to persevere with the program, having had encountered initial problems in applying it to their data; when a statement such as 'LISREL is not an easy program to learn how to use . . . When I run LISREL I presume I have made an error. I check and recheck my results' is made by the author of a well known text on causal modelling (Kenny, 1979), the potential difficulties likely to be encountered by mere mortals become very clear.

Against this background, the purpose of the present paper is threefold. First, to discuss the major steps associated with the formulation and testing of a causal model using the LISREL framework. Second, to illustrate the application of the LISREL approach with a concrete example. Third, to sensitize the reader against 'mechanically' fitting LISREL models and to encourage a critical attitude when applying the technique.

In terms of statistical/mathematical background, it is assumed that the reader is familiar with the basic principles of confirmatory factor analysis (as described in, for example, Long, 1983b) and causal models with observed variables (as described in, for example, Duncan, 1975 or Asher, 1985); these are really minimum prerequisites for effectively using LISREL, as is a grasp of matrix algebra (the reason for the latter will become clear later). Considerable patience also helps.

Stages in LISREL modelling: an overview

Judging from the author's own experience, the best way of getting to know LISREL is to decompose the overall modelling task into more or less distinct components; while the latter are obviously interlinked, focusing on one component at a time is much less overwhelming than trying to absorb everything at once. Figure 12.1 shows an eight-step procedure associated with the formulation and testing of a comprehensive LISREL model.

Step 1 focuses on the development of the substantive hypotheses linking the constructs of interest (i.e. the latent variables) and the operationalization of the latter in terms of empirical indicators (i.e. the manifest variables). Step 2 involves the construction of a path diagram in which a visual representation of the hypotheses and measurement scheme is given, according to certain conventions; while this step can be omitted, for reasons that will become clear later, it is strongly recommended that a path diagram is always produced. Step 3 involves the formal specification of the model and thus describes the nature and number of parameters to be estimated. Step 4 addresses the issue of identification, that is, it ascertains the extent to which the information

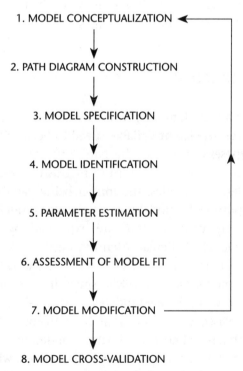

FIGURE 12.1 LISREL modelling sequence

provided by the data is indeed sufficient to enable parameter estimation. Assuming that the model is identified, then one can proceed with parameter estimation in Step 5. Step 6 involves the assessment of model fit using a variety of fit measures; both the quality of the measurement model and the soundness of the structural model in terms of supporting the postulated hypotheses must be evaluated at this stage. Step 7 considers whether modifications to the model may be called for in the light of the results obtained at the previous stage. The final step, involves the cross-validation of the model with another data set; the same data set should not be used both for model development and model testing purposes.

In the sections that follow, each of the eight steps in Figure 12.1 will be expanded using a hypothetical model for illustration purposes and blending the discussion with excerpts from LISREL output. The model used is 'typical' of modelling causal applications based on survey data. (The model used as an example has been deliberately selected to provide an initial bad fit to illustrate the various concepts involved, and its sole purpose is expository.) However, LISREL can also be applied to experimental designs as well as pure measurement models; for a discussion of the former in a marketing context, the reader is referred to Bagozzi (1977), Bagozzi and Yi (1989) and Bagozzi *et al.* (1991), while the review papers by Darden *et al.* (1984) and Steenkamp and van Trijp (1991) provide good expositions of how LISREL can be applied to measurement models of marketing constructs.

Model conceptualization

In conceptualizing a LISREL model, two aspects need to be considered. First, the linkages between the latent variables need to be specified, reflecting the substantive hypotheses of interest. This part of the conceptualization relates to the structural model. Here, one must distinguish between the exogenous and endogenous latent variables, the former being variables which are *not* explained by the postulated model (i.e. act always as independent variables) and the latter being variables that are explained by the relationships contained in the model. Particular attention needs to be paid at this stage to make sure that no important exogenous and/or endogenous variables are omitted from the model (James, 1980), since 'if an omitted independent variable is correlated with included independent variables, one's estimates of parameters will be biased and inconsistent. If, on the other hand, the omitted independent variable is not correlated with included independent variables, the parameter estimates for causal paths, while unbiased, will have an upward bias on their variances' (Bagozzi, 1980, p.97). Omission of important variables is a major cause of what is known as specification error, i.e. a lack of correspondence between the model under study and the 'true' model in the population. Other causes of model misspecification are selecting the incorrect form of the mathematical relationship (covariance structure modelling assumes linear functions of relationships); misrepresentation (or lack of modelling) of error terms; inclusion of irrelevant variables; and omission of relevant linkages or inclusion of irrelevant ones. These problems reemphasize the importance of theory when developing a LISREL model to minimize specification errors.

The second part of the conceptualization process relates to the measurement model and describes the way in which the latent variables are operationalized (i.e. represented by manifest variables). In covariance structure modelling, the manifest variables are reflective indicators, that is, it is assumed that one (or, sometimes, more) underlying unobservable constructs 'cause' the observed variables (Bagozzi and Fornell, 1982). Since, in most instances, a single indicator is likely to be inadequate in terms of capturing the construct involved, one should opt for multiple indicators when operationalizing the latent variables (Howell, 1987). Ideally, one would like a variety of quite distinct observable measures (possibly also reflecting different data collection methods) to ensure a well rounded operationalization of each construct. Regarding the number of variables to be included in a LISREL model, this, of course, depends on the area of substantive interest; however, it has been suggested by Bentler and Chou (1987) that in areas where knowledge is limited, models should contain at most 20 variables (i.e. 5–6 constructs each measured by 3–4 indicators).

For illustration purposes, it is assumed that a thorough literature search has been undertaken and the following hypothetical structural model has been specified based upon theoretical considerations ('generic' terminology is used for variable names to facilitate exposition and subsequent interpretation of LISREL output): there are two endogenous variables ETA-1 (η_1) and ETA-2 (η_2) which are hypothesized to be linked in a recursive fashion with ETA-1 and expected to have a positive influence on ETA-2. 4. A recursive system implies that there are no feedback loops or reciprocal (i.e. two-way) linkages and, thus, assumes one-way causation; moreover, error terms are assumed to be independent of each other and all exogenous variables (Darden, 1983). In nonrecursive models, mutual linkages are allowed (i.e. two endogenous variables can be both causes and effects of each other). The reader wishing to pursue nonrecursive modelling with LISREL would do well to first consult Berry (1984).

In addition, there are three intercorrelated exogenous variables KSI-1 (ξ_1), KSI-2 (ξ_2) and KSI-3 (ξ_3) which are hypothesized to impact on ETA-1 and ETA-2 as follows: KSI-1 has a positive effect on ETA-1 and a negative effect on ETA-2; KSI-2 has a negative effect on ETA-2; and KSI-3 has a positive effect on ETA-2; according to the postulated theory, neither KSI-2 nor KSI-3 are expected to impact on ETA 1.

With regard to the measurement model, each of the latent variables is assumed to be operationalized by means of two empirical indicators, as follows: X-1 and X-2 are indicators of KSI-1; X-3 and X-4 are indicators of KSI-2; X-5 and X-6 are indicators of KSI-3; Y-1 and Y-2 are indicators of ETA-1; and Y-3 and Y-4 are indicators of ETA-2. All indicators are measured at, at least, interval level and a covariance matrix based upon a sample of 100 observations is used as input.

While LISREL has facilities for dealing with ordinal variables via its preprocessor PRELIS (Jöreskog and Sörbom, 1988) or through applying rescaling algorithms (Yadar, 1992) and can accept data in a variety of forms (e.g. correlation matrices), these options are better handled by the more familiar user; moreover, 'the general rule is that the covariance matrix should be analyzed' (Jöreskog and Sörbom, 1989a).

Path diagram construction

Following the conceptualization of the model, the next step is to construct a path diagram, i.e. a graphical representation of how the various elements of the model relate to one another. While a path diagram is not a formal requirement for LISREL modelling, the benefits it offers are far too important to ignore. Specifically, the system of hypotheses contained in the model is much more easily comprehended in visual form than in either verbal or mathematical terms. A path diagram may also help improve the conceptualization of the model by drawing attention to omitted links and/or excluded variables, thus reducing the chances for specification error. Finally, with models characterized by a large number of variables interconnected by complex linkages, a path diagram is invaluable in helping detect mistakes in the computer program instructions.

Figure 12.2 shows the path diagram for the illustrative model developed in the previous section, based upon conventional notation and standard construction rules (see Appendix 12.1); it can be seen that the entire model is composed of two confirmatory factor models (one each for the latent exogenous and endogenous variables respectively) linked by a structural equations model.

Consistent with the model's conceptualization, no paths are included between KSI-2 and KSI-3 and ETA-1. The remaining structural paths reflect

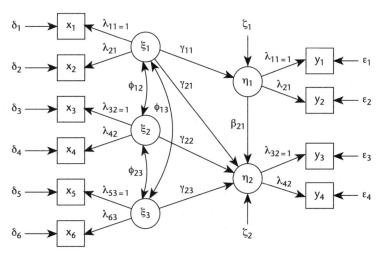

FIGURE 12.2 Path diagram for illustrative model

the substantive hypotheses (thus, it is expected that $\beta_{21}>0$, $\gamma_{11}>0$, $\gamma_{21}<0$, $\gamma_{22}<0$ and $\gamma_{23}>0$); the ζs are known as 'errors in equations' and reflect random disturbances (i.e. they indicate that the endogenous variables are not perfectly explained by the independent variables). With regards to the measurement, this is described by the λs which indicate the relationships between the five latent variables and their ten indicators, the δs and εs are known as 'errors in measurement' and reflect measurement error in the indicators for exogenous and endogenous variables respectively. Note that, for each latent variable, one of the λs has been set equal to 1 in order to fix the unit of measurement in relation to an observed indicator (because, being unobserved, latent variables have no definite scale).Finally, the correlations among the latent exogeneous variables (ϕ_{ij}, i, j = 1, 2, 3, i $\neq$ j) are reflected in the curved two-way arrows. Note that as the ϕs do not represent causal linkages, but merely covariances, their subscripts can be interchanged, i.e. $\phi_{ij} = \phi_{ji}$.

Model specification

The relationships shown in the path diagram must now be translated into a linear equations system so that the formal specification of the model can be obtained. Based upon the rules described in Appendix 12.2, the following sets of equations provide the mathematical specification of the model depicted in Figure 12.2.

Structural equations:

$$\eta_1 = \gamma_{11}\xi_1 + \zeta_1 \tag{1}$$

$$\eta_2 = \beta_{21}\eta_1 + \gamma_{21}\xi_1 + \gamma_{22}\xi_2 + \gamma_{23}\xi_3 + \zeta_2 \tag{2}$$

Measurement equations for the endogenous variables:

$$y_1 = \eta_1 + \varepsilon_1 \tag{3}$$

$$y_2 = \lambda_{21}\eta_1 + \varepsilon_2 \tag{4}$$

$$y_3 = \eta_2 + \varepsilon_3 \tag{5}$$

$$y_4 = \lambda_{42}\eta_2 + \varepsilon_4 \tag{6}$$

Measurement equations for the exogenous variables:

$$x_1 = \xi_1 + \delta_1 \tag{7}$$

$$x_2 = \lambda_{21}\xi_1 + \delta_2 \tag{8}$$

$$x_3 = \xi_2 + \delta_3 \tag{9}$$

$$x_4 = \lambda_{42}\xi_2 + \delta_4 \tag{10}$$

$$x_5 = \xi_3 + \delta_5 \tag{11}$$

$$x_6 = \lambda_{63}\xi_3 + \delta_6 \tag{12}$$

Since model specification in LISREL is done by means of parameter matrices (see below), equations (1)–(12) must be converted into matrix form (this is where brushing-up on matrix algebra can make life much easier); the relevant matrix equations are:

Structural model

$$\begin{bmatrix} \eta_1 \\ \eta_2 \end{bmatrix} = \begin{bmatrix} 0 & 0 \\ \beta_{21} & 0 \end{bmatrix} \begin{bmatrix} \eta_1 \\ \eta_2 \end{bmatrix} + \begin{bmatrix} \gamma_{11} & 0 & 0 \\ \gamma_{21} & \gamma_{22} & \gamma_{23} \end{bmatrix} \begin{bmatrix} \xi_1 \\ \xi_2 \\ \xi_3 \end{bmatrix} + \begin{bmatrix} \zeta_1 \\ \zeta_2 \end{bmatrix}$$

Measurement model for the endogenous variables

$$\begin{bmatrix} y_1 \\ y_2 \\ y_3 \\ y_4 \end{bmatrix} = \begin{bmatrix} 1 & 0 \\ \lambda_{21} & 0 \\ 0 & 1 \\ 0 & \lambda_{42} \end{bmatrix} \begin{bmatrix} \eta_1 \\ \eta_2 \end{bmatrix} + \begin{bmatrix} \varepsilon_1 \\ \varepsilon_2 \\ \varepsilon_3 \\ \varepsilon_4 \end{bmatrix}$$

Measurement model for the exogenous variables

$$\begin{bmatrix} x_1 \\ x_2 \\ x_3 \\ x_4 \\ x_5 \\ x_6 \end{bmatrix} = \begin{bmatrix} 1 & 0 & 0 \\ \lambda_{21} & 0 & 0 \\ 0 & 1 & 0 \\ 0 & \lambda_{42} & 0 \\ 0 & 0 & 1 \\ 0 & 0 & \lambda_{63} \end{bmatrix} \begin{bmatrix} \xi_1 \\ \xi_2 \\ \xi_3 \end{bmatrix} + \begin{bmatrix} \delta_1 \\ \delta_2 \\ \delta_3 \\ \delta_4 \\ \delta_5 \\ \delta_6 \end{bmatrix}$$

In summary notation, the general form of the full LISREL model can be described as follows:

$\eta = B\eta + \Gamma\xi + \zeta$ *(Structural model)*
$y = \Lambda_y\eta + \epsilon$ *(Measurement model for latent endogenous variables)*
$x = \Lambda_x\xi + \delta$ *(Measurement model for latent exogenous variables)*

Note Ethat the mathematical specification of the illustrative model is directly derived from its path diagram. This is reflected in the subscripts of the various path coefficients which correspond directly to the locations (i.e. the row/column positions) of the coefficients in the matrices B, Γ, Λ_y and Λ_x. The absence of a path is indicated by entering zero in the corresponding matrix location, while, for path coefficients fixed *a priori* to a given value (e.g. the λs used to fix the units of the latent variables), the latter are entered directly in the relevant matrices (i.e. the 1s in the Λ_y and Λ_x matrices).

The formal specification of the model must now be translated into LISREL language so that the computer program can be used for estimation purposes. Parameter specification in LISREL is in the form of eight matrices (Table 12.1). Four of these are the coefficient matrices representing the paths in one's model (i.e. B, Γ, Λ_y and Λ_x above), while the other four are simple variance–covariance matrices for the exogenous variables (i.e. the ξs) and the error terms

TABLE 12.1 Parameter matrices of a comprehensive LISREL model

Mathematical Notation	Name	LISREL Notation	Description
Λ_y	LAMBDA-y	LY	a (pxm) matrix containing the coefficients linking the y- to the η-variables
Λ_x	LAMBDA-x	LX	a (qxn) matrix containing the coefficients linking the x- to the ξ-variables
B	BETA	BE	a (mxm) matrix containing the coefficients representing causal links between η-variables
Γ	GAMMA	GA	a (mxn) matrix containing the coefficients representing causal links between ξ- and η-variables
Φ	PHI	PH	a (nxn) matrix containing the covariances between the ξ- variables
Ψ	PSI	PS	a (mxm) matrix containing the covariances between the ζ- variables
Θ_ε	THETA-EPSILON	TE	a (pxp) matrix containing the covariances between the ε-variables
Θ_δ	THETA-DELTA	TD	a (qxq) matrix containing the covariances between the δ-variables

where p, q, m and n is the number of y-, x-, η- and ζ-variables respectively (i.e. the ζs, ϵs and δs). Depending upon the specification of these matrices, different types of models can be estimated with the LISREL program. For example, if $\mathbf{B} = 0$, $\mathbf{\Gamma} = 0$, $\mathbf{\Psi} = 0$, $\mathbf{\Lambda_y} = 0$ and $\mathbf{\Theta_\epsilon} = 0$, then the factor-analytic model results. This is commonly known as 'submodel 1 of the general LISREL model' and involves only the parameter matrices $\mathbf{\Lambda_x}$, $\mathbf{\Phi}$ and $\mathbf{\Theta_\delta}$.

Given a particular model specification, the elements in eight matrices imply a certain covariance matrix $\mathbf{\Sigma}$ (i.e. the model-based covariance matrix); estimation involves fitting $\mathbf{\Sigma}$ to the sample covariance matrix $\mathbf{S}$ (i.e. the covariance matrix based on the empirical data at hand).

The model-based covariance matrix $\mathbf{\Sigma}$ consists of four submatrices containing the variances/covariances between the x- and y-variables, as follows:

$$\mathbf{\Sigma} = \begin{bmatrix} \mathbf{\Sigma_{yy}} & \mathbf{\Sigma_{yx}} \\ \mathbf{\Sigma_{xy}} & \mathbf{\Sigma_{xx}} \end{bmatrix}$$

Each of these submatrices can be expressed in terms of the parameter matrices in Table 12.1 and all eight parameter matrices enter the final expression; while the latter is so complex that it will not be reproduced here (for a derivation, see Long, 1983a), it is important to bear in mind that any changes in the model will result in a modified and, thus, a different fit to the data.

Within the eight parameter matrices described in Table 12.1, a distinction can be drawn between fixed, constrained and free parameters. Fixed parameters are given a certain value *a priori*, so they are not estimated as part of the model; the absence of causal paths (represented by zero values) and assignment of units of measurements to latent variables (represented by λs set equal to 1) are typical examples of fixed parameters. Restricted parameters are estimated by the model but are specified to be equal to another (or more) parameter(s); for example, theory may suggest that two independent variables (e.g. ξ_1 and ξ_2) have the same impact on a dependent variable (e.g. η_1), which could be incorporated in the model by specifying $\gamma_{11} = \gamma_{12}$. Note that, with restricted parameters it is only necessary to actually estimate one of them (as this automatically determines the value of the other parameter). Finally, free parameters are those which have unknown values and which need to be estimated by the program. With LISREL there is also the possibility of specifying entire matrices in a particular way. Thus a matrix can be initially declared as fixed (or free) and then individual parameters may be freed (or fixed) to derive the desired model specification; moreover depending upon the particular matrix under consideration, one can choose a certain form from a number of available options (e.g. symmetric, diagonal, zero, etc).

Table 12.2 shows the LISREL control file for the model depicted in Figure 12.2. The first line is a title line. The second line specifies the data characteristics in terms of number of manifest variables (ten in this instance), sample size (100 in this case) and type of matrix to be analysed (covariance matrix). The third line indicates the form of the data input (a symmetrical covariance matrix) and the file in which it is contained (here DATA.COV). The LA, LE and LK lines simply mean that variable labels for the manifest and latent variables are listed in the next line (here they reflect the variables names used in the conceptualization of the illustrative model). The MO line gives the overall specification of the model by indicating (1) the number of indicators representing latent endogenous and exogenous variables (here 4 and 6 respectively), (2) the number of latent endogenous and exogenous variables (here 2 and 3 respectively), and (3) the overall form of the parameter matrices. With regards to the latter, only specifications departing from the default settings are given. Specifically, given the recursive nature of the model, **B** is specified as a subdiagonal matrix and **Ψ** as a diagonal matrix. (A subdiagonal (or triangular) matrix is a full matrix with zeros in and above the diagonal and all other elements free; in the present example, this specification means that only β_{21} (but not β_{12}) will be estimated. A diagonal matrix has free elements in the diagonal and all other elements equal to zero; in the present example, this specification precludes the intercorrelation of the error terms Z_1 and Z_2 (i.e. $\psi_{12} \neq 0$). For the remaining six matrices, the default settings are used. Specifically, **Γ** is full and free, **Λ_y** and **Λ_x** are full and fixed, **Θ** is symmetrical and free, and **Θ_ε** and **Θ_δ** are both diagonal matrices. There are different default

TABLE 12.2 LISREL control commands for illustrative model

Illustrative LISREL model for *JMM* special issue
DA NI = 10 NO = 100 MA = CM
CM SY FI = DATA.COV
LA
Y–1 Y–2 Y–3 Y–4 X–1 X–2 X–3 X–4 X–5 X–6
MO NY = 4 NX = 6 NE = 2 NK = 3 BE = SD PS = DI
FR LY(2,1) LY(4,2) LX(2,1) LX(4,2) LX(6,3)
FI GA(1,3) GA(1,2)
VA 1 LY(1,1) LY(3,2) LX(1,1) LX(3,2) LX(5,3)
LE
ETA-1 ETA-2
LK
KSI–1 KSI–2 KSI–3
OU ME = ML SE TV RS MI SS SC

---

modes in LISREL regarding which parameter matrices are fixed and which free and the same holds for the default form of different matrices; for details, see Jöreskog and Sörbom (1989a, 1989b). The next two lines (FR, FI) free (fix) specific elements in the various parameter matrices to reflect the particular specification of the model, while the VA line assigns non-zero values to certain fixed parameters (here values of 1 are given to certain λs to fix the units of the latent variables). The final line controls the output to be produced; as edited portions of this latter will be discussed in later sections, the contents of the OU line can be ignored for the moment.

As a LISREL run based on the commands shown in Table 12.2 will produce more than ten pages of printout, only the key portions of the output will be discussed in this and subsequent sections. Initially, the program reproduces the command file (i.e. Table 12.2) and the matrix to be analysed (i.e. here the covariance matrix contained in file DATA.COV). Next, the parameter specifications are listed (Table 12.3) and these should be immediately inspected against the path diagram and/or matrix equations to make sure that no errors in the intended specification have been made. Each free parameter is numbered sequentially, while fixed parameters are indicated by zeros; constrained parameters, if any, are given the same number. This does not mean that the value of the fixed parameter is necessarily set to zero; for example, as can be seen from Table 12.3, λ_{11} and γ_{12} are both indicated by zeros, although their values have been fixed at 1 and 0 respectively (see matrix equations). Constrained parameters, if any, are given the same number.

In the present example, a total of 28 independent parameters need to be estimated in the model; however, before estimation can proceed, the question of whether there is enough information to estimate the model needs to be addressed. This issue is dealt with in the next section and is *very* important, because 'attempts to estimate models that are not identified result in arbitrary estimates of the parameters and meaningless interpretations' (Long, 1983b).

Model identification

Identification revolves around the question of whether the information provided by the empirical data (e.g. variances and covariances of the observable variables) is actually sufficient to allow for a unique solution of the system of equations containing the model parameters. If a model is not identified, then it is not possible to determine the model parameters in a meaningful sense. Since a system of equations can only be solved if the number

TABLE 12.3 Parameter specifications for illustrative model

Illustrative LISREL model for *JMM* special issue

0 PARAMETER SPECIFICATIONS

0   LAMBDA Y

0		ETA–1	ETA–2			
+	Y–1	0	0			
	Y–2	1	0			
	Y–3	0	0			
	Y–4	0	2			

0   LAMBDA X

0		KSI–1	KSI–2	KSI–3		
+	X–1	0	0	0		
	X–2	3	0	0		
	X–3	0	0	0		
	X–4	0	4	0		
	X–5	0	0	0		
	X–6	0	0	5		

0   BETA

0		ETA–1	ETA–2			
+	ETA–1	0	0			
	ETA–2	6	0			

0   GAMMA

0		KSI–1	KSI–2	KSI–3		
+	ETA–1	7	0	0		
	ETA–2	8	9	10		

0   PHI

0		KSI–1	KSI–2	KSI–3		
+	KSI–1	11				
	KSI–2	12	13			
	KSI–3	14	15	16		

0   PSI

0	ETA–1	ETA–2				
+	17	18				

0   THETA EPS

0	Y–1	Y–2	Y–3	Y–4		
+	19	20	21	22		

0   THETA DELTA

0	X–1	X–2	X–3	X–4	X–5	X–6
+	23	24	25	26	27	28

of equations is at least equal to the number of unknowns, to obtain a unique solution of the parameters in a covariance structure model, it is necessary to have at least as many unique (i.e. linearly independent) equations relating observable variables to the model parameters as there are parameters.

Consequently, 'a necessary condition for identification is that the number of independent parameters being estimated is less than or equal to the number of nonredundant elements of **S**, the sample matrix of covariances among the observed variables' (Long, 1983a). Thus if t parameters are to be estimated (N.B. this reflects the number of independent parameters, i.e. constrained parameters should only be counted once), the *minimum* condition for identification is:

$$t \leqslant s$$

where $s = ½ (p+q) (p+q+1)$
        p = number of y-variables
        q = number of x-variables

If $t = s$, the set of parameters is said to be 'just-identified', i.e. there is one and only one estimate for each parameter (because there are as many equations as there are unknowns). If $t<s$, the model is said to be 'overidentified', i.e. it is possible to obtain several estimates of the same parameter (since there are more equations than unknowns). Lastly, if $t>s$, the model is 'unidentified' (or underidentified), i.e. an infinite number of values of the parameter would satisfy the equations (there are more unknowns than equations).

In the case of a just-identified model, all the information available is used in the estimation of parameters and there is no information left that can be used to test the model (i.e. there are zero degrees of freedom). In contrast, with overidentified models there are positive degrees of freedom (equal to $s-t$) and, therefore, one set of estimates can be used to test the model. With unidentified models, although some of the parameters may be identified and could still be estimated, 'it is recommended to deal with such models by adding appropriate conditions so as to make all the parameters identified' (Jöreskog and Sörbom, 1989a). This can be done by, for example, including more manifest variables (i.e. empirical indicators) in the model, setting certain parameters to zero (the most widely used approach), or setting parameters equal to each other (Aaker and Bagozzi, 1979). It goes without saying that 'all these strategies are viable only if they can be justified by substantive theory . . . one must not sloppily add constraints just to achieve identification' (Kenny, 1979).

It should be emphasized that while the condition t ≤ s is necessary for the identification of a LISREL model, it is not a sufficient condition. In fact, 'no easily applicable sufficient, or necessary and sufficient, conditions for the full covariance structure model are available' (Long, 1983a). From the user's perspective, it is fortunate that the LISREL program has a number of diagnostics that provide warnings about identification problems; for example, if any of the parameter matrices in Table 12.1 cannot be inverted (i.e. are not positive-definite) an appropriate message is printed and the same happens if a particular parameter is found to be unidentified. As this section only gives a basic treatment of identification issues, the reader is referred to Bollen (1989) for a more comprehensive description.

In the present example, $t=28$ (see Table 12.3), $p=4$ and $q=6$. The total number of available variances and covariances is ½ $(4+6)$ $(4+6+1)=55$ which is greater than the number of parameters to be estimated; in fact, the illustrative model is overidentified with $55-28=27$ degrees of freedom. During the program run all matrices were found to be positive-definite and no warning messages concerning unidentified parameters were encountered. Thus estimation of the model can proceed.

Parameter estimation

Simply put, the problem of estimation is that of finding values for the eight parameter matrices in Table 12.1 (i.e. Λ_y, Λ_x, $\mathbf{B}$, Γ, Φ, Ψ, Θ_ε and Θ_δ) that are consistent with the constraints imposed on the model (as described by the specification of the various fixed, free and constrained parameters) and 'generate an estimated covariance matrix Σ that is as close as possible to sample covariance matrix $\mathbf{S}$' (Long, 1983a). A function that shows how closely Σ is to $\mathbf{S}$ is known as a fitting function and designated as F($\mathbf{S}$; Σ). Different estimation procedures have different fitting functions and the LISREL 7 program offers a choice among the following: instrumental variables (IV), two-stage least squares (TSLS), unweighted-least squares (ULS), generalized least squares (GLS), maximum likelihood (ML), generally weighted least squares (WLS) and diagonally weighted least squares (DWLS). For details of specific fitting functions, see Jöreskog and Sörbom (1989a) and Bollen (1989) and the references therein.

The most widely used estimation method in LISREL modelling is the maximum likelihood (ML) approach. ML is an iterative procedure whereby final parameter estimates are obtained through a numerical search which successively improves initial estimates (starting values); the latter can be supplied by the user, or automatically through the LISREL program which calculates starting values through two-stage least squares (TSLS). ML provides consistently efficient estimation of parameters under the assumption of multivariate normality and is relatively robust against departures from the latter; moreover, it is accompanied by a whole range of fit statistics which enable one to assess the degree to which one's theoretical model is in fact consistent with the data. For these reasons, ML was used to obtain the parameter estimates of the illustrative model (Table 12.4). To save space, the initial TSLS estimates are not shown (their interpretation is comparable to that of the ML estimates); note that the output has been edited so that only parameter estimates are shown (fit statistics are discussed in the next section).

Looking at Table 12.4, the unstandardized parameter estimates are shown first, for each of the eight matrices describing the model (see Table 12.1 earlier); the covariance matrix of the latent variables is also displayed at this stage (note that the lower-right triangle contains the covariances among the ξ variables, i.e. the elements of the Φ matrix). The interpretation of the unstandardized parameters is straightforward, i.e. they show the resulting change in a dependent variable from a unit change in an independent variable, all other variables being held constant. Unstandardized coefficients are computed with all variables in their original metric and, therefore, describe

> the effect that variables have in an absolute sense, and can be used to compare similar models in other populations. However, these estimates are tied to the measurement units of the variables they represent. Any change in the measurement unit for either independent or dependent variable changes the value and, hence, comparability of parameters across populations.
>
> (Bagozzi, 1977)

With regard to the specific estimates obtained, it can be seen the signs of the parameters in the **B** and **Γ** matrices are consistent with expectations (see section on model conceptualization) and that the exogenous variables are all positively related to one another; moreover, no 'unreasonable' estimates (such as negative variances) are to be seen. Note that for the fixed parameters the preset values are reproduced (e.g. $\gamma_{13}=0$).

Next, the standard errors of the free parameters are displayed; these are correct under assumptions of multivariate normality but otherwise need to be interpreted with caution. Standard errors show how accurately the values of the parameters have been estimated; the smaller their value the better the estimation. In the present case, most standard errors are small relative to the size of the parameter they relate to.

Third, the t-values (i.e. value of the parameter divided by its standard error) associated with the free parameters are listed. With a large sample size, these are approximately normally distributed with a mean of 0 and a variance of 1; despite their designation, they do not follow a t-distribution (Long 1983a, 1983b). T-values between -1.96 and $+1.96$ indicate that the corresponding parameters are not significantly different from zero (at the 5 per cent level). In the example under consideration, the vast majority of the t-values (24 out of

TABLE 12.4 Parameter estimates for illustrative model

Illustrative LISREL model for *JMM* special issue

0 LISREL ESTIMATES (MAXIMUM LIKELIHOOD)

0   LAMBDA Y

	ETA–1	ETA–2
Y–1	1.000	0.000
Y–2	0.922	0.000
Y–3	0.000	1.000
Y–4	0.000	1.139

0   LAMBDA X

	KSI–1	KSI–2	KSI–3
X–1	1.000	0.000	0.000
X–2	1.277	0.000	0.000
X–3	0.000	1.000	0.000
X–4	0.000	1.014	0.000
X–5	0.000	0.000	1.000
X–6	0.000	0.000	1.489

0   BETA

	ETA–1	ETA–2
ETA–1	0.000	0.000
ETA–2	1.017	0.000

0   GAMMA

	KSI–1	KSI–2	KSI–3
ETA–1	0.563	0.000	0.000
ETA–2	−1.160	−0.070	0.933

0   COVARIANCE MATRIX OF ETA AND KSI

	ETA–1	ETA–2	KSI–1	KSI–2	KSI–3
ETA–1	2.952				
ETA–2	2.592	3.696			
KSI–1	0.553	−0.168	0.982		
KSI–2	0.458	−0.473	0.813	1.173	
KSI–3	0.281	0.758	0.498	0.092	1.134

0   PSI

	ETA–1	ETA–2
	2.640	0.125

0   THETA EPS

	Y–1	Y–2	Y–3	Y–4
	0.252	0.119	0.136	0.198

0   THETA DELTA

	X–1	X–2	X–3	X–4	X–5	X–6
	0.381	0.360	0.203	0.536	0.288	0.170

—STANDARD ERRORS

0   LAMBDA Y

	ETA–1	ETA–2
Y–1	0.000	0.000
Y–2	0.036	0.000
Y–3	0.000	0.000
Y–4	0.000	0.034

TABLE 12.4 Parameter estimates for illustrative model (continued)

0	LAMBDA X			
0		KSI–1	KSI–2	KSI–3
+	X–1	0.000	0.000	0.000
	X–2	0.109	0.000	0.000
	X–3	0.000	0.000	0.000
	X–4	0.000	0.101	0.000
	X–5	0.000	0.000	0.000
	X–6	0.000	0.000	0.103

0	BETA		
0		ETA–1	ETA–2
+	ETA–1	0.000	0.000
	ETA–2	0.053	0.000

0	GAMMA			
0		KSI–1	KSI–2	KSI–3
+	ETA–1	0.181	0.000	0.000
	ETA–2	0.245	0.178	0.125

0	PHI			
0		KSI–1	KSI–2	KSI–3
+	KSI–1	0.191		
	KSI–2	0.155	0.209	
	KSI–3	0.132	0.127	0.203

0	PSI		
0		ETA–1	ETA–2
+		0.414	0.087

0	THETA EPS				
0		Y–1	Y–2	Y–3	Y–4
+		0.056	0.040	0.043	0.057

0	THETA DELTA						
0		X–1	X–2	X–3	X–4	X–5	X–6
+		0.069	0.087	0.084	0.111	0.062	0.106

—T-VALUES

0	LAMBDA Y		
0		ETA–1	ETA–2
+	Y–1	0.000	0.000
	Y–2	25.759	0.000
	Y–3	0.000	0.000
	Y–4	0.000	33.752

0	LAMBDA X			
0		KSI–1	KSI–2	KSI–3
+	X–1	0.000	0.000	0.000
	X–2	11.723	0.000	0.000
	X–3	0.000	0.000	0.000
	X–4	0.000	10.011	0.000
	X–5	0.000	0.000	0.000
	X–6	0.000	0.000	14.471

TABLE 12.4 Parameter estimates for illustrative model (continued)

0	BETA					
0		ETA–1	ETA–2			
+	ETA–1	0.000	0.000			
	ETA–2	19.307	0.000			
0	GAMMA					
0		KSI–1	KSI–2	KSI–3		
+	ETA–1	3.106	0.000	0.000		
	ETA–2	−4.730	−0.392	7.437		
0	PHI					
0		KSI–1	KSI–2	KSI–3		
+	KSI–1	5.140				
	KSI–2	5.244	5.616			
	KSI–3	3.769	0.730	5.575		
0	PSI					
0		ETA–1	ETA–2			
+		6.382	1.425			
0	THETA EPS					
0		Y–1	Y–2	Y–3	Y–4	
+		4.545	2.981	3.188	3.491	
0	THETA DELTA					
0		X–1	X–2	X–3	X–4	X–5	X–6
+		5.489	4.128	2.418	4.820	4.643	1.604

—COMPLETELY STANDARDIZED SOLUTION

0	LAMBDA Y		
0		ETA–1	ETA–2
+	Y–1	0.960	0.000
	Y–2	0.977	0.000
	Y–3	0.000	0.982
	Y–4	0.000	0.980
0	LAMBDA X		
0		KSI–1	KSI–2	KSI–3
+	X–1	0.849	0.000	0.000
	X–2	0.904	0.000	0.000
	X–3	0.000	0.923	0.000
	X–4	0.000	0.832	0.000
	X–5	0.000	0.000	0.893
	X–6	0.000	0.000	0.968
0	BETA		
0		ETA–1	ETA–2
+	ETA–1	0.000	0.000
	ETA–2	0.909	0.000
0	GAMMA		
0		KSI–1	KSI–2	KSI–3
+	ETA–1	0.325	0.000	0.000
	ETA–2	−0.598	−0.039	0.516

TABLE 12.4 Parameter estimates for illustrative model (continued)

0	CORRELATION MATRIX OF ETA AND KSI					
0		ETA–1	ETA–2	KSI–1	KSI–2	KSI–3
+	ETA–1	1.000				
	ETA–2	0.785	1.000			
	KSI–1	0.325	−0.088	1.000		
	KSI–2	0.246	−0.227	0.758	1.000	
	KSI–3	0.153	0.370	0.472	0.080	1.000

Reprinted with Permission from *Journal of Marketing Management*. © Westburn Publishers Ltd

28) fall outside this range and, thus, the parameters associated with them can be considered as having non-zero values.

Finally, the standardized parameter estimates are shown (a standardized parameter equals the value of the raw/unstandardized parameter multiplied by the ratio of standard deviations of the independent to the dependent variable), including the correlation matrix among the latent variables (given the space limitations, the error matrices Ψ, Θ_ε and Θ_δ have been excluded). Unreasonable estimates are indicative of fundamental problems with the model and/or data, such as misspecification, strong departures from normality, small sample sizes or empirical underidentification due to strong multi-collinearity (Long, 1983a). The standardized parameter estimates reflect the resulting change in a dependent variable from a standard deviation change in an independent variable. Here, both the latent and the manifest variables have been standardized producing what is known as the completely standardized solution (in the standardized solution only latent variables are standardized and the manifest variables are left in their original metric). Note that

> standardized parameters are appropriate only when one desires to compare the relative contributions of a number of independent variables on the same dependent variable and for the same sample of observations. They are not appropriate and can lead to false inferences when one wishes to make comparisons across populations or samples
>
> (Bagozzi, 1980)

In the current example, the pattern of standardized parameter estimates corresponds closely to that of the unstandardized estimates discussed earlier and, again, no 'improper' parameter values (e.g. correlations greater than unity) are encountered. One additional benefit is that the relationships between the latent variables are now much easier to interpret as they are cast in terms of correlations rather than covariances.

Assessment of model fit

In assessing model fit, attention needs to be paid both to the measurement and the structural parts of the model. Whether this should be done simultaneously or sequentially is still a point of debate in the literature. The majority view seems to be that the measurement model and the substantive (structural) model should be evaluated simultaneously (Fornell, 1987), however, it has been argued that

> proper specification of the measurement model is necessary before meaning can be attached to the analysis of the structural model. That is, good measurement of the latent variables is prerequisite to the analysis of the causal relations among the latent variables
>
> (Anderson and Gerbing, 1982)

While this stepwise approach is not without merits (see Anderson and Gerbing, 1988; Gerbing and Anderson, 1988), for present purposes, the conventional way of assessing model fit will be followed, i.e. on the basis of a single LISREL run incorporating both the measurement and structural components of the illustrative model.

Table 12.5 shows the typical indicators in the LISREL output that, together with the information on the parameter estimates (see previous section) and examination of residuals (see below) can be used to assess the extent to which the specified model fits the data.

TABLE 12.5 Measures of fit for illustrative model

Illustrative LISREL model for *JMM* special issue

0	SQUARED MULTIPLE CORRELATIONS FOR Y-VARIABLES				
0	Y–1	Y–2	Y–3	Y–4	
+	0.921	0.955	0.965	0.960	
0	TOTAL COEFFICIENT OF DETERMINATION FOR Y-VARIABLES IS 0.999				
0	SQUARED MULTIPLE CORRELATIONS FOR X-VARIABLES				

0	X–1	X–2	X–3	X–4	X–5	X–6
+	0.720	0.817	0.853	0.692	0.797	0.936

0	TOTAL COEFFICIENT OF DETERMINATION FOR X-VARIABLES IS 0.998
0	SQUARED MULTIPLE CORRELATIONS FOR STRUCTURAL EQUATIONS

0	ETA–1	ETA–2
+	0.105	0.966

0	TOTAL COEFFICIENT OF DETERMINATION FOR STRUCTURAL EQUATIONS IS 0.921
0	CHI SQUARE WITH 27 DEGREES OF FREEDOM = 48.95 (P = 0.006)
0	GOODNESS OF FIT INDEX = 0.924
	ADJUSTED GOODNESS OF FIT INDEX = 0.845
	ROOT MEAN SQUARE RESIDUAL = 0.444

Regarding the measurement models for the latent endogenous and exogenous variables respectively, the squared multiple correlations for the y- and x-variables indicate the extent to which the individual manifest variables are free from measurement error. They therefore represent the reliabilities (convergent validities) of the measures. These coefficients lie between 0 and 1 (the closer to 1, the better the variable concerned acts as an indicator of the latent construct). In the present case they are all high, which provides evidence that none of the measures used to operationalize the latent variables is a poor indicator. The coefficient of determination for the y- and x-variables indicates how well the manifest variables as a group serve as measures for the latent endogenous and exogenous variables respectively; again, the closer to 1, the better. Here, the relevant values are very close to unity, which indicates that, collectively, the chosen indicators do a good job of capturing both the endogenous and exogenous constructs. Although not provided by the LISREL program and not considered here, a number of additional statistics can be computed to evaluate the overall quality of the measurement part of the overall model; for relevant discussions and formulae see Fornell and Larcker (1981a, 1981b), Anderson and Gerbing (1982), Hunter and Gerbing (1982), Danes and Mann (1984) and Gerbing and Anderson (1988).

Shifting attention to the structural model, the squared multiple correlations for structural equations indicate the amount of variance in each endogenous latent variable accounted for by the independent variables in the relevant structural equation; the total coefficient of determination, on the other hand, shows the strength of the relationships for all structural relationships taken together. In this context, it can be seen that, while the total coefficient of determination is very high in the present case, this is largely attributable to the high squared multiple correlation (0.966) for the ETA–2 variable; in contrast, only a small proportion of the variance in ETA–1 (0.105) is explained by the independent variable which impacts on it (i.e. by KSI–1).

The chi-square value, goodness of fit index (raw and adjusted) and the root mean square residual provide information on the extent to which the model as a whole provides an acceptable fit to the data. These statistics are known as measures of overall fit and, therefore,

> do not express the quality of the model judged by any internal or external criteria . . . Furthermore, if any of the overall measures indicate that the model does not fit the data well, it does not tell what is wrong with the model or which part of the model is wrong
> (Jöreskog and Sörbom, 1989a)

Under assumptions of multivariate normality, a sufficiently large sample size and a covariance matrix as input, the chi-square statistic tests 'the hypothesis H_0 that the observed covariance matrix was generated by the hypothesized model against the alternative hypothesis H_1 that the covariance matrix is an unrestricted matrix' (Long 1983a). The relevant degrees of freedom are $\frac{1}{2}(p+q)$ $(p+q+1)-t$, where $p+q$ = number of manifest variables and t = number of independent parameters to be estimated (see also section on Model identification above). Rejection of the null hypothesis implies that the model-based covariance matrix Σ does not adequately reproduce the observed (i.e. sample-based) covariance matrix **S**. However

> although the χ^2 measure may be viewed theoretically as a test statistic for testing the hypothesis that Σ is of the form implied by the model against the alternative that Σ is unconstrained . . . it must be emphasized that such a use of χ^2 is not valid in most applications.
>
> (Jöreskog and Sörbom, 1989b)

Reasons for this include the sensitivity of the chi-square statistic to departures from mutivariate normality, sample size and problems related to the power of the test, given its 'reverse-testing' logic (i.e. one looks for a non-significant chi-square to support one's model). Thus, chi-square values should be interpreted with caution and used

> as an indicator of how well the model reproduces the observed covariance matrix **S**, rather than as a formal test of a hypothesis. A large value of χ^2 indicates a poor reproduction of **S** and a small value indicates a good reproduction.
>
> (Long, 1983b)

This interpretation is particularly appropriate when the model under investigation is only tentative and the key concern is fitting the model to the data, assessing whether the fit is adequate, and perhaps modifying the model to improve the fit (Jöreskog and Sörbom, 1989a, 1989b). With specific reference to Table 12.5, the chi-square value is high and significant, implying that, on the whole, the model does not fit the data well; this view is supported by the other fit criteria elaborated below.

The goodness of fit index (GFI) is an indicator of 'the relative amount of variances and covariances jointly accounted for by the model' (Jöreskog and Sörbom, 1982); it thus shows how closely the proposed model comes to perfectly reproducing the observed covariance matrix. The adjusted goodness of fit index (AGFI) is simply the GFI adjusted for the degrees of freedom in the model. Both these indices take values between 0 and 1 and the closer to unity, the better the model fit. In the present case, GFI = 0.924 but AGFI = 0.845, which is a substantial drop for simply adjusting for the degrees of freedom; this again raises questions about the overall fit of the model.

In contrast to both the GFI and AGFI, the root mean squared residual (RMSR) is a measure of residual variance, reflecting the average amount of variances and covariances not accounted for by the model. Although, the closer to zero the better the fit, it needs to be borne in mind that RMSR must be interpreted in relation to the sizes of the observed variances and covariances and, therefore, the measure works best with standardized manifest variables (Jöreskog and Sörbom, 1989a). For the illustrative model, RMSR = 0.444 which is quite high and indicates that the fit of the model to the data may be suspect. As was the case with the evaluation of the measurement part of the model, a number of additional overall fit measures are available (but not computed by the LISREL program); Bollen (1989) and the collection of papers in Bollen and Long (1993) provide excellent overviews of these.

An analysis of residuals also provides useful insights regarding model fit. Table 12.6 provides summary statistics for fitted and standardized residuals as

TABLE 12.6 Residual analysis for illustrative model

Illustrative LISREL model for *JMM* special issue
—SUMMARY STATISTICS FOR FITTED RESIDUALS
  SMALLEST FITTED RESIDUAL   = −0.279
    MEDIAN FITTED RESIDUAL = 0.010
    LARGEST FITTED RESIDUAL = 1.326
—STEMLEAF PLOT
  − 2|82
  − 0|9540966432200000000000000
    0|1112223346122
    2|
    4|899
    6|160779
    8|45
    10|226
    12|3
—SUMMARY STATISTICS FOR STANDARDIZED RESIDUALS
  SMALLEST STANDARDIZED RESIDUAL = −2.328
    MEDIAN STANDARDIZED RESIDUAL = 0.111
    LARGEST STANDARDIZED RESIDUAL = 4.236
—STEMLEAF PLOT
  − 2|33
  − 1|8772
  − 0|98876430000000000000
    0|1112223336779
    1|
    2|
    3|144456777788
    4|0222

well as a Q-plot of the latter. The fitted residuals represent the difference between the sample covariance matrix **S** and the covariance matrix Σ calculated from the model (i.e. the fitted covariance matrix); if the model fit is good, the fitted residuals should be small in comparison to the magnitude of the elements in **S**. A problem with interpreting fitted residuals is that their size varies with the unit of measurement and the latter can vary from variable to variable. This problem is avoided by looking at the standardized residuals each of which 'can be interpreted as standard normal deviate and considered "large" if it exceeds the value 2.58 in absolute value' (Jöreskog and Sörbom, 1989a). In the current case, no fewer than 17 standardized residuals have values greater than 2.58, indicating specification error; moreover, they are decidedly non-normal as reflected in the relevant stem and leaf plots.

The overall picture is perhaps best obtained by looking at the Q-plot which plots the standardized residuals (horizontal axis) against the quantiles of the normal distribution (vertical axis). The best possible fit is obtained when all residuals lie in a straight vertical line (i.e. parallel to the ordinate), while the worst possible fit is indicated when the residuals lie in a horizontal straight line (i.e. parallel to the abscissa); an acceptable fit is indicated when the residuals lie approximately along the diagonal, with steeper plots (i.e. greater than 45 degrees) representing better fits. If the pattern of residuals is non-linear this is indicative of departures from normality, linearity and/or specification errors in the model. For the illustrative model, the residual plot is both shallower than 45 degrees and clearly non-linear; this confirms the conclusion drawn based on the overall fit measures, i.e. that the model as presently specified does not fit the empirical data adequately. The issue is now whether a better fit can be obtained by effecting changes in the original specification of the model.

Model modification

At this stage it is important to stress that the nature of the analysis is no longer confirmatory (i.e. testing a predetermined system of hypotheses as reflected in the original model specification) but becomes exploratory in nature. The process of using the results from the estimation from the original (i.e. rejected) model to develop a better fitting (or so it is hoped) model is known as specification search (Leamer, 1978; MacCullum, 1986). A specification search aims to identify and remedy specification errors, thus producing a 'new' model which has a better fit to the data and is interpretable from a substantive point of view. This 'new' model, however, must be regarded as tentative and, before it can be accepted, it will have to be verified on a second, independent, sample.

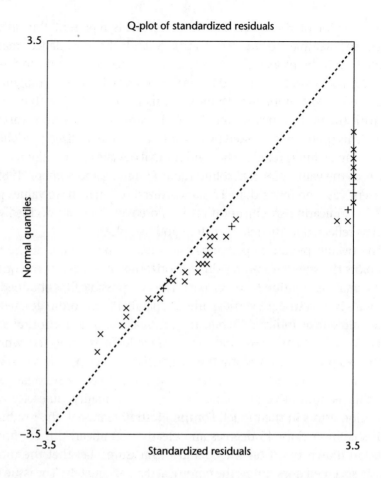

Q-plot of standardized residuals

There are two basic ways in which modifications can be effected to a model, namely by deleting or adding parameters. In both cases, it is important that theoretical considerations guide the specification search because 'even if the model initially suggested by substantive theory is rejected, there are generally some parameters that are definitely required on the basis of past research, and some parameters that make no sense to include' (Long, 1983a).

Insights into which parameters to eliminate can be gained by looking at nonsignificant t-values. To the extent that these parameters contribute little in terms of explanatory power in the model, restricting them to zero will influence the estimation of the remaining parameters which may lead to a better model fit. However, one should be aware that

> if the substantive theory suggests that a particular parameter should be included in the model, it is probably better to retain it even

though it is not significant, because the sample size may be too small to detect its real significance.

(Jöreskog and Sörbom, 1989a)

Once a particular parameter has been deleted and the model re-estimated, the effect of the deletion on the model fit can be evaluated by comparing the chi-square values of the two models; specifically, the difference in chi-squares (D^2) can be evaluated as a chi-square with 1 degree of freedom (Jöreskog and Sörbom, 1989a). In the example at hand, a potential candidate for deletion is parameter γ_{22} which, although it has a sign consistent with expectations (i.e. KSI–2 has a negative influence on ETA–2), also has a low t-value (-0.392); however, in this case, it is assumed that γ_{22} represents a theoretically essential link in the postulated model and, therefore, on substantive grounds, it is retained.

Insights into which parameters to add to the model can be gained by looking at the modification indices (Table 12.7). These show, for each fixed (and constrained) parameter, the decrease in the chi-square that would result if the parameter in question was freed, with all other parameters maintaining their present values; the accompanying estimated changes in the fixed/constrained parameters is also shown. The modification indices 'may be judged by means of a χ^2-square distribution with 1 degree of freedom. The fixed parameter corresponding to the largest such index is the one which, when relaxed, will improve fit maximally' (Jöreskog and Sörbom, 1989a); as was the case with deleting parameters, the improvement in fit from relaxing the parameter can be assessed with the D^2 statistic (which will be close to the modification index). Needless to say that, it should make substantive sense to relax a parameter, so sole reliance on the size of the modification index is not recommended for adding parameters to the model; moreover, 'it is suggested that only one parameter is relaxed at a time, since freeing one parameter may reduce or eliminate the improvement in fit possible by freeing a second parameter' (Long, 1983b). An excellent discussion on model modification is contained in Bollen (1989).

As Table 12.7 shows, the parameter with the largest modification index is γ_{13}, suggesting a link between KSI–3 and ETA–1. Assuming that it is theoretically defensible, a substantial improvement in fit may result from incorporating this link in the model. In this instance, relaxing γ_{13} may be particularly desirable as it is likely to also improve the low coefficient of determination for ETA–1 (see Table 12.5 above). Table 12.8 shows the fit statistics resulting from re-estimating the illustrative model with γ_{13} set free; the LISREL command file is identical to the one in Table 12.2, the only difference being that GA(1,3) is no longer included in the FI line.

TABLE 12.7 Modification indices for estimated model

Illustrative LISREL model for *JMM* special issue
—MODIFICATION INDICES AND ESTIMATED CHANGE

0   MODIFICATION INDICES FOR LAMBDA Y

	ETA–1	ETA–2
Y–1	0.000	2.032
Y–2	0.000	0.117
Y–3	1.798	0.000
Y–4	1.798	0.000

0   ESTIMATED CHANGE FOR LAMBDA Y

	ETA–1	ETA–2
Y–1	0.000	0.082
Y–2	0.000	−0.018
Y–3	0.073	0.000
Y–4	−0.084	0.000

0   MODIFICATION INDICES FOR LAMBDA X

	KSI–1	KSI–2	KSI–3
X–1	0.000	0.056	0.559
X–2	0.000	0.090	0.049
X–3	0.094	0.000	0.063
X–4	0.094	0.000	0.063
X–5	0.638	0.000	0.000
X–6	0.638	0.000	0.000

0   ESTIMATED CHANGE FOR LAMBDA X

	KSI–1	KSI–2	KSI–3
X–1	0.000	−0.032	−0.064
X–2	0.000	0.051	−0.024
X–3	−0.070	0.000	−0.021
X–4	0.071	0.000	0.021
X–5	0.058	0.000	0.000
X–6	−0.087	−0.000	0.000

0   MODIFICATION INDICES FOR BETA

	ETA–1	ETA–2
ETA–1	0.000	13.373
ETA–2	0.000	0.000

0   ESTIMATED CHANGE FOR BETA

	ETA–1	ETA–2
ETA–1	0.000	0.709
ETA–2	0.000	0.000

0   MODIFICATION INDICES FOR GAMMA

	KSI–1	KSI–2	KSI–3
ETA–1	0.000	0.057	14.167
ETA–2	0.000	0.000	0.000

0   ESTIMATED CHANGE FOR GAMMA

	KSI–1	KSI–2	KSI–3
ETA–1	0.000	−0.067	0.703
ETA–2	0.000	0.000	0.000

MAXIMUM MODIFICATION INDEX IS 14.17 FOR ELEMENT (1, 3) OF GAMMA

TABLE 12.8 Measures of fit for modified model

Modified illustrative LISREL model for *JMM* special issue

0	SQUARED MULTIPLE CORRELATIONS FOR Y-VARIABLES					
0	Y–1	Y–2	Y–3	Y–4		
+	0.922	0.954	0.972	0.969		
0	TOTAL COEFFICIENT OF DETERMINATION FOR Y-VARIABLES IS 0.999					
0	SQUARED MULTIPLE CORRELATIONS FOR X-VARIABLES					
0	X–1	X–2	X–3	X–4	X–5	X–6
+	0.727	0.827	0.854	0.691	0.816	0.918
0	TOTAL COEFFICIENT OF DETERMINATION FOR X-VARIABLES IS 0.998					
0	SQUARED MULTIPLE CORRELATIONS FOR STRUCTURAL EQUATIONS					
0	ETA–1	ETA–2				
+	0.244	0.972				
0	TOTAL COEFFICIENT OF DETERMINATION FOR STRUCTURAL EQUATIONS IS 0.929					
0	CHI-SQUARE WITH 26 DEGREES OF FREEDOM = 33.48 (P = 0.149)					
0	GOODNESS OF FIT INDEX = 0.944					
	ADJUSTED GOODNESS OF FIT INDEX = 0.882					
	ROOT MEAN SQUARE RESIDUAL = 0.134					

Comparing Table 12.8 with Table 12.5, it can be seen that the chi-square value is now much lower and nonsignificant. The improvement in fit is reflected in the difference in the chi-square values of the original and modified models; this comes to $D^2 = 48.95 - 33.48 = 15.47$ with $27 - 26 = 1$ degrees of freedom. The value of D^2 is close to the value of the modification index for γ_{13} and is significant at $p < 0.001$. The GFI and AGFI have also improved and, perhaps most visibly, there has been a substantial reduction in RMSR (down to 0.134 from 0.444). Further, the coefficient of determination for ETA–1 has more than doubled in magnitude and, although not shown, the Q-plot of the residuals is now much improved. Thus, on the whole, a substantial improvement in the model fit to the data was attained by adding a structural parameter; of course, a new sample is now needed to test the revised model before it can be accepted.

At this point it should be pointed out that a specification search can be much more extensive than what was done in relation to the illustrative example. Thus one may add to the model, one at a time, links that were hypothesized not to exist and delete from the model, one at a time, links hypothesized to exist and evaluating the resulting changes in fit by means of incremental difference chi-square (i.e. D^2) tests with 1 degree of freedom (Sawyer and Page, 1984). However, an obsessive desire to obtain a good fit at all costs must be firmly resisted because a good fit for a model *proves nothing*. There are conceivably many models that could fit as well – or in some cases – better. In fact, a poor fit would tell you more; this would be more conclusive evidence that the model is not supported by the data.

(Darden, 1983; emphasis in the original)

Model cross validation

The last stage in LISREL modelling is (or, in any case, should be) the cross-validation of one's model with a new (different) data set. In practice, this is usually done through randomly splitting the sample into two parts, whereby 'one part is used for deriving the model, while the other is used for evaluating the derived model. In this sense, cross-validation simulates prediction of an independent sample' (Yi and Nassen, 1992). The LISREL program has a facility for multisample analysis and this can be used to conduct cross-validation tests. However, given that this can be quite complex, for present purposes, only key issues associated with cross-validation will be discussed (i.e. without actually running a LISREL multigroup analysis).

Cross-validation is important not only when modifications in the original model have been undertaken following an initially poor fit but also when the model has provided an acceptable fit in the first place. The reason for this is that the observed fit may largely reflect the specific characteristics of one's data set rather than a generalizable structure in the population (Backhaus *et al.*, 1989). Cross-validation can also be used to compare competing models in terms of predictive validity and, thus, facilitate the selection of a model that best approximates the structure in the population.

Following Cudeck and Browne (1983), the process of cross-validation can be summarized as follows. First, the sample is split into two subsamples (usually halves). This can be done either randomly or through the application of sample-splitting procedures (e.g. Snee's (1977) DUPLEX algorithm) that ensure that the two subsamples have similar statistical properties and neither contains a subset of observations that could bias the results. Next, one sample is designated as the derivation (i.e. analysis) sample while the other is the validation (i.e. hold-out) sample; often, each of the two samples is used in turn as the derivation and validation sample (a process known as double-cross-validation). In the third step, the derivation sample is used to estimate the model parameters. In the fourth step, the derived model is applied to the validation sample with some or all the parameter estimates fixed at the values obtained from the derivation sample. Here, one has to decide which parameters to fix and which to set free when running the model on the validation sample and three main strategies are available. Under the first while the same measurement and structural paths are used in the validation sample and the derivation sample, the parameters are set free and estimated on the validation sample. Under the second strategy, critical parameters reflecting measurement and structural paths are fixed to the values estimated from the derivation sample, but other parameters (e.g. error terms) are set free and subsequently estimated on the validation sample. Under the third (and most restrictive) strategy, all parameters are fixed at the values estimated from the derivation sample. Next, a cross-validation index (and, often, also a double cross-validation index) is computed which reflects the difference between the covariance matrix from parameters generated by the derivation sample and the actual covariance matrix of the validation sample. Thus the cross- and double cross-validation indices provide summary measures of the extent to which the model under consideration is stale.

If multiple models are to be compared, the procedure involved is a straightforward extension of the steps outlined above. Each of, say, k models would be cross-validated and doubly cross-validated individually and k cross- and double cross-validation indices computed. Subsequently, the model with the lowest indices would be selected as the best approximation to the 'true' model in the population. A potential problem with this approach is that two different models may score differently in the two cross-validations, so none can be selected as 'optimal'; while the chances of inconsistent results on the cross-validation and double cross-validation indices are much lower when a formal sample-splitting algorithm is applied to split the sample, other properties of the competing models, such as interpretability and parsimony, should also be considered (Balderjahn, 1988).

The principles of cross-validation can also be applied to compare the differences between samples belonging to different populations, what is known as validity generalization (Yi and Nassen, 1988) or to assess the impact of moderating variables (Sharma *et al.*, 1981). In both instances, the model would be estimated first with all parameters set equal between the two groups and, then, by relaxing the equality constraints; if the difference in chi-square values turns out to be significant, then the population characteristic or moderating variable is important.

Cross-validation is not without limitations, however. First, and most obvious, it implies access to the raw data and not just the covariance/ correlation matrix; otherwise, it is not possible to split the sample and generate separate covariance matrices for the developmental and validation subsamples. Second, the sample size must be large enough to enable reliable estimates to be generated within each subsample; in this context, it has been found that cross-validation works best when the sample size has between 300 and 500 observations (Homburg, 1991). Lastly, bias may be introduced if sample splitting is done randomly; although, as noted, there are algorithms available to guard against this, they tend to be very intensive in terms of computer time. To cope with such problems, a single sample cross-validation index has been proposed (Browne and Cudeck, 1989), which measures 'the discrepancy between the fitted covariance matrix in the analyzed sample and the expected covariance matrix that would be obtained in another sample of the same size' (Jöreskog, 1993).

Conclusions

This paper has sought to introduce the uninitiated reader to the principles of covariance structure modelling using the LISREL approach and computer program, while keeping technical details to a minimum. It is hoped that at least some of the mystery has been taken out of LISREL modelling and an awareness created of the benefits and pitfalls of the approach. In this context, while a number of issues relating to constructing, estimating and interpreting a LISREL model were examined, several important topics had, inevitably, to be left out. Equivalent models, interpretational confounding and effect decomposition are only three examples of topics that were not even mentioned, given the introductory nature of the paper and the space limitations. There is much more to covariance structure modelling than what was covered here and, it is hoped, that the literature pointers provided will be followed up by the reader.

It seems appropriate to conclude with a quote from a pioneering article on covariance structure modelling:

> it is relatively easy to find a structural model which fits the data quite closely . . . it is extremely difficult to demonstrate (a) that a model simulates reality, (b) that it provides better simulation than another model, (c) that the constructs defined in the model have greater explanatory power from the observed variables from which they are derived, and (d) that these constructs are in any sense useful in promoting better research.
>
> (Werts *et al.*, 1974)

Reader beware.

References

Aaker, D. and Bagozzi, R.P. (1979), Unobservable variables in structural equation models with and application in industrial selling, *Journal of Marketing Research*, Vol. **16**, pp. 147–58

Anderson, J.C. and Gerbing, D.W. (1982), Some methods for respecifying measurement models to obtain unidimensional construct measurement, *Journal of Marketing Research*, Vol. **19**, pp. 453–460

Anderson, J.C. and Gerbing, D.W. (1988), Structural equation modeling in practice: a review and recommended two-step approach, *Psychological Bulletin* Vol. **103**, pp. 411–23

Arora, R. and Cavusgil, S.T. (1985), Image and cost factors in the choice of mental health-care organizations: a causal model, *Journal of the Academy of Marketing Science*, Vol. **13**, pp. 119–29

Asher, H.B. (1985), *Causal Modeling*, second edition, Beverly Hills: Sage

Backhaus, K., Erichson, B., Plinke, W., Suchard-Fisher, C. and Weiber, R. (1989), *Multivariate Analysemethoden: Eine einwendungs- orientiertes Einführung*, fifth edition, Berlin: Springer

Bagozzi, R.P. (1977), Structural equation models in experimental research, *Journal of Marketing Research*, Vol. **14**, pp. 209–226

Bagozzi, R.P. (1980), *Causal Models in Marketing*, New York: Wiley

Bagozzi, R.P. and Fornell, C. (1982), Theoretical concepts, measurements, and meaning, in *A Second Generation of Multivariate Analysis: Measurement and Evaluation*. Fornell, C. (Ed.) New York: Praeger

Bagozzi, R.P. and Yi, Y. (1988), On the evaluation of structural equation models, *Journal of the Academy of Marketing Science*, Vol. **16**, pp. 77–94

Bagozzi, R.P. and Yi, Y. (1989), On the use of structural equation models in experimental designs, *Journal of Marketing Research*, Vol. **26**, August, pp. 271–284

Bagozzi, R.P., Yi, Y. and Singh, S. (1991), On the use of structural equation models in experimental designs: two extensions, *International Journal of Research in Marketing*, Vol. **8**, No. 2, pp. 125–140

Balderjahn, I. (1988), Die Kreuzvalidierung von Kausalmodellen, *Marketing – Zeitschrift für Forschung und Praxis*, Vol. **10**, February, pp. 61–73

Bentler, P.M. (1980), Multivariate analysis with latent variables. Causal models, *Annual Review of Psychology*, Vol. **31**, pp. 419–56

Bentler, P.M. (1985), *Theory and Implementation of EQS: A Structural Equations Program*, Los Angeles: BMDP Statistical Software, Inc.

Bentler, P.M. and Chou, C.P. (1987), Practical issues in structural modeling, *Sociological Methods and Research*, Vol. **16**, pp. 78–117

Berry, W.D. (1984), *Nonrecursive Causal Models*, Beverly Hills: Sage

Bielby, W.T. and Hauser, R.M. (1977), Structural equation models, *Annual Review of Sociology*, Vol. **3**, pp. 137–61

Bollen, K.A. (1989), *Structural Equations with Latent Variables*, New York: Wiley

Bollen, K.A. and Lang, J.S. (1993), *Testing Structural Equations Models*, Beverly Hills: Sage

Bone, P.F., Sharma, S. and Shimp, T.A. (1989), A bootstrap procedure for evaluating goodness-of-fit indices of structural equation and confirmatory factor models, *Journal of Marketing Research*, Vol. **26**, February, pp. 105–11

Box, G.E.P. (1949), A general distribution theory for a class of likelihood criteria, *Biometrika*, Vol. **36**, pp. 317–46

Browne, M. W. and Cudeck, R. (1989), Single sample cross-validation indices for covariance structure, *Multivariate Behavioral Research*, Vol. **24**, pp. 445–55

Cudeck, R. and Brown, M.W. (1983), Cross-validation of covariance structures, *Multivariate Behavioral Research*, Vol. **18**, pp. 147–57

Danes, J.E. and Mann K.O. (1984), Unidimensional measurement and structural equation models with latent variables, *Journal of Business Research*, Vol. 12, pp. 337–52

Darden, W.R. (1983), Review of behavioral modeling in marketing, in: *Research Methods and Causal Modeling in Marketing.* W.R. Darden, K.B. Monroe, and W.R. Dillon, (Eds), Chicago: American Marketing Association

Darden, W.R., Monroe, K.B. and Dillon, W.R. (Eds) (1983), *Research Methods and Causal Modeling in Marketing*, Chicago: American Marketing Association

DeBrentani, U. and Droge, C. (1988), Determinants of the new produce screening decision: a structural model approach, *International Journal of Research in Marketing*, Vol. **5**, No. 2, pp. 91–106

Dubinsky, A.J., Howell, R.D., Ingram, T.N. and Bellenger, D.N. (1986), Salesforce socialization, *Journal of Marketing*, Vol. **50**, pp. 192–207

Duncan, O.D. (1975), *Introduction to Structural Equation Models*, New York: Academic Press

Fornell, C. (1987), A second generation of multivariate analysis: classification of methods and implications for marketing research. In: *Review of Marketing.* M.J. Houston, (Ed.) Chicago: American Marketing Association, pp. 407–50

Fornell, C. and Larcker, D.F. (1981a), Evaluating structural equation models with unobservable variables and measurement error, *Journal of Marketing Research*, Vol. **18**, pp. 440–52

Fornell, C. and Larcker, D.F. (1981b), Structural equation models with unobservable variables and measurement error: algebra and statistics, *Journal of Marketing Research*, Vol. **18**, pp. 382–88

Förster, F., Fritz, W., Silberer, G. and Rafeé, H. (1984), Der LISREL Ansatz der Kausalanalyse und seine Bedeutung für die Marketing-Forschung, *Zeitschrift für Betriebswirtschaft*, Vol. **54**, pp. 346–67

Fraser, C. (1980), *COSAN User's Guide*, Armidale, Australia: Center for Behavioural Studies, University of New England

Gerbing, D.W. and Anderson, J.C. (1988), An updated paradigm for scale development incorporating unidimensionality and its assessment, *Journal of Marketing Research*, Vol. **25**, May, pp. 186–92

Goldberger, A.S. (1971), Econometrics and psychometrics: a survey of communalities, *Psychometrika*, **36**, pp. 83–107

Goldberger, A.S. (1972), Structural equation methods in the social sciences, *Econometrica*, Vol. **40**, pp. 979–1001

Good, L.K., Sisler, G.F. and Gentry, J.W. (1988), Antercendents of turnover intentions among retail management personnel, *Journal of Retailing*, Vol. **64**, pp. 295–314

Han, C.M. (1988), The role of consumer patriotism in the choice of domestic versus foreign products, *Journal of Advertising Research*, Vol. **28**, pp. 25–32

Hayduk, L.A. (1987), *Structural Equation Modelling with LISREL: Essentials and Advances*, Baltimore: The Johns Hopkins University Press

Homburg, C. (1991), Cross-validation and information criteria in causal modeling, *Journal of Marketing Research*, Vol. **28**, May, pp. 137–44

Howell, R.D. (1987), Covariance structure modeling and measurement issues: a note on 'Interrelations among a channel entity's power sources', *Journal of Marketing Research*, Vol. **24**, pp. 119–26

Hunter, J.E. and Gerbing, D.W. (1982), Unidimensional measurement, second-order factor analysis, and causal models, in: *Research in Organizational Behavior.* B.M. Staw and L.L. Cummings (Eds.), JAI Press, Vol. **4**, pp. 267–99

James, L.R. (1980), The unmeasured variables problem in path analysis, *Journal of Applied Psychology*, Vol. **65**, pp. 415–21

Jöreskog, K.G. (1993), Testing structural equations models, in: *Testing Structural Equations Models*. K.A. Bollen and J.S. Lang (Eds.) Beverly Hills: Sage

Jöreskog, K.G. and Sörbom, D. (1982), Recent developments in structural equation modeling, *Journal of Marketing Research*, Vol. **19**, pp. 404–16

Jöreskog, K.G. and Sörbom, D. (1988), *PRELIS: A Preprocessor for LISREL*, second edition, Mooresville: Scientific Software Inc.

Jöreskog, K.G. and Sörbom, D. (1989a), *LISREL 7: A Guide to the Program and Applications*, Chicago, IL: SPSS, Inc.

Jöreskog, K.G. and Sörbom, D. (1989b), *LISREL 7 User's Reference Guide*, Scientific Software, Inc., Mooresville

Jöreskog, K.G. and Van Thillo, M. (1972), *LISREL: A General Computer Program for Estimating a Linear Structural Equation System Involving Multiple Indicators of Unmeasured Variables*, Princeton, NJ: Educational Testing Service

Jöreskog, K.G. and Wold, H. (1982), *Systems Under Indirect Observation: Causality, Structure, Prediction*, Amsterdam: North-Holland Publishing Co.

Kenny, D.A. (1979), *Correlation and Causality*, New York: Wiley

Leamer, E.E. (1978), *Specification Searches: Ad hoc Inference with Non-Experimental Data*, New York: Wiley

Lohmöller, J.B. (1984), *LVPLS 1.6 Program Manual: Latent Variables Path Analysis with Partial Least-Squares Estimation*, Cologne: Zentralarchiv für Empirische Sozialforschung, Universität zu Köln

Long, J.S. (1983a), *Confirmatory Factor Analysis: A preface to LISREL*, Beverly Hills: Sage

Long, J.S. (1983b), *Covariance Structure Models: An Introduction to LISREL*, Beverly Hills: Sage

MacCullum, R. (1986), Specification searches in covariance structure modeling, *Psychological Bulletin*, Vol. **100**, pp. 107–120

MacKenzie, S.B. and Lutz, R.J. (1989), An empirical examination of structural antecedants of attitude towards the ad in an advertising pretesting context, *Journal of Marketing*, **53**, April, pp. 48–65

Michaels, R.E., Day, R.L. and Joachimsthaler, E.A. (1987), Role stress among industrial buyers: an integrative model, *Journal of Marketing*, Vol. **51**, pp. 28–45

Muthén, B.O. (1987), *LISCOMP: Analysis of Linear Structural Equations with a Comprehensive Measurement Model*, Mooresville: Scientific Software, Inc.

Oliver, R.L. and Swan, J.E. (1989), Consumer perceptions of interpersonal equity and satisfaction in transactions: a field survey approach, *Journal of Marketing*, Vol. **53**, pp. 21–35

Pfeifer, A., and Schmidt, P. (1987), *LISREL: Die Analyse Komplexer Strukturgleichungmodelle*, Stuttgart: Gustav Fischer Verlag

Sawyer, A.G. and Page, T.J. Jr. (1984), The use of incremental goodness of fit indices in structural equation models in marketing research, *Journal of Business Research*, Vol. **12**, pp. 297–308

Schoenberg, R. (1982), *MILS: A Computer Program to Estimate the Parameters of Multiple Indicator Linear Structural Models*, Bethesda MD: National Institute of Health

Schul, P.L. and Babakus, E. (1988), An examination of the interfirm power–conflict relationship: the intervening role of channel decision structure, *Journal of Retailing*, Vol. **64**, pp. 381–404

Sharma, S., Durand, R.M. and Gur-Arie, O. (1981), Identification and analysis of moderator variables, *Journal of Marketing Research*, Vol. **18**, August, pp. 291–300

Snee, R.D. (1977), Validation of regression models: methods and examples, *Technometrics*, Vol. **19**, pp. 415–428

Steenkamp, J-B E.M. and van Trijp, H.C.M. (1991), The use of LISREL in validating marketing constructs, *International Journal of Research in Marketing*, Vol. **8**, No. 4, pp. 283–99

Steiger, J.H. (1989), *EzPATH: A Supplementary Module for SYSTAT and SYGRAPH*, Evanston, IL: SYSTAT, Inc.

Walters, R.G. and MacKenzie, S.B. (1988), A structural equations analysis of the impact of price promotions on store performance, *Journal of Marketing Research*, Vol. **25**, pp. 51–63

Werts, C.E., Linn, R.L. and Jöreskog, K.G. (1974), Quantifying unmeasured variables. In: *Measurement in the Social Sciences: Theories and Strategies*. H.M. Blalock, (Ed.) Chicago IL: Aldine-Atherton

Wright, S. (1960), Path coefficients and path regressions: alternatives or complementary concepts?, *Biometrics*, Vol. **16**, pp. 189–202

Yadav, M.S. (1992), The effect of rescaling on the measurement and fit statistics of causal models: an exploratory study. in: *Enhancing Knowledge Development in Marketing*. R.P. Leone, and V. Kumar, (Eds) Chicago IL: American Marketing Association

Yi, Y. and Nassen, K. (1992), Multiple comparison and cross-validation in evaluating structural equation models, in: *Developments in Marketing Science XV*. V.L. Crittenden, (Ed.) Chestnut Hill MA: Academy of Marketing Science

Appendix 12.1: Path diagram construction for a LISREL model

1. An *endogenous* latent (unobservable) variable is denoted by η (read: eta) and placed in a circle.

2. An *exogenous* latent (unobservable) variable is denoted by ξ (read: ksi) and placed in a circle.

3. A *manifest* (observable) variable used as an indicator of a endogenous latent variable is denoted by y and placed in a box.

4. A *manifest* (observable) variable used as an indicator of an exogenous latent variable is denoted by x and placed in a box.

5. The *error* (residual) term for a latent endogenous variable is denoted by ζ (read: zeta); this reflects 'error in equations' i.e. (random disturbances).

6. The *error* (residual) term for an indicator y of a latent endogenous variable is denoted by ε (read: epsilon) and for a latent exogenous variable by δ (read: delta); these reflect 'errors in measurement'.

7. A *causal linkage* between two variables is represented by a one-way straight arrow starting from the (hypothesized) cause and pointing to the (hypothesized) effect. Each linkage is referenced by a small Greek letter (see 8. below) and two subscripts, the first indicating the target of an arrow (i.e. the effect) and the second its origin (i.e. the cause). No one-way arrow can point to a latent exogenous variable ξ.

8. A *causal relationship* between two endogenous latent variables is denoted by β (read: beta), while that between an exogenous and an endogenous latent variable is denoted by γ (read: gamma).

9. The relationships between latent variables and their *measures* (i.e. the manifest variables) are represented by one-way straight arrows originating from the latent variables and denoted by λ (read: lambda).

10. The impact of *residual terms* is also represented by straight arrows, always originating from the error variables ζ, δ and ε and pointing to the relevant latent or manifest variables (i.e. η, *y* and *x* respectively).

11. A *non-causal linkage* between two variables is represented by a curved double arrow, connecting the variables concerned. Such linkages are only permitted between the exogenous latent variables (i.e. ξ) and between error terms (see 12 below).

12. A *non-causal relationship* between two exogenous latent variables is denoted by φ (read: phi) and between the error terms of endogenous latent variables by ψ (read: psi).

13. The *measurement model* for the exogenous latent variables, specifying the relationships between the ξ- and *x*-variables is always placed to the left of the path diagram.

14. The *measurement model* for the endogenous latent variables, specifying the relationships between the η- and *y*-variables is always placed to the right of the path diagram.

15. The *structural model*, specifying the relationships between the ξ- and η-variables is placed in the centre of the path diagram.

Appendix 12.2: Mathematical specification for a LISREL model

1. Each *dependent* variable can be described by a single linear equation; dependent variables are those to which a one-way arrow points (i.e. *x*-, *y*- and η-variables).

2. Variables to which a one-way arrow points (i.e. dependent variables) are placed to the left of the equality operator, whereas variables from which a one-way arrow originates (i.e. independent variables) are placed to the right of the equality operator. Note that ξ-variables, being exogenous, can never be dependent variables; in contrast η-variables can function both as dependent and independent variables in different equations.

3. The arrows in the path diagram, representing the linkages between the variables in the model are mathematically represented through *coefficients* (i.e. the λs, γs and βs, as described in Appendix 12.1), the sign and magnitude of which reflect the nature and strength of the postulated relationships.

4. If a dependent variable is affected by a *number* of independent variables, the cumulative impact of the independent variables is assumed to be additive and the number of terms in the right hand side of the equation is equal to the number of one-way arrows leading to the variable concerned.

5. It is assumed that *error terms* (i.e. ζ, ε and λ) are mutually uncorrelated; that ζ and δ are uncorrelated with ξ; and that ε is uncorrelated with η.

6. In matrix notation, any LISREL model can be described by means of three matrix equations, reflecting (a) the measurement model for the ξ-variables, (b) the measurement model for the η-variables and (c) the structural model.

7. The matrix equation for the *measurement model* of the exogenous latent variables links the vector of the x-variables to the vector of ξ-variables by means of the coefficient matrix Λ_x (containing the λ_x parameters) and the vector of error terms δ.

8. The matrix equation for the *measurement model* of the endogenous latent links the vector of y-variables to the vector of η-variables by means of the coefficient matrix Λ_y (containing the λ_y parameters) and the vector of error terms ε.

9. The matrix equation for the *structural model* links the vector of η-variables to (i) the vector of η-variables by means of the coefficient matrix $\mathbf{B}$ (containing the β parameters), (ii) the vector of ξ-variables by means of the coefficient matrix $\mathbf{\Gamma}$ (containing the γ parameters), and (iii) the vector of residuals ζ.

10. In all the above matrices, the *row* and *column* positions for each coefficient correspond directly to the *subscripts* of the coefficient in the path diagram (e.g. γ_{21} which represents the path between ξ_1 and η_2 is located in the first column of the second row of the $\mathbf{\Gamma}$ matrix). Arrows which are not included in the path diagram (i.e. reflecting the absence of a relationship among the variables concerned) are denoted by zeros in the relevant matrices.

11. In addition to the matrices described above, four variance–covariance matrices are part of the complete LISREL model (see Table 12.1 in text).

 **Part 2**

13

Measuring Consumer Involvement with Grocery Brands: Model Validation and Scale-Reliability Test Procedures

Dr Simon Knox, David Walker and Charles Marshall

This paper identifies how consumer involvement measuring techniques can be adapted for use with fast-moving consumer goods. The discussion opens with a review of the recent theoretical developments in involvement and their applications in a number of different product areas. A contemporary measuring device is identified from the extant literature and applied to grocery products. The researchers report on a data reduction step which enabled us to eliminate over one third of the measured items without apparent loss in reliability. Using this modified approach, significant differences in the levels of involvement were found across grocery product categories. The managerial implications of these results are discussed and further uses of the measuring device suggested.

Introduction

The concept of involvement has played an increasingly important role in explaining consumer behaviour. The level of consumer involvement has been hypothesized as affecting brand loyalty, information search, decision process complexity and the predictive ability of attitude models (Assael, 1987). Early attempts at empirical verification of the concept as a mediator of purchasing decisions have been of limited value. Problems in definition and measurement techniques have restricted much of this research to a qualitative level (Cohen, 1983; Antil, 1984; Costley, 1988). Recently, significant progress has been made in clarifying the definition and providing new methods of measurement (Bloch and Richins, 1983; Laurent and Kapferer, 1985; Mittal and Lee, 1989; Mittal, 1989). Whilst these measuring devices have proved to be robust, their application has been very limited, particularly in grocery product markets.

The research question posed in this paper is whether or not contemporary measurement techniques are sufficiently sensitive to detect significant differences in consumer involvement with grocery products. The paper opens with an evaluation of the converging theory on consumer involvement and its application in the grocery sector. Whilst recognizing that researchers are divided in their opinions about how involved consumers are with these products, we argue that, in principle, differing levels of involvement could be detected.

In the second part of the paper, we discuss the research procedures that we used to measure consumer involvement across a number of grocery product categories. Initially, we present evidence to support the validity of the chosen model. However, because of consumer fatigue (due to the length of the self administered questionnaire), a data reduction step was undertaken to shorten the questionnaire whilst maintaining the structure of the original model. The reliability of this reduced-item measure is assessed. Involvement scores are then presented and cross-comparisons between products discussed. Although the product categories were all considered medium to low involvement, significant differences in the levels of involvement were found.

Finally, we discuss how our approach to measuring involvement can be used by marketing management and academics to advance understanding of grocery product purchasing.

Consumer involvement: a converging theory

Despite differences in nuances, there seem to be some common threads emerging from the multifarious definitions of consumer involvement. A number of authors (Antil, 1984; Zaichkowsky, 1985; Celsi and Olson, 1988) emphasize the importance of product possession, usage and purchasing situation to the consumer. This reflects the perceived value attached to the particular stimulus or situation that manifests as consumer interest. Peter and Olson (1987) also recognize the saliency of perceived consequences that may result. Their definition of involvement is: 'the degree of personal relevance which a stimulus or situation is perceived to help achieve consequences and values of importance to the consumer'. So involvement with a product can be regarded as the extent to which consumers' product knowledge is related to their self knowledge about desirable values and needs. Peter and Olson argue that the more closely that product knowledge about attributes and functional consequences is connected to abstract psychosocial and value consequences, the more involved the consumer is with the product. Product involvement can thus be expressed as a means–end of product knowledge. (Figure 13.1) Consumers probably perceive relatively few products to be directly linked to their terminal values. Most products are strongly linked to functional and psychosocial ends and, occasionally, instrumental values (de Chernatony and Knox, 1989). Product (or enduring) involvement develops as the means–end relationships are established through the experiences gained in possessing, using or consuming the product. Purchasing involvement (situational involvement), on the other hand, is the interest taken in making the brand selection and is context specific. For instance, buying a gift may activate certain values and goals that are not relevant in other use situations. The level of situational involvement is temporarily felt and is fashioned by the association of brand knowledge (attributes and functional consequences) with relevant self knowledge appropriate to the purchasing context. Consumer involvement (Figure 13.2) is considered to be a function of the base level of enduring involvement interacting with the level of situational involvement caused by the physical and social context of purchase (Bloch and Richins, 1983).

Involvement with grocery products

Many marketing practitioners seem to believe that consumers choose their products and brands in a highly discriminating and deliberate fashion, none more so than marketers of grocery products. McKinsey have estimated that some 23 per cent of costs for a major food manufacturer were directly or

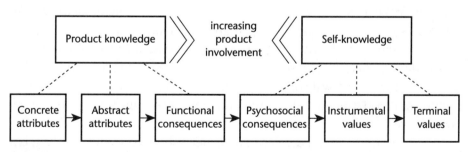

FIGURE 13.1 Product involvement as a means–end chain

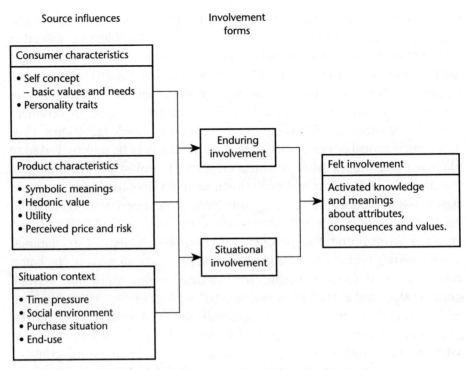

FIGURE 13.2 Basic model of consumer involvement

indirectly attributable to building their brands' added values (Davis, 1986). If consumers were not in some sense prepared to pay for that differentiating activity or if the brand differences were not sufficiently valued, they argue there would not be the economic justification for either manufacturers or retailers to engage in expensive branding exercises. Recent research on price recall of grocery brands and own labels suggests that consumers can readily discriminate between product categories in assessing price-perceived value relationships (de Chernatony, Knox and Chedgey, 1992). Whether this level of discrimination exists between individual brands within product categories has yet to be reported for grocery products. Clearly, manufacturers and retailers subscribe to this view (perhaps based on proprietary consumer research) since brands within product categories are differentially priced in store. McWilliam (1991) presents a very strong argument for carrying out this type of research amongst consumers using involvement to establish whether brand differentiation translates into differentiated values based on brand knowledge.

Academics do appear divided in their views about consumer involvement with grocery products. For instance, the Kassarjians have stated categorically that consumers simply 'don't give a damn' about most grocery products (Kassarjian and Kassarjian, 1979). Barwise and Ehrenberg are of a similar view (Barwise, 1984). They argue that most grocery goods are so risk-free and, through direct experience of them, so similar that any perceived difference (no matter how trivial) is likely to generate some trial on a 'why not' basis. In contrast, Kapferer and Laurent (1984) are able to distinguish between grocery product categories based on their involvement profile approach. For instance, they found that consumers showed significant differences in the level of situational involvement when purchasing pasta or shampoo. The latter was found to be more highly involving. In a similar study, Mittal (1989) showed significant differences in situational involvement when wine was bought for a special occasion rather than as an ordinary purchase. However, neither of the researchers measures enduring involvement, so the level of felt involvement (Figure 13.2) remains unclear.

In addition to enduring and situational involvement, there are a number of source influences that are regarded by academics as having an effect on the

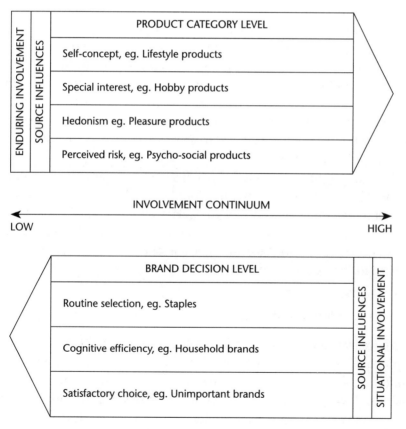

FIGURE 13.3 Involvement continuum for grocery products

level of felt involvement with grocery products. They are categorized in Figure 13.3 according to the direction of influence on the involvement continuum and are discussed in the next section.

Source influences and high involvement

Source influences that contribute towards high involvement with grocery products have been discussed in the literature for the past 20 years. However, empirical validation is scant. There are only a few grocery product studies that provide evidence to support the argument. For example, Knox, Tait and Amps (1989) cite the case of UK mineral waters being positioned as 'bistro' brands to exploit social recognition and sports drinks as being associated with fitness and health. Both are examples of lifestyle products that provide routes to self concept enhancement through product symbolism (Lannon and Cooper, 1983). Laurent and Kapferer (1985) report differences in the pleasure values associated with chocolate and detergents, with high and low ratings respectively. In the same study, detergents were also found to be devoid of any risk components.

In his meta-analysis of risk and information search, Gemunden (1985) concludes that, for convenience goods in general, perceived risk usually seems to remain below a tolerated threshold. This may be due to the fact that manufacturers of grocery products have clearly understood the importance of consistency and quality to remove the threat of adverse functional consequences. However, psychosocial risk may still remain within the family and among friends which could lead to increased consumer involvement with particular product categories.

In contrast to the research on consumer durables, the evidence for grocery products points towards medium-low enduring involvement if the effects of source influences are any guide. However, it would be inappropriate to be too emphatic since consumer involvement is multifaceted and the source factors cited here do not take into consideration the situational influences discussed in the next section.

Source influences and low involvement

The source influences which mediate low consumer involvement tend to be situational for grocery products. In other words, they relate more to the level of information processing associated with brand choice and purchasing decisions. However, there is an inherent paradox associated with each one of these source effects. Cognitive efficiency, for example, implies that consumers strive to minimize effort in decision making, particularly when purchasing grocery products (Hoyer, 1984); the role of the brand in this process is potentially considerable. Essentially this role is a recoding process (Millar, 1956) whereby each 'bit' of information is organized by learning into 'chunks'. It is the 'chunk' which is subsequently used as shorthand for a compendium of information; brands can be viewed as 'informational chunks' for functional performance, pleasurable experiences, self concept, etc. Millar's logic suggests that the stronger the brand's added values, the lower the situational involvement. It is quite possible that low situational involvement (in terms of cognitive effort) masks a good deal of enduring involvement. Routine purchasing, a consequence of routine selection, implies that repeat purchasing becomes the norm unless poor product performance or a simple desire for 'change' forces a re-analysis of the original decision. For example, a new advertising campaign from a competing staple (e.g. fruit sugar rather than common sugar) may just be sufficient to trigger such a purchasing switch and a new process of information 'chunking' through user experiences.

It would seem from this brief literature review that consumers could, in principle, exhibit differing levels of involvement with grocery products. What little empirical evidence there is seems to point towards some differences in both the enduring and situational forms, judging from the arguments presented about source influences.

In carrying out the exploratory research reported in this paper, our main objective has been to determine whether significant variations in the levels of consumer involvement can be obtained for grocery products, i.e. to test the sensitivity of the most appropriate measurement device. We wished to measure both situational and enduring involvement directly, as well as the saliency of source influences, so it was necessary to validate not only the measurements across product categories but also at the brand-decision level.

In the next section we review the measuring devices that have been developed in recent years and discuss their application to grocery products.

Measuring involvement

In early research when quantitative indicators of involvement were used, the instruments were often single scale (Vaughn, 1980; Zaichkowsky, 1985) or a single-item measurement of perceived importance (Agostini, 1978; Lastovicka and Bonfield, 1982). More recently, in their seminal paper on involvement measurement, Laurent and Kapferer (1985) challenge this assumption and posit the idea of an 'involvement profile' as a more appropriate measurement device. They argue that since their profile is multidimensional, it must provide a more complete description of the relationship between the consumer and the product. The authors identify four sources of involvement derived both from the literature and from interviews with marketing management; the profile is based on a measurement of each of these four sources. Whilst their work represents a significant step forward, their modelling approach is vulnerable to criticism. Mittal and Lee (1989) argue that because the researchers implicitly define involvement by source, there can be no distinction between situational and enduring involvement in their theory. This is important when considering products which are to be consumed in radically different situations. For instance, compare wine purchased by the layman for personal consumption to wine purchased by the same person for a dinner party or the wine purchased by a connoisseur. In each case, the characteristics of purchase are different yet the consumer remains the same in two out of the three cases. Mittal and Lee offer two further criticisms. Firstly, they argue that the perceived product importance measured by Laurent and Kapferer as a source is, in fact, a part-measure of enduring involvement itself. They give the example of a refrigerator which can be perceived as important but may not evoke much interest (i.e. be involving). Secondly, they point out that it is artificial not to distinguish explicitly between sources and forms of involvement. In their paper, Mittal and Lee present a causal model of involvement derived from the work of Laurent and Kapferer (1985) and Bloch and Richins (1983) but which takes into account both sources and forms of involvement. The model is outlined in Figure 13.4.

In the study by Mittal and Lee (1989), the levels of involvement across five products were measured amongst a convenience sample of 100 consumers. The researchers were then able to validate the causal network using LISREL VI for two consumer durable product groups. In essence, they recognize both forms of involvement (as per Figire 13.2) and establish that enduring involvement is an antecedent of situational involvement. Their three source influences of enduring involvement are remarkably similar to three of the items identified previously by researchers (Figure 13.3). (Product utility in the causal model identifies category benefits and opportunity loss of not using these products rather than a direct measure of perceived risk). With regard to sources of situational involvement, the consumer's cognitive processing (or lack of it) is replaced by evaluations of functional and psychosocial consequences of brand selection and purchase. The researchers make no attempt to explicitly measure the extent of information processing or the degree of satisfaction in the choice procedure that have been identified in prior theory. Whilst we could level this as a criticism of the model, we also recognize the enormous complexity of providing suitable

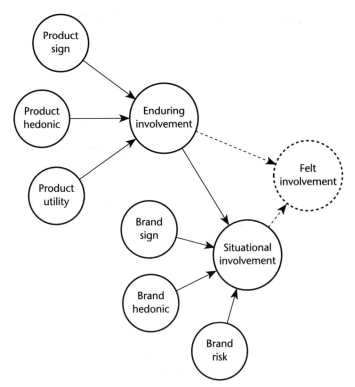

FIGURE 13.4 A causal model of consumer involvement (Adapted from Mittal and Lee, 1989)

measuring devices. In the end, researchers need an instrument that is practicable, straightforward for consumers to understand and is quick to complete.

Interestingly, Mittal and Lee were able to demonstrate that these source influences were able to explain a substantial portion of the variance in situational involvement for consumer durables; sufficient evidence to accept the model for our exploratory purposes. Measures of all eight involvement related constructs (six source, two form) lead to the final identification of three scale items for each construct. So, in total, 24 items were measured in Mittal and Lee's self administered questionnaire.

Given that this questionnaire had been developed using involving products, our research objective was to adapt this measurement tool for use among grocery products. The research procedure described in the following two sections was designed, firstly, to validate the dimensionality of the model across several grocery product categories and, secondly, to determine whether significant differences in sources and forms of involvement could be detected.

Research procedures and model validation

Seven high-penetration product categories were selected for inclusion in the research described in this chapter. They had previously been considered by expert opinion as representative of the full range of involvement levels amongst grocery products. They are grouped below according to how they had been categorized prior to field research:

Low	←	Level of involvement	→	Medium
Kitchen towels		detergents	newspapers	cigarettes
	tinned tomatoes	breakfast cereals		toothpaste

For each of the seven product categories, a random, convenience sample of 25 respondents was asked to complete the Mittal and Lee questionnaire. This provided us with 168 usable cases for analysis. Respondents were selected only if they were responsible for the household grocery purchases and had bought/used the products in the last four weeks. The self completed questionnaire (24 items) was left with respondents and collected two days later. All items were recorded on a seven-point, bipolar scale (strongly agree . . . strongly disagree) and comments about the length and content of the questionnaire were collected in an open-ended question at the end. The data was then analysed using the Genstat 5.21 suite of programs.

In order to provide evidence in support of the dimensionality of the model for grocery products, we examined the convergent and discriminant validity of the measured items. The multitrait–multimethod matrix (MT–MM) approach was used (Campbell and Fiske, 1959). They suggest four criteria to imply convergent and discriminant validity from the correlation matrix. Table 13.1 shows the extent to which the data satisfy these four criteria.

TABLE 13.1 Validity measures

Criteria for correlations	Extent criteria satisfied (%)
1. Validity coefficients: significant and sufficiently large	100
2. Validity coefficients: greater than all different trait, different method correlations in the same row and column	100
3. Validity coefficients: greater than different trait same method variables	94
4. Same pattern of correlations evidenced between all triangles	75

MEASURING CONSUMER INVOLVEMENT WITH GROCERY BRANDS **273**

Whilst caution must be exercised in drawing categorical conclusions from this test (multiple item scales do not strictly qualify as maximally different methods), the analysis provides strong evidence to support the dimensional structure of the involvement model.

Next, in assessing the reliability of the scale when applied to grocery products, Cronbach's coefficient alpha (α) was calculated for the items measuring each source and form of involvement. These reliability coefficients are shown in Table 13.2. With the exception of the brand hedonic and brand risk items, the reliability coefficients are extremely good

A major problem we found with the questionnaire was that the number and similarity of the measured items (all relating to the underlying construct of involvement) led to a high level of respondent frustration. This was evidenced both through the difficulty in getting respondents to complete the questionnaire and through comments collected in the open-ended question at the end of the process. The problem of respondent fatigue is, perhaps, highlighted in our research since the sample we used was made up of householders rather than MBAs with whom the scale was originally developed. It was clear to us that for any large-scale survey of this type, the number of items in the questionnaire would have to be substantially reduced. This item reduction process is briefly described below, prior to discussion of the involvement scores in the next section.

In order to minimize the loss in reliability of either form or source of involvement, only items showing very high convergence within a construct were removed (>0.65, significant at $p=0.001$). Using this criterion, ten items were dropped from the original questionnaire (see Appendix 13.1 for the retained items). For the two constructs with the lowest α coefficients (brand hedonic and risk), all three items remain. In contrast, only one item is retained within the three constructs with the highest α values. To allay any concern

TABLE 13.2 Reliability measures

Measurement item	α value
1. Enduring involvement	0.94
2. Situational involvement	0.94
3. Product utility	0.89
4. Product sign	0.87
5. Brand sign	0.87
6. Product hedonic	0.84
7. Brand hedonic	0.72
8. Brand risk	0.72

about loss of reliability, we carried out a test–retest analysis using this shortened questionnaire. A second convenience sample was asked to complete the questionnaire on two occasions, separated by two weeks, which provided us with 2 × 84 usable responses. The test–retest reliability coefficients are shown for each of the constructs in Table 13.3. The figures strongly support the reliability of the measure in its reduced form.

In addition to these reliability calculations, a two-way analysis of variance (ANOVA) was undertaken on the test–retest data for individual products. No significant differences were found. Both tests together provide strong evidence to suggest that the measurement device is, indeed, robust. In subsequent involvement surveys of grocery products, we recommend that the original Mittal and Lee questionnaire is shortened to these 14 items (Appendix 13.1).

Measuring involvement with grocery products

Given that we now had a reliable measurement approach for grocery products, we wished to establish whether significant differences in consumer involvement could be measured. From the data collected in the initial questionnaire (based on the 14 item measure), values for enduring and situational involvement were calculated using ANOVA for six of the seven product fields. The three source values for both forms of involvement have also been reported (Table 13.4). Building upon the premise that enduring involvement is the more influential form of involvement (Mittal and Lee, 1989), we anticipated significant differences in the scores between product groups for this construct. This was found to be the case for toothpaste, newspapers, detergents and cereals when compared to either tinned tomatoes or kitchen towels. However, there were no significant differences within these four product categories on

TABLE 13.3 Test–retest reliability coefficients

Measurement item	Reliability coefficient (r_{kk})
1. Enduring involvement	0.98
2. Situational involvement	0.91
3. Product utility	0.97
4. Product sign	0.99
5. Brand sign	0.99
6. Product hedonic	0.99
7. Brand hedonic	0.99
8. Brand risk	0.97

TABLE 13.4 Forms and sources of involvement for grocert products

Involvement		Prduct categories/Mean scores*								
Form	Source	Kitchen towels	Tinned tomatoes	Cereals	Detergent	Toothpaste	Newspapers	Six category mean	S.E.D.[†]	L.S.D.[‡]
Enduriong involvement		5.58	4.88	3.92	3.46	3.04	3.33	4.32	0.534	0.87
Situational involvement		5.29	4.50	3.33	3.21	2.71	2.75	3.98	0.556	0.91
	Product sign	5.83	6.00	5.10	4.83	4.42	3.27	4.92	0.475	0.78
	Product hedonic	6.45	6.58	5.60	6.39	6.29	5.27	6.14	0.371	0.61
	Product utility	2.88	3.54	3.38	2.00	1.79	2.63	3.22	0.436	0.71
	Brand sign	5.25	5.67	4.54	4.38	4.71	2.46	4.49	0.518	0.84
	Brand hedonic	5.15	4.97	3.69	4.15	3.78	2.90	4.11	0.438	0.71
	Brand risk	5.36	4.97	4.82	4.17	4.01	4.15	4.58	0.457	0.74

*Low scores, more involving; high scores, less involving.
[†]S.E.D., Standard error of difference.
[‡]L.S.D., Least significant difference ($P = 0.05$)

this construct measurement. At the source level (product sign, hedonic and utility), the data are more revealing. For instance, the sign value of newspapers was significantly higher than for toothpaste, detergents or cereals which, in turn, were each significantly higher than for tinned tomatoes. Similarly, the product utility value of toothpaste was significantly above cereals (as was detergents). So our measurement of enduring involvement, when linked with source influences, indicates a hierarchy of product categories which are also reflected by the situational involvement measures. Toothpaste and newspapers, with the highest situational interest, scored significantly higher than tinned tomatoes (or kitchen towels). At source level, broadly the same pattern emerges; newspapers have significantly higher brand sign and hedonic values than cereals which, in turn, have higher brand values across these constructs than tinned tomatoes (or kitchen towels).

Whilst there are variations in the hierarchy of the product groupings due to source influences, there is an underlying consistency based on the measures of the two forms of involvement; both measures place each of the six products in an identical order. By considering both forms and sources of involvement, three clusters of product categories emerge on the involvement continuum (Figure 13.5). Both tinned tomatoes and kitchen towels are low involvement categories according to either measure. Cereals can be distinguished as more involving, primarily due to attributed hedonic and sign values, whilst toothpaste, newspapers and detergents are the most involving of the six product categories.

In comparison to the measurements of situational involvement carried out by Mittal (1989), all the six grocery product categories here have medium to high scores relative to the consumer durables in that particular study (e.g. spectacles (0.73); lawnmower (1.53); bicycle (1.97) . . . toothpaste (2.71); kitchen towels (5.29)). This implies a medium to low level of situational involvement for grocery products. Intuitively, we would expect this to be the case but it is very reassuring to find this level of separation in the scores between durables and groceries. We are not aware of any other empirical studies where such direct comparisons can be made (Laurent and Kapferer's questionnaire approach and involvement profile scores remain unpublished).

It is clear from this pilot study that the 14-item questionnaire is sufficiently sensitive to produce significant variations in the levels of influencing sources and forms of involvement across the grocery products in question. The managerially derived involvement hierarchy for the product

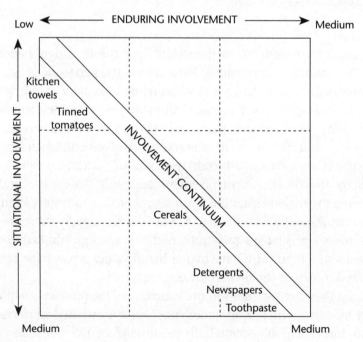

FIGURE 13.5 Clustering product categories on the involvement continuum

categories has been confirmed in four out of six cases. The measures of enduring involvement proved slightly less sensitive at the source level. Nonetheless, significant differences between product categories at the medium and low end of the involvement continuum were observed. These differences also correspond to prior expectations. So, within the confines of our research procedures (limited by sample size and representativeness), our research objective has been met.

In the concluding comments, we draw together prior theory and discuss the practical implications of our findings for practitioners and academic researchers.

Conclusions

Recently, significant progress has been made by researchers both in reaching agreement about a suitable definition of consumer involvement and providing new methods of measuring it. Building on these recent works, Mittal and Lee have now developed a causal model that distinguishes between forms and sources of involvement and which has been validated for consumer durables. The research question which we have addressed is whether or not this measurement device is sufficiently sensitive to detect significant differences in the levels of consumer involvement with grocery products. Prior theory suggested that, in principle, this should be possible despite the divided opinions that characterize the academic research in this area. Indeed, a number of individual researchers have identified differences in situational involvement and sources of enduring involvement in relation to grocery products.

So far as we are aware, our exploratory study is the first time that both sources and forms of consumer involvement have been measured using a multidimensional device in grocery markets. In the study, seven product categories were selected for testing and a 24-item questionnaire used to measure the involvement constructs. We have been able to confirm both the validity of the involvement model and the reliability of the measurement device when applied to grocery products. Subsequently, ten items were dropped from the questionnaire without apparent loss of reliability. Finally, using this 14-item questionnaire, we have shown that it is possible to measure significant differences in the sources and forms of consumer involvement with grocery products. The measurement of situational involvement and its influencing sources was particularly sensitive. This finding will be of practical interest to practitioners since it relates to brand-decision involvement, i.e. differences between brands within a product category. In the questionnaire, 8 of the 14 items relate to these constructs. Where appropriate, the questionnaire could be shortened in this way for use among consumers in developing promotional strategies to modify search and purchasing behaviour at the brand level. At the product category level, the 14-item questionnaire could be used to segment the market. Rather than merely indicating medium-low involvement divisions of the market, the measuring device allows identification of consumers high on some source constructs but low on others. This provides a better understanding of the dynamics of consumer involvement, i.e. a better understanding of where involvement originates and provides clues as to which types of appeals should be used in communications with each segment.

At a broader level, as the measure of involvement becomes more firmly established, so can the causal relationships with behavioural consequences (such as purchase loyalty, purchase frequency and brand purchasing portfolios). In grocery product markets, such knowledge would undoubtedly become the key to effective and efficient management of brands and product groups.

Acknowledgments

The authors gratefully acknowledge the financial assistance of the Isle of Man Government Department of Education and the Cranfield School of Management.

References

Agostini, J.M. (1978), Communication publicitaire et implication du consommateur. Conséquences pratiques pour la conception des messages et le choix des media. *IREP, Proceedings of the 18th Annual Conference*, 79–86

Antil, J.H. (1984), Conceptualization and operationalization of involvement, in: T. Kinnear (ed.), *Advances in Consumer Research*, **11**, 203–09. Ann Arbor: MI

Assael, H. (1987), *Consumer Behavior and Marketing Action*, New York: Wadsworth

Barwise, T.P. (1984), 'Mass attitudes and routine choice behaviour', Unpublished thesis, London Business School

Bloch, P.H. and M. Richins (1983), A theoretical model for the study of product importance perceptions, *Journal of Marketing*, **47**, Summer, 69–81

de Chernatony, L. and Knox, S.D. (1989), Using the extended Fishbein model to develop a strategy in the mineral water market, *Proceedings of the 129th E.S.O.M.A.R. Seminar: Is marketing keeping up with the customers?* 67–80. Vienna

de Chernatony, L., Knox, S.D. and Chedgey, M. (1992), Brand pricing in a recession, *European Journal of Marketing*, **26**, 2, 5–14

Celsi, R.L. and J.C. Olson (1988), The role of involvement in attention and comprehension process, *Journal of Consumer Research*, **15**, 210–24

Campbell, D.T. and Fiske, D.W. (1959), Convergent and discrimnant validation by the multitrait, multimethod matrix. *Psychological Bulletin*, **56**, March, 81–105

Cohen, J.B. (1983), Involvement and you: 1000 great ideas, in: R. Bagozzi and A. Tybout (Eds.), *Advances in Consumer Research*, **10**, 325–328. Ann Arbor: MI

Costley, C.L. (1988), Meta analysis of involvement research, in: M. Houston (Ed.), *Advances in Consumer Research*, **15**, 554–562. Ann Arbor MI

Cronbach, L.J. (1951), Coefficient alpha and the structure of tests. *Psychometrika*, **16**, September, 297–334

Davis, I. (1986), Does branding pay? *Admap*, December, 44–8

Gemunden, H.G. (1985), Perceived risk and information search: a systematic meta analysis of the empirical evidence. *International Journal of Research in Marketing*, **2**, 79–100

Hoyer, W.D. (1984), An examination of consumer decision making for a common repeat purchase product. *Journal of Consumer Research*, **11**, December, 822–29

Kapferer, J-N. and Laurent, G. (1984), Marketing analysis of the basis of consumers' degree of involvement. *Proceedings of the 37th E.S.O.M.A.R. Seminar, What we have learned from the recession*, 223–246. Rome

Kassarjian, H.H. and Kassarjian, W. (1979), Attitudes under low commitment conditions, in: J. Maloney and B. Silverman (Eds.), *Attitude Research Plays for High Stakes*, American Marketing Association, 3–15

Knox, S.D., Tait, J. and Amps, P. (1989), 'Market segmentation criteria in the U.K soft drinks market'. Paper read at the biannual conference of food marketing on 6 January; Silsoe College, Cranfield Institute of Technology, UK

Lannon, J. and Cooper, P. (1983), Humanistic advertising: a holistic cultural perspective, *International Journal of Advertising*, **2**, 195–213

Lastovicka, J.L. and Bonfield, E.H. (1982), Do consumers have brand attitudes? *Journal of Economic Psychology*, **2**, 57–75

Laurent, G. and Kapferer, J-N. (1985), Measuring consumer involvement profiles, *Journal of Marketing Research*, **22**, 41–53

McWilliam, G. (1991), Consumer's involvement in brands and product categories, in: F. Bradley *et al.* (Eds.) *Marketing Thought around the World*, **2**, 404–425

Millar, G.A. (1956), The magic number seven, plus or minus two: some limits on our capacity for processing information, *The Psychological Review*, **36**, 2, 81–97

Mittal, B.I. (1989), Measuring purchase-decision involvement. *Psychology and Marketing*, **6** (2), 147–62

Mittal, B.I. and Lee, M.S. (1989), A causal model of consumer involvement. *Journal of Economic Psychology*, **10**, 363–389

Nunally, J. (1967), *Psychometric Methods*, New York: McGraw Hill

Peter, J.P. and Olson, JC. (1987), *Consumer Behavior, Marketing Strategy Perspectives*, Illinois: Irwin

Vaughn, R.I. (1980), How advertising works: a planning model, *Journal of Advertising Research*, **20**, 27–33

Zaichkowsky, J.L. (1985), Measuring the involvement construct, *Journal of Consumer Research*, **12**, 341–352

Appendix 13.1

Measures for the forms and sources of involvement for grocery products

1. Enduring involvement
    I have a strong interest in . . . . .
2. Situational involvement
    I would choose my . . . . . very carefully.
3. Product sign
    3.1 Using . . . . . helps me express my personality.
    3.2 Knowing whether or not someone uses . . . . . tells a lot about that person.
4. Product hedonic
    4.1 I would give myself great pleasure by purchasing . . . . .
    4.2 To buy . . . . . would be like giving myself a present or treat.
5. Product utility
    Using . . . . . would be beneficial.
6. Brand sign
    You can tell a lot about a person from the brand of . . . . . s/he buys.
7. Brand hedonic
    7.1 I believe differing brands of . . . . . would give different amounts of pleasure.
    7.2 All brands of . . . . . would not be equally enjoyable.
    7.3 No matter what brand of . . . . . you buy, you get the same pleasure.
8. Brand risk
    8.1 When you buy . . . . . , it is not a big deal if you buy the wrong brand by mistake.
    8.2 It is very annoying to buy a . . . . . which isn't right.
    8.3 A bad buy of . . . . . could bring you trouble.

Nunnally (1967) argues that for basic research, reliability coefficients of 0.7–0.8 are sufficient.

Cigarettes were dropped from this part of the analysis since the dipolar responses, arising from health concerns, tended to confuse the results.

All items used 7 point strongly agree/disagree scales.

■ □ ▨ ■ 14

Individual Attitude Variations Over Time

S.B. Castleberry, N.R. Barnard, T.P. Barwise, A.S.C. Ehrenberg,
F. Dall'Olmo Riley

When consumers are reinterviewed about their attitudinal beliefs
towards different brands, such as whether it 'tastes nice' or is 'good
value for money', only about half mention the same brand as
before. This great variability of consumers' expressed attitude does
not seem to reflect any systematic erosion of their liking of the
brand, but mainly a degree of as-if-random or stochastic variation.

Background and Expectations

Introduction

A major interest in studying consumer attitudes is how such attitudes change,
possibly as correlates of changes in each consumer's buying or using the item
in question.

Systematic attitudinal tracking studies are common, but they almost
never involve reinterviewing the same sample of people because of concerns
about possible conditioning, sample attrition, and higher costs. Apart from pre
and post tests of advertisements, few studies of consumers have sought to
measure and compare the attitudes of the same individuals at different points
in time (Achenbaum, 1972; Biel, 1970; Channon and Bullen, 1985; Holmes,
1974; Katona, 1979; Lievesly and Waterton, 1986; Mills and Nelson, 1977).
Most of the studies have not been on a substantial scale, e.g. in the number of
products covered.

Yet measuring individual attitude changes is not difficult or risky, at least
not when done experimentally. It would seem of the essence for understanding
some of the dynamics of marketing. Our aim here is to report on two simple

282 QUANTITATIVE METHODS IN MARKETING

but extensive reinterviewing studies which we have carried out in the UK and America. These show how beliefs about brand attributes, intentions to buy the brand, and claimed buying behaviour varied over time for the same groups of consumers, for a variety of brands and products under normal market conditions.

The background of previous research is summarized in the rest of this section, together with our resulting expectations or hypotheses about individual attitude changes in mature, steady-state markets. The design of the studies is described next, followed by the findings of the research. The paper concludes with a brief general discussion.

Aggregate stationarity versus individual variation

Reinterviewing the same consumers either about their attitudes to a brand or about their buying behaviour has in the past yielded two highly contrasting results: steady aggregate responses but highly variable individual ones. This has been noted consistently by the few researchers who have examined reinterview attitude data. A similar pattern has been found for buying behaviour for frequently purchased categories (e.g. from consumer diary or scanner panels). But the variability of individual attitudinal responses over time has been widely ignored both by practitioners and academics.

The steady picture at the aggregate level, that much the same overall percentage of consumers state an attitude towards a brand at two different points in time, is widely confirmed by many routine tracking studies which periodically monitor usage and attitudes over time but for different samples of consumers (e.g. Brown, 1985).

In contrast, when data are collected from the same consumers over time, a picture of great 'change' or variability emerges at the individual level. Many or sometimes even most consumers alter their attitudinal responses from one interview to the next. The degree of this has been strikingly consistent: in all of the studies (see references in the Introduction to the chapter), something between 40 per cent to 60 per cent of consumers gave a different answer at two different points in time. Much the same degree of variability has also occurred for attitudes to social issues (Lievesly and Waterton 1986), and even for some more 'factual' market research questions (Samuels, 1988).

The interpretation of such individual change has, however, varied considerably among researchers. Certain researchers believe that systematic changes occur which compensate each other over large groups (Katona, 1979). In particular, some (e.g. Biel, 1970) presuppose that external factors motivate not only an irreversible loss of some of the brand's customers but also their replacement, sometimes only partial, by the conversion of new customers. This is what is known as the 'leaky bucket' theory, where some customers 'leak away' and have to be replaced by others just to keep the level of the water (or of sales) steady. Their attitudes would presumably vary in line.

Various forms of Markov chain analysis, such as a mover–stayer model or chains of different orders, are at the base of other tentative explanations, in terms of more stochastic but still systematic changes of attitude (e.g. Lievesly and Waterton, 1986).

Mills and Nelson (1977) mention a general 'volatility' in consumers' attitudes, Channon and Bullen (1975) compared the variability of individual attitude responses to the widely observed variability in consumers' purchase incidence and brand choice which was already known to underlie overall stable brands shares, with theory to match (e.g. Ehrenberg, 1972; 1988). Here it is assumed that individual consumers have different but stable propensities to buy a particular brand, with their actual purchasing behaviour varying as if probabilistically.

Our expectations

Against this background, we formulated two main hypotheses for our reinterviewing studies, the first concerning the kind of results to be expected, the second their interpretation.

We firstly hypothesized that much the same phenomenon (stability of the attitudinal results at the aggregate level but great variability at the individual) would recur and that it would closely replicate for (1) the two different countries covered by us (US and UK); (2) different kinds of frequently purchased packaged goods (e.g. food versus non-food) as well as for services; (3) in spite of different usage characteristics (e.g. by the housewife or by individual household members); (4) different brands in each product category; (5) different time spans between the two interviews; (6) differences in the breadth of the samples (e.g. selected local neighbourhoods in Athens, Georgia in the US, versus countrywide in the UK); (7) variously experienced interviewers (professionals in the UK, specially trained novice students in the US); (8) the timing of the studies (1984/5 in the UK, versus 1986/8 in the US); (9) the measurement; and (10) the nature of the variables (various specific attribute beliefs, as well as overall buying intentions and claimed buying behaviour).

Secondly, we postulated that the data would support an interpretation in stationary, zero-order stochastic and heterogeneous terms, i.e. results consistent with stable individual propensities towards making a particular attitudinal or purchase claim, but with large differences between the purchase propensities of consumers, and with observed variations over time so irregular that they could be summarized as being stochastic, i.e. as if probabilistic. We expected neither any marked systematic erosion (e.g. 'wear-out' or 'forgetting') in individuals' propensities over time, nor yet any systematic growth (e.g. 'learning' or 'purchase feedback') under normal market conditions.

This hypothesis contrasts both with the 'leaky bucket' theory, where there are highly systematic (or 'real') changes in individual consumers' propensities to make an attitudinal claim, and with the more dynamic notion of systematic validity in consumers' attitudes.

Method

Overall design

In each of two countries (the UK and the USA), a sample of consumers was interviewed twice (in one subsample three times: see below), about a range of brands, products and services.

The questions covered consumers' beliefs regarding ten or so attributes of each brand, their expressed likelihood to buy the brand, and measures of their recency and frequency of buying it, after a filter question whether the product category was ever bought. The questionnaire format was modelled on that used by the British Market Research Bureau in their Advertising Planning Index (a service previously supplied to US advertisers) and by other practitioners since, for example in the Millward–Brown tracking studies (e.g. Brown, 1985) and in many companies' 'usage and attitude' surveys.

At the aggregate level we then compared the response levels at each of the two interviews, i.e. the percentages of respondents who expressed a specific attribute belief etc. for a given brand. At the individual level we calculated repeat rates, i.e. the number of respondents giving the same answer again as a percentage of those who gave it the first time.

Product categories

Data were collected in the UK for about ten leading brands of each of five frequently purchased product categories: breakfast cereals, laundry detergents, toothpastes, canned soups, and carbonated soft drinks. In the US, data were collected for ten or so brands of two of the same products (breakfast cereals and laundry detergents) as a close replication, and also for two services (ten or so different fast food restaurant chains, and ten TV news programmes) as highly differentiated extensions, one of which (non cable TV) did not require any direct payment from the consumer.

Subjects

The UK sample was selected by the British Market Research Bureau (BMRB) among the universe of housewives aged 25 to 59 who claimed to buy at least three of the five selected product categories and who were on the telephone. Six matched subsamples from different locations throughout Great Britain were selected, totalling 784 respondents.

Four out of the six split samples were reinterviewed after 1, 3, 6, and 12 months respectively, using mostly the same professionally trained and experienced BMRB interviewers throughout. The 6 month subsample was interviewed for a third time after 12 months. (The other two subsamples were interviewed only once, to compare the response levels from ranking and scaling techniques with the free-choice ones used here, as reported elsewhere (Barnard and Ehrenberg, 1990). In the present paper we report results for those UK subjects (about two-thirds, i.e. 537) who were successfully reinterviewed. Checks on the data for respondents who could be interviewed only once showed no marked effects of attrition.

The US sample was drawn from selected neighbourhoods in Athens County, Georgia, avoiding depressed areas and apartment complexes. First, 461 consumers were interviewed at their homes in June 1986, and 219 (about half) were successfully reinterviewed some 18 months later. Two sets of previously inexperienced students of the University of Georgia were specially trained and supervised by one of the authors to interview respondents each time.

Variables measured

Three different types of variables were measured for the 100 or so brands in the study:

1. overall purchase intentions for each brand;
2. beliefs about the same set of ten or so attributes for each brand within each product category (from now on called 'attribute beliefs'), but largely differing from category to category;
3. claimed purchase behaviour.

The questionnaire format and the range of questions asked were kept essentially the same in the two countries and at each interview. The details were as follows.

Purchase intentions and attribute beliefs

Respondents were presented with a list of leading brands in each product category and asked to indicate which one(s) they were likely to buy in the future, and which one(s) they believed were characterized by each of ten or so attributes read out by the interviewer (e.g. 'tastes nice', 'is good value for money', etc. (for more detail see Barnard and Ehrenberg, 1990)).

The concept of attitudinal beliefs about brand attributes follows Joyce's (1967) definition of attitudes as 'the consumer's system of beliefs, associations, images and memories concerning the brand'. This definition has three distinctive features: (1) it does not refer to a propensity to act in any given way; (2) attitudes are supposed to mean more than the overall evaluation of the product by the consumer; (3) it implies that attitudes can be inferred or measured by research methods which are different from establishing the consumer's choice in purchasing situations.

The first and the last assumptions above make a clear distinction between the concept of 'attitude' and the concept of 'purchase intention' or 'purchase propensity'. This differs from the structural approach (Lutz, 1981) that considers intended behaviour as one of the three components of the attitude variable, and also from Azjen/Fishbein's multiattribute approach to purchase intentions (e.g. Tuck, 1976).

Claimed purchase behaviour

Claimed buying data were collected by first questioning respondents about the recency of the last purchase of the product category as a whole, and then of each itemized brand. There were seven possible responses ranging from 'in the last seven days' to 'more than a year ago' (plus 'don't know'). The claimed frequency of buying the product category as a whole and each brand was then assessed in a similar way, with possible responses ranging from 'once a week or more often' to 'less than once a year' (plus 'don't know').

The buying behaviour variables used in this study are therefore for claimed purchase recency or frequency, rather than actual specific purchases (as measured through diaries or scanners or similar means). Although there is evidence that consumers tend to overreport their buying behaviour when interviewed, the brands' relative rank order appears to be largely unaffected (Wind and Lerner, 1979).

For each of the three types of variable just described, the data were analysed across brands, beliefs about attributes, products, and countries. In this paper we will focus on the results for the average attribute belief, and for the average brand in each of the product categories studied in each country. Variations for specific brands and specific attributes are themselves very regular (mostly of a double jeopardy kind, e.g. Ehrenberg *et al.*, 1990) and will be reported on separately (e.g. Dall'Olmo Riley *et al.*, 1998). They do not affect the results discussed in the present paper.

Results

In the following sections we summarize the results for the variation from interview to interview for the average attributes and the average brand in each product category, in terms of the two parts of our first hypothesis in the Introduction to the chapter, namely:

- stability at the aggregate response level;
- variability at the individual level, i.e. 'low' repeat.

We then report on evidence relating to the second, interpretative hypothesis, namely that there is no consistent (and large) erosion in either the aggregate response levels or the repeat rates with increasing time intervals between the two interviews.

Aggregate stability

Table 14.1 summarizes all the response levels for all the variables at each of the two interviews, across the nine product categories and two countries. The variation between the two sets of results in Table 14.1 has a correlation of 0.997, i.e. the average response levels for the first and second interviews

TABLE 14.1 Attitudinal responses to a brand at two interviews (The average brand)

	Attribute beliefs*		Purchase intentions		Claimed buying**	
Interviews	1st	2nd	1st	2nd	1st	2nd
UK	%	%	%	%	%	%
Breakfast cereals	22	24	36	35	30	30
Laundry detergent	17	19	19	19	15	15
Canned soups	18	19	25	27	15	17
Toothpaste	27	28	22	23	16	17
Carbonated soft drinks	16	18	27	29	27	23
US						
Breakfast cereals	22	25	28	34	16	17
Laundry detergents	24	29	21	29	11	13
Fast food restaurants	45	49	54	62	32	33
TV news	44	50	58	67	69	71
Average	26	29	32	36	26	26

*The average belief.
**Once a month or more often

generally vary closely together. The response levels for each of the individual attributes of a brand were generally also steady from the first to the second interviews (see Dall'Olmo Riley, 1995). Much the same is the case for intentions and claimed purchasing. Overall, the average response levels for the different measures are almost steady. This is especially apparent in the UK (e.g. 20 per cent and 21 per cent for the average attribute belief, or 26 per cent and 27 per cent for the average purchase intention).

There is, however, a systematic subpattern in Table 14.1 for the US data, where the attitudinal response levels at the second interview are on average some 6 to 8 percentage points higher. This is unlikely to be positive conditioning (i.e. consumers tending to be more likely to say it at the second interview just because they have said it at the first), given that there was an elapsed interval of 18 months, and that questions were asked about 100 brands and for 100 variables.

A possibility is that with different novice (but trained) student interviewers each time in the US study, some 'learning' occurred in questionnaire administration, leading to fractionally more responses. This is in principle checkable with other such experiments. The closure of one of the fast food chains (D-Lites) and an exceptionally high response level for the US detergent Cheer at the second interview (presumably it was being highly promoted just then) also contributed to the higher US response levels.

Variable individual responses

In contrast with the basically steady response levels shown in Table 14.1, Table 14.2 summarizes how on average only about half of those giving a response in an interview do so again at the next. By the same token, about half of those saying a brand 'tastes nice', say, at the second interview had not said so at the first.

For example, while at the first interview 72 respondents mentioned Kellogg's corn flakes among the brands that 'taste nice' only 39 of them (or 54 per cent) mentioned Kellogg's corn flakes again at the second interview. Similar findings apply to both free-choice measures (i.e. attribute beliefs and purchase intentions) and to forced choice questions (i.e. claimed buying).

For fast food chains, and TV news in the US, the repeat-rates for intentions (to visit or to view) were higher, at 70 per cent. For fast food, this may be due to a 'location effect', namely that consumers patronize restaurants that are convenient in terms of their location, either near the workplace, or the home, or a regular shopping mall, etc. They may, in practice, eat in each restaurant only rather occasionally, but intend to do so whenever they are in its

TABLE 14.2 Average repeat rates
(For the average brand)

		Attribute beliefs*	Purchase intentions	Claimed buying**
UK				
Breakfast cereals	%	41	54	57
Laundry detergents	%	43	57	57
Canned soups	%	47	59	49
Toothpaste	%	50	58	48
Carbonated soft drinks	%	39	56	51
USA				
Breakfast cereals	%	39	53	44
Laundry detergents	%	42	49	32
Fast food restaurants	%	54	73	47
TV news	%	57	72	77
Average	%	46	59	51

* The average belief.
** Once a month or more often.

neighbourhood. Hence perhaps the high response level for intentions to buy in Table 14.1 and the high repeat in Table 14.2.

The relatively high TV repeat rate of 72 per cent for intentions to view is, we think, partly due to the very high potential viewing frequency in Table 14.1 (seven out of the nine programmes were nightly ones, which their viewers might see several times a week). There is also a specific form of overclaiming for regular TV programmes: people's viewing claims tend to ignore evenings when they are out or not viewing TV at all: 'I always watch it [when I'm at home and watching television]' (Barwise and Ehrenberg, 1988). But otherwise, the average repeat levels in Table 14.2 are all rather close to the 50 per cent level.

Little or no 'leaky bucket' erosion

Our second hypothesis in the section on product categories postulated that these mostly rather low repeat rates would sustain an interpretation in stationary but stochastic terms. Individual propensities to give a particular attitudinal response or purchase claim should then be stable in successive periods, with no signs of being either systematically eroded or enlarged over time, as for instance in the 'leaky bucket' or 'conditioning' interpretation, respectively.

Support for this interpretation is found from the repeat interview data at different points in time in the UK, where matched split-samples were re-interviewed after 1, 3, 6, and 12 months, respectively. Furthermore, the 6 month split-sample was interviewed for a third time after 12 months.

The results are summarized in Table 14.3 for the average attribute belief across the brands in each UK product category, and also for purchase intentions and claimed buying frequency.

Apart from a consistent drop after one month (discussed below), the results across all product fields show that the frequency with which attitudinal claims are repeated (i.e. on average about 45 per cent of the time for the attribute beliefs) is not greatly affected by the length of the time period (e.g. 3, 6, 12 months), nor yet for the third interview. There are some wobbles, but nothing either very large or very consistent. Yet on any erosion (or 'learning') theory, repeat rates from the first interview (at time zero) should all show continuing trends.

One possible interpretation of the 10 point or so drop in repeat rates in Table 14.3 after just a single month is that some 10 per cent more interviewees might then have remembered their previous response, compared with reinterviews after the longer intervals. But this seems to us unlikely to be a marked effect, since at each interview, beliefs about some 500 brand attributes were covered (i.e. ten or so attributes for each of ten brands in five product fields). Giving a response at one interview, might however reinforce the awareness and salience of the brand in the respondent's mind, in a way which still affects her responses to a measurable extent after a month.

TABLE 14.3 Average repeat rates
(Average across all brands and attribute beliefs)

		2nd interview (months later)				3rd interview
		1	3	6	12	
Attribute Beliefs						
Breakfast cereals	%	52	42	44	41	46
Laundry detergents	%	54	47	46	43	45
Canned soups	%	56	46	50	47	51
Toothpastes	%	60	50	49	50	48
Carbonated soft drinks	%	50	40	42	39	43
Average attribute	%	54	45	46	44	47
Average intention	%	75	61	63	55	62
Average buying class	%	73	68	63	62	60

An additional, and perhaps more likely, explanation might be that after just one month quite a few consumers might have not yet made a further purchase of the product category, and especially not one of some other brand. Since attitudinal responses about a brand appear to be related to the recency of purchasing the brand (Castleberry and Ehrenberg, 1990), after a month respondents could be less conditioned to change their responses. This possible explanation could, we believe, be explored and tested in future research, e.g. with yet shorter time intervals. As shown in Table 14.3, however, a time lag of three months between interviews is sufficient to eliminate any effects of 'conditioning', or memory, or increased level of awareness.

The critical information in Table 14.3 is, we believe, that repeat rates after one month or more are in the main remarkably stable. This supports the hypothesis of stationary, but stochastically variable, individual propensities to respond. It is also in line with the well established stationary stochastic models of reported or recorded buying behaviour (e.g. Ehrenberg, 1972, 1988).

Discussion and conclusions

In this paper we have reported how both in the UK and the USA, attitudinal responses to brands are generally steady in the aggregate, but highly variable at the individual level. On average only some 50 per cent of the people mention the same brand as they did 1 to 18 months before, both for branded products and also for services.

The question is why such a consumer should sometimes mention that 'brand X tastes nice' and sometimes not. In part this could be due to what is often loosely referred to as 'error of measurement'. Alternatively, it could be caused by some inherent variability or 'volatility' in people's responses (e.g. Mills and Nelson, 1977). If consumers buy a brand only occasionally, they might wish to mention that 'it tastes nice' only occasionally.

Most consumers buy several brands more or less habitually (with one or two of them probably more often than others, e.g. a 'favourite'). Nonetheless, people could express their beliefs (e.g. that 'it tastes nice') consistently about each of the brands all the time. One's attitudes about a brand could be more consistent than one's buying behaviour (i.e. all the brands in one's habitual repertoire could 'taste nice'). But the results show that this is not so at all, at least as far as consumers' highly variable expressed attitudinal responses go (as measured in our free-choice questioning here).

We discuss elsewhere how these attitudinal variations appear to be somewhat correlated with the more or less equally stochastic variations in consumers' buying (or claimed buying) behaviour for the brand in question (Barnard *et al.*, 1999). Some tentative explanations now are:

1. That consumers are affected by more or less irregular 'as-if-random' factors such as being exposed to some advertising, seeing a brand in a store or at a neighbour's, or the concurrent or recent usage or purchase of the different brands. There is extensive evidence, for example, that attitudinal responses are related to the recency and/or frequency of buying the brands (e.g. Bird and Ehrenberg, 1966; Barwise and Ehrenberg, 1985; Castleberry and Ehrenberg, 1990).

2. That expressing a positive belief about a brand all the time, if a respondent does not buy the brand all the time, could lead to cognitive dissonance (e.g. Festinger, 1957), or to difficulties if one's beliefs are self-descriptions of one's behaviour (Bem, 1968).

At this stage our interpretation of the findings is that the attributed responses analysed here represent consumers' propensities to respond about a given brand for a particular attribute where these propensities differ across people, but are stable for each individual in the medium term. If we assume that responses at successive interviews are more or less independent, a propensity or probability of 0.6 of stating that brand X, say, 'tastes nice', means that the consumer in question would, to a first approximation, say so in 60 per cent of possible interviews, in a more or less random manner. More definitive answers to these complex questions need to be sought in future research.

Our interpretation of the findings so far is both parsimonious and consistent with known patterns of buying behaviour. Future research, however, should also seek definitive explanations for two subpatterns found in this study, namely: (1) some nonstationarity in aggregate measured responses in the US, perhaps due to the use of nonprofessional interviewers there; and (2) some short-term 'conditioning' for time spans shorter than three months.

References

Achenbaum, A.A. (1972), Advertising doesn't manipulate consumers, *Journal of Advertising Research*, **12** (April), 3–13

Barnard, N.R. and Ehrenberg, A.S.C. (1990), Robust measures of consumer brand beliefs, *Journal of Marketing Research*, **27** (November), 477–84

Barnard, N.R., Dall'Olmo Riley, F., Castleberry, S.B. and Ehrenberg, A.S.C. (1999), Attitude Changes and Behaviour Change (in preparation)

Barwise, T.P. and Ehrenberg, A.S.C. (1988), *Television and Its Audience*, Newbury Park, CA, and London: Sage

Bem, D.J. (1968), Attitudes as self-perceptions: another look to the attitude–behavior link, (Eds.), in *Psychological Foundations of Attitudes*, A.G. Grenwald, T.C. Brook, and T.M. Ostrom (Eds.), New York: Academic Press

Biel, A.L. (1970), 'The dynamic of change: a longitudinal study of attitudes and behaviour', paper presented at the International Marketing Congress of the American Marketing Association

Brown, G. (1985), Tracking studies and sales effects: a UK perspective, *Journal of Advertising Research*, **25** (February/March), 52–64

Castleberry, S.B. and Ehrenberg, A.S.C. (1990), 'Brand usage: a factor in consumer beliefs,' *Marketing Research*, June 1990, 14–19

Dall'Olmo Riley, F. (1995), '*Changing attitudes in steady markets*', Ph.D. thesis, London University

Dall'Olmo Riley, F., Barnard, N.R., Barwise, T.P., Castleberry, S.B. and Ehrenberg, A.S.C. (1993), Double jeopardy in attitudinal repeat-rates, *Journal for Consumer Research* (to be submitted)

Dall'Olmo Riley, F., Barnard, N.R., Barwise, T.P., Castleberry, S.B. and Ehrenberg, A.S.C. The variability of attitudinal repeat rates, *International Journal of Research in Marketing*, (in press)

Channon, C. and Bullen, T. (1985), 'Qualitative use of quantitative data', paper presented at the 18th Marketing Research Society Conference

Ehrenberg, A.S.C. (1972, 1988), *Repeat-Buying: Facts, Theory and Applications*, second edition, London: Griffin; New York: Oxford University Press

Ehrenberg, A.S.C., Goodhardt, G.J. and Barwise, T.P. (1990), Double jeopardy revisited, *Journal of Marketing*, **54** (3), 82–91

Festinger, L. (1957), *A Theory of Cognitive Dissonance*, Stamford: University Press

Goodhardt, G.J., Ehrenberg, A.S.C. and Chatfield, C. (1984), The dirichlet: a comprehensive model of buying behaviour, *Journal of the Royal Statistical Society*, **A147**, 5, 621–655

Holmes, C. (1974), 'A statistical evaluation of rating scales', paper presented at the 17th Marketing Research Society Conference

Joyce, T. (1967), Brand images, in *Consumer Behaviour*, A.S.C. Ehrenberg and F.G. Pyatt (Eds.), London: Penguin, 123–38

Katona, G. (1979), Toward a macropsychology, *American Psychologist*, **34** (February), 118–26

Lievesly, D.D. and Waterton, J.J. (1986), Advantages and limitations of a panel approach in an attitude survey, paper presented at the 29th Marketing Research Society Annual Conference

Lutz, R. (1981), The role of attitude theory in marketing, in *Perspectives in Consumer Behavior*, H.H. Kassarjian and T.S. Robertson (Eds.), Glenview IL: Scott, Foresman and Company

McPhee, W.N. (1963), *Formal Theories of Mass Behavior*, New York: Free Press

Mills, P. and Nelson, E. (1977), 'Re-interviewing in attitude surveys: an experimental study,' paper presented at the ESOMAR Seminar on Social Research

Samuels, J. (1988), Social class in the future, *Admap*

Tuck, M. (1976), *How Do We Choose?* London: Methuen

Wind, Y. and Lerner, D. (1979), On the measurement of purchase data: surveys versus purchase diaries, *Journal of Marketing*, **16** (February), 39–47

■ ☐ ■ ■ 15

Role of Motives and Attributes in Consumer Motion Picture Choice

K.E. Kristian Möller and Pirjo Karppinen

The study focuses on consumer motion picture motives and choice criteria. Its purpose can be specified into the following objectives: (1) to examine the motivational basis of cinema attendance (2) to examine the predictive ability of movie motives and consumers' attribute importances in preference regressions of four types of movie, (3) to carry out a motion picture choice analysis by predicting audience membership with discriminant analysis. The data is based on a convenience sample of Finnish consumers (N = 228) attending one of the following types of movie: adventures/thrillers, human/ social dramas, sex movies, entertainment movies.

The results of a group of multivariate analyses (factor analysis, canonical correlation, preference regression, and discriminant analysis) indicate that consumers attending different types of films have distinctly separate motivation bases, as well as attribute importance profiles, underlying their movie choices. Each movie type had a specific preference structure, expressed by the regression coefficients. Finally, the discriminant analysis suggests that the general motive and attribute variables are effective also in predicting motion picture choice. On balance, the results were mutually supportive and exemplify the managerial usefulness of quantitative consumer analysis also in the case of such abstract leisure products as motion pictures.

Introduction

This study focuses on consumers' motion picture preferences. It seems that very little is known about how consumers choose motion pictures, what kind of evaluative criteria they use, and how the audience could be segmented. Only one exception is known to us, the Choffray and Pras (1980) study on the determinants of market success for commercial movies. On the other hand, a multitude of studies have investigated the above issues in relation to television viewing, concentrating on program type and preference analysis (e.g. Ehrenberg, 1968; Frank *et al.*, 1971; Lehmann, 1971) and on audience characteristics and segmentation (e.g. Stanton and Lowenhar, 1974; Gensch and Ranganathan, 1974; Villani, 1975; Frank and Greenberg, 1979; and Bryant and Gerner, 1981). Television study results cannot, however, be generalized over consumers' movie attendance as the audiences and programme types are different. Further, we believe that the movie choice is more active and potentially complex than television programme choice. This is certainly the situation in most European countries, particularly Scandinavia, where the number of television channels is limited compared to the cinema options.

Two basic issues made the motion picture (or movie or film) choice interesting to us. First, this choice can be regarded as a complex buying process of a predominantly intangible 'product'. The films available on the market exhibit great variety, and the perception of any specific film varies distinctively between consumers. Moreover, each film is a unique product and the comparison between alternatives is bound to be subjective because the actual evaluation of a film can take place only during and after the viewing experience. This abstractness forms a challenge for the explanation and prediction of movie preferences (Beard, 1980). Second, cultural officials concerned with motion pictures as well as marketing management of the motion picture industry could benefit from answers to basic questions such as (1) what criteria do consumers use in choosing between movies; (2) how well do these criteria predict the preferences of movie types and specific movies; and (3) do these criteria vary between audience types (segments) and/or between movie types? On balance, there are both theoretical and managerial rationales for the present study. Before stating the objectives in detail the variables characterizing motion picture choice are briefly outlined.

The movie choice is seen as a process guided by contextual factors and consumer variables. The contextual variables, especially reference groups and general movie supply and 'culture', together with a person's values, personality and lifestyle, influence the motion picture attendance and choice. 'Movie motivation' consists of the needs and reasons why people go to the movies. In addition to the relaxation and change, interest in history, technology, or in human and social dramas, a wish to have a 'horror' or aesthetic experience are examples of potential motives related to the cinema. Factor analysing 17 movie characteristics, Choffray and Pras (1980) received three general criteria in evaluating movies: overall quality, relaxation, and intellectual satisfaction. Villani (1975), researching television viewing, noted three tentative categories of viewer groups as follows: change oriented, non violence, and action oriented. In their comprehensive survey of television audience, Frank and Greenberg (1979) found nine interest factors (based on a factor analysis of 139 items): socially stimulating, status enhancement, creative accomplishment, escape from problems, family ties, understanding others, greater self acceptance, escape from boredom, intellectual stimulation and growth.

It seems evident that a person's motivation base can be multidimensional: at different times different dimensions or needs may dominate the choice process. Motivations are further related to the supply of motion pictures. If only 'westerns' are available no multidimensional motivation can evolve or survive.

The motion picture related beliefs and attitudes represent an internal information source accumulated through viewing experiences and external information. Beliefs contain information about movie attributes (such as actors, directors, critiques, characteristics of movie types or genres, popularity etc.) and the attitudes represent fairly stable affective tendencies (preferences) towards both the attributes and movie types. The motives and attitudes are interrelated. Cumulating experience may change the beliefs and attitudes, and gradually affect the motive base.

The demographic and socioeconomic variables are not expected to have a notable direct effect on movie preferences. Of course age and education do influence movie behaviour, but the causal impact is asssumed to be channelled through socialization, personality, and reference groups which further affect motion picture motivation.

We argue that the motives play a dominant role in shaping consumers' general preferences towards types or genres of movies. They are used as criteria when the consumer dichotomizes his or her evoked set of movies into acceptable/non-acceptable sets. Depending on the multidimensionality of his or her motives a person may at various times find different genres acceptable and also consider more than one genre acceptable at a time. Based on Howard and Sheth (1969), Choffray and Pras (1980) suggest a three staged movie choice process: awareness of available movies and their characteristics, perception of characteristics and formation of preferences, choice among available movies. We think that this is too simplistic a view because it omits the genre level.

Moreover, the motives and movie attributes are interlinked. Motivation affects the emphasis a person gives to various movie attributes. In this way it is evident that both motives and attributes are used as choice criteria when making decision on specific motion pictures.

The relationship between motives and attributes is decisive for understanding movie preferences. Both these constructs should have a key role in segmenting the motion picture market. The ability to classify the heterogeneous cinema audience into meaningful subaudiences would enhance the planning of cultural policy actions, as well as the targeting of the product development and marketing communication of the film industry.

Concerning our scant knowledge of movie choice and the general nature of the above conceptualizations several exploratory issues emerge.

- Which motivational dimensions and movie attributes form the determinant choice criteria, and what is the relationship between these two construct types?
- Do the preference structures (defined by criteria) differ between various types of movies and can the cinema audience be segmented into more homogeneous subgroups according to the choice criteria?
- How well do the motives and attribute importances predict movie type preferences and choice?

These issues are dealt with in the empirical part of the study.

Data

The empirical analyses of the study are based on the data collected in Turku (a Finnish town with a population of 160 000) among the audiences of the four movies: *Sheriff and the Satellite Kid, Sun Wind, The Front Page*, and *Emmanuelle in Tabu Island*. The first movie was an action type western with the actors Bud Spencer and Terence Hill. The second was a Finnish science fiction movie; its theme combined both psychological and social issues and resembled Tarkovski's *Solaris* a little. *The Front Page* was Billy Wilder's comedy about the newspaper world including a lot of funny jokes. Finally, *Emmanuelle* represents the new wave of bold but soft sex movies.

These movies were selected by a group of experts to represent adventures/thrillers, human/social dramas, light entertainment movies, and sex movies. The typology adopted is based on the report of a Finnish committee on cinema policy including factor analytic research results (Komiteanmietinto, 1973). A convenience sample of 600 weekend audience members (i.e. 150 each per movie) was given a questionnaire in the cinema before the show. The respondents were requested to answer the questions at home and return the questionnaire by mail. A satisfactory return of 288 usable questionnaires gave a 48 per cent response rate (*Sheriff and the Satellite Kid*: 27 per cent, *Sun Wind*:

27 per cent, *The Front Page*: 31 per cent, *Emmanuelle in Tabu Island*: 15 per cent).
As respondent names were not collected, the nonresponse bias could not be
checked.

The questionnaire consisted of batteries of 15 motive and 14 movie
attribute statements (depicted in tables 15.1 and 15.2), and a question of movie
type preference. The choice of statements was based on qualitative audience
interviews and on earlier Finnish factor analytic studies on motion picture and
theatre attendance (Pietila, 1967; Artell *et al.*, 1973; Artell, 1974). In case of
motives the following construct was used: 'How well do these statements
describe the reasons why you go to the movies?', measured with a five-point
scale with anchors 'very well'/'not at all'. The attribute importance was
measured by: 'How much attention do you pay to the following factors when
you choose a movie?', rated with another five-point scale with anchors 'very
much'/'not at all'. The preference of the four general movie types (adventures/
thrillers, human/social dramas, light entertainment movies, and sex movies)
was again measured with a five-point scale.

TABLE 15.1 Factor analysis of the motion picture motives

Variable	Factor I	Factor II	Factor III	Factor IV	Communality h_2
Knowledge of social issues	0.63	0.23	0.25	0.17	0.55
Excitement	0.02	−0.58	0.30	−0.17	0.46
Knowledge of history, nature, technology	0.25	0.01	0.40	0.24	0.28
Escape daily worries	−0.05	−0.77	0.03	−0.03	0.60
Aesthetic experiences	0.38	0.03	0.05	0.68	0.61
Understand myself and world	0.82	0.15	−0.01	0.24	0.76
Extend views and opinions	0.84	0.09	−0.03	0.23	0.76
New experiences and impressions	0.67	−0.04	0.04	0.34	0.56
Relaxation	−0.07	−0.75	−0.05	0.06	0.57
Form of art and culture	0.41	0.23	0.17	0.60	0.61
Friends like movies	−0.10	−0.18	0.45	−0.00	0.24
Enhances understanding among people	0.56	0.06	0.44	0.11	0.52
Exposes human issues	0.68	0.13	0.24	0.12	0.56
To get change	−0.29	−0.60	0.09	−0.15	0.47
Maintains ideals and values	0.31	−0.03	0.47	0.03	0.32
Eigenvalues	3.57	2.04	1.03	1.22	7.86
Percentage of total variation	24%	14%	7%	8%	53%

TABLE 15.2 Factor analysis of the motion picture attribute importances

Variable	Factor Communality I	Factor II	Factor III	h_2
Topic	0.00	0.10	0.16	0.04
Actors	0.19	0.03	0.48	0.27
Director	−0.52	0.34	0.41	0.56
Music	0.15	0.02	0.39	0.17
Title	0.47	−0.10	0.20	0.27
Finnish/foreign	0.52	−0.13	0.25	0.35
Country of origin	0.40	0.06	0.30	0.26
Critiques	−0.24	0.68	0.13	0.54
Awards	0.16	0.55	0.24	0.38
Colour/black & white	0.68	0.02	0.16	0.49
Popularity	0.67	0.33	−0.04	0.57
Media publicity	0.24	0.64	−0.03	0.47
Debate aroused	−0.12	0.69	0.05	0.49
Based on well-known novel, person, incident	0.30	0.23	0.24	0.20
Eigenvalues	2.15	1.97	0.94	5.06
Percentage of total variation	15%	14%	7%	36%

It should be noted that both the motivation and attribute relevance measures assess respondents' reasons for going to the cinema and their choice criteria only in general terms, not related to any movie type or specific film. This limitation restricts the subsequent analyses. The rest of the questionnaire covered a number of cinema attendance questions, not used in the present study, and basic demographic and socioeconomic variables.

Analysis and results

In view of the scarce *a priori* knowledge an exploratory plan of analysis was developed. The first part is fairly descriptive including factor analyses of movie motives and attribute importance ratings and a subsequent mapping of various subaudiences into the 'motive' space. The relationship between motives and attributes is further examined.

With only a two-dimensional data matrix (consumers' motive and attribute ratings) we could not make the ordinary 'brand' or in our case movie analysis, requiring a 'consumer attribute ratings per brands' matrix, but concentrated on audience analysis by canonical correlation. Secondly, the motive and attribute importance ratings are used as explanators in preference regressions of the four movie types. Thirdly, discriminant analysis is used to predict the audience membership of the respondents. This gives us a view of how well the general motives and attribute ratings can predict movie choice.

The overlapping of the analyses is intentional. We wanted to compare the preference structures indicated by regression and discriminant coefficients and further the dimensions of 'movie audience spaces' defined by factors and discriminant functions respectively.

Consumers' motion picture motives and attribute importance

The motives guiding cinema attendance were studied by factor analysing the ratings of the 15 motive statements with the principal axis method. A varimax rotated four factor solution, described in Table 15.1, was chosen on the basis of eigenvalues and interpretability. The solution accounts for 52 per cent of total variation.

The first factor (interest and information) seems to delineate intellectual curiosity and willingness to acquire new information and experiences (cf. the 'uses and gratifications' study of media behaviour by Katz *et al.*, 1973–74). The second factor summarizes relax and change based motivation, whereas the third, social relationships is primarily related to friends and company, and to understanding ideals and values. The last factor describes aesthetics and art related motivation. The interpretability of the factor solution is fairly straightforward.

To evaluate the homogeneity of respondents' motivations the respondents were partitioned into subaudiences according to the movie they attended, their age, education, and frequency of attending the cinema. The projected subaudience positions in the motion picture motivation space (based on the mean factor scores) are presented in Figure 15.1. Respondents evidently have widely varying movie motivations depending on their favourite movie types, education and age.

Concentrating first on the four movie audiences it can be noted that adventure/thriller audiences are characterized by being low on interest and information and aesthetics and art, and high on relax and change, whereas the profile of human/social drama audiences is just the opposite. Light entertainment audiences are low on interest and information and high on social relationships, while the sex movie audiences represent an in-between case except being lowest on social relationships.

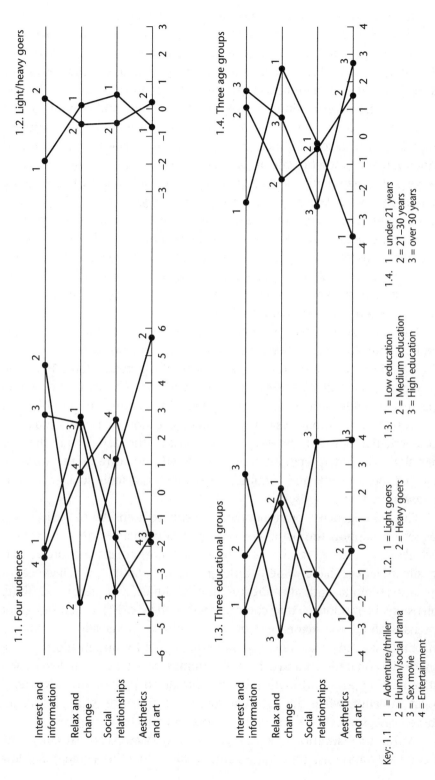

1.1. Four audiences

Interest and information

Relax and change

Social relationships

Aesthetics and art

1.2. Light/heavy goers

1.3. Three educational groups

Interest and information

Relax and change

Social relationships

Aesthetics and art

1.4. Three age groups

Key: 1.1 1 = Adventure/thriller
        2 = Human/social drama
        3 = Sex movie
        4 = Entertainment

1.2. 1 = Light goers
       2 = Heavy goers

1.3. 1 = Low education
       2 = Medium education
       3 = High education

1.4. 1 = under 21 years
       2 = 21–30 years
       3 = over 30 years

FIGURE 15.1 Motion picture motivation space: subaudience analysis

The interpretation of the other subaudience profiles can be done in a similar way. Concerning education the high education audiences (college or university degree) are high on interest and information, social relations and aesthetics and art, and low on relax and change, whereas the profiles of low and medium education audiences (vocational schools or courses; technical, commercial and other institute degree) are fairly similar and opposite to the one of the high education group. Within the three age groups the youngest (under 21 years) have a distinctive profile with low values on interest and information and aesthetics and art, and high on relax and change. The other two age groups have fairly identical patterns, which are opposite to the young but more moderate. The frequency of movie attendance partitioning did not disclose significant variances in the motives of light v heavy cinema goers.

Both the factor analysis and the subsequent motivational mapping of the subaudiences produced empirically sensible results. The revealed motivation patterns provide invaluable managerial information both for undertaking marketing communication programs for specific films or cinemas and for planning audience segmentation strategy.

The analysis discussed previously was repeated over the respondents' motion picture attribute importance beliefs. Factor analysis of the 14 attribute ratings produced a three-factor varimax solution depicted in Table 15.2. The first factor gets high loadings primarily with colour/black and white, popularity, and director. It is labelled popularity, colour and anti-director. The second factor summarizes critiques and debate aroused as motion picture choice criteria, whereas the last factor portrays the actors and director dimension. The interpretations must be viewed with care as the variance explained (36 per cent) and communalities are considerably smaller than in the case of motive analysis.

The homogeneity of respondents' attribute importance beliefs was analysed by mapping the factor score means of subaudiences into an 'attribute space' illustrated in Figure 15.2. Looking at the four submaps one can see that the subaudiences have widely different views about the relevance of popularity, colour and anti-director and critiques and debate attribute dimensions in motion picture choice, whereas there exists a high degree of consensus about the actors and director attribute dimension. Adventure/ thriller and sex movie audiences are high on popularity, and in addition, the former is low on critiques and debate. The human/social drama audience has a distinctively opposite attribute relevance profile to that of the adventure/ thriller audience, while the light entertainment audience represents an in-between case, somewhat stressing the actors and director dimension.

Within the education groups, high education viewers are extremely low on popularity and high on critiques and debate, while the medium and low

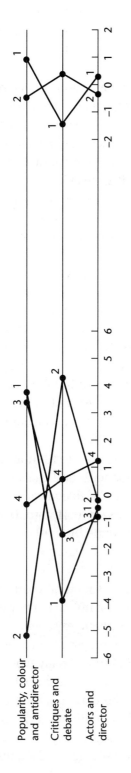
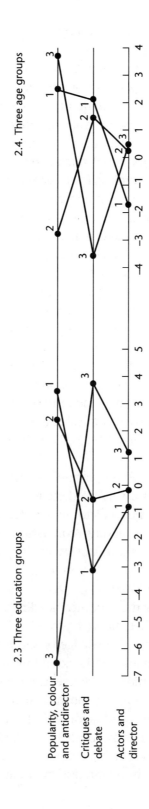

2.1. Four audiences

2.2. Light/heavy goers

2.3 Three education groups

2.4. Three age groups

Popularity, colour and antidirector

Critiques and debate

Actors and director

Key: 2.1 1 = Adventure/thriller
2 = Human/social drama
3 = Sex movie
4 = Entertainment

2.2. 1 = Light goers
2 = Heavy goers

2.3. 1 = Low education
2 = Medium education
3 = High education

2.4. 1 = under 21 years
2 = 21–30 years
3 = over 30 years

FIGURE 15.2 Motion picture attribute importance space: subaudience analysis

education audiences have opposite views. The 21–30 age group is low on popularity, while the old (over 30) are high on that dimension and low on critiques and debate. The frequency of cinema going did not have a significant impact on the importance of attribute dimensions.

The results indicate that there are two basic dimensions underlying the attributes people use to evaluate motion pictures: general popularity of the movie, and the critiques the movie receives and the debate it arouses. Different subaudience types varied remarkably in the relevance they related to these dimensions. The findings have again practical implications for motion picture marketing and cinema management. Moreover, it seems likely that such the interest and information motivation dimension as well as aesthetics and art are related to critiques and debate, as are relax and change to popularity. To examine the potential relationships in detail canonical correlation analysis was conducted on the two variable groups.

The canonical analysis was run by using both original variables and factor scores as input data. Only the results of the former analysis are reported, the runs based on factor scores supported the following suggestions but were more difficult to interpret. Table 15.3 describes the results with the 15 motivation statements as predictor set and the 14 attribute statements as criterion set. Only two variant pairs are reported (although four were significant) as the redundancy achieved by the third pair was already low (0.10). For a discussion on interpretation of canonical analysis results see Lambert and Durand (1975), Johansson and Sheth (1977), Fornell (1978), Green (1978), and Kuylen and Verhallen (1981).

The sum of the proportion of explained variance in the criterion set given the predictor set is 0.17 (Redundancy1 + Redundancy2) and the sum of the redundancy for the predictor set is 0.24. This amount of shared variance could be interpreted as finding correlation coefficients of 0.41 and 0.49. The redundancy scores compare favorably with those found by Sparks and Tucker (1971), Alpert and Peterson (1972), Lambert and Durand (1975), and Schaninger *et al.* (1980).

Looking at the canonical loadings (called also structural coefficients) it can be noted that the first prediction variate is mainly characterized by a positive interest in knowledge of social issues, aesthetic experiences, understanding oneself and world extending views, art and culture, and disinterest (negative correlation) in charge, excitement and escape of daily worries. This variate seems to combine the interest and information with the aesthetics and art movie motivation factors (cf. Table 15.1). The corresponding criterion variate is dominated by positive attention on director, critiques and debate and negative on colour/B&W, and popularity. In other words, people whose movie motivation is based on interest, information, and aesthetics tend to emphasize

TABLE 15.3 Canonical analysis of motion picture motivation and attribute importance

Variables	Variate I		Variate 2	
	w_1	l_1	w_2	l_2
Predictor Set (x)				
Knowledge of social issues	0.21	0.65	0.01	0.29
Excitement	−0.17	−0.46	0.09	0.45
Knowledge of history, nature etc.	−0.09	0.18	0.46	0.64
Escape daily worries	−0.04	−0.42	0.13	0.49
Aesthetic experiences	0.18	0.63	0.17	0.37
Understand myself and world	−0.07	0.67	0.05	0.32
Extend views and opinions	0.27	0.71	0.23	0.40
New experiences and impressions	0.07	0.57	−0.05	0.34
Relax	−0.04	−0.34	0.28	0.45
Form of art and culture	0.35	0.79	−0.05	0.23
Friends like movies	0.00	−0.16	0.16	0.37
Enhances understanding	−0.01	0.43	0.04	0.38
Exposes human issues	0.07	0.56	0.12	0.36
To get change	−0.25	−0.64	0.31	0.39
Maintains ideals and values	−0.16	0.03	0.17	0.47
Criterion Set (y)				
Topic	0.11	0.20	0.21	0.36
Actors	−0.12	−0.12	0.11	0.38
Director	0.39	0.79	0.04	0.07
Music	0.14	0.07	0.17	0.41
Title	−0.11	−0.40	0.35	0.50
Finnish/foreign	−0.03	−0.37	−0.01	0.23
Country of origin	−0.02	−0.20	−0.03	0.22
Critiques and debate	0.32	0.67	0.27	0.34
Awards	0.08	0.22	0.09	0.50
Colour/black and white	−0.27	−0.57	0.14	−0.11
Popularity	−0.24	−0.46	0.05	0.47
Media publicity	−0.05	0.09	0.31	0.57
Debate aroused	0.18	0.51	−0.13	0.24
Based on well known novel etc.	0.09	−0.01	0.41	0.66

Canonical variates	Rc	R_c^2	R_{dy}	R_{dx}	Wilks' lamloda	X^2	df	P
1st variate pair	0.79	0.63	0.105	0.176	0.098	633	210	0.001
2nd variate pair	0.62	0.38	0.065	0.063	0.264	364	182	0.001

director, critique, and debate when choosing the film. The canonical loadings reflect the direct linear correlation of an observed variable in the set with the canonical variate (score) of the set. They are unaffected by the direct influence of multicollinearity and suppression phenomenon because they ignore the correlation between other variables and variates.

The second canonical variate pair indicates that people who want to get excitement, change, and knowledge of history, nature etc. and maintain ideas and values are prone to pay attention to whether the film is based on a well known novel, person or incident, to its media publicity, popularity, awards and title . The relationship highlighted by the first variate pair supports the *ad hoc* expectations based on the motivation and attribute importance mapping. The outcome of the second pair is more novel and not so straightforward. As the redundancy coefficients of the variate pair are relatively low, the relationships disclosed can be considered more marginal.

To summarize, the canonical analysis indicates that significant relationships exist between motion picture motivation and relative attribute importance beliefs. Consumers' whose motivation is based on intellectual curiosity and interest in human and social issues or on aesthetics and 'film as a form of art' tend to emphasize director, critiques and debate aroused, whereas those seeking excitement, change and relaxation value popularity and media publicity. For the latter, the film must be a colour film while the film being black and white may not be a decisive drawback for the interest, information and aesthetics minded. On balance, the motion picture motivation and attribute importance findings seem to have remarkable managerial potential in segmentation and promotional planning. This potential can be further evaluated by carrying out movie type preference and choice analysis.

Consumer preference for basic motion picture type

Consumer preference for adventures/thrillers, human/social dramas, sex movies and light entertainment movies was studied by conducting preference regressions for each movie type using the general motive and attribute ratings as explanators and the movie type preference measure as dependent variable. Three model versions were fitted: attribute model, motive model, and combined model. The latter model combined the three best explanators of the first two models and in addition included the age, education and income of the respondents. It was expected that the motive model would outperform the attribute model because the task concerned movie type not specific movie preference.

In all 12 runs a stepwise version of the linear additive model was used. The predictive ability of the model versions is summarized in Table 15.4. The

TABLE 15.4 Summary of motion picture type preference regressions: coefficients of multiple determination

Model	1^{1}	2	3	4
Attribute model	0.34^{2}	0.47	0.07	0.35
Motive model	0.42	0.54	0.08	0.36
Combined model	0.54	0.55	0.15	0.46

[1] 1 = Adventures/thrillers, 2 = Human/social dramas, 3 = Sex movies, 4 = Entertainment movies.
[2] All R2s are significant at the 0.001 level except the coefficients of sex movies; these are significant at the 0.01 level.

expected relationship between the motive model and the attribute model is supported in the cases of adventures/thrillers and human/social dramas but is unclear in the two other cases.

It seems that the preference for sex movies cannot be explained by the variables used in the present study but requires a tailor made approach, preferably based on personal interviews. This movie type will be excluded from further analysis. Otherwise the degree of preference explanation can be regarded as satisfactory especially when it is noted that the prediction is based on general movie motive and attribute importance responses. This indicates that the linear model can be used to model motion picture preferences in pragmatic studies.

Table 15.5 shows the summary of preference structures produced by the attribute model. The preference structures of adventures/thrillers and light entertainment are fairly similar. The film belonging to these genres obviously should be a colour film and not praised by critiques (the more a person emphasizes critiques as choice criterion the less likely he/she is to prefer these types of movie). Further, the popularity and publicity of adventures/thrillers increase their preference. Actors have the same impact on light entertainment movies, whereas the valuation of directors has a notable negative effect on their preference. Finally, the preference structure of human/social dramas is opposite to those of adventures/thrillers and light entertainment movies.

It is important to note the role of black and white films. The audiences of other movie types, except human/social dramas, evidently use this variable to dichotomize movie alternatives into acceptable versus nonacceptable categories. In general, the results denote that various types of movies have different preference structures. When comparing the present outcome with the results derived by mapping movie audiences into an attribute space, in Figure 15.2, it can be noted that the principal directions are similar. The two analyses support each other giving internal validity to the results.

TABLE 15.5 Summary of motion picture type preference structures: beta coefficients of attribute model and motive model

Attribute model

Variables	1[a]	2	4
Colour/black & white	0.26[b]	−0.23	0.29
Critiques	−0.27	0.33	−0.16
Popularity	0.18	0.10	
Based on well-known novel, person, incident		0.12	−0.10
Director		0.22	−0.28
Finnish/foreign	0.13	−0.10	0.13
Actors			0.20
Media publicity	0.15		0.13
Media publicity	0.15		0.13
Debate aroused	−0.17		
Topic		0.18	
Music		0.12	

Motive model

Variables	1[a]	2	4
Aesthetic experiences	−0 24[b]	0.55	
Excitement	0.47	−0.18	0.12
Knowledge of history, nature, technology			0.12
To get change	0.17		0.12
Knowledge of social issues	−0.20	0.21	−0.19
Enhance understanding among people		0.11	−0.16
Extend views and opinions			0.18
Form of art and culture			−0.23
Relax			0.19
Escape daily worries			−0.10
Maintain ideals and values		−0.17	0.12
Friends like movies			0.20
New experiences and impressions			0.21

[a] 1 = Adventures/thrillers, 2 = Human/social dramas, 4 = Entertainment movies.
[b] All standardized regression coefficients (betas) are sigmficant at least at the 0.05 level. They can be directly compared within a movie type but not across the types.

The summary results of the motive model, in Table 15.5, show clearly that consumers have different motives for preferring adventures/thrillers, human/social dramas, and light entertainment movies. The preference of adventures/thrillers is dominated by the wish to experience excitement and change, whereas the emphasizing of aesthetic experiences or social issues decreases the preferences. Subsequently the liking of human/social dramas is based on the need for aesthetic experiences and the wish to have information on social issues.

The motive structure underlying the preference for light entertainment movies is more diverse. Positive dimensions include the wish to have a good time with friends and relax, the negative ones the wish to avoid 'art and cultural' movies, and the handling of social issues. The relatively small variance in the magnitude of beta coefficients may indicate that the light entertainment movies represent a too wide and thus obscure category. This is reflected in the lower coefficients of determination (R2s) in Table 15.4. In possible future studies this category should be reclassified into at least two subcategories.

The above results can be compared with the mapping of the subaudiences into a motivation space (shown in Fig. 15.1). The outcomes support each other strongly and provide internal validity to the results. The relative importance of the standardized regression coefficients should, however, be viewed with care as there is notable multicollinearity in the motive model.

The last model version, the combined model, included the three best explanators from the previous models and age, education, and income as potential regressors. The background variables were included in order to check their direct impact on movie preferences. As shown in Table 15.6, education was a significant regressor in case of all three movie types. The negative sign against human/social dramas indicates that increasing education is related to increasing preferences. The magnitudes of the background variables are low except in adventures/thrillers. Also, age had some effect on the preferences of this movie type, aging reducing the preference.

On balance, the background variables did not increase the rate of preference explanation remarkably except in the case of adventures/thrillers. This was to be expected as it was assumed that their effect was channelled through motivations. The relative emergence of education is explainable because education (and the social consequences related to it) is closely connected to one's socialization and reference groups and through these to motion picture motivation.

TABLE 15.6 Summary of motion picture type preference structures: beta coefficients of combined model

Variables	[Combined model] 1[1]	2	4
Excitement	0.35[2]		
Education	0.20	−0.09	0.14
Aesthetic experiences	−0.17	0.31	
Colour/black & white	0.17	−0.19	0.21
Age	−0.14		−0.09
Critiques	−0.14	0.15	
Popularity	0.12		
Extend views and opinions		0.31	
Escape daily worries		−0.08	
Form of art and culture			−0.21
Relax			0.21
Director			−0.19
Actors			0.13

[1] 1 = Adventures/thrillers, 2 = Human/social dramas, 4 = Entertainment movies.
[2] All standardized regression coefficients (betas) are significant at least at the 0.05 level. They can be directly compared within a movie type but not across types.

To summarize, the preference regressions confirmed the expectation that different movie types have varying preference structures. The predictive ability of the simple linear model proved to be satisfactory even when using the general attribute importance and movie motivation ratings as explanatory variables. By collecting specific evaluations about each motion picture alternative under study the predictive validity of the model should easily be increased. The sex movie was, however, an exception. It seems that the preference of that movie type cannot be accounted for by the explanatory variables available in the present study. Finally, all the principal preference structure results were indirectly corroborated by the corresponding attribute and motivation mapping analyses.

Predicting motion picture choice by multiple discriminant analysis

Multiple discriminant analysis was adopted to predict the audience membership of the respondents (the sex movie was not included). A model based on 12 explanators, selected from the pool of 15 movie motive and 14 attribute importance variables was fitted (after testing the equality of the underlying covariance matrices). The summary results are shown in Table 15.7. Both discriminant functions are significant at the 0.001 level, the first accounting for approximately 70 per cent of the total discrimination. The canonical correlation coefficients define the correlation between the discriminant functions and the grouping variable (coded as a set of binary dummies). To facilitate the interpretation of the functions, loadings (also called structural coefficients) expressing the correlations between predictors and the discriminant axes were derived.

The first discriminant function represents a bipolar continuum characterized by a wish to experience change and excitement, and to avoid artistic and aesthetic experiences, and the handling of social issues. Further, the function is negatively correlated with critiques and positively with colour. It seems that the first discriminant function combines the principal elements of three motivation factors: interest and information, relax and change and aesthetics and art (cf. Table 15.1), and the critique and debate attribute factor (cf. Table 15.2).

The second discriminant function is characterized by such motives as knowledge of social issues, history, nature and technology, and understanding among people; and by attributes like actors, well known novel, and awards (negative sign). This function covers some of the elements in the social relationship motivation factor and in the actors and director attribute factor (Tables 15.1 and 15.2).

TABLE 15.7 Discriminant analysis of three motion picture audiences

Variables	1st discriminant function		2nd discriminant function	
	Weights	Loadings	Weights	Loadings
Form of art and culture	−0.30	−0.75	−0.19	0.01
To get change	0.35	0.68	0.27	0.13
Knowledge of social issues	−0.20	−0.51	0.47	0.39
Critiques	−0.33	−0.64	−0.25	−0.14
Excitement	0.23	0.51	−0.53	−0.13
Aesthetic experiences	−0.32	−0.65	0.24	0.22
Actors	0.13	0.25	0.45	0.43
Awards	0.12	−0.11	−0.56	−0.28
Knowledge of history, nature, technology	0.09	−0.19	0.36	0.42
Enhances understanding among people	0.31	−0.22	0.27	0.32
Based on well known novel, person, incident	−0.26	−0.05	0.13	0.36
Colour/black & white	0.16	0.48	0.30	0.20

Discriminant functions	% of total discrimination	Eigen- values	χ^2	df	p	R_c	Wilk's lamloda	$F_{(24,4s8)}$	P
1st discriminant function	69%	0.50	96.3	13	0.001	0.58			
2nd discriminant function	31%	0.23	49.1	11	0.001	0.43	0.54	6.90	0.001

The projection of the three audiences into the resultant discriminant space, given in Figure 15.3, shows that the first axis discriminates effectively between the respondents attending the adventure/thriller movie and the human/social drama movie. Along the second axis there exists more overlapping but the axis helps to classify the Entertainment movie respondents. To facilitate the interpretation of the discriminant space the loadings of the independent variables are also projected into the space. Risking simplication, the first axis could be labelled as Information and art v escape, and the second as Content and social relations. The outcome is indirectly corroborated by the audience mappings into motivation and attribute important spaces (cf. Figures 15.2 and 15.3).

Moreover, the discriminant weights are supported by the preference regressions. The dominant beta coefficients of adventures/thrillers and

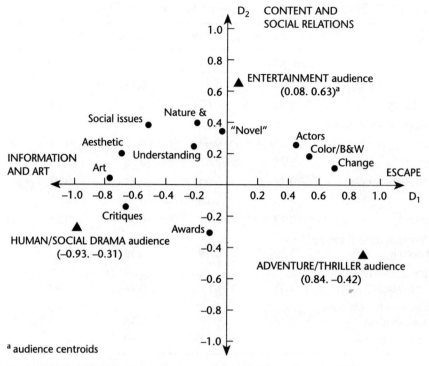

FIGURE 15.3 Discriminant space of three motion picture audiences

human/social dramas (in Table 15.5) cover neatly the principal weights of the first discriminant function. The relationship between. the second function is, however, weaker.

The classification matrix, depicted in Table 15.8, indicates that the discriminant model was able to predict correctly 60 per cent of the audience memberships. This is significantly better than 35 per cent achieved by a chance model (cf. Mosteller and Bush, 1954). Looking at the proportions, it can be

TABLE 15.8 Classification matrix of audience members

Actual audience	Predicted audience membership			Total
	[1[1]]	[2]	[4]	
1	47 (62%)	8 (11%)	22 (23%)	77
2	9 (12%)	47 (65%)	21 (22%)	77
4	20 (26%)	17 (24%)	52 (55%)	89
Total	76(100%)	72 (100%)	95 (100%)	243

1. 1 = Adventure/thriller audience, 2 = Human/social drama audience, 4 = Entertainment movie audience.

noted that respondents belonging to the entertainment movie audience are most difficult to classify. This audience overlaps with both the adventure/thriller and human/social drama audiences. The latter are mutually disassociated but overlap with the light entertainment audience. The relationships reflect clearly the discriminant space (Figure 15.3).

The discriminant analysis results indicate that the general movie motivation and attribute importance measures can be used to explain and predict consumers' choice of motion pictures. The predictive ability received is, however, bound to be inflated because we selected, from a pool of 29 variables, 12 discriminators which best fitted the present sample (cf. Frank *et al.*, 1965). To check the stability of discriminant coefficients and the potential sample bias, the data should be split into two subsamples, one used for coefficient estimation and the other for validation.

In the present case the discriminant coefficients were indirectly supported by the preference regressions and the motion picture motivation and attribute importance factor analyses. Further, the availability of motive and attribute evaluations of specific movie options should increase the predictive ability of the discriminant model.

Discussion

The results of this exploratory study indicate that consumers' preferences for abstract leisure services/products such as motion pictures can be explained by the simple linear model. The factor analysis of respondents' movie motivation and the subsequent mapping of subaudiences into motivation space (Figure 15.1) suggest that consumers attending different types of movie and belonging to different education and age categories have distinctly different motivation bases underlying their movie choices. The corresponding attribute importance analysis disclosed the same phenomenon in attributes: subaudiences differing in their age, education, and movie audience membership had varying attribute importance profiles (Figure 15.2). These results can be directly used in planning segmentation and marketing communications for both specific films and cinemas.

The preference regressions of four movie types (adventures/thrillers, human/social dramas , sex movies, light entertainment movies) corroborated the audience mappings: each movie type had a specific preference structure, expressed by the beta coefficients, differing especially in the case of motives but also in the attributes (Tables 15.5 and 15.6). Sex movies, however, were an exception; their preference could not be explained by the variables available in the present study.

Finally, the discriminant analysis suggests that the general motive and attribute variables are effective also in predicting motion picture choice. The two-dimensional discriminant space (Figure 15.3) had a close resemblance to the audience motive and attribute mappings.

The outcomes produced by the set of analyses are mutually supportive, which lends internal validity to the results. Moreover, the directions of the findings are interpretable and empirically sensible. In general, the results exemplify the usefulness of this kind of customer research approach to the motion picture industry and cinema management.

Concerning the generalization of the present results, certain limitations must be kept in mind. First, the predictive results have not been cross-validated with any hold-out data samples, and second, there may exist cross-cultural differences in film motives. The first problem can be overcome even within the present data but the second calls for cross-cultural research efforts. Any future studies in this area should include saved data prediction and the collection of motion picture specific motive and attribute measurements enabling the researcher to carry out movie space analysis in addition to the audience space. Moreover, a richer set of background variables including relevant AIOs, media usage patterns and use of competing leisure activities would be useful in segmentation analysis and promotion targeting.

Concerning more theoretical research, the film choice process should be studied in detail. We suggest that this phenomenon can be modelled as a two-phase process comprising a rejection phase and a preference phase. In the first phase the consumer is assumed to evaluate the perceived alternatives in his/her evoked set and to dichotomize them into acceptable/nonacceptable sets. We believe that movie type related motives form the dominant criteria at this phase. The rejection subprocess could be approximated with such satisfactory judgemental rules as conjunctive and disjunctive models.

If there are two or more acceptable movie alternatives, these have to be placed in order of preference. At this stage both motives and attributes are assumed to be used as criteria. If all alternatives belong to a similar genre we believe that attributes are dominant. The linear compensatory model can be used to approximate this preference phase. The above suggestions are partly speculative. They should be tested by collecting protocol data about the movie choice process and fitting the appropriate judgemental rules.

Acknowledgements

The authors wish to thank W. Fred van Raaij and two *JEP* reviewers for their helpful comments.

References

Alpert, M.L. and Peterson, R.A. (1972), On the interpretation of canonical analysis, *Journal of Marketing Research* **9**, pp. 187–192

Artell, P. (1974), Elokuvan osakulttuureita onko niitä (Subcultures of the cinema – do they exist), Unpublished Master's thesis, Department of Social Sciences, University of Tampere, Finland

Artell, P., Myyryläinen, P. and Soramäki, M. (1973), Elokuovat ja yleisö (Motion pictures and the audience), Working paper no. 56/1973, Research Institute, University of Tampere, Finland

Beard, A.D. (1980), Judgements of visual aesthetic stimuli: the end of the linear additive model's ubiquitous application, Working paper, Centre for Business Research Services

Bryant, W.K. and Gerner, J.L. (1981), Television use by adults and children: a multivariate analysis, *Journal of Consumer Research* **8**, pp. 154–161

Choffray, J-M. and Pras, B. (1980), Determinants of market success for commercial movies. *Der Markt* **73**, pp. 3–13

Ehrenberg, A.S.C., (1968), The factor analytic search for program types, *Journal of Advertising Research* **8**, pp. 55–63

Fornell, Claes, (1978), Three approaches to canonical analysis, *Journal of Market Research Society* **20**, pp. 166–181

Frank, R.E. and Greenberg, M.C. (1979), Interest-based segments of TV audiences, *Journal of Advertising Research* **19**, pp. 43–52

Frank, R.E., Becknell, J.C. and Clokey, J.D. (1971), Television program types, *Journal of Market Research* **8**, pp. 204–11

Frank, R.E., Massay, W.F. and Morrison, D.G. (1965), Bias in multiple discriminant analysis, *Journal of Marketing Research* **2**, pp. 250–58

Gensch, D.H. and Ranganathan, B. (1974), Evaluation of television program content for purpose of promotional segmentation, *Journal of Marketing Research* **11**, pp. 390–408

Green, P.E. (1978), *Analyzing multivariate data*, Hinsdale, IL: Westburn

Howard, J.A. and Sheth, J.N. (1969), *The Theory of Buyer Behavior*, New York: Wiley

Johansson, J.K. and Sheth, J.N. (1977), Canonical correlation and marketing research, in J.N. Sheth (Ed.), *Multivariate Methods for Market and Survey Research*. Chicago IL: American Marketing Association

Katz, E., Bluner, J.G. and Curevitch, M. (1973–74), Uses and gratifications research, *Public Opinion Quarterly*, **37**, pp. 509–23

Komiteanmietintö, (1973), Elokuvapoliittisen komitean I osamietintö, Helsinki: 1973/121

Kuylen, A.A.A. and Verhallen, T.M.M. (1981), The use of canonical analysis, *Journal of Economic Psychology* **1**, pp. 217–37

Lambert, Z.V. and Durand, R.M. (1975), Some precautions in using canonical analysis, *Journal of Marketing Research*, **12**, pp. 468–75

Lehmann, D.R. (1971), Television show preference publication of a choice model, *Journal of Marketing Research* **8**, pp. 47–55

Mosteller, F. and Bush, R.T. (1954), Selective quantitative techniques. In: Gardner

Pietilä,V. (1967), Elokuvissa kavijän anatomiaa (The anatomy of the motion picture attendant), *Projektion*, no. 4/1967

Schaninger, C.M., Lessig, V.P. and Panton, D.B.C. (1980), The complementary use of multivariate procedures to investigate nonlinear and interactive relationships between personality and product usage, *Journal of Marketing Research*, **17**, pp. 119–124

Sparks, D.L. and Tucker, W.T. (1971), A multivariate analysis of personality and product use, *Journal of Marketing Research* **8**, pp. 67–70

Stanton, J.L. and Lowenhar, J.A. (1974), Psychological need–product congruence as a basis for product planning', Proceedings, AIDS National Meeting, Atlanta, GA

Villani, K.E.A. (1975), Personality/life style and television viewing behavior, *Journal of Marketing Research*, **12**, pp. 432–39

■ □ ▨ ■ 16

A Factor Analytic Study of Consumers' Location Specific Values: A Traditional High Street and a Modern Shopping Mall

Paul M.W. Hackett and Gordon R. Foxall

Within the social sciences Factor Analysis is a widely used statistical technique. It is employed in analyses to reveal possible multiple dimensions of similarities or dissimilarities between variables (variance) within a data set. In the present paper the factor analysis procedure is first detailed. This is followed by the reporting of a factor analysis procedure which was undertaken in order to analyse responses to a questionnaire viewing consumers' location specific shopping values.

The survey was conducted in the high street of Worcester city centre and in the modern shopping mall at Merry Hill. Factor analysis showed respondents to structure their shopping location values using different dimensions (different in the type and number of factors present) between the two types of shopping location. In the high street four significant factors were discovered: service quality, access and facilities, social aspects, choice and variety. However, in the mall three significant factors were revealed: store variety, comfort and convenience, ancillary convenience.

The factor analytic approach is demonstrated as a tool for enabling a greater understanding of consumer values within shopping locations. The differential factor structure to responses between the two locations demonstrates that even when using similar research instruments, in different locations situational factors may significantly affect consumers' responses.

Introduction

Within the United Kingdom the retail shopping mall is a relatively new form of shopping centre. Within the United States the mall has for many years constituted a significant aspect of retail patronage. The 'pulling power' (the decision to mall shop) has been explained in terms of a gravitational theory. This stated that (within the context of the United States) 'the size of a trading area and driving time/distance to that area offered a suitable prediction of patronage' (Stolman *et al.*, 1991). However, Gautschi (1981) amongst others, has criticized gravitational attraction to retail settings as it fails to allow for qualitative distinctions between retail settings. Aspects such as the image of a shopping area (Wee, 1985), a customer's previous learning history (Meoli *et al.*, 1991) demands for quality, value and variety of goods (May, 1989) and tenant mix (Brown, 1992; Dawson, 1983) are just a few of the qualitative differences which have been found to be influential in the choice of shopping locations. (See also Hackett *et al.*, 1993.)

In the United Kingdom, the high street shop setting represents a more traditional retail location with the retail mall only appearing from the early 1980s. The high street shopping area is also often of comparable size to the area covered by the shopping mall, and with a similar variety and mix of retail outlets. The high street and the mall now stand in direct competition attempting to attract retail patronage to a comparable store mix from a similar public.

It has already been suggested that there are significant quantitative factors which to some extent determine consumer patronage of a shopping location (e.g. distance and access time). The qualitative differences noted above have also been claimed as influential. Foxall and Hackett (1992) addressed the psychological and behavioural differences which may be present between the mall and high street. Their investigation viewed the locational effects of the two settings upon consumers' cognitive mapping and shop-finding abilities. They discovered differential types and levels of performance between the settings. This raises the important point that significant differences in the experience and behaviour, whether these be termed quantitative or qualitative, exist for shoppers between the mall and the high street shopping area. Our earlier investigation was undertaken at Worcester city centre and Merry Hill shopping mall near Dudley, West Midlands. The study reported here was a follow up and also involved these centres.

The city centre of Worcester, an historic city in the English Midlands was selected as one of the study locations. The shopping area itself is made up from a series of main pedestrian streets with a small number of alleys and sidestreets running between, all of which are bounded by traffic-carrying roads. The streets adjoin at irregular angles and contain churches, public houses, museums, statues, public service utilities (fire and police) and a cathedral, as well as retail outlets. Two recently constructed small shopping squares also now exist and emphasize the wide time period over which the centre has been developed in an unplanned, organic manner through its admix of architectural styles.

Merry Hill is a modern shopping mall, also in the English Midlands (lying approximately 30 kilometres from Worcester). Its construction is very different to Worcester as whilst a similar number and variety of retail outlets exist (and a comparable variety of cafés and snack bars are present) no non-retail units such as churches, public houses and museums, etc. are included in the mall. The mall is of recent construction, dating from the mid-1980s, and has been designed to embody a single architectural style, with uniform shopfronts and walkway design. However, perhaps the single greatest distinguishing feature of the highly planned shopping mall is the controlled nature of lighting levels, cleanliness, thermal and other weather features within its environment.

The physical structure of the two shopping centres, whilst possessing essential similarities (similar shops, supermarkets, utilities, etc.), is very different. The differences in the nature of the two centres are shown in the two maps of the shopping centres at Worcester and Merry Hill, (Figures 16.1 and 16.2, respectively).

Furthermore, consumer experience and behaviour within the two has been found to differ along at least two criteria (cognitive mapping and wayfinding). Due to the mall's hermetic and the city's non-hermetic atmospheres the experience and behaviour of shoppers would also be expected to differ upon other dimensions. Furthermore, as a consequence of these physical, behavioural and cognitive differences expectation may be that the aspects or features of the two shopping centres 'valued' by shoppers whilst in their respective shopping centres would be different. The present study is concerned with the valued aspects of the shopping experience whilst shopping within each of these locations (i.e. the aspects and features that respondents from the mall and the city centre locations report as being valued components of the experience of being 'out shopping').

Value as a psychological concept has been defined in many varied ways. Contemporary research in the area of human social and personal values has defined a value as a thing which is assessed as being of importance. Elaborations of this definition have been made which have enabled, for instance, something to be valued for itself (in itself) or for the attainment of a greater, more superordinate or more distant goal (valued instrumentally)

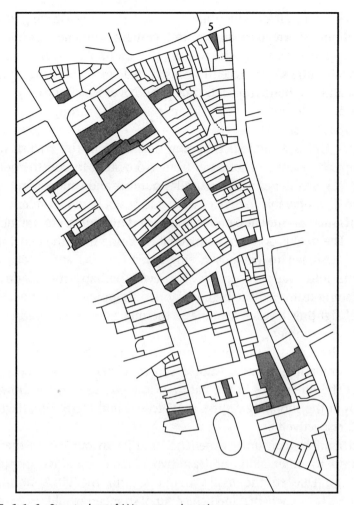

FIGURE 16.1 Street plan of Worcester shopping centre

e.g. Hackett and Florence, 1991; Levy, 1985, 1986; Levy and Guttman, 1981). Within the context of this paper, this definition of a value will be accepted. Shopping values and features or aspects of the shopping environment which are valued will be defined as those which are identified as being important by respondents for the achievement of their immediate shopping goals or those which will facilitate in the achievement of some more distant goal, desire or need. (See also Foxall and Hackett, 1994.) Thus, this study is concerned with asking shoppers what aspects of their shopping environment they value. The next section of this paper reports upon the development of a research instrument and the execution of a procedure to undertake this task. The

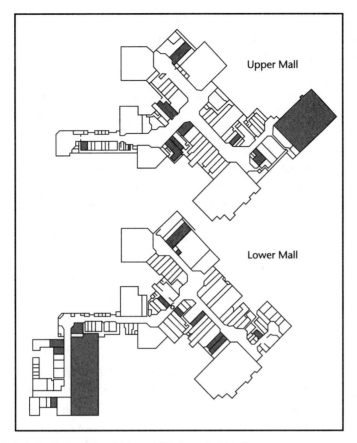

FIGURE 16.2 Floor plan of Merry Hill shopping mall

analytic technique which will be used in this exploratory study of factor analysis will also be introduced.

Design and method

It was decided that in order to assess consumers' value preferences with various aspects of shopping locations a questionnaire study formed the most appropriate format. Through reference to retail trade journals (e.g. *Shop Equipment News, The Grocer*, etc.) a standard 'non-location specific' questionnaire was therefore developed which addressed this content area (i.e. a questionnaire that may be used without modification at different shopping locations). This resulted in a 33 item instrument being assembled. Questions were included which covered a wide range of activities undertaken during shopping and aspects of the shopping situation. Standard demographic details were also collected as were other qualitative shopping preference data (see Appendix 16.2 for a copy of the questionnaire). The analyses of the data from these ancillary questions are not reported in the present paper (these and other further details are available from the authors).

Questionnaires were distributed at the two shopping locations described earlier: Worcester city centre and Merry Hill shopping mall. Respondents for the study were assembled on an opportunity basis at both locations. Concern was with the internal structure of the evaluations made by respondents, and not with the overall levels of importance they ascribed. It was therefore considered by the researchers that an opportunity sample which approximated the proportions of the general demographic features of shoppers (e.g. gender, age) present on survey days and which was comparable between the two survey sites, was sufficient. Thus, no attempts towards the systematic stratification of the samples were made. Interviewers did endeavour to assemble a sample which reflected the gender and age splits at each setting. This procedure resulted in the following samples: Total–204, Worcester 103 respondents, Merry Hill 101 respondents; Gender total–46 male, 157 female (1 missing).

Respondents were approached by an interviewer at locations throughout the two shopping areas at all times of the day between 8.30 a.m. and 6 p.m. and asked to complete the questionnaire *in situ*. Assistance to complete the questionnaire was provided by the interviewer as it was needed. However, care was taken not to guide or cue responses. The days on which the survey was run covered all week days (Monday to Saturday) for both of the locations over a two week period in August 1992. During this time no heavy rain or other adverse weather was encountered at either site.

The 33 item questionnaire was designed to contain questions which addressed a wide variety of different aspects of shopping behaviour and experience. It was expected, therefore, that an univariate analysis of this content (e.g. any simple tabulation of the responses from the questionnaire, etc.) would obscure the respondent imposed subcategories present within these responses. Rather, a statistical procedure is required which will allow for these respondent-defined categories to structure results. One such technique is factor analysis, details of which will now be outlined.

Factor analysis

There are many forms of factor analysis and it is beyond the scope of the present article to provide details of these. Rather, principal component factor analysis alone will be mentioned as this is both the most widely used analysis format and also the one which will later be used in this study. The reader with an interest in the techique is guided to a text concerned solely with this subject, for instance: Cureton (1983); Gorsuch (1983); Harman (1976); McDonald (1984). DeVellis (1991) provides an overview of the use of factor analysis in the understanding of scale scores, and Churchill Jr (1976) and Kinnear and Taylor (1987) give details of the procedure as used within marketing research. Also of interest to readers of the present paper are studies which have been undertaken which have investigated the structural dimensions of both and built natural consumer environments using a similar factor approach (e.g. Canter, 1972).

Factor analysis is a data simplification technique. Given a data set with n variables it attempts to reduce the number of significant variables to n^f (where n^f is a number significantly smaller than n). This it does by assuming that whilst a set of n items, which all measure different things, all address a similar content area (for instance, shopping values) then subsets of these items, or the total set of items, together measure more general content. These general or latent variables are the factors which structure a content area.

To continue the example of shopping values, a series of ten questions addressing the importance of various aspects of shopping could be asked. It may then be discovered if the responses are intercorrelated that the coefficients so produced would all be positive and of varying magnitude. This would be indicative of the presence of a factor which could be labelled 'shopping values'.

Inspection of the size of intercorrelations may suggest that whilst all variables are positively related (i.e. measure a single content area) the magnitude of correlation between any pair of items differs. Suppose further that a series of items which all address shopping in outdoor locations all have relatively high intercorrelations, whilst the same is true of a set of items on indoor shopping activities. Furthermore, the items which comprise these two sets are found to have low between set correlations. This would be indicative of the presence of two subsets (factors) one of which may be labelled 'indoor shopping', the other 'outdoor shopping'. In such a case the responses to the original ten items can be seen as being influenced by respondent orientation to the two factors. In such a case exploratory factor analysis has been undertaken: the technique has been used to explore a new domain (an area not subjected, previously, to factor analysis). It is this exploratory type of study which will be conducted.

It should be pointed out that the example given above is highly simplistic; if such a simple solution to shopping values existed there would be little point conducting the complex statistical procedure of factor analysis. Shopping values may indeed refer to indoor or outdoor behaviours and in this case the two factors would be independent and uncorrelated as a shopping value can only refer to one of these factors. However, as is the case with most social behaviours, a set of variables or items which address shopping values may also be broken down simultaneously by other latent variables. To give another fictitious and simplistic example, either an indoor or an outdoor shopping behaviour may be undertaken whilst being in the company of others or alone. As this is the case, if a factor reflecting the 'socialness' of shopping emerged during analysis as being a superbly identifiable source of variance in test scores, then this would not be an independent source of variance as it is correlated with the other two factors. Factor analysis attempts to identify factors which are as independent from each other as is possible in order to enable an understanding of the structure of a specific content area.

Results

The results from the survey were coded and entered for statistical analysis. This took the form of descriptive statistical analysis (e.g. cross tabulations) and factor analysis. The descriptive analyses are not commented upon in this paper, however, further information may be attained in this regard from the first author. The general procedure of factor analysis has been described in the previous section. At this point the results alone will be presented. In the discussion the use of factor analysis in order to enhance the understanding of consumer experience of shopping locations will be elaborated.

Results of factor analysis

Principal component factor analysis with varimax rotation (see Appendix 6.1) was performed on the survey data. Independent analyses were conducted for each of the two locations. The results of these analyses will now be separately presented for the two survey sites.

Merry Hill

Factor analysis of the Merry Hill data set produced a solution of 11 factors with eigen values of unity and greater (see Appendix 6.1, note 2). Inspection of a scree plot (see Figure 16.3) of eigen values suggested that three of the factors should be retained and used as descriptors of the variance in the data. Scree plots are formed by plotting the number of factors against their respective eigen values. In so doing it is often possible to discern an elbow in a line drawn to connect these points. It is after this joint that progressively smaller gain is achieved in terms of variance which is accounted for by the retention of

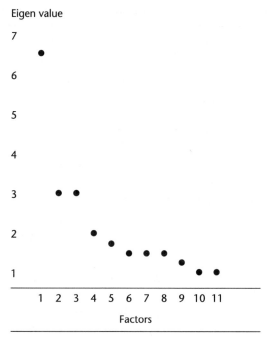

Eigen value

FIGURE 16.3 Scree plot of Merry Hill factor eigen values

subsequent factors. Keeping a large number of factors is not desirable as the greater the number of factors the lesser the reduction in sources producing variances (as already stated, one of the aims of factor analysis is to simplify a variable set by reducing this to one or more latent variables which represent a significant amount of the variance in the total data set). Furthermore, factors with relatively low eigen values are hard to label as often there is only one item with a significant loading on this factor.

In the present analysis an elbow in the scree plot suggests the retention of three factors (factors one to three may be connected by a line in a more vertical plane, whilst factors four to eleven join in a more horizontal plane). Together the three factors accounted for 35 per cent of the cumulative variance. The eigen values for the three factors were as follows: factor 1 (6.12), factor 2 (2.80), factor 3 (2.63). Table 16.1 gives factor loadings for all of the 33 variables.

Worcester

Factor analysis of the data from the Worcester sample produced 11 factors with eigen values of unity and greater. The scree plot of eigen values (Figure 16.4) suggested that four factors should be retained (this is again shown by the elbow in a line drawn to connect all points in the plot). The eigen values for the four

TABLE 16.1 Factor loadings for 33 questionnaire variables for Merry Hill and Worcester samples

Question	Merry Hill Factors			Worcester factors			
	1	2	3	1	2	3	4
1 staying dry	0.11	**0.81**	0.07	0.05	−0.01	−0.05	−0.08
2 high quality goods	0.17	−0.10	0.14	**0.62**	0.16	−0.27	0.18
3 value for money	0.15	0.14	−0.13	0.58	−0.13	−0.15	0.01
4 helpful staff	0.07	0.04	0.19	**0.89**	0.07	0.05	0.02
5 clean shopping areas	−0.05	0.22	0.15	**0.70**	0.20	−0.07	0.18
6 a wide choice of goods	**0.78**	−0.04	−0.04	0.34	−0.01	0.04	**0.78**
7 shops being close to your home	0.06	**0.52**	0.17	0.03	0.02	0.09	0.16
8 staying warm	0.14	**0.77**	0.07	0.26	0.09	0.24	0.25
9 good road links	0.02	0.10	−0.08	0.19	**0.47**	−0.03	0.23
10 small specialist stores	−0.01	−0.40	0.10	0.19	−0.16	0.04	−0.05
11 convenient parking	0.17	0.08	−0.04	0.18	**0.54**	−0.19	−0.05
12 being able to easily find the shops you are looking for	**0.62**	0.24	−0.05	0.03	0.13	0.00	**0.58**
13 friendly staff	0.22	0.13	−0.09	**0.83**	0.14	0.19	0.13
14 places to sit down	0.00	0.11	0.07	0.04	0.24	**0.49**	−0.00
15 easy access to information about shops and the goods they offer	0.04	**0.51**	0.10	0.17	0.16	0.09	0.08
16 cafes	0.00	−0.03	−0.07	−0.11	−0.07	0.28	−0.04
17 an attractive looking shopping area	0.12	−0.09	−0.12	0.32	−0.00	0.05	0.08
18 toilets	0.32	−0.00	0.10	0.16	0.18	−0.06	0.16
19 a wide choice of shops	**0.80**	0.13	0.01	0.24	0.02	0.12	**0.68**
20 large supermarkets/hypermarkets	0.32	0.18	**0.61**	−0.05	0.17	0.12	0.08
21 a baby feeding/changing area	−0.07	0.21	**0.70**	0.03	**0.85**	0.02	−0.03
22 good public transport links	−0.07	−0.18	0.33	0.05	0.30	**0.41**	0.08
23 places to meet others	0.05	−0.14	0.16	0.05	0.12	**0.84**	0.10
24 shopping with friends	0.32	0.02	0.11	−0.02	−0.03	**0.73**	0.17
25 getting a bargain	**0.44**	0.06	0.12	0.06	−0.01	0.24	0.14
26 enjoying yourself	0.04	0.07	−0.03	**0.43**	−0.18	0.34	0.18
27 large departmental stores	**0.63**	0.28	0.32	0.08	0.07	0.06	0.12
28 litter-free shopping areas	0.11	−0.08	0.39	0.28	0.15	0.06	0.13
29 a place to leave children	−0.18	0.02	**0.56**	0.12	**0.79**	0.18	0.07
30 security staff	0.18	0.01	**0.62**	0.16	**0.64**	0.07	0.17
31 short distances between shops	0.26	0.10	0.29	−0.14	0.17	0.17	**0.54**
32 pedestrian zones	0.15	0.16	0.33	0.00	0.28	0.31	**0.43**
33 public houses	0.03	0.06	0.01	−0.06	−0.16	**0.70**	−0.02

Items with loadings >0.4 are highlighted.

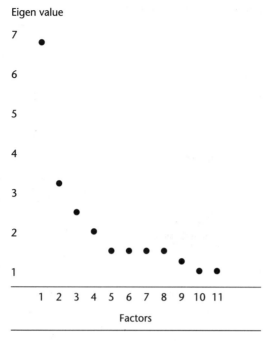

FIGURE 16.4 Scree plot of Worcester factor eigen values

factors were: factor 1 (6.72), factor 2 (3.26), factor 3 (2.58), factor 4 (2.10) which together accounted for 44 per cent of the cumulative variance. Table 16.1 shows the factor loadings for the 33 variables. A full list of the cumulative

TABLE 16.2 Eigen values and cumulative variance explained by factors for both samples

Worcester factor	Merry Hill eigen	cum var	eigen	cum var
1	6.72	20.4	6.12	18.5
2	3.26	30.3	2.80	27.0
3	2.58	38.1	2.63	35.0
4	2.10	44.4	1.93	40.9
5	1.63	49.4	1.73	46.1
6	1.47	53.9	1.58	50.9
7	1.40	58.1	1.42	55.2
8	1.36	62.2	1.42	59.5
9	1.25	66.0	1.28	63.4
10	1.08	69.3	1.12	66.8
11	1.04	72.5	1.07	70.0

TABLE 16.3 Factor composition: Merry Hill

Factor 1. Store variety			
19 a wide choice of shops	**0.80**	0.13	0.01
6 a wide choice of goods	**0.78**	−0.04	−0.04
27 large departmental stores	**0.63**	0.28	0.32
12 being able to easily find the shops you are looking for	**0.62**	0.24	−0.05
25 getting a bargain	**0.44**	0.06	0.12
Factor 2. Comfort and convenience			
1 staying dry	0.11	**0.81**	0.07
8 staying warm	0.14	**0.77**	0.07
7 shops being close to your home	0.06	**0.52**	0.17
15 easy access to information about shops and the goods they offer	0.04	**0.51**	0.10
10 small specialist stores	−0.01	**−0.40**	0.10
Factor 3. General facilities and convenience			
21 a baby feeding/changing area	−0.07	0.21	**0.70**
30 security staff	0.18	0.01	**0.62**
20 large supermarkets/hypermarkets	0.32	0.18	**0.61**
29 a place to leave children	−0.18	0.02	**0.56**

Factor loadings >0.4 are highlighted.

percent of variance explained by factors (for both samples) is given in Table 16.2.

In Tables 16.3 and 16.4 are provided the listings of the variables which load on the significant factors for each of the two survey locations. A factor loading of greater than or equal to 0.4 has been used to determine the cut-off point for assigning variables to factors. This is in line with Walsh (1989). However, criteria of 0.3 to 0.5 have been suggested by other authors (Child, 1970; Norusis, 1988). A comparison between the factors present at the two survey locations is provided in Table 16.5.

Discussion

Factor analysis is a technique which does not assume that all covariance within a data set (see Appendix 16.1, note 3) is due to any single source or theme. In the present context it would not be assumed that covariation in the data arising from the administering of a questionnaire viewing consumer values was all due to one unified source. Rather, multiple 'latent variables' (variables

TABLE 16.4 Factor composition: Worcester

Factor 1. Service quality				
4 helpful staff	**0.89**	0.07	0.05	0.02
13 friendly staff	**0.83**	0.14	0.19	0.13
5 clean shopping areas	**0.70**	0.20	−0.07	0.18
2 high quality goods	**0.62**	0.16	−0.27	0.18
3 value for money	**0.58**	−0.13	−0.15	0.01
26 enjoying yourself	**0.43**	−0.18	0.34	0.18
Factor 2. Access and facilities				
21 a baby feeding/changing area	0.03	**0.85**	0.02	−0.03
29 a place to leave children	0.12	**0.79**	0.18	0.07
30 security staff	0.16	**0.64**	0.07	0.17
9 good road links	0.19	**0.47**	−0.03	0.23
Factor 3. Social				
23 places to meet others	0.05	0.12	**0.84**	0.10
24 shopping with friends	−0.02	−0.03	**0.73**	0.17
33 public houses	−0.06	−0.16	**0.70**	−0.02
14 places to sit down	0.04	0.24	**0.49**	−0.00
22 good public transport links	0.05	0.30	**0.41**	0.08
Factor 4. Choice and variety				
6 a wide choice of goods	0.34	−0.01	0.04	**0.78**
19 a wide choice of shops	0.24	0.02	0.12	**0.68**
12 being able to easily find the shops you are looking for	0.03	0.13	0.00	**0.58**
31 short distances between shops	−0.14	0.17	0.17	**0.54**
32 pedestrian zones	0.00	0.28	0.31	**0.43**

Factor loadings >0.4 are highlighted.

TABLE 16.5 Factors present at the two shopping locations

Worcester	Merry Hill
Service quality	Store variety
Access and facilities	Comfort and convenience
Social	General facilities and convenience
Choice and variety	

not specifically nominated as variables or questions within the research design/ questionnaire) are allowed to account for observed variation and the technique attempts to identify these.

Of the 33 questions or variables in the research, instrument factor analysis identified three latent variables or factors to account for 35 per cent of covariance in questionnaire responses at Merry Hill. Responses to the same questionnaire at Worcester produced four latent variables or factors explaining 44.4 per cent of covariance. Moreover, not only was the number of significant factors identified at each location different but so were the items comprising these. As a consequence of the differential composition of factors it may be said that consumers' structure values differently and along different dimensions between the traditional high street shopping centre and the innovative shopping mall. The ability of factor analysis to identify latent variables greatly reduces the number of variables which have to be considered when trying to understand variation in a set of responses.

Thus it is possible to make statements on the basis of the responses to individual questions. For instance, the average value of staying dry may be calculated and this may be subdivided by location, gender, age, etc. However, factor analysis of the same data enables the allocation of this particular item to the comfort and convenience factor for the Merry Hill sample, whilst the item was not present within a factor of Worcester (furthermore there was no comfort or convenience factor for Worcester respondents). From this, several conclusions may be drawn. The absence of a comfort and convenience factor for Worcester respondents shows this not to be a pertinent dimension of their shopping values (the converse is true at Merry Hill). This is lent intuitive support by the fact that comfort and convenience have been designed into Merry Hill, whilst they fail to emerge as a coherent latent variable in the traditional high street shopping area where comfort and convenience are allowed to emerge, or not, on an *ad hoc* basis.

Differences in factor structure between the two settings

Inspection of Tables 6.3 and 16.4 shows which items loaded on which factor for their respective survey locations. There was some overlap, or similarity, between factors. For instance, factor 1 at Merry Hill (store variety)has similarities to factor 4 at Worcester (choice and variety). Both of these factors contain items 6, 19, 12, all of which are questions which are clearly addressing choice in shops and goods. At Merry Hill these items were supplemented with those concerned with departmental stores (27) and bargains (25). In the high street of Worcester supplementary items were intershop distances (31) and pedestrian zones (32). This illustrates how an analogous concept (in this case consumer choice) can have different specific meanings. It further shows how this concept will be affected by the consumer environment and how factor analytic procedures are able to reveal such differences.

This latter point is further illustrated by factor 2 at Merry Hill which embodied items addressing customer comfort and convenience. This factor was composed of items all of which were not to be found, singularly or in groups, in any of the factors in the Worcester data analysis. Factor 3 at Merry Hill (general facilities and convenience) provides another example of the contextual influence present in the factors. Three of the four items in this factor are the same as three of the four items in factor 2 (access and facilities: Worcester). In the mall large supermarkets and hypermarkets (20) supplement facility and convenience items. These forms of large markets are both found in abundance at the mall but not in the high street. In the high street, however, the supplementary item in the factor is good road links (9), an issue that may perhaps be more of a difficulty in this organically developed shopping environment, but of little difficulty in the highly planned mall with its good road and public transport links and abundant car parking.

The social factor present at Worcester (factor 3) was not represented at Merry Hill. This is interesting as it suggests that social aspects of shopping are a dimension used by customers to structure their values in the high street but not in the mall.

From the factors presented in Table 16.5 it can be seen that whilst the same questionnaire and survey procedure was carried out at Worcester and Merry Hill, at the same times of the day, week and year, the factor sets which emerged at the two locations were very different. With such similarity in the research design it is possible to state that the differences in response structure (factors) was due to the two gross physical locations of the survey: the mall and the high street (see Appendix 6.1, note 4).

Furthermore, the factors may be identified as being locational specific. This may be observed in the fact that in the shopping location which has been highly manipulated (in its design) in order to produce customer comfort, a factor emerged which showed customers to evaluate this retail environment in these terms. However, in the open-air, *ad hoc* designed atmosphere of the city centre of Worcester, no such factor was present. Rather, in this latter location, the factors which were discovered reflected the quality of service, access and facilities, and social aspects of the shopping experience; these criteria were not embodied as distinct factors in the analyses for the Merry Hill respondents.

Consumer experience of shopping has been shown to be highly influenced by the gross type of physical area within which an individual is shopping. Not only will the same aspects of the shopping area by area receive different ascriptions of importance dependent upon where the consumer is shopping, but a whole different set of dimensions will be employed in order to structure their evaluations of what aspects of a shopping area they personally value. It should be noted at this point that the caveat issued earlier (see Appendix 6.1, note 4) regarding the need for replication studies to be conducted with structured samples in order to allow claims for the generality of the findings, be followed.

Conclusion

This paper began by considering the importance of several factors in shopper choice of retail location. The gravitational theory of store attraction was first considered. In this the time and distance a potential shopper must travel in order to use a specific retail location with the largest retail area is seen as the determinant of store choice and patronage. Qualitative aspects of the shopping environment were also considered as determinants of store choice. These included store image, variety and value and tenant mix. Finally, consumers' psychological and behavioural variables of wayfinding and cognitive mapping were noted as aspects of the experience of shopping and mooted as possible influential factors in shop location choice.

The present results have shown that shoppers within either a mall or high street setting, when asked to report the importance of various aspects of the shopping experience, do so differentially. Factor analysis has demonstrated that different criteria or dimensions are present in such evaluations between settings. As a consequence of these findings it may be claimed that simply measuring consumer attitude toward travelling to the nearest and largest specified shopping location (gravitational attraction) may obscure the reasons for the response given. The results have also afforded considerable support to the importance of qualitative aspects of the shopping environment (such as image, variety and value) as also being of significance in influencing retail location patronage. Finally, the results demonstrated that psychological value structures for shopping locations existed and were easily accessible using the factor analytic technique. These structures synergized the qualitative and quantitative components of the mall and high street into location specific consumer values.

The research presented has shown the factor analytic approach to be an applicable tool for exploring and enhancing understanding of consumers' location specific shopping values. The differential factor structure found to underlie responses at the two locations demonstrates that even when using the same research instrument in different locations, the location or what may be called situational factors may significantly affect consumers' responses. Thus to make generalizations regarding the things that shoppers value or find important in the shopping situation may be very hard to do with any degree of confidence.

Acknowledgements

Thanks go to the owners and authorities at Crown Gate, Worcester, and Edward Erdman, Merry Hill.

References

Brown, S. (1992), Tenant mix: tenant placement and shopper behaviour in a planned shopping centre, *The Service Industries Journal*, **12**, No. 3, pp. 384–403

Canter, D. (1972), Royal Hospital for Sick Children, Yorkhill, Glasgow: a psychological analysis, *Architects Journal*, 4 February 1970, pp. 299–301

Child, D. (1970), *The Essentials of Factor Analysis*, London: Holt, Rinehart and Winston

Churchill, Jr, G.A. (1976), *Marketing Research: Methodological Foundations*, Hillsdale IL: Westburn

Cureton, E.E. (1983), *Factor Analysis: An Applied Approach*, Hillside NJ: Lawrence Erlbaum

Dawson, J.A. (1983), *Shopping Centre Development*, London: Longman

DeVellis, R.F. (1991), *Scale Development: Theory and Applications*, Applied Social Research Methods Series, **26**. Newbury Park, CA: Sage Publications

Foxall, G.R. and Hackett, P.M.W. (1992), Consumers' perceptions of microretail location: wayfinding and cognitive mapping in planned and organic shopping environments, *The International Review of Retail, Distribution and Consumer Research*, **2**, No. 3, pp. 309–27

Foxall, G.R. and Hackett, P. (1994), Sources of consumer satisfaction with Birmingham's international conference centre, *The Service Industries Journal*, **14**, 389–401

Gautschi, D.A. (1981), Specification of patronage models for retail centre choice, *Journal of Marketing Research*, **18**, May, pp. 162–74

Gorsuch, R.L. (1983), *Factor Analysis*. Hillside NJ: Lawrence Erlbaum

Hackett, P.M.W. and Florence, S.J. (1991), The facet theoretical analysis of green values: theoretical implications and empirical findings, Paper presented at the First Workshop on Values and Lifestyle Research in Marketing; European Institute for Advanced Studies in Management; Brussels, 4–15 October 1991

Hackett, P., Foxall, G.R. and Van Raaij (1993), Consumers in retail environments, in T. Gärling, and R.G. Golledge, *Behaviour and Environment: Psychological and Geographical Approaches*. Amersterdam: North-Holland

Harman, H.H. (1976), *Modern Factor Analysis*. Chicago: University of Chicago Press

Kinnear, T.C. and Taylor, J.R. (1987), *Marketing Research: An Applied Approach*, New York: McGraw Hill Book Company

Levy, S. (1985), A faceted cross-cultural analysis of some core social values, In: D. Canter (Ed.) *Facet Theory: Approaches to Social Research* New York: Springer

Levy, S. (1986), *The Structure of Social Values*, Jerusalem, Israeli Institute of Applied Social Research

Levy, S. and Guttman, L. (1981), Structure and levels of values of rewards and allocation criteria in several life areas, in I. Borg (Ed.) *Multidimensional Data Representations: When and Why*, Ann Arbor MI: Mathesis Press

May, E. (1989), A retail odyssey, *Journal of Retailing*, **65**, Fall, pp. 356–67

McDonald, R.P. (1984), *Factor Analysis and Related Methods*. Hillside NJ: Lawrence Erlbaum

Meoli, J., Feinberg, R.A. and Westgate, L. (1991), A reinforcement-affect model of retail mall patronage, *Advances in Consumer Research*, **18**, pp. 441–49

Norusis, M.J. (1988), *SPSS/PC+ Advanced Statistics v2.0: for the IBM PC/XT/AT and PS2.* Chicago IL: SPSS Inc.

Stolman, J.J., Gentry, J.W. and Anglin, K.A. (1991), Shopping choices: the case of mall choice, *Advances in Consumer Research*, **18**, pp. 434–40

Walsh, A. (1989), *Statistics for the Social Sciences: With Computer Applications*, New York: Harper and Row Publishers

Wee, Chou Hou (1985), Shopping area image: its factor analytic structure and relationships with shopping trips and expenditure behaviour, *Advances in Consumer Research*, **13**, pp. 48–52

Appendix 16.1

1. Principal component analysis and varimax rotation are factor analytic procedures. Having determined the number of factors to retain in an analysis (see 2 below on eigen values and scree plots) the factor analytic procedure is run in order to maximize the variance of squared loadings (the correlation of items with factors). In this form of analysis the vectors (factors) in an analysis are located in order to account for as much of the total variance in the data set as is possible. When the factors are uncorrelated the vectors may be rotated orthogonally so as to account for successively greater amounts of the variance remaining within a data set without distorting the underlying patterns of covariance. Varimax is the most common rotation technique used in factor analysis when factors are orthogonal (as in our analysis where the factors are largely uncorrelated).

2. Eigen values are the sum of the squares of all loadings on a factor. The value of the first factor's eigen value is the greatest, with all subsequent eigen values reducing sequentially. This is due to the nature of factor analysis which attempts to account for the maximum possible variance by each factor in turn. As the eigen value is a factor's sum of squares it is a representation of the amount of total variance within a data set which is accounted for by the factor. As such this has been used as one of the criteria for determining the number of factors to extract (there are, however, many more criteria which may be employed in order to determine the number of factors which should be extracted). When these

criteria are used, factors with an eigen value above unity (1) are extracted as only these factors are considered as being common factors (Child, 1970). In the present study this would result in the adoption of 11 factors for each of the studies. One of the other criteria for judging the appropriate number of factors to be retained is that of the scree test. In this the number of factors is plotted in a graph against the eigen values, and the shape of the curve formed used to judge the cut-off point.

3. Covariance is a measure of the unstandardized variance between any two items from a matrix of items which are being compared. This may be made easier to understand if we consider a covariance matrix. In this, all items to be compared are plotted against each other to form a rectangular matrix (X_1, X_2, X_3 ... X_n by X_1, X_2, X_3 ... X_n). In such a matrix the values along the leading diagonal are all variances (covariances of items with themselves) whilst of-diagonal values are covariances between item pairings (this contains the same information as a correlation matrix of the same variable set but in an unstandardized form).

4. A warning regarding the opportunity sampling used in this study must be given. None of the systematic stratification of the sample in the study was undertaken. As a consequence, caution must be employed when attempting to generalize from the present results to members of the public in general. The opportunity sample which was used does not negate the factor differences discovered. Furthermore, there were no great differences in the two samples assembled which it may be supposed could alone have accounted in the differential structures discovered between the two sites.

ppendix 16.2: Questionnaire to measure consumers' cation specific values

When you are shopping, how important are the following to you –

	very important	to	very unimportant
staying dry	1	2	3	4
high quality goods	1	2	3	4
value for money	1	2	3	4
helpful staff	1	2	3	4
clean shopping areas	1	2	3	4
a wide choice of goods	1	2	3	4
shops being close to your home	1	2	3	4

staying warm	1	2	3	4
good road links	1	2	3	4
small specialist stores	1	2	3	4
convenient parking	1	2	3	4
being able to easily find the shops you are looking for	1	2	3	4
friendly staff	1	2	3	4
places to sit down	1	2	3	4
easy access to information about shops and the goods they offer	1	2	3	4
cafes	1	2	3	4
an attractive-looking shopping area	1	2	3	4
toilets	1	2	3	4
a wide choice of shops	1	2	3	4
large supermarkets/hypermarkets	1	2	3	4
a baby feeding/changing area	1	2	3	4
good public transport links	1	2	3	4
places to meet others	1	2	3	4
shopping with friends	1	2	3	4
getting a bargain	1	2	3	4
enjoying yourself	1	2	3	4
large departmental stores	1	2	3	4
litter-free shopping areas	1	2	3	4
a place to leave children	1	2	3	4
security staff	1	2	3	4
short distances between shops	1	2	3	4
pedestrian zones	1	2	3	4
public houses	1	2	3	4

age _____ gender _____ married   Y   N

Occupation _____ children   Y   N

residence _____ car owner   Y   N

main shopper in household?   Y   N

frequency they visit the interview area _____

what is their favourite area to shop in _____

for them, what is the most important aspect of a shopping area _____
_____

what is their favourite shop _____

Thank you.

■ □ ▥ ■ 17

On the Derivation of a Common Space of Competing Leisure Attraction Types

Andreas H. Zins

This study investigates day trippers' attitudes toward different types of leisure attractions. The analysis of 15 attraction types generated one common perceptual space whose axes were interpreted as underlying competing dimensions. Data were collected by self administered computer-assisted interviews using the technique of individual grouping which consists of an unconstrained sorting task of the stimuli. Nonmetric multidimensional scaling (MDS) procedures were employed in order to reveal a three dimensional configuration. Besides the direct stimuli comparisons, attribute data were generated for avoiding a completely subjective interpretation of the perceptual map. Individual difference scaling (INDSCAL) procedures were applied for an *a priori* segmentation approach which resulted in remarkable perceptual differences among the analysed sub-groups. The MDS configuration suggests that despite the obvious unique character of every leisure attraction the decision process for visiting a particular attraction site is based upon a few perceptual dimensions. Implications of these results for marketing purposes are briefly discussed.

Introduction

Multidimensional Scaling (MDS) approaches have been widely used for marketing research purposes in general (Green and Carmone, 1969) and are recognized in the field of tourism and leisure research as well (Fenton and Pearce, 1988). MDS techniques are applied in order to reveal a perceptual map of a set of objects (products, brands). These objects vary depending upon the orientation of the study.

Revealing structural relationships among leisure activities (Ritchie, 1975; Becker, 1976) or among attitudes and motivations toward leisure (Iso-Ahola, 1980; Crandall and Slivken, 1980; Pyo, Mihalik and Uysal, 1989) is one major concern in leisure research. In tourism research these objects consist of tourist attractions (Stumpf, 1975), tourist destinations (Haahti, 1986; Gartner, 1989), travel packages (Anderssen and Colberg, 1973), or tour operators.

One favourable function of MDS is the conversion of weakly ordered similarities judgements into metric scaled distances allowing the structure of the perceptions to be represented in graphical form which helps in interpreting the results. Whereas these advantages are appealing to the marketer some serious research problems arise around the use of MDS: (1) the data gathering process is one key factor for good and valid result; (2) especially with field studies, the data collection process is imposed by certain restrictions which may leave the researcher without or with little empirical information for interpreting the graphical solutions.

As regards the first problem, there are several data gathering techniques (Coombs, 1964) available in order to generate the appropriate input data for the MDS procedure. Most of them are very time consuming and burdensome for the respondent (Mazanec, 1978). The interviewing time grows progressively with additional objects under consideration. Limiting the number of objects (stimuli) and/or attributes (if any) may influence negatively the respondent's ability to reproduce his or her map of the reality. If the study allows only for attribute rating and not for (additional) direct stimuli comparisons it is difficult to determine an adequate set of attributes with which each respondent has to differentiate his or her perception (Aaker and Day, 1980). In this case the MDS map can only reproduce the preselected criteria, though the interpretation task will be supported by empirical information for attributes.

The second research problem, which is directly related to the former issues, has further implications. As the interviewing time is restricted because of cost limits and/or limits of the willingness to participate in an interview, there are three aspects to be considered: (1) If the set of objects is too small the computational model is underdetermined; (2) on the other hand, specifying a set of items large enough may cause the interviewing time to explode, which deters valid information; and (3) this may force the respondent to judge over objects that had never represented an element of the consumer's awareness (Spiggle and Sernall, 1987), consideration (Woodside and Sherell, 1977), action set (Woodside and Lysonski, 1989), or decision set (Moutinho, 1987).

As the choice set structures are dynamic across consumers, time and contexts, an improvement for the measurement process consists in the free elicitation of the specific objects and/or attributes (Reilly, 1990) by the respondent.

The present study tried to overcome some of the above mentioned problems which will be discussed in detail in the next section. The major concern referred to a methodological comparison of three different data gathering techniques: attribute rating, conditional rank ordering and individual grouping of 15 leisure attraction types. This article concentrates on the presentation of the grouping approach. Due to the level of funding, the study was based on rather small convenience samples. It is this reason, as well as the geographical and cultural context, that entails some restrictions for generalizing the results.

The study presents a demonstration of MDS techniques for assessing basic attitudinal structures that daytrippers apply in the decision-making process for leisure attraction participation. The interpretation of the MDS configuration does not stop at the point of determining the number and content of the underlying valuative dimensions but tries to stress the view of the interrelationship and competing areas among attraction types (Fodness, 1990) and demonstrates the use of MDS as a means for customer benefit segmentation.

Methodology

Reducing structural relationships between leisure activities as well as tourist attractions does not imply a new research problem. The literature review reveals several approaches from which some fundamental insights can be drawn. Lew (1987) classifies the applied research methods into three categories: ideographic listing, the organization, and the tourist cognition of attractions. Depending on the classification level more or less general ideographic characteristics can be determined. Ritchie and Zinns (1978) employ the following traits: natural beauty and climate; culture and social characteristics; sport, recreation, and educational facilities; shopping and commercial facilities; infrastructure; price levels; attitudes toward tourists; and accessibility. This kind of grid allows a very general classification of attractions which therefore lacks insight into other fields such as tourist motivations and preferences for different attractions.

Some other studies examined common structures for leisure activities (Ritchie, 1975; Becker, 1976; Russell and Hultsman, 1987). These approaches have only limited use for the investigation of leisure attraction perception because for every visit to a particular attraction an individual bundle of activities will be combined as well as additional benefits will be perceived.

However, some dimensions seem to be essential as they appear in several studies. They can be expressed as bipolar scales: solitude–social interaction, active–passive, relaxing–stimulating. Another most basic distinction between attractions emerges from studies that are targeted for tourist attraction research (Perry, 1975; Gunn, 1979; Stumpf, 1975); that of nature versus human orientation.

As these ideographic approaches do not provide information for perceptual as well as spatial relationships among attractions a cognitive perspective was introduced into this study. Respondents were asked to rate their perceptions of those attraction types which they had in fact recently visited. The intention was to address the real criteria behind the selection and decision process for visiting a particular attraction type without, for the first step, directing the respondent's mind to a set of specified attributes or attitudes.

This approach should reveal a more differentiated map including customer interchange data (Fodness, 1990) as input material for the MDS procedures. However, in the Florida study, it was only possible to reproduce some geographical aspects of consumers' perception of tourist attractions. This leaves a serious shortfall in the information required for product positioning and advertising strategy decisions. In addition, the perceived geographical location can exhibit both competitive and agglomerative relationships according to the results from Kim and Fesenmaier (1990).

The rating task was settled in order to minimize difficulties and inconvenience for the respondent. Hence, the data gathering technique called individual grouping was applied for obtaining similarity data for a set of attraction types. The rating task consisted of classifying the individually selected attraction types by putting attractions together in one group that appeared for any reason to be very similar and to separate those which were found not to be compatible in one group. There were no restrictions imposed such as a minimum number of groups or a particular criteria for the classification job with the exception that any attraction type could only appear in one group. Every group pattern was preprocessed with the F77-program DIGROUP (Mazanec, 1978) which is based on the individual height of partition (Burton, 1975) in order to derive weakly ordered dissimilarities. After averaging the dissimilarities matrices over all respondents the aggregated matrix served as input data for the following nonmetric MDS procedure.

The aggregated dissimilarity data matrix was subject to a nonmetric multidimensional scaling procedure. Using the ALSCAL algorithm within the statistical package SPSS the nonmetric classical symmetric multidimensional scaling model (Kruskal, 1964) was specified. In order to determine the optimal number of dimensions of the MDS configuration, two quality measures stemming from the MDS analysis were inspected. Stress values for the different configurations were used as a badness of fit measure (Kruskal and Wish, 1988) and RSQ values as 'an index of the variability in the input data matrix accounted for by the spatial distances among . . .' the attraction types '. . . in the MDS solution' (Russell and Hultsman, 1987).

A second data level was generated by inviting the respondents to rate the individually constructed groups of attractions by a list of attitudinal criteria. In order to minimize again the interviewing effort these criteria could be assigned to each group only on a dichotomous basis. This second source of empirical information had two functions: (1) Aggregating the criteria data for each attraction type resulted in profiles that were useful in interpreting the MDS solution; (2) Matching the n-dimensional MDS configuration with the m-dimensional profile data with the PROFIT-program (Carroll and Chang, 1970) should test the presence of some important dimension in the MDS configuration that is not covered by the prespecified criteria list.

The pragmatic rationale of this study incorporated the investigation of substitutional relations among different attraction types from the point of view of Vienna day trippers choosing some destination within a reasonable distance. Therefore, every attraction identified as a day trip destination within a radius of 60 miles of Vienna was recorded. Only those attractions were admitted which represented a permanent facility or at least a seasonal but not a one-off event. If it were a singular and short-term attraction it could not serve as a regular competitor to other destinations. Different attractions (e.g. historical museum, arts museum, technical museum) were accumulated to one attraction type or category in order to present a concise set of available options to the respondent. Those attraction types were separated for which *a priori* a substantial perception difference had been considered. The final set consisted of 15 attraction types which are listed in Table 17.1.

With reflection to the proposed limits of the size of a distinct choice set (Howard and Sheth, 1969) the respondents were asked to choose only 7 to 10 personally known and attended attraction types out of the list of 15.

The set of criteria for the rating task that can be seen in Table 17.2 was derived in a two-step process. In the first step a group of experts listed independently numerous attitudinal attributes with reference to the visit of any attraction type. After compilation of all proposals every notion was subject to a semantic association test with another sample of 15 individuals. The analysis of this material allowed the criteria list to be reduced to eight items.

TABLE 17.1 List of pre-selected leisure attraction types

	Leisure attraction
1	Zoo
2	Water theme park
3	Open-air concert
4	Wildlife park (native animals)
5	Product trade show
6	Archaeological site
7	Sports event
8	Danube arts festival
9	Cultural or art exhibition
10	Amusement park
11	Summer theatre festival
12	Safari park (exotic animals)
13	Museum
14	Traditional funfair
15	Open-air museum

TABLE 17.2 Attitudinal criteria for attraction rating

	Rating criteria
1	Relationship to nature
2	Interest in the particular field
3	Ease of access quality
4	Entertainment value
5	Recreation value
6	Price value
7	Pleasure
8	Suited for children

Besides the well established application of MDS techniques for assessing a spatial map of a stimuli set this study included a subsequent objective. The once generated dissimilarity data could uncover individual differences in the perception of the attraction types. As there was no interest in every single respondent pattern cases were aggregated by two different criteria (overall day trip frequency per year, special interest in travelling). The divided data matrices were input to the appropriate INDSCAL procedure (Carroll and Chang, 1970; Young, 1987) resulting in dimension weights for the individual subgroups. These weights can be interpreted as the particular importance that is attributed to a specific dimension by one group of respondents. If a correlation between a split criteria and the dimension weights can be observed the first step in the customer benefit segmentation process (Fitzgibbon, 1987) is done.

The final purpose of this study consisted in the application of PC-based interviewing techniques (Zins, 1991). The questionnaire was programmed with Ci2–500 (Sawtooth Software Inc.) for IBM compatible PCs for self administering computer-aided interviews. This interviewing technique allowed a sophisticated data gathering procedure without the employment of well trained interviewing staff and without introducing any interviewer bias (Huisman, 1988). Data collection took place at one weekend in October 1988 at Carnuntum, an archaeological site of the Roman era outside Vienna. Two IBM compatible PCs served as parallel interview stations where a total of 28 interviews were gathered. After eliminating interrupted or incomplete interviews the operative portion of the sample shrank to 22 cases.

Findings

The results for configurations in one to five dimensions are presented in Table 17.3 which shows the appropriate stress and RSQ values. The improvement of the results is considerable through the first four dimensions. As the three dimensional solution fell into Kruskal's good category of fit (Kruskal and Wish, 1988) this was preferred to the four dimensional configuration in favour of the less complicated graphical presentation and interpretation.

After determining the number of axes of an MDS solution, the next task consisted of the interpretation of the dimensions. Thus, for a first examination the coordinates for the 15 attraction types of the three

TABLE 17.3 Goodness-of-fit values for dissimilarity data of attraction types

Number of dimensions	Stress	RSQ
1	0.286	0.801
2	0.159	0.860
3	0.075	0.945
4	0.038	0.980
5	0.029	0.986

dimensional configuration were combined with the profile data using the linear PROFIT algorithm (Miller, Shepard and Chang, 1964). This procedure performs a linear regression of each property in the *n*-dimensional space such that the projections of the *m*-stimuli points on the regression vector correspond optimally with the given property values. For the eight criteria an average correlation of 0.70 was computed. Therefore, it can be argued that the main proportion of the MDS solution can be explained by the *a priori* defined criteria.

A more detailed analysis was performed by running multiple regression procedures for every single criterion. The coordinates on the three dimensions were input into the model as the independent variables and the average values for each criteria as the dependent. The resulting coefficients and multiple correlations for the regression analysis are presented in Table 17.4. High multiple correlations are one condition necessary to interpret a dimension. Best values were obtained for the recreation and relationship to nature (multiple correlation: 0.917, $p < 0.001$; 0.801, $p < 0.01$) criteria. A poor correlation was observed for the ease of access and the entertainment quality.

The second qualification for the interpretation incorporates the regression coefficients on the particular dimension. The first dimension shows a considerable association with pleasure, recreation, and interest in the particular field. The second dimension is strongly related to the criteria relationship to nature, recreation, and suitability for children. The third dimension reveals no distinct correlation between any criteria. There is a moderate negative relationship to the ease of access and the price value criteria.

TABLE 17.4 Multiple regression of profile data on dimensions of attraction map

Regression and multiple correlation coefficients for equation

Rating Criteria	DIM 1	DIM 2	DIM 3	Mult.Corr.	Sign.Level
Relationship to nature	−0.148	0.752	0.201	0.801	0.005
Interest in the particular field	−0.508	0.290	−0.396	0.773	0.010
Ease of access	−0.041	0.152	−0.557	0.531	0.248
Entertainment	0.331	0.056	−0.130	0.397	0.543
Recreation	−0.375	0.780	0.317	0.917	0.000
Price Value	−0.017	0.459	−0.469	0.655	0.072
Pleasure	0.481	0.450	−0.272	0.779	0.009
Suitability for Children	−0.126	0.728	0.098	0.766	0.012

These results support the visual inspection of the MDS configuration. Figure 17.1 presents the plot for the 15 attraction types in three dimensions. Despite the fact that the price value criterion is somewhat associated to the third dimension, the horizontal axis can be identified as a trade-off continuum: the more emotional and adventure aspects attributed to the attraction the less dominant the cost factor seems to be. Indoor and open-air museums including archaeological sites as well as exhibitions of any kind obviously do not offer that magnitude of excitement and are therefore located close together at the left end of dimension one. Opposite to these attractions, water theme parks, amusement parks, safari parks, open-air concerts, and sports events are positioned on the more pleasureful edge. Daytrippers making their choice for these types of attractions are less concerned with value for money considerations. This can be deduced because the observed entrance fees

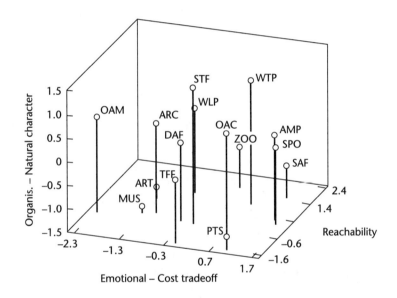

Label	Leisure attraction	Label	Leisure attraction
ZOO	Zoo	WTP	Water theme park
OAC	Open-air concert	WLP	Wildlife park
PTS	Product trade show	ARC	Archaeological site
SPO	Sports event	DAF	Danube arts festival
AMP	Amusement park	STF	Summer theatre festival
SAF	Safari park	MUS	Museum
TFF	Traditional funfair	OAM	Open-air museum
ART	Art exhibition		

FIGURE 17.1 MDS configuration for group of 15 leisure attractions

for the latter ones are comparatively higher. It can be concluded that visitors are predisposed to spend more money for more adventuresome benefits.

For the second dimension it can be inferred that visitors expect a certain degree of free movement without restricting regulations. These benefits are expected especially while visiting a wildlife park or an archaeological site. On the other hand, leisure facilities, such as (open-air) museums, exhibitions, safari parks, zoos and trade shows are perceived to be more organized and technically supported requiring a more regulated behaviour from the visitor.

The ease of access represented by the third dimension should not be viewed as the objective travel distance or time, but as the extent of inconvenience accepted by the daytrip traveller to get to the particular leisure attraction. This dimension may be regarded as an indicator of attractiveness: the more attractive a facility seems to be, the more effort will be considered acceptable to go there. On the positive side are located safari parks, water theme parks, zoos, and wildlife parks. Whereas attractions like a product trade show, a sports event, a traditional fun fair, or an archaeological site are positioned on the other side signalling the importance of the ease of access quality.

The final analysis was directed toward the investigation of perceptual differences for subgroups of the sample. Two separate matrices of dissimilarity data were computed for frequent and less frequent daytrippers. For the subgroups of respondents interested and not interested in travel, the data were processed accordingly. These matrices were separately submitted to the INDSCAL model in order to reveal different weights on the previously found dimensions. The numerical results indicating the different dimension weights are presented in Table 17.5.

The first segmentation approach uncovered significant differences in the perceptual maps of leisure attractions. Visitors making day trips at least several times per month have a strong orientation toward dimensions two and three while less frequent daytrippers concentrate completely on dimension one,

TABLE 17.5 INDSCAL results of attraction types for subgroups

Subgroups	n	Stress	RSQ	Dimension weights		
				Dim 1	Dim 2	Dim 3
Frequent day-trips	8	0.129	0.984	0.000	0.867	0.481
Less frequent day trips	14	0.275	0.930	0.964	0.000	0.000
Highly interested in travelling	13	0.220	0.955	0.935	0.265	0.105
Less interested in travelling	9	0.208	0.962	0.529	0.627	0.537

identified as the trade-off between price value aspects and emotional benefits. The second segmentation between travel and not-travel interested respondents resulted in similar clear differences in dimension weights. It can be concluded that people with a high interest in travelling place most emphasis on the first dimension (value for money versus emotional expectations). Less importance is attributed to the relationship to nature, the recreational potential, as well as the ease of access quality when choosing a leisure attraction. Visitors who are less interested in travelling consider all three attitudinal dimensions with an equal significance. Without disposing of real importance data that differentiate between several benefit factors this analysis reveals a respectable contribution to perceptual differences between particular customer segments.

The presented results deriving from small samples cannot claim to be representative. Nevertheless, the utility of the MDS approach may be appraised. For attraction managers, it is important to know the psychological position of their own and their surrounding attraction facilities. The MDS technique allowed the reduction of the visitors' perceptual map to a three dimensional configuration. Despite the obvious uniqueness of every leisure attraction the decision process for attending a particular attraction is guided by only a few basic benefit factors. It is this reason why some different attraction types operate on a close competitive level. Appraising these structural relationships between leisure attractions, managers will have practical guidelines at their disposal for positioning strategies and communication policies. Whether strengthening the actual market position or moving toward the position of an attractive competitor, it is important to take into account the strengths and weaknesses perceived by the present and potential visitor.

In order to differentiate marketing activities for leisure attractions a benefit segmentation approach can give useful recommendations. If the segmentation reveals an important association between one or several perceptual dimensions and population subgroups marketers can incorporate these findings for tuning their marketing mix programmes.

Conclusions

This study investigated the substitutional relations among 15 different leisure attraction types. It was demonstrated that there are a few fundamental dimensions upon which the selection for visiting a particular attraction is based. In order to improve response validity interviews were accomplished under field conditions using individual grouping, a less time consuming data gathering technique for MDS purposes.

Given the cultural and spatial context, three attitudinal factors were found. The first dimension was interpreted as a trade-off between perceived emotional benefits and spending propensity. A second axis was highly correlated with recreation, relationship to nature, and suitability for children. The third factor was identified as the perceived effort of bridging the distance between one's residence and the attraction site.

This approach should provide managers in the leisure and attraction business with some insight into how types of leisure attraction compete with each other. The perceptual map of attraction facilities can be seen as a tool for revealing strengths and weaknesses of past and future marketing strategies. Repositioning or differentiation policies may be supported by these findings. As well, market entry programs for new attractions may draw relevant information from this kind of analysis.

Additionally, an *a priori* segmentation using individual difference scaling algorithms delivered some significant distinctions in the perception of attractions. Day trip frequency and interest in travelling were used for a demonstration of this kind of analysis. Both criteria accounted for remarkable perceptual differences.

It was mentioned in the introductory section that this study was conducted with a convenience sample. Further studies with a larger sample size using the same survey instrument should test the reliability of the reported results. Some bias effects can only be eliminated if repeated surveys (1) at different locations, (2) at several time periods over the year, and (3) with and without computer assistance are accomplished.

This study was conceptualized for a limited choice of attraction types. It is a question of the measurement level (product brand or product category) and the aggregation task over respondents that would allow or prohibit the completely free elicitation of objects. Obviously, only this alternative could avoid that respondents are forced to rate attractions far from being an element of the individual choice set.

Further improvements can be added. In a similar vein to the individualized sets of objects, this approach can be applied for the descriptive attributes as well (Reilly, 1989; Boecker and Schweikl, 1988). An extension of the present study consists in the introduction of a magnitude scale instead of the dichotomous rating of attributes. A final proposal concerns the additional measurement of importance weights for product attributes which could meet the requirements of the attitudinal model of Fishbein (1967). All three suggestions could improve the reproduction of individual perceptions and the assessment of intersegment differences.

References

Aaker, D. and Day, G. (1980), *Marketing Research – Private and Public Sector Decisions*, New York: Wiley

Andersson, P. and Colberg, R. (1973), Multivariate analysis in travel research: a tool for travel package design and market segmentation, in *Fourth Annual Conference Proceedings*, (Sun Valley), The Travel Research Association, pp. 225–240

Becker, B.W. (1976), Perceived similarities among recreational activities, *Journal of Leisure Research*, **8**, pp. 112–122

Boecker, F. and Schweikl, H. (1988), Better preference prediction with individualized sets of relevant attributes, *International Journal of Research in Marketing*, **5**, pp. 15–24

Burton, M.L. (1975), Dissimilarity measures for unconstrained sorting data, *Multivariate Behavioral Research*, **10**, pp. 409–24

Carroll, J.D. and Chang, J.J. (1970), Analysis of individual differences in multi-dimensional scaling via an N-way generalization of Eckart–Young decomposition, *Psychometrika*, **35**, pp. 283–319

Carroll, J.D. and Chang, J.J. (1970), *How to Use PROFIT, A Computer Program for Property Fitting, by Optimizing Nonlinear or Linear Correlation*, Murray Hill: Bell Telephone Laboratories

Coombs, C.H. (1964), *A Theory of Data*, New York: Wiley

Crandall, R. and Slivken, K. (1980), Leisure attitudes and their measurement, in S.E. Iso-Ahola (Ed.), *Social Psychological Perspectives on Leisure and Recreation*, Springfield, IL: Charles C. Thomas

Fenton, M. and Pearce, P. (1988), Multidimensional scaling and tourism research, *Annals of Tourism Research*, **15**, pp. 236–54

Fishbein, M. (1967), A behavioral theory approach to the relations between beliefs about an object and the attitude toward the object, in M. Fishbein (Ed.), *Readings in Attitude Theory and Measurement*, New York: John Wiley

Fitzgibbon, J.R. (1987), Market segmentation research in tourism and travel, in J.R. Ritchie and C.R. Goeldner (Eds.) *Travel, Tourism, and Hospitality Research*, New York: John Wiley

Fodness, D. (1990), Consumer perceptions of tourist attractions, *Journal of Travel Research*, **28**(4), pp. 3–9

Gartner, W.C. (1989), Tourism image: attribute measurement of state tourism products using multidimensional scaling techniques, *Journal of Travel Research*, **28**(2), pp. 16–20

Gunn, C.A. (1979), *Tourism Planning*, New York: Crane Russak

Green, P.E. (1975), Marketing applications of MDS: assessment and outlook, *Journal of Marketing*, **39**, pp. 24–31

Green, P.E. and Carmone, F.J. (1969), Multidimensional scaling: an introduction and comparison of nonmetric unfolding techniques, *Journal of Marketing Research*, **VI**, pp. 340–1

Haahti, A. (1986), Finland's competitive position as a destination, *Annals of Tourism Research*, **13**, pp. 11–35

Howard, J.A. and Sheth, J.N. (1969), *The Theory of Buyer Behavior*, New York: John Wiley

Huisman, D. (1988), PC-based research in Europe and the USA now and after 1992: strengths, weaknesses, fairy-tales. in *The Impact of New User-Oriented Computer Facilities on Market Research*, Amsterdam: ESOMAR, pp. 95–112

Iso-Ahola, S.E. (1980), Toward a dialectical social psychology of leisure and recreation: in *Social Psychological Perspectives on Leisure and Recreation*, Springfield IL: Charles C. Thomas

Kim, S. and Fesenmaier, D. (1990), Evaluating spatial structure effects in recreation travel, *Leisure Sciences*, **12** pp. 367–81

Kruskal, J.B. (1964), Multidimensional scaling: a numerical method, *Psychometrika*, **29**, pp. 115–129

Kruskal, J.B. and Wish, M. (1988), *Multidimensional Scaling*, Beverly Hills: Sage

Lew, A.A. (1987), A framework of tourist attraction research, *Annals of Tourism Research*, **14**, pp. 553–75

Mazanec, J. (1978), Strukturmodelle des Konsumverhaltens, in G. Schweiger and G. Theuer (Eds.) *Absatzwirtschaftliche Schriftenreihe Nr. 3* Wien: Orac

Miller, J.E., Shepard, R.N. and Chang, J.J. (1964), An analytical approach to the interpretation of multidimensional scaling solutions, *American Psychologist*, **19**, pp. 579–80

Moutinho, L. (1987), Consumer behaviour in tourism, *European Journal of Marketing*, **21**,10, pp. 1–44

Perry, M. (1975), Planning and evaluating advertising campaigns related to tourist destinations, in: S.P. Ladany (Ed.), *Management Science Applications to Leisure Time Operations*, New York: American Elserion Publishing Co.

Pyo, S., Mihalik, B.J. and Uysal, M. (1989), Attraction attributes and motivations: a canonical correlation analysis, *Annals of Travel Research*, **16**, pp. 277–282

Reilly, M.D. (1990), Free elicitation of descriptive adjectives for tourism image assessment, *Journal of Travel Research*, **28**(4), pp. 21–6

Ritchie, B.J.R. (1975), On the derivation of leisure activity types – a perceptual mapping approach, *Journal of Leisure Research*, **5**, pp. 128–164

Ritchie, B.J.R. and Zinns, M. (1978), Culture as a determinant of the attractiveness of a tourism region, *Annals of Tourism Research*, **5**, pp. 252–67

Russell, R.V. and Hultsman, J.T. (1988), An empirical basis for determining the multidimensional structure of leisure, *Leisure Sciences*, **10**, pp. 69–76

Spiggle, S. and Sewall, M.D. (1987), A choice sets model of retail selection, *Journal of Marketing*, **51**, pp. 97–111

Stumpf, R.V. (1975), 'Perceptions and preferences of tourist attractions: a nonmetric multidimensional scaling approach', Claremont Dissertation, Claremont Business School

Woodside, A.G. and Lysonski, S. (1989), A general model of traveler destination choice, *Journal of Travel Research*, **27**(4), pp. 8–14

Woodside, A.G. and Sherrell, D. (1977), Traveler evoked, inept and inert sets of vacation destinations, *Journal of Travel Research*, **16**(1), pp. 14–18

Young, F.W. (1987), *Multidimensional Scaling, History, Theory and Application*, Hillside NJ: Lawrence Erlbaum Associates

Zins, A. (1991), *Multidimensionale Skalierung von Freizeiteinrichtungen. Ein Methodenvergleich unterschiedlicher Datengewinnungsverfahren*, Wien: Service Fachverlag

■ □ ■ ■ 18

Consumer Perceptions of ATMs: An Application of Neural Networks

Luiz Moutinho and Bruce Curry

This paper reports on the results of research aimed at using neural network methods to model consumer attitudes towards automated teller machines (ATMs). The approach is based on an analogy of the workings of the human brain, using a set of interconnected neurons. It involves quantifying the interconnections by means of a statistically based learning procedure. The model was tested on data derived from a consumer survey, and the results obtained were encouraging.

Introduction

Bank services automation is becoming a critical factor in the process of trying to attain cost effectiveness which can then be used as a strategic competitive weapon in the financial services market. Many financial institutions have clearly embarked on the development of technology driven strategies which they hope will be translated in terms of customer preference and, consequently, higher returns and higher market penetration.

Automated teller machines (ATMs) have been playing a pioneering and pivotal role in the advancement of this technological transformation of the banking scene. At the same time, bank marketing managers need to continuously assess the customer's decision-making process as well as the formation of attitudes, preferences and satisfaction with these new automated services. The key building blocks of this bank customer behaviour model are related to service expectations, perceived risk, consumer confidence, usage rate and long-term satisfaction.

This paper reports on the application of neural network (NN) techniques as a means of modelling such consumer perceptions. The NN approach is one of a number of branches of artificial intelligence, which are attracting increasing interest in the marketing literature. The main focus of attention so far has been expert systems (ES) which have been discussed by a number of authors. Models developed for a wide range of decision problems, for example, international negotiations (Rangaswamy *et al.*, 1989), site location analysis (Curry and Moutinho, 1991a), competitive positioning advertising (Cook and Schleede, 1988), and export market selection, (Mitri *et al.*, 1991). As regards Neural Networks, Kennedy(1991) suggests that this approach may have some potential, but actual models in the marketing field using the technique are as yet in their infancy. (See for example Ellis, Lemay and Arnold's (1991) report on development of a working model dealing with transportation backhaul pricing.)

This paper examines the theoretical base of the NN technique. A model is then suggested to represent consumers' perceptions of and responses to ATMs. The model has been tested using data obtained from a consumer survey. The results provide encouragement for further work in the field.

Previous research

Deregulation of the financial sector has led to intense competition to attract and keep customers. One of the methods of obtaining customers is for banks to provide increased convenience in banking via electronic means. Automated teller machines are well established, while remote banking is making inroads with corporate customers. Marr and Prendergast (1990) conducted a study in the New Zealand financial system to determine why and how often customers use alternative delivery mechanisms, especially human tellers. Over 30 per cent of a large sample of ATM cardholders said they had problems with their bank, such as long queues and slow or rude service. The findings indicate weaknesses in the banks' current system of human tellers. The main reasons for using a human teller were a preference for dealing with humans and the branch bank being closer in location than an ATM. These facts point to a failure by banks to view new product developments from a customer perspective.

The banking industry has tried to take advantage of the productivity and customer service gains associated with technology with the provision of ATMs which consumers can use to carry out day to day banking transactions. Leonard and Spencer (1991) found that a great majority of consumers perceived banks with automated teller machines as being either very successful or somewhat successful. However, while these new technologies may offer significant advantages to the consumer, many are unwilling to adopt them. A large number of consumers are resistant to new ways of doing their banking, especially when the new way represents loss of personal contact. Moutinho and Meidan (1989) found a segment of the market who placed importance on the 'human factor' in banking. Murdock and Franz (1983) identified a large class of customers who found it 'embarrassing and/or degrading' using ATMs – implying that they preferred more personal service.

A unique finding by these authors was that a particularly strong correlation was found between the psychological/social risk perception that using an ATM is 'degrading and/or embarrassing'.

The ATM has not wholly replaced the teller as many had projected. A major problem could be due to the comparable rate of increase in the number of ATM transactions per month with the increases in the total number of ATMs and card bases. According to some ATM industry analysts, it takes two ATM transactions to displace one teller transaction, thus requiring roughly 8000 ATM transactions per month just to break even. The reluctance to use ATMs affects deposit volume and usages for withdrawals. The same industry analysts attribute this reluctance to poor marketing. That some banks charge fees for ATM transactions is evidence that ATMs have achieved acceptance, but the practice repels some customers. Still, offsite ATMs, strategically placed, have successfully boosted volume.

Marr and Prendergast (1991) found that around 60 per cent of card holders are regular users of ATMs. The vast majority of these only withdraw money. This low usage rate suggests a serious misuse of bank resources. Thus, while ATMs are at the maturity stage of the product life cycle, usage rates are still well short of their potential.

Stevens, Warren and Martin (1989) have analysed nonadopters of the innovation of the ATM in a research study. They found that two psychographic characteristics differentiate users of ATMs from nonusers. Users are not as concerned about safety when conducting business at an ATM and are less likely to enjoy going to the bank to conduct financial business. These characteristics also differentiate laggards from nonadopters, with laggards being more similar to users. Along demographic dimensions, users: (1) are younger; (2) are better educated; (3) have higher incomes; (4) are more likely to reside in a household where the female is employed and there are children; (5) are more likely to be male; and (6) are somewhat more likely to be married. A similar profile differentiates laggards from nonadopters, except that nonadopters: (1) do not have lower incomes; (2) are much more likely to be married; (3) reside in a household where the female is not employed; and (4) are female. It is estimated that between 10.2 per cent and 17.4 per cent of consumers fall into the nonadopter category.

Leblanc (1990) has analysed the perceptions of users and nonusers of an automated service. He found that the main reason for using the ATM was accessibility. The user group believed that the ATM improves quality of service, reduces costs, presents no risks to customers, and is fast and easy to use. The nonusers saw no advantage to using the ATM and preferred dealing with humans. The user group was generally more educated. It is apparent that financial institutions must develop different strategies for user and nonuser groups. Nonusers should be educated on how to operate the machines. Human tellers, while offering personalized service, could demonstrate the functions of the ATM. In addition, the machines could be placed inside the bank near the human teller in order to entice usage.

Kutler (1982) found that usage of ATMs can be increased by opening more locations. While many banks have tried to boost transaction volumes at ATMs by locating them in an ever widening variety of places, some are going a step further by promoting the use of ATMs for purposes other than banking. For example, in Portland, Oregon, bus commuters can get monthly passes as well as cash from ATMs and the programme has been successful. A growing number of banks are reviving ATM promotions in hopes of luring customers away from competitors and offsetting heavy expenditures on the equipment.

With the passage of time, society is being confronted with an accelerated shift from an industrial to an information technology orientation. A new breed of consumer, who is more demanding and technologically aware, has emerged. For many customers the most visible symbol of how the electronic age has affected banking is still the ATM. No longer are ATMs only to be found sprouting through the walls of banks and building societies. Increasingly they are being installed in remote sites such as motorway service areas, where they are some distance from the nearest bank premises but close to the point of demand. Consumers are becoming more sophisticated and discriminating in their evaluation of banking services. So, as they become more attuned to the benefits and possibilities of electronic banking, they will expect to have access to a wider range of such services.

That more and more consumers are at ease with robotic tellers, and that they are becoming ATM literate, is suggested by figures quoted in a *Financial Times* survey (1988) which reported that the number of cash withdrawals made through ATMs has increased from 12 million in 1976 to 507 million in 1987. And as proprietary ATM networks continue to give way to shared networks, there is little doubt that ATMs will remain an important feature of the electronic banking landscape for some time to come. The move away from proprietary networks of ATMs and towards shared networks offers banks a way of sharing the high cost of installing ATMs and providing better availability and convenience.

Automated teller machines have risen from their early beginnings to a position of prominence in the retail banking field. Two major constructs for ATM cost justification are: (1) traditionally, ATMs are economically rational because they replace brick and mortar and tellers; and (2) the rationale for ATMs needs to come from increasing revenue. Traditional strategies, such as increasing the card base, may be refined by identifying barriers to increased penetration and segments to target and by promoting nonwithdrawal transactions for increased ATM usage. Under the second construct, individual ATM deployers and card issuers are feeling the pinch as top management looks at these cost centres and wonders about the return on investment.

The most controversial issue concerning ATM marketing revolves around an effective pricing strategy. The successful ATM pricing strategy has to: (1) create a positive customer attitude towards ATM usage; (2) overcome the consumer perception of exploitation when fees are imposed; and (3) generate significant investment of consumers from the teller line to the ATM. The basic components of a positive ATM pricing strategy are an annual, fixed fee, with a rebate programme for each ATM cardholder and a per charge transaction fee for any nonproprietary, foreign ATM transaction. A cardholder's fee places some value on the ATM service and creates the opportunity for a rebate as a reward mechanism for full function usage. The fixed fee establishes clearly the total cost of using the ATM service. It is critical that the positive pricing strategy be implemented as a complete and ongoing programme (Nease, 1989).

Different types of ATM pricing include: (1) periodic card fee; (2) 'us on us' transaction fees; (3) 'us on others' transaction fees; and (4) no fees at all. Sophisticated pricing of traditional transaction services under circumstances of unusual time or place convenience could provide revenue to meet the goals of the newer ATM construct (Lederman, 1989).

The introduction of new financial services such as electronic fund transfer at point of service (EFTPOS), home banking and ATMs has greatly decreased the interface of the bank with its customers. These services will not build customer franchises, but will lower the bank's direct involvement with the customer and may, in turn, affect patterns of customer loyalty (Howcroft and Lavis, 1986). Indeed, a trend of depersonalization is emerging in the banking industry, and as such, its impact on the way in which banking business will be conducted is unknown. Moreover, it will become more difficult for customers to differentiate the services offered by one bank from those of another, as any technological advantage gained will be short lived (Moutinho and Meidan, 1989). Laroche *et al.* (1986) found that service related factors such as speed of delivery and efficiency proved to be an effective way of attracting and retaining bank customers.

The nature and direction of the satisfactions that are delivered to customers of bank services were explored by Moutinho and Brownlie (1989) using a nonmetric multidimensional scaling technique. Interviews were conducted with 250 established bank customers to identify variables that influence customer satisfaction.

These authors found in their bank customers' evaluation of currently provided services that there existed a high level of satisfaction with regard to the location and accessibility of ATMs. The respondents' evaluation of ATM services indicated a willingness to accept the incorporation of new functions and services to be provided to them through ATMs (i.e., loan requests, credit card payment and the transfer of funds). Bank customers' perception of safety when depositing cash in ATMs seemed to be increasing, and they appeared to be more willing to make deposits through ATMs. In their study, the Euclidean distance attached to the withdrawing of money from ATMs has indicated that bank customers seemed to be only moderately satisfied with this provision of service. This result may be due either to the recognition of a routinized behaviour or to occasional errors detected in bank statements. A low level of satisfaction was attached by bank customers to the factor associated with their experience of having to queue when using an ATM. A negative perception of safety related to the deposit of cheques in automated teller machines has been found.

These authors have also draw attention to the important role of ATMs in conditioning consumers' perceptions of the services offered by banks. Further, despite many well publicized negative incidents with ATMs, and an historically conservative banking public that is only now becoming computer literate, it would seem that customers are favourably inclined towards the use of ATMs for conducting other business with banks.

Howcroft (1991) found that bank customers emphasized the breakdown in automated teller machines (ATMs) as an important source of service dissatisfaction, but subsequently, it was established that, to some extent, their opinions were not necessarily based on the banks' current generation of ATMs. This raises the distinct possibility of an important gap in communications between the bank and its customers on ATM policy. The reasons for being loyal to a bank are changing as a result of increased competition and the application of new technology in the provision of bank services. Not only is it becoming easier to switch banks and to make use of the services of several banks, but consumers are also becoming more willing to do so.

Neural networks

Neural network models can be looked at from a number of viewpoints. In the first place they can be regarded as attempts to copy the structure and workings of the human brain, which is taken to comprise an interconnected set of neurons. The interconnections are referred to as synapses: the neural network approach is also loosely described as connectionism. Neural network models attempt to replicate the brain's own problem solving processes, whereby 'input neurons' receive direct stimuli which are then fed into them through a pattern matching process to produce a conclusion or response. For example, the NN approach has been successfully applied to computer vision. A noteworthy achievement in this direction is reported by Pomerleau (1989), who reports on the use of NN techniques to develop ALVINN (autonomous land vehicle in a neural network) a vehicle with a vision system which allows it to negotiate obstacles.

The essence of this approach is that the vehicle operates a number of electronic sensors, the signals from which are input into a neural network which can identify certain patterns. These patterns consist of obstacles and the shape of the road to be negotiated. The software uses the patterns to derive the optimal direction for the vehicle to steer. Pattern matching operations such as this translate conveniently into the marketing environment, to the extent that we are concerned with perceptions, cognition and stimuli. It is therefore natural to seek to examine consumer perceptions through this route.

The second useful perspective views neural networks in computational terms. Here, the important feature can be referred to as 'parallel distributed processing', which also relates to the brain analogy described above (see McClelland and Rumelhart, 1986). The neurons which make up the brain, although connected together, are physically independent. Computationally, parallel processing offers an escape from the bottlenecks which arise in serial machines, and is likely to be more prominent in the computing mainstream over the early years of the 21st century.

Third, NNs can usefully be examined from a statistical viewpoint. It is possible to regard a network model as a specialized version of a simultaneous equation multiple regression model, with a number of input variables influencing a set of output variables. As noted below this amounts to a specialized structure because of the existence of a hidden layer of nonmeasured variables and because of the threshold effects which operate for each node. The statistical procedures required involve non linear search over the parameter space. The strength of the approach lies in the fact that it provides a statistical foundation for the use of quantitative methods in examining cognitive processes. The simplest form of NN consists solely of two sets or 'layers' of neurons, the 'input ' and 'output' layers. Each input is potentially linked to each output, as shown in Figure 18.1 below.

In the ALVINN project mentioned above, the input neurons record or are activated by the electronic sensors of the vehicle. The output neurons would relate either to specific recognized shapes or to decisions regarding directions to steer. This simple model is referred to as the 'perceptron' model (see, for example, Minsky and Papert, 1969). It suffers from the serious weakness, however, that it is incapable of representing a number of commonly encountered structures. For example, it cannot represent 'XOR' problems in which neurons are to be connected by means of 'exclusive OR 'operators which allow either one combination or another but not both (see, for example, Touretski and Pomerleau, 1989). In formal terms, the simple perceptron can cope only with linearly separable structures.

A solution to this problem, which brings with it a number of additional advantages regarding the modelling process, is to insert an optional number of intermediate layers in between the input and output layers, as shown in Figure 18.2 below. These layers are described as 'hidden' layers in that they do not contain directly measurable variables. In terms of the brain analogy of the connectionist approach they can be related to the internal workings of the brain rather than its physical exterior.

In addition to the fact that it provides a richer modelling platform, permitting the inclusion of more real world structures, the multilayer model has the advantage that the intermediate layers may frequently be linked to important concepts. This is particularly valuable where these concepts are not susceptible to direct measurement (see Touretski and Pomerleau, 1989). The hidden layers may add valuable features. For example, the Kohonen self-organizing network contains a first layer which

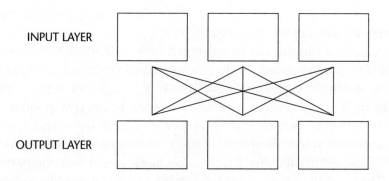

FIGURE 18.1 A simple 2 layer network

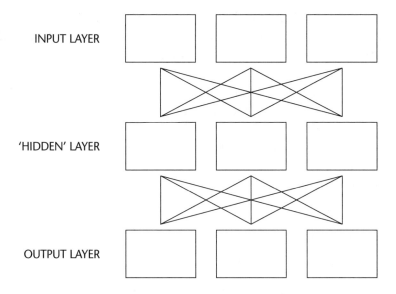

INPUT LAYER

'HIDDEN' LAYER

OUTPUT LAYER

FIGURE 18.2 A network with hidden layers

is seen to direct stimuli towards those neurons which are particularly able to process certain patterns (Kohonen, 1988). This again may be a valuable feature of physical brains which one would wish to see replicated in a computer model.

Implementation of NNs

In formal terms an NN model may be expressed in terms of the interconnections between its neurons. These interconnections can be regarded as weights. For a particular layer above the first input layer we therefore have each neuron functionally dependent on neurons in the layer immediately below it.

Hence $X(i,j) = \Sigma\,(\,wi,j-1\,X(i,j-1))$

for the value of the ith neuron at level j
where the wi,j constitute a vector of constant weights.

In the simplest approach the $X\,(i,j)$ are limited to the values one or zero, in which case there is an overlap with the formal framework of Boolean logic. The implications of this are that there is a sizeable area of overlap between NNs and rule based expert systems. It is also generally the case that the structure of the equation above is taken to be linear, partly for the sake of computational convenience and partly because a linear form can provide a valid approximation. For a formal framework through which higher order neural models can be effected see Jeffries (1989).

Where the NN approach certainly differs from the rule based ES approach is that the value of a neuron is subject to a threshold effect. Thus a neuron will take on the value '1' only if the weighted sum of its inputs exceeds a threshold value. A common formulation of this threshold effect involves use of the logistic function.

In formal terms, we have:

$$X(i,j) = 1 \text{ if NET}(i) > Ki$$
$$= 0 \text{ otherwise}$$

where $\text{NET}(i) = \Sigma \ (wi,j-1 \ X(i,j-1))$

and can be interpreted as the total input to neuron i, which is only 'activated' if the input exceeds the threshold value Ki. The logistic function implies that

$$X \ (i, j) = 1 \ / \ (1 + \exp-(\text{NET}(i))$$

A threshold model embodies a greater degree of 'fuzziness' as compared with a simple Boolean model of change. The work on ATMs described in this paper, however, makes use of an 'analogue' variant of the NN approach, whereby the variables may be measured in continous terms. This makes the model more closely resemble a conventional multivariate statistical model.

A vital feature of the approach is that the values of the weights are established by 'learning', whereby they are induced from example connections. In 'supervised learning', the network is fed training pairs of related inputs and outputs. In unsupervised learning it is forced to rely solely on input vectors and learns by means of clustering methods (see e.g. Kohonen, 1984). The fact that a network can learn from experience, which is said to obviate the need for an extensive process of knowledge acquisition, serves as an advantage of the approach as compared with rule based systems, even though the latter may operate on rules derived inductively from examples. However, the learning aspects of the NN approach may also be easily overstated. Learning depends very heavily on correct selection of training examples. The particular cases, variables or categories chosen by the system developer will be important, and the choices may be subject to arbitrary or subjective factors.

Learning takes place through a statistically based procedure of iteratively adjusting the weights. For supervised learning this is carried out in order to arrive at values for the weights which minimize the distances between actual output levels of neurons in the 'training set' and the values of the output neurons predicted from the inputs. An integral part of the definition of a particular network is therefore the learning process by which the weights are adjusted.

A specific problem which arises in this context concerns the hidden intermediate layers, for which the learning algorithm needs a value at each iteration. The most commonly used solution to this problem is the 'back propagation' algorithm whereby inputted values are calculated for hidden layer neurons. By definition it is not possible directly to calculate error factors for these layers, so imputed error values are calculated at each iteration for each layer by using values of neurons in the previous layer.

At each iteration, the values of the input layer nodes yield values for hidden layer nodes through the current set of weights. This in turn yields a predicted set of values for the nodes in the output layers and hence a vector of prediction errors for this layer. The next step is to 'propagate' the output layer errors backwards through the hidden layers, i.e. to estimate the prediction errors for these layers. This is achieved by apportioning each output layer error to the hidden layers according to the strengths of the connections.

A neural network approach to ATMs

As a first step in applying the NN approach we have constructed a model with four output nodes and four input nodes. The input nodes are respectively

> EXPECT: Consumer expectations of the machines
> RISKFUNCT: The degree of functional risk involved
> CONFID: The extent of customer confidence
> RISKFIN: The degree of financial risk

The output nodes are

> RECOMM : Recommendation of ATMs to others
> SATIS: The degree of satisfaction
> USAGE: The extent of usage
> CONTINUE: Intentions to continue using the machines

The software used for this research was Neuroshell, from Ward Systems Inc. This runs on standard PC equipment, although it will run very slowly without a maths coprocessor and convergence may be difficult to achieve. The particular machine used was a 33 megahertz 486 DX machine (having an onboard coprocessor), with 8 megabytes of RAM.

Neuroshell uses the back propagation algorithm as outlined above, with the following additional features:

1. There is a single hidden layer, although the user may specify the number of nodes in this layer. By default, the number of nodes will be set by a formula which depends on the number of input and output nodes.

2. The user may set the learning rate, which as described above denotes the change in a weight as a proportion of the prediction error at each iteration.

3. In addition the user may set the learning 'momentum', which is an extra refinement whereby the adjustment to a weight depends not only on the prediction error but also, proportionately, on the adjustment carried out at the previous iteration. In formal terms:

   New weight change = learning rate * error
   + momentum * (last change).

4. The user may set the 'learning threshold'. Learning stops when the errors for all sample cases fall below this level.

Although the connectionist approach has its roots in a parallel model of the brain, actual implementations generally use conventional serial computing methods. Indeed, NNs may be put into practice using standard PCs. This means that the although the effective use of parallel processing is lost the approach is perfectly accessible to most computer users without the need for specialized hardware. It should be noted, however, that the training process may impose excessive computational burdens on lower grade machines.

Data collection

A nonprobability sampling procedure was used in the study and the respondents were selected through the utilization of a quota sample approach. Personal interviews were carried out with 200 individuals of both sexes of 18 years of age or over. In terms of age brackets, the sample comprised: 18–35 age group: 26 per cent; 36–54 age group: 43 per cent; and 55 and over: 31 per cent. The questionnaire was administered to a sample of bank customers at three main locations in the city of Cardiff, Wales (two of these sites were located in the city centre). To ensure quality, the interviewers received six hours of training by project staff. In addition, a supervisor was present at all times while the interviews were conducted. The respondents were qualified to answer the questionnaire on the basis that they had to be established bank customers

(EBCs) in possession of a 24 hour teller bank card and of their degree of usage of ATMs (heavy, moderate and light users). After the completion of the editing of the questionnaires, the study comprises an achieved sample of 199 respondents.

An introductory statement related to the explanation of the purpose of the study was used as an opener designed to secure respondent cooperation. Interval scaled responses were collected, in which the differences between scale values could be meaningfully interpreted. Still, verifying whether respondents' mental or psychological perceptions of the differences between adjacent response categories are equal is somewhat difficult. The computation and the interpretation of the results are legimate because the relationships among the differences hold regardless of the particular constants chosen. The study variables were measured through the use of itemized five point rating scales.

Results

The tentative conclusions drawn here are limited since the variables were measured at a single point in time despite the fact that the satisfaction formation process is generally believed to occur over time (Andreasen, 1977). Additional antecedents of satisfaction should be investigated as well, particularly those related to customer expectations and disconfirmation of complaining behaviour related to ATM usage.

The results obtained so far are quite reasonable. Figure 18.3 below shows the Neuroshell screen which summarizes the learning carried out. In addition to the features descibed above it gives a frequency distribution for the prediction error and charts the learning history. The error referred to is the average error over all sample cases, and 'learning events' refer to iterations of the learning procedure.

The learning threshold value of 0.15 was the best achievable convergence level for this particular set of data. Also available in Neuroshell are implied R-squared values for each of the output nodes. For the current case these are as follows

$$[\, 0.765 \quad 0.496 \quad 0.905 \quad 0.722 \,]$$

Figure 18.4 below shows the final calculated weights for the entire system, as displayed in Neuroshell. As noted above, the hidden layer of the network allows the model to be applied to a much wider range of problems, without the restriction of liner separability.

In addition, the nodes in the hidden layer may be regarded as intermediate variables which are impossible or very difficult to measure. The

—————————————————————— Summary of Learning Error Factors ——————————————————————

Error range		Count	Percent	Histogram
1.0001	99999.0000	0	0.00	
0.5001	1.0000	0	0.00	
0.1001	0.5000	26	13.07	
0.0501	0.1000	65	32.66	
0.0201	0.0500	33	16.58	
0.0101	0.0200	10	5.03	
0.0051	0.0100	64	32.16	
0.0001	0.0050	1	0.50	
0.0000	0.0001	0	0.00	

Neurons:		Factors:		Average error → Training:		Testing:
Input	4	Learnt rate	0.6	Last error	0.04934	------
Hidden	4	Momentum	0.9	Minimum error	0.04934	------
Output	4	Threshold	0.15	Events since min.	0	------
Problem: ATM1		Cases: 199		Presentation: random		

FIGURE 18.3 Summary of learning for ATM model

strength of the NN approach is that it avoids these measurement problems, and permits the testing of deeper cognitive models. In the case of ATMs there is still work to be done on the theoretical role of the the hidden layer nodes. Our current suggestion is that they represent the self image of the consumer and factors relating to service involvement.

Analysis of the findings

Figure 18.4 shows the final neural network connection weights based on the total and single contributions of each input neuron on each of the four hidden nodes, as well as the total and single contributions of these hidden modes on the final output neurons as hypothesized in the original NN framework model.

The connection weights should be interpreted as either inhibitory factors (−) or excitory factors (+) within the structure of the equation model. The amount of bias associated with the hidden nodes and the output neurons can be analogically described as intercept values or to put it in NN language, it represents the state of a node which is always 'switched on'.

The final implied R-squared values for each of the four output modes are quite significant, in particular those related to the recommendation of ATMs to others, the extent of usage and the intentions to continue using the machines.

EXPECT				
FROM:	−28.6	12.4	−7.42	−26.4
CONTRIBUTION:	74.8			
RISKFUNC				
FROM:	0.21	−130.5	−53.6	−0.69
CONTRIBUTION:	185.0			
CONFID				
FROM:	7.20	−23.5	−6.18	13.5
CONTRIBUTION:	50.3			
RISKFIN				
FROM:	−18.8	−18.0	−7.28	−11.6
CONTRIBUTION:	55.8			
Hidden node # 1				
BIAS:	14.1			
TO:	−28.6	0.21	7.20	−18.8
FROM:	−1.00	−0.38	0.35	0.09
Hidden node # 2				
BIAS:	59.4			
TO:	12.4	−130.5	−23.5	−18.0
FROM:	−1.09	3.26	−0.22	1.76
Hidden node # 3				
BIAS:	16.8			
TO:	−7.42	−53.6	−6.18	−7.28
FROM:	−1.06	−5.99	−6.03	−4.84
Hidden node # 4				
BIAS:	−3.79			
TO:	−26.4	−0.69	13.5	−11.6
FROM:	2.54	−2.17	−2..30	1.31
RECOMM				
BIAS:	0.61			
TO:	−1.00	−1.09	−1.06	2.54
SATIS				
BIAS:	0.26			
TO:	−0.38	3.26	−5.99	−2.17
USAGE				
BIAS:	1.09			
TO:	−0.35	−0.22	−6.03	−2.30
CONTINUE				
BIAS:	0.53			
TO:	0.09	1.76	−4.84	1.31

FIGURE 18.4 Network connection weights

After having analysed all the connection weights within the neural network in terms of inhibitory and excitory factors, we were able to apply on a posterior labelling approach to the four hidden modes. We have labelled the four nonobservable endogenous variables respectively: user innovativeness, risk recognition, situation contingencies and consumer cognitive analysis (evaluation of processed information).

The highest total weight contribution of the input neurons comes from the amount of functional risk perceived by consumers when using ATMs (185.0), followed by the formation of service expectations (74.8), the degree of financial risk (55.8) and the extent of consumer confidence (50.3).

User innovativeness is not particularly affected by previous expectations nor by a percussive perception of financial risk when using ATMs. On the other hand, service innovators feel confident when utilizing the machines and are willing to accept the inherent functional risk associated with automated teller machines.

Consumer risk recognition which subsequently may trigger risk reduction strategies is inversely related to the perceived amounts of functional and financial risks as well as to the degree of confidence when using an ATM. This psychological non directly observable variable is positively associated with the formation of consumer expectations. The strongest connection weight affecting the neural network was found here (-130.5 between input neuron 2 and hidden mode 2) reflecting that a low risk recognition level experienced by the consumer carries the probability of originating a high perceived functional risk.

Situational contigencies (3) which may include factors such as non habitual ATM usage locations, the utilization of machines which belong to a shaped ATM network but not a proprietary network (i.e., the customer's bank) as well as the consumer's perception of high technical uncertainty, may be directly interrelated and consequently have a negative effect on the formation of consumer's expectations and his or her degree of confidence when using the machines. Furthermore, these situational contingencies may also increase the consumer's perception of functional and financial risks.

The amount of cognitive analysis developed by the consumer in terms of processing and evaluating ATM information contained in his or her long-term memory can help reduce perceived functional and financial risks as well as the shaping of previously formed service expectations. On the other hand, this cognitive activity carried out by the consumer can increase his or her overall level of confidence when using the machine.

The analysis of the findings related to the output neurons suggests that consumers do not recommend the usage of ATMs to others when they perceive themselves as innovators, when they experience a high level of risk recognition or when they are confronted with specific contigencies. Conversely, if consumers are engaged in a high level of cognitive activity and information processing, they are more inclined to make recommendations of ATM usage to other people. User innovativeness (here described as a personality trait of the ATM user) does not necessarily derive overall satisfaction from using the machines. Consumers who perceive themselves as innovators may like to explore new ATM functions which may or may not disconfirm their service expectations. Also, certain situational contigencies (or the higher the degree of occurence of these contingencies) may lead to service dissatisfaction. Furthermore, the amount of cognitive activity and behavioural effort spent by the consumer may negatively affect the perceived overall satisfaction level derived from ATM usage. Risk reduction strategies used by the consumer can have a positive effect on the amount of prolonged satisfaction related to the utilization of automated machines.

The lack of consumer risk reduction strategies, the occurence of particular situational contigenicies and the amount of consumer cognitive activity and behavioural effort can all reduce the extent of ATM usage, whereas the degree of user innovativeness can in fact increase the usage rate of ATMs.

Finally, the degree of user innovativeness, the adoption of risk reduction strategies as well as the amount of information processed and evaluated by the consumer, can all positively affect his or her intentions to continue using the machines. Only specific situational contigencies can inhibit these usage intentions.

Conclusions

The empirical results obtained from Neuroshell are of an acceptable quality, and provide encouragement regarding the potential for applying NN technology in the marketing field. The greatest potential seems to lie in modelling consumer perceptions, either of particular products or of advertising campaigns, etc (See Curry and Moutinho, 1992). The specific advantages of the NN approach arise because of its strength in the field of cognitive psychology. McClelland and Rumelhart (1986) discuss a whole range of relevant models. The approach provides a platform capable of describing and analysing various cognitive processes while at the same time being susceptible to empirical/quantitative analysis. Of particular interest is the role of the hidden layer of network nodes, which add computational richness, but which are also capable of providing theoretical interpretations. In the present case, the hidden layer nodes can be interpreted as: the specific advantage of the NN model is that it casts light on these non-measurable variables, in a manner analagous to the often neglected multivariate technique of canonical correlations.

Implications

The research has two major implications. First, as has previously been assumed, consumers' previous expectations about the performance of ATMs seem to shape the degree of prolonged satisfaction with the financial service. This finding calls for marketing managers to undertake further research on the issue of how consumers' service performance expectations are formed so that the critical performance expectations can be better matched with the attributes of the end service. Second, the outcome of consumers' prolonged satisfaction calls for development of effective service improvement programmes and new product developments based on multi function operations so that the level of prolonged satisfaction with the service as perceived by consumers could be maintained or even raised.

The clearest general implication which emerges is the need for designing appropriate approaches to measuring customer satisfaction. *A posteriori* aggregate measures such as volume of ATM transactions cannot specify the pure influence of specific service aspects on consumer behaviour. For this reason it may be desirable to descend to the level of individual measures, such as satisfaction or customer complaints.

Individual measures such as prolonged satisfaction help explain what takes place at the level of the decision maker, and as such provide additional evidence to the more aggregate indicators of service performance. In most markets, the competitive energy is not aimed at reducing dissatisfaction but at obtaining higher degrees of satisfaction.

Are the strategies used in the past necessarily appropriate for the future? When ATMs were launched in the US and UK, emphasis was on large scale promotional campaigns and lavish giveaways to encourage trial. Such strategies were largely resisted by some banks, for example in New Zealand, which preferred to adopt a more 'soft sell' approach centred on issuing consumers with a card and then letting them adopt ATMs in their own time.

By providing information that customers value directly related to expectations and evaluations through advertising and direct communication efforts, prolonged satisfaction can be enhanced. The same marketing communication efforts could be designed to balance out the negative effects of ATM usage over time.

Some key marketing implications of the findings related to usage rate and long-term satisfaction with ATMs are described below.

- Service quality takes on increased importance for consumers because of the frequency of contact they may have with a single provider of ATM services. The total perceived quality in this case encompasses critical factors ranging from the operational effectiveness of the system (i.e., number of breakdowns) to the number of times that the customer finds the machine 'closed' and the associated length of time for it to reopen and from the number of mistakes related to ATM withdrawals found in the customer's statement to the average waiting time to use an ATM due to the limited availability of other machines.
- Financial services organizations should promise certain actions or responsibilities in the event of service failure.
- A customer's satisfaction with an organization's complaint handing response may influence both intention to increase or maintain the usage rate and word of mouth behaviour.
- Service that is personalized (for example, by greeting the user through the displaying of the customer's name on the screen of the machine) can add substantially to the bottom line while increasing customer satisfaction as well.
- The financial services should place ATMs in more convenient locations and should target untapped demographic/psychographic groups. For example, Schram (1991) found that despite the attraction of credit cards and free banking, students often seek the availability of automated teller machines (ATMs) when choosing a bank. As a result, some banks have invested heavily in placing ATMs on college campuses.
- Financial services organizations should develop and install ATMs which would perform more banking functions in order to obtain sufficient transaction volume to justify its operating costs (e.g. the Touch-Bank system developed by Barclays).
- Financial institutions will be able to improve ATMs. Customers may one day find themselves talking with a video of the bank manager about pension plans or other financial products. Multimedia systems will soon appear in the high street and will take customers from interfacing to interaction. The system uses multimedia, which involves the integration of text, graphics, sound, animation and video.

References

Andreasen, A.R. (1977), A taxonony of consumer satisfaction/dissatisfaction measures, *Journal of Consumer Affairs*, **11** (Winter): pp. 11–24

Cook, R.L. and Schleede, J.M. (1988), Application of expert systems to advertising, *Journal of Advertising Research* (June/July) pp. 47–55

Curry, B and Moutinho, L. (1991a), Expert systems and marketing strategy: an application to site locations, *Journal of Marketing Channels*, Volume 1 No. 1

Curry, B and Moutinho, L. (1991b), Artificial intelligence in marketing: an application to strategic analysis, in M.C. Gilly *et al.* (Eds.), *Enhancing Knowledge Development in Marketing*, Vol.2, Chicago: IL: American Marketing Association

Ellis, R., LeMay, S. and Arnold, D. (1991), A transportation backhaul pricing model: an application of neural network technology, in C. Johnson, F. Karakaya and M. Laric (Eds.) *Proceedings of the 1991 AMA Micro Computers in Marketing Education Conference*, C. Johnson, F. Karakaya and M. Laric (Eds.) Chicago, IL: American Marketing Association

Financial Times (1988), Survey of plastic cards, Section 3 (15 September): p. 5

Howcroft, B. (1991), Customer Service in selected branches of a UK clearing bank: a pilot survey, in the services–manufacturing divide: synergies and dilemmas, *Proceedings of the Service Industries Management Research Unit Conference*, Cardiff Business School, University of Wales College of Cardiff, 25–26 September

Howcroft, J.B. and Lavis, J. (1986), *The New Revolution in Structure Strategy*, Oxford: Blackwell

Jeffries, C. (1989), An alternative formation of high order neurodynamics, *International Journal of Neural Networks*, 1

Kennedy, M.S. (1991), Artificial intelligence in media planning: an exploration of neural networks, in *Enhancing Knowledge Development in Marketing*, C. Gilly *et al.* (Eds.), *American Marketing Association Educators' Summer Conference Proceedings* Vol. 2, Chicago IL: American Marketing Association

Kohonen, T. (1988), *Self-Organization and Associative Memory*, New York: Springer

Kutler, J. (1982), Consumers' acceptance of ATMs, *Credit* (January/February): pp. 24–5

Laroche, M., Rosenblatt, J.A. and Manning, T. (1986), Services used and factors considered important in selecting a bank: an investigation across diverse demographic segments, *International Journal of Bank Marketing*, 4, 1: pp. 35–55

Leblanc, G. (1990), Customer motivations: use and non-use of automated banking, *International Journal of Bank Marketing*, 8,4: pp. 36–40

Lederman, C.J. (1989), ATM strategies: looking ahead, *Journal of Retail Banking*, 11, 4 (Winter): pp. 17–26

Leonard, M. and Spencer, A. (1991), The importance of image as a competitive strategy: an exploratory study in commercial banks, *International Journal of Bank Marketing*, 9, 4 pp. 25–29

Marr, N.E. and Prendergast, G. (1990), Human tellers: who needs them? *International Journal of Bank Marketing*, 8, 2, pp. 32–39

Marr, N.E. and Prendergast, G.P. (1991), Strategies for retailing technologies at maturity: a retail banking case study, *Journal of International Consumer Marketing*, 3, 3, pp. 99–125

McClelland, J.L. and Rumelhart, D.E. (1986), *Parallel Distributed Processing: Explorations in the Microstructure of Cognition*, Volumes 1 and 2, Cambridge MA: MIT Press/ Bradford Books

Minski, M. and Papert, S. (1969), *'Perceptions'*, Cambridge MA: MIT Press

Mitri, M, Evrigen, C. and Tamer Cavusgill, S. (1971), 'The country consultant: an expert system for the international marketing executive', AMA Conference on Microcomputers in Marketing Education, San Diego

Moutinho, L. and Brownlie, D.T. (1989), Customer satisfaction with bank services: a multidimensional space analysis, *International Journal of Bank Marketing*, 7, 5, pp. 23–27

Moutinho, L. and Meidan, A. (1989), Bank customers' perceptions, innovations and new technology, *International Journal of Bank Marketing*, 7, 2, pp. 22–27

Murdock, G. and Franz, L. (1983), Habit and perceived risk as factors in the resistance to the use of ATMs, *Journal of Retail Banking*, 5, 2 (Summer), pp. 20–29

Nease, C.B. (1989), A positive pricing strategy for ATMs, *Bank Marketing*, **21**, 2 (February) pp. 26–29

Rangaswamy, A., Eliashberg, J., Burke, R.R. and Wind, J. (1989), Developing marketing expert systems: an application to international negotiations, *Journal of Marketing*, **53** (October) pp. 24–39

Schram, J. (1991), How students choose their banks, *United States Banker* **101**, 10 (October) pp. 75–78

Stevens, R.E., Warren, W.E. and Martin, R.T. (1989), Nonadopters of automatic teller machines, *Akron Business and Economic Review* **20**, 3 (Fall) pp. 55–63

Touretski, D.S. and Pomerleau, D.A. (1989), What's hidden in the hidden layers? *BYTE*, **14**, p. 8

Wasserman, P.D. (1989), *Neural Computing: Theory and Practice*, New York: Van Nostrand Reinhold

■ □ ▪ ■ 19

External Moderation of Associations among Stakeholder Orientations and Company Performance

Gordon E. Greenley and Gordon R. Foxall

A recent survey of the treatment accorded to the stakeholder concept across the business administration literature, by Donaldson and Preston (1995), concluded that there is an implicit assumption that stakeholder orientation is positively associated with company performance, but that this assumption has not been empirically tested. In the marketing literature studies by Kohli *et al.* (1993) and Slater and Narver (1995), of the association of the market orientation with performance, also concluded that empirical evidence is needed about wider stakeholder orientation and performance, to expand our understanding of market orientation. The study reported in this article provides such evidence from a sample of UK companies. The theory tested addresses stakeholder orientation to consumers, competitors, employees, and shareholders, the potential association of these orientations with company performance, and potential moderation of these associations from the external environment. The results indicate that stakeholder orientation *per se* is not associated with performance *per se*, but that different types of stakeholder orientation are associated with different measures of performance, and that these associations are moderated by the external environment.

Introduction

While the recent marketing literature has focused on only two stakeholders, consumers and competitors in the form of market orientation, there have been calls from leading scholars in the field, Kohli *et al.* (1993) and Slater and Narver (1995), that this research domain should be expanded to incorporate other key stakeholders. In a comprehensive review of the treatment accorded to stakeholder orientation across the business administration literature, Donaldson and Preston (1995) concluded that there is a general assumption that companies must address the individual interests of all stakeholder groups in order to be successful, and that these orientations will be positively associated with performance. However, they also found that there has been no empirical testing of this assumption, despite the potential implications for company performance.

The overall aim of the study reported in this paper was to extend our understanding of market orientation, by investigating associations between different stakeholder orientations and company performance.

Background to the study

The stakeholder groups of any organization represent a wide and diverse range of interests, given that each stakeholder group has its own unique set of expectations, needs and values (Clarkson, 1995; Freeman, 1984; Harrison and St.John, 1994; King and Cleland, 1978). While the marketing literature has, of course, focused on a single stakeholder group, there have been claims from leading marketing scholars in the field of market orientation that it should be extended to incorporate other stakeholders. A conclusion of Kohli *et al.* (1993) was that the market orientation research domain, focusing on consumers and competitors, should be extended to incorporate other stakeholders, in order to expand understanding further. The same conclusion was drawn by Slater and Narver (1995). While they found that market orientation is an important cultural foundation for organizational learning, they also concluded that: 'to be a powerful foundation for a learning organization and to provide the opportunity for generative learning, the scope of market orientation must include all stakeholders and constituencies'.

There are two major reasons for incorporating wider stakeholder orientations into this research domain of marketing. First, at the corporate level the interests of a particular stakeholder group, such as consumers, cannot be considered in isolation from those of other stakeholders (Kotter and Heskett, 1992; Miller and Lewis, 1991; Mintzberg, 1983; Polonsky, 1995), given that many diverse interests must be addressed (Clarkson, 1995; Freeman, 1984; Harrison and St.John, 1994). Therefore, orientation to a particular stakeholder group must be developed with respect to orientation to the other groups (Aupperle *et al.*, 1985; Posner and Schmidt, 1984), while particular stakeholder groups, such as consumers, are likely to be in competition with other groups for scarce resources and managerial attention. Second, success in achieving an effective orientation to the consumer stakeholder group is likely to be partly dependent on orientations to other groups. In the original Kohli and Jaworski (1990) conceptualization of market orientation, employees were included as antecedents. For example, market orientation will be more effective if companies educate all employees to recognize marketing as an element of their jobs (Canning, 1988), and to see their roles as serving consumers as much as their companies (Kelley, 1992; Miller and Lewis, 1991). Also, effective communication and coordination among employees is essential for market orientation (Masiello, 1988; Shapiro, 1988), as employees are the means for generating, communicating and distributing products and services for successful consumer satisfaction (Day, 1994). Such employee orientation should contribute to effective marketing, which will help to protect employees' long-term security and remuneration interests. Consumer orientation will also be partly dependent on shareholder orientation. While dividend payout of profits to shareholders may reduce investment for enhancing consumer benefits, satisfaction of shareholders' interests is clearly essential for long-term company development, which in turn will protect consumer interests (Kotter and Heskett, 1992; Samuels *et al.*, 1990). Indeed, consumer orientation can only be sustained when there is satisfaction of shareholder payout and share price interests (Kotter, 1990; Kotter and Heskett, 1992).

The generic model of strategic management assumes that, in order to be successful, companies should address the interests of all stakeholder groups (Chakravarthy, 1986; Clarkson, 1995; Donaldson and Preston, 1995; Evan and Freeman, 1993). It has even been argued that, in order to be successful, it is critical for companies to address diverse stakeholder interests, and that failure to do so may be detrimental to company performance (Chakravarthy, 1986; Clarkson, 1995; Evan and Freeman, 1993; Harrison and St.John, 1994; Kimberly, *et al.*, 1993; Kotter, 1990). However, addressing this diverse range of interests may be problematic, especially when there are conflicting stakeholder interests (Greenley and Foxall, 1996), and where there is a scarcity of resources (Amit and Schoemaker, 1993; Barney, 1991; Grant, 1995; Mahoney and Pandian, 1992).

Donaldson and Preston (1995) completed a comprehensive review of the treatment accorded to the stakeholder concept across the business administration literature. One of their conclusions was that there is a general assumption in the literature that companies that adopt stakeholder principles and practices perform better than companies that do not. However, they also discovered that associations among stakeholder orientations and company performance have not been empirically investigated, despite the potentially detrimental effect on performance of not giving adequate attention to the diverse range of stakeholder interests. Consequently, they suggest that such evidence is needed, in order to develop understanding within this domain. Although there is an absence of evidence, relevant empirical results are available from studies of the association of market orientation with company performance, where market orientation is a combined measure of customer and competitor orientations. In two major studies of market orientation and performance by Kohli *et al.* (1993) and Slater and Narver (1995), it was similarly concluded that evidence is needed about associations between other stakeholder orientations and performance. Therefore, there is a compelling case for an empirical study of the association of stakeholder orientation with company performance.

Empirical evidence from the market orientation studies

Located in the marketing literature but limited to the consumer and competitor stakeholder groups, empirical evidence from this stream of research provides a basis for developing stakeholder theory. Market orientation research has followed four themes: developing an instrument for measuring market orientation; testing the instrument; investigating main effects of market orientation on performance, and investigating external moderation of the market orientation/performance association. The two main instruments that have been reported are those developed by Kohli and Jaworski (1990), Kohli *et al.* (1993), and by Narver and Slater (1990), although a more recent instrument had been developed by Deng and Dart (1994). With respect to testing their instruments both Deng and Dart and Kohli and Jaworski report empirical refinement of their scales and evidence of validity and reliability (Deng and Dart, 1994; Jaworski and Kohli, 1992 and 1993). Although Narver and Slater (1990) also report empirical refinement of their scale and subsequent evidence of validity and reliability, an independent empirical test by Siguaw and Diamantopoulos (1995) did not confirm the theoretical dimensionality of this scale.

Empirical evidence about the association of market orientation with performance and about external moderation is available from four US and two UK studies, and is summarized in Table 19.1. There is clearly some equivocality in these results. Main effects of market orientation on performance were found in all of the US studies. However, Jaworski and Kohli (1992 and 1993) did not find any external moderation of the association, and concluded that the linkage between market orientation and performance appears to be robust

TABLE 19.1: Market orientation studies

Study	Country	Sample	Market orientation/ performance association	Moderator effects
Jaworski and Kohli (1992 and 1993)	US	Sample 1: 220 companies	Positive	None identified
		Sample 2: 230 companies	Positive	None identified
Narver and Slater (1990)	US	113 SBUs in one company	Positive	Not investigated
Slater and Narver (1994)	US	81 SBUs in one company; 36 SBUs in another	Positive	Effects identified
Ruekert (1992)	US	5 SBUs in one company	Positive	Not investigated
Greenley (1995)	UK	240 companies	Moderated association	Effects identified
Hart and Diamantopoulos (1993)	UK	87 companies	Weak association	Effects identified

across contexts characterized by varying levels of external environmental change. Although Slater and Narver (1994) identified main effects of market orientation on performance, unlike Jaworski and Kohli (1993) they identified some external moderation effects. However, despite these results they concluded that there is little support for the proposition that the competitive environment has an effect on the strength and nature of the market orientation/performance relationship. In the UK study by Greenley (1995) main effects were not identified. However, external moderation effects were identified, which suggest that the influence of market orientation on performance is contingent on external environment variables, and that market orientation may only be advantageous in certain types of external environments. Similarly, in the UK study by Hart and Diamantopoulos (1993) external moderator effects were also identified, with only a very weak main effect.

Although these results provide a basis for developing stakeholder theory, there are several inadequacies of the market orientation approach, which further support a wider stakeholder approach. First, as mentioned earlier, at the corporate level the interests of particular stakeholder groups, such as consumers and competitors, cannot be considered in isolation from those of other stakeholders (Campbell and Yeung, 1991; Donaldson and Preston, 1995; Miller *et al.*, 1985; Miller and Lewis, 1991; Mintzberg 1983). Second, market orientation involves only a limited set of corporate culture issues, albeit an important set (Hunt and Morgan, 1995). Corporate culture, by contrast, encompasses a much broader set of managerial issues and expectations which relate to a wider range of stakeholders (Alvesson, 1989; Schein, 1985; Wong and Saunders, 1993). As corporate culture influences strategic decision making, a wider understanding of stakeholder issues beyond consumers and competitors is necessary. Third, Hunt and Morgan (1995) have suggested that market orientation can only provide a competitive advantage if it is rare among competitors. Therefore, developing a planned orientation to a wider range of stakeholders ought to provide a greater potential for developing a competitive advantage that is rare and difficult to imitate. Fourth, Slater and Narver (1995) argue that market orientation may not encourage a sufficient willingness for managers to take risks and suggest that it needs to be balanced with entrepreneurial activity, which encourages managers to develop a broader concept of organizational culture that focuses the firm outwards (Webster, 1994). A wider stakeholder orientation in turn provides the basis for broadening the cultural emphasis of the firm, and for addressing risks in decision making.

Conceptualization of stakeholder orientation

Although several definitions of stakeholders have been proposed, the common theme is that a stakeholder is any group or individual who can affect, or be affected by, a particular organization, such as shareholders, employees, competitors, consumers, suppliers and government agencies (Clarkson, 1995; Freeman 1984; Rhenman 1968). The stakeholder groups of any organization represent a wide and diverse range of interests, given that each stakeholder group has its own unique set of expectations, needs and values (Clarkson 1995; Freeman 1984; Harrison and St.John 1994; King and Cleland 1978). Despite the diversity of the range of these interests, relatively little consideration has been given to approaches that companies use to address the interests of their stakeholder groups. This consideration is largely conceptual and normative, providing a range of key organizational issues, which companies should consider with respect to their stakeholder groups. These key issues are discussed below, and provide a conceptualization of orientation to each stakeholder group.

Understanding stakeholders

Clarkson (1995) and Harrison and St.John (1994) have emphasized the difficulty of analysing and understanding the diverse interests of stakeholder groups. However, the latter advocate that a comprehensive understanding of stakeholder interests is essential to an effective strategic management process, which should be an ongoing and interactive process. Indeed, informational inputs are obviously essential to all decision making throughout strategic management (Grant, 1995; Mintzberg, 1990; Pettigrew and Whipp, 1993). Unfortunately empirical studies of how companies achieve an understanding of their stakeholders are not available, although conceptual models for understanding stakeholders have been proposed (Freeman and Reed, 1983; Harrison and St. John 1994). However, before such models can be used, information obviously needs to be acquired, and judgements made, to provide inputs for using these models to achieve an understanding. Empirical evidence about how companies gain an understanding of stakeholders has not hitherto been available.

Corporate culture

The plans that companies develop to address the interests of stakeholders also depend on the beliefs, values and expectations of managers, within the context of corporate culture (Alvesson, 1989; Cleland and King, 1979; Guth and MacMillan, 1986; Kotter and Heskett, 1992; Schein, 1985). Although Gordon and DiTomaso (1992) identified much ambiguity in the various descriptions of corporate culture, its importance is well expounded in the literature (Hassard and Shariffi, 1989). Deshpande *et al.* (1993) found that companies with a customer orientated culture perform better than companies without, while Jones (1995) argues that acceptance of responsibility for stakeholders can lead to a competitive advantage. McDonald and Leppard (1991) reported that certain beliefs and values within a corporate culture can provide a barrier to effective strategic planning.

Where the personal beliefs, values and expectations of managers are openly discussed throughout the organization, within the context of corporate culture, there will be an opportunity to compare the values and needs that are held internally with those of stakeholders (Kotter and Heskett, 1992; Miller and Lewis, 1991). However, empirical evidence about the importance of stakeholder groups in corporate culture is not available.

Corporate mission

A theme of the strategic management literature is that an effective mission statement is central to developing strategies for addressing stakeholder interests (Campbell and Tawadey, 1990; Campbell and Yeung, 1991; Harrison and St.John, 1994). Hence, the approach advocated by Pearce (1982) is that stakeholder interests should be the first inputs for formulating a mission statement, and hence they are at the starting point of strategic planning. Pearce (1982) proposes a 'claimant' approach, wherein managers should attempt to identify all stakeholder groups and the claims that they have on the company (King and Cleland, 1978). However, as it is argued that some stakeholder claims may not be legitimate, not all may be included in the mission (Donaldson and Preston, 1995; Hooley and Saunders, 1991). There remains, nevertheless, a paucity of empirical evidence about the relative importance of stakeholder groups in mission statements.

Stakeholder planning

Several researchers have identified and explicated the importance of strategic planning, both as a process and as a predictor of performance (Dutton and Duncan, 1987; Dyson and Foster, 1982; Greenley, 1994; Ramanujam and Venkatraman, 1987; Sinha, 1990). Miller and Lewis (1991) see the core problem of addressing stakeholder interests as one of planning a balance between satisfying the firm's own needs and values, and addressing the diverse range of stakeholder interests. Clarkson (1995) emphasizes the importance of planning for stakeholders, while Polonsky (1995) suggests a planning procedure for addressing stakeholders. Harrison and St. John (1994) go further, by advocating that the whole scope of strategic planning should encompass plans for addressing stakeholder interests. Part of this process includes the relative extent of planning for addressing each stakeholder group, given the availability of resources (Amit and Schoemaker, 1993; Barney, 1991; Grant, 1995; Mahoney and Pandian, 1992), which may need to be rationed among stakeholders. Therefore, the relative extent of planning for each stakeholder group reflects attention accorded to stakeholders.

Model and hypotheses

Empirical evidence from the market orientation studies implies that any associations among stakeholder orientations and performance are likely to be moderated by variables from the external environment. This is consistent with the theoretical proposition of Jones (1995), that associations among stakeholder management and its outcomes, such as performance, will be influenced by the market environment, given that changing market conditions are likely to affect the firm's ability to address stakeholder interests. This is likely to be exacerbated where there is conflict in stakeholder interests (Greenley and Foxall, 1996), and where there is a scarcity of resources (Amit and Schoemaker 1993; Grant 1995). Indeed, this is also consistent with general theory in business administration, in which associations among organizational variables are expected to be contingent upon other endogenous and exogenous variables (Boyd *et al.*, 1993; Hansen and Wernerfelt, 1989). Within such associations the key parameters are the complexity and dynamism of the environmental variables; complexity means the number of relevant variables from the environment, whereas dynamism means the extent of change within these variables (Clark *et al.*, 1994). The model tested in this study is shown in Figure 19.1. This depicts the set of stakeholders on which the study is based as consumers, competitors, employees and shareholders (see Method section below); orientations to each stakeholder group based on the key organizational issues discussed above; competitor hostility, market growth and market turbulence as potential moderators; and four measures of company performance (see Method section below).

Jones (1995) predicts that competitive hostility will be a key external variable in empirical studies of stakeholders, which is consistent with theory discussed in the wider literature on competitive rivalry (Day and Wensley,

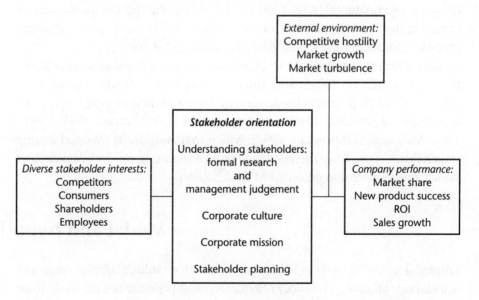

FIGURE 19.1 Model of stakeholder orientation

1988; Day and Nedungadi, 1994; Hunt and Morgan, 1995; Kukalis, 1991). Competitive hostility was also operationalized in the market orientation empirical studies, as it was included in the original Kohli and Jaworski (1990) conceptualization study of market orientation. Kohli and Jaworski (1990) argue that the greater the competitive hostility, the more aggressive a company must be in understanding the interests of its customers and competitors, and hence in developing its market orientation. Therefore, the more hostile the competition the more companies will need to be orientated to their consumers and competitors in order to sustain performance. Competitive hostility was also found to be a moderator in the Narver and Slater (1990) empirical study. This gives the following hypotheses:

H1a Consumer orientation will be positively associated with performance at high levels of competitive hostility.

H1b Competitor orientation will be positively associated with performance at high levels of competitive hostility.

Although writers such as Chakravarthy (1986), Clarkson (1995), Kimberly *et al.* (1983) and Kotter (1990) argue that companies should address the interests of all stakeholder groups in order to be successful, Miller and Lewis (1991) argue that imbalances of attention and resource allocation are likely to occur at certain times. Such a situation is likely in times of high levels of competitive hostility, where more attention and resources will need to be allocated to consumers and competitors than to other stakeholders such as employees and shareholders, in order to overcome these hostile competitive conditions and to sustain performance. Such diversion, through competitive hostility, is likely to be exacerbated if there is a shortage of resources, which in itself is likely to result in a selective prioritization of attention to stakeholder interests (Campbell and Yeung, 1991). Another view is that the power of respective stakeholder groups to influence the firm will be different at different times, and that companies will need to prioritize their allocation of attention and resources to different stakeholders with respect to this power (Mintzburg, 1983; Polonsky, 1995). Therefore, in times of high competitive hostility consumers and competitors will have more power than other stakeholders such as employees and shareholders, as the company seeks to overcome hostile competitive conditions and to sustain performance. Consequently, both views suggest that in such conditions employees and shareholders will receive less attention. Therefore:

H1c At high levels of competitive hostility, employee orientation will be negatively associated with performance.

H1d At high levels of competitive hostility, shareholder orientation will be negatively associated with performance.

Other changing market conditions that are likely to influence the firm's ability to address stakeholder interests are market turbulence and market growth (Anderson, 1982; Davis, *et al.*, 1991; Hunt and Morgan, 1995; Jones, 1995; Kukalis, 1991; Webster, 1992), especially if there is conflict among stakeholder interests (Greenley and Foxall, 1996) and if there are scarce resources (Amit and Schoemaker, 1993; Grant, 1995). These two potential moderators were included in the original Kohli and Jaworski (1990) conceptualization study of market orientation. Market turbulence is defined as the extent of change of consumer needs per period of time. Kohli and Jaworski (1990) conceptualize that where there are stable consumer needs a relatively low market orientation can sustain performance, but with increasing turbulence more attention will need to be given to consumers and competitors. Although market turbulence did not exhibit a moderator effect in the Jaworski and Kohli (1993) empirical study, market turbulence moderator effects were found in the Greenley (1995) and Slater and Narver (1994) empirical studies. Hence:

H2a Consumer orientation will be positively associated with performance at high levels of market turbulence.

H2b Competitor orientation will be positively associated with performance at high levels of market turbulence.

High levels of market turbulence, like competitive hostility, are likely to lead to an imbalance in attention and resource allocation to stakeholder groups, and to a shift in the relative power of the groups, as discussed above. Therefore, high levels of market turbulence are also likely to divert attention and resources away from stakeholders such as employees and shareholders, as companies seek to overcome turbulent market conditions and to sustain performance by closely addressing consumers and competitors. This gives:

H2c At high levels of market turbulence, employee orientation will be negatively associated with performance.

H2d At high levels of market turbulence, shareholder orientation will be negatively associated with performance.

Kohli and Jaworski (1990) conceptualize that where companies experience a high level of demand they can 'get away with' a minimum level of market orientation and still achieve an acceptable level of performance; conversely, where there is low market growth then higher levels of attention must be given to consumers and competitors in order to sustain performance. Consequently, less attention is likely to be given to other stakeholders, in such conditions of low market growth. However, unlike conditions of high competitive hostility and market turbulence, high market growth conditions will give more opportunity to address shareholders' dividend and wealth interests, and employees' security and remuneration interests. In the Greenley (1995) and the Slater and Narver (1994) empirical studies, market growth was found to be a moderator, but not in the Jaworski and Kohli (1993) study. This gives the final set of hypotheses:

H3a Consumer orientation will be positively associated with performance at low levels of market growth.
H3b Competitor orientation will be positively associated with performance at low levels of market growth.
H3c Employee orientation will be positively associated with performance at high levels of market growth.
H3d Shareholder orientation will be positively associated with performance at high levels of market growth.

Method

Three sets of variables were operationalized in order to measure stakeholder orientation, the potential external moderators and company performance.

Stakeholder orientation

The conceptualization of stakeholder orientation discussed above was operationalized into the following measures:

Research

The importance of formal research for understanding the interests of each stakeholder group. Scale: 1 not important, through to 7 very important.

Management judgement

The importance of management judgement for understanding the interests of each stakeholder group. Scale: 1 not important, through to 7 very important.

Corporate culture

The extent of open managerial discussions about each stakeholder group, when addressing corporate culture. Scale: 1 no discussions, through to 7 extensive discussions.

Corporate mission

The relative importance of each stakeholder group in the corporate mission. Scale: 1 not important, through to 7 very important.

Stakeholder planning

The extent of planned strategies for addressing the interests of each stakeholder group. Scale: 1 not developed, through to 7 highly developed.

The respondents were asked to compare company practice with respect to four stakeholder groups; competitors, consumers, employees, and shareholders, which were identified in the pilot study as the key stakeholders (see section on Procedure below). For each stakeholder group the responses to the above measures were aggregated across the sample with equal weighting, to give an overall measure of orientation to each of the four stakeholder groups.

External moderators

Boyd *et al.* (1993) concluded that managers' perceptions of their environments are more critical than objective measures, especially in the context of interpreting information and decision making. Indeed, managerial perceptions of the external environment were measured in the market orientation studies to represent potential moderators (Greenley, 1995; Narver and Slater, 1990). Each of the hypothesized variables was operationalized with respect to change, to reflect dynamism in the environment (Clark *et al.*, 1994), as follows:

Competitive hostility

The extent to which the marketing operations of key competitors have changed over the last three years (Day and Nedungadi, 1994; Jones, 1995; Narver and Slater, 1990). Scale: 1 little change, through to 7 extensive change.

Market turbulence

The extent to which consumer needs have changed over the last three years (Miller, 1987; Narver and Slater, 1990). Scale: 1 little change, through to 7 extensive change.

Market growth

A measure of the average annual rate of change in market size, over the last three years (Narver and Slater, 1990; Hooley *et al.*, 1992). Measured on a percentage scale.

Company performance

Previous studies have taken either a subjective or an objective approach to measuring performance. The subjective approach has been used extensively in empirical studies, based on executives' perceptions of performance, and has been justified by several writers. Studies by Covin *et al.* (1994), Dess (1987), Dess and Robinson (1984), Golden (1992), Hart and Banbury (1994), Powell (1992), Venkatraman (1990), Venkatraman and Ramajuman (1986), and Verhage and Waarts (1988) for instance, have all found consistency between executives' perceptions of performance and objective measures. Also, Speed (1991) found consistency between managers' assessments of their performance and that of their peers, while Doyle *et al.* (1989) observed frankness among businessmen when discussing performance. Another argument in favour of the subjective approach is that objective measures in company accounts are generally flawed and are not suitable for research purposes (Fisher and McGowan, 1983), while Day and Wensley (1988) suggest an absence of suitable objective measures. Yet another argument is that managerial perceptions are more important than objective reality in decision making (Day and Nedungadi, 1994). As the subjective approach has been widely adopted, and as it was used in the market orientation studies (Greenley, 1995; Hart and Diamantopoulos, 1993; Jaworski and Kohli, 1992; Narver and Slater, 1990), it is also appropriate for this study. The performance measures were operationalized from these studies. Consequently, the respondents were asked to state how their companies' market share, new product success rate, return on investment and sales growth compare to that of their competitors, in their principal market. Measures consisted of percentage differences in performance, compared to competitors.

Procedure

The questions were piloted through personal interviews with the managing directors/CEOs of eight UK companies. After completing the questionnaire the respondents were asked about the validity of the measures for addressing the variables, ambiguity and difficulty in responding. The questionnaire was modified accordingly. They were also asked to select their key stakeholder groups. As the key groups were found to be competitors, consumers, employees, and shareholders, the study focused on these groups, in order to ensure a questionnaire of reasonable length and to avoid respondent fatigue.

A sample of 1,000 companies was randomly drawn from the Dunn and Bradstreet data base of UK companies with more than 500 employees. As this was an initial empirical study careful consideration was given to the unit of analysis. The managing director/CEO was chosen for two reasons. First, as this position holds considerable executive responsibility for addressing and satisfying the diverse interests of stakeholder groups, there will be a high level of commitment to balancing these interests with respect to corporate objectives and available resources (Deshpande *et al.*, 1993). Second, researchers such as Boyd *et al.* (1993), Day and Nedungadi (1994), Glick *et al.* (1990) and Huber and Power (1985), advise that responses from the most knowledgeable respondent can be more accurate than taking an average of several informants in an organization. Consequently, a questionnaire and personal letter were mailed to the managing director/CEO of each company. A total of 242 companies responded, which yielded a usable response of 230 fully completed questionnaires. The sample has similar proportions of service and manufacturing companies, and all companies were represented by their Managing Directors/CEOs. To test for nonrespondent bias the results from the later respondents were compared to those of the early respondents (Armstrong and Overton, 1977). No significant difference was identified between the two sets on any of the measures.

Validity and reliability

Content validity

As explained earlier, the questionnaire was piloted prior to data collection, during which the respondents were asked about the validity of the measures for addressing the variables, question ambiguity, and difficulty in responding. Consequently modifications to the questionnaire were made to address these issues.

Discriminant validity

A single-factor test was performed on the survey data, in order to test for discriminant validity (Podsakoff and Organ, 1986). The stakeholder orientation, external and performance variables were factor analysed together, using principal components analysis. Owing to the sample size factor loadings below 0.35 are not significant (0.05 significance level, 80 per cent power level, and allowing for inflation of the standard errors), and therefore loadings below this level were suppressed (Hair *et al.*, 1995). If the variables load onto a single factor that accounts for substantial variance, then little discrimination on the part of respondents is evident, and common method variance is a likely problem. The analysis produced four factors with eigenvalues greater than unity, which account for 64 per cent of the variance, as shown in Table 19.2. A very clean solution resulted as the performance, stakeholder orientation and external variables loaded onto different factors, and as virtually unique significant factor loadings resulted. Therefore, the results suggest that the respondents discriminated among the stakeholder orientation, external and performance constructs, suggesting discriminant validity within the measures.

Convergent validity

For each of the stakeholder orientation scales, construct validity was tested in two ways. First, all pairwise correlations between the items within each of the scales were examined. All these correlations are significant at the $p < 0.05$ level, while 85 per cent are significant at the $p < 0.01$ level, which suggests convergence within each scale. Second, for each stakeholder orientation scale, item to total correlations were calculated for each respective item. These within

TABLE 19.2 Results of single-factor test for discriminant validity

Variables	Factor 1	Factor 2	Factor 3	Factor 4
Sales growth	0.87			
Market share	0.86			
ROI	0.75			
NPS	0.70			
Competitor orientation		0.76		
Employee orientation		0.70		
Consumer orientation		0.68		
Shareholder orientation		0.56		
Competitive hostility			0.80	
Market turbulence			0.78	
Market growth				0.85
Eigenvalue	2.86	1.79	1.42	1.1
Percentage of variance	26.0	16.3	12.9	9.2

stakeholder group correlations were compared to those of alternative scales made up of the organizational issues (research, planning, corporate culture and corporate mission) across the range of stakeholder groups. Evidence of convergent validity in the stakeholder orientation scales will be demonstrated if they feature higher correlations than those of the alternative organizational issue scales. These results are given in Table 19.3, and indeed show that the stakeholder orientation scales feature higher item to total correlations than the organizational issue scales. Also, the alpha coefficients for all the organizational issue scales are unacceptably low, and do not meet the prerequisite for validity. Therefore, both tests suggest convergent validity within each of the stakeholder orientation scales.

Convergent validity of the performance measures was also tested in two ways. First, pairwise correlations between the measures of performance were examined, and all were found to be significant at the $p < 0.001$ level, which reflects the high factor loadings on factor 1 (see Table 19.2). Second, a retest of the measures of performance were obtained from a quarter of the sample, but the results were not significantly different from the original results. Therefore, the results suggest convergent validity within the performance construct.

TABLE 19.3 Item to total correlations and reliability analyses

Scales	Research	Planning	Culture	Mission
(a) *Stakeholder orientation scale*				
Competitor orientation scale; alpha 0.72	0.46	0.58	0.43	0.58
Consumer orientation scale; alpha 0.64	0.40	0.48	0.43	0.48
Employee orientation scale; alpha 0.67	0.40	0.50	0.40	0.51
Shareholder orientation scale; alpha 0.67	0.51	0.57	0.36	0.44
(b) *Organizational issue scales*				
Research scale; alpha 0.50	0.36	0.30	0.35	0.25
Planning scale; alpha 0.62	0.43	0.49	0.48	0.31
Corporate culture scale; alpha 0.31	0.28	0.33	0.05	0.07
Corporate mission scale; alpha 0.59	0.36	0.51	0.37	0.38

Reliability

The reliability of each of the four stakeholder orientation scales was tested using Cronbach's coefficient alpha (Churchill, 1979; Nunnally, 1967). The results are given in Table 19.3. As these responses are from a new type of investigation using a new research instrument, the range of coefficients, from 0.72 to 0.64, is acceptable (Churchill, 1979; Nunnally, 1967), and the coefficients are consistent with those reported in leading marketing journals (Peterson, 1994; Slater, 1996). They are also consistent with scales that are made up of a small number of items (Norusis, 1990). In order to test the reliability of the construct of performance the four performance measures were combined into a scale. The resultant coefficient of 0.82 is consistent with acceptable reliability.

Results

The testing of the hypotheses requires the investigation of the influence of external variables on the form of the relationship between each of the stakeholder orientations and performance. The appropriate statistical technique for such investigations is hierarchial moderated regression analysis (Arnold, 1982; Hair *et al.*, 1995; Hellevik, 1984; Schoonhoven, 1981; Sharma *et al.*, 1981). This technique requires the examination of three models of multiple regression equations, which in this study are:

Model 1:
$$Y = a + b_1 X_1 + b_2 X_2 + b_3 X_3 + b_4 X_4 + e$$

where Y is the dependent variable (performance) and X_1 through X_4 are the predictor variables of competitor, consumer, employee and shareholder orientations respectfully.

Model 2:
$$Y = a + b_1 X_1 + b_2 X_2 + b_3 X_3 + b_4 X_4 + b_5 X_5 + b_6 X_6 + b_7 X_7 + e$$

where X_5 is market growth, X_6 is competitive hostility and X_7 is market turbulence.

Model 3:
$$Y = a + b_1 X_1 + b_2 X_2 + b_3 X_3 + b_4 X_4 + b_5 X_5 + b_6 X_6 + b_7 X_7 + b_8 X_1 X_5 \ldots b_{19} X_4 X_7 + e$$

where b_8 to b_{19} are the regression coefficients of the interaction terms among the stakeholder orientations and market growth, competitor hostility and market turbulence, with the external variables being potential moderator variables. Where an interaction term is significant it identifies either a quasi or pure moderator effect on the form of the relationship between the respective stakeholder orientation and performance, from the respective moderator variable. If the external variable (market growth, competitive hostility or market turbulence) corresponding to the significant interaction term in model 3 is not significant in model 2 then it is a pure moderator; if it is significant in model 2 then it is a quasi moderator. A pure moderator is not related to either the dependent or predictor variables but interacts with the predictor variable to modify the form of the relationship. A quasi moderator not only interacts with the predictor variable, but is also a predictor itself (Sharma *et al.*, 1981).

Where moderator effects are identified then further analysis can identify monotonicity in the form of the relationship between the predictor variable (a stakeholder orientation) and the dependent variable (performance), over the range of the moderator (market growth, competitive hostility or market turbulence). Monotonicity cannot be identified by simply inspecting the signs and magnitudes of the regression coefficients, as recommended by Schoonhoven (1981), but can be determined from a partial derivative of model 3, for example;

$$dY/dX_1 = b_1 + b_8X_5 \tag{1}$$

where b_1 and b_8 are unstandardized regression coefficients.

For each of the four dependent variables three regression models were built. For models 1 and 2 the variables were entered simultaneously. For model 3 stepwise entry of the interaction terms was used, with PIN set at 0.05 and POUT at 0.10. For models 1 and 2, where main effects were investigated, the VIF of all the independent variables was less than 2 (far below the threshold of 10 stipulated by Hair *et al.*, 1995), indicating that multicollinearity is not problematic. As moderator effects were investigated in model 3 with unstandardized coefficients, any multicollinearity introduced by the interaction terms is not problematic (Golden, 1992; Schoonhoven, 1981; Sharma *et al.*, 1981). Moreover, as multicollinearity reduces the likelihood of obtaining significant interaction terms, the analyses produce conservative tests. In order to test the stability of the results the sample was randomly split and the same analyses were performed on each half. As expected some differences were found in these results (Hair *et al.*, 1995), but the moderator effects were upheld in these analyses. The results are given in Tables 19.4 to 19.7, and the resultant moderator effects are summarized in Table 19.8.

TABLE 19.4 Unstandardized regression coefficients on market share

					B	Sig
Model 1	R^2 0.04	F 2.4	NS			
Model 2	R^2 0.07	F 2.2	p 0.03			
	Employee orientation				−0.15	NS
	Shareholder orientation				0.20	NS
	Competitor orientation				0.16	NS
	Consumer orientation				0.31	NS
	Market growth				0.16	0.05
	Competitive hostility				−0.07	NS
	Market turbulence				0.11	NS
Model 3	R^2 0.12	F 2.9	p 0.00			
	Employee orientation				−0.13	NS
	Shareholder orientation				1.2	0.00
	Competitor orientation				−0.89	0.08
	Consumer orientation				0.41	NS
	Market growth				0.14	NS
	Competitive hostility				1.05	0.01
	Market turbulence				−1.04	0.06
	Shareholder orientation* competitive hostility				−0.21	0.00
	Competitor orientation* market turbulence				0.21	0.03

TABLE 19.5 Unstandardized regression coefficients on new product success

					B	Sig
Model 1	R^2 0.02	F 1.3	NS			
Model 2	R^2 0.04	F 1.3	NS			
	Employee orientation				−0.13	NS
	Shareholder orientation				0.07	NS
	Competitor orientation				0.17	NS
	Consumer orientation				0.18	NS
	Market growth				0.11	NS
	Competitive hostility				−0.04	NS
	Market turbulence				0.09	NS
Model 3	R^2 0.11	F 2.1	p 0.05			
	Employee orientation				−1.08	0.01
	Shareholder orientation				0.10	NS
	Competitor orientation				0.17	NS
	Consumer orientation				0.28	NS
	Market share				0.10	NS
	Competitive hostility				−0.04	NS
	Market turbulence				−0.97	0.03
	Employee orientation* market turbulence				0.20	0.02

TABLE 19.6 Unstandardized regression coefficients on ROI

					B	Sig
Model 1	R^2 0.02	F 1.3	NS			
Model 2	R^2 0.07	F 1.98	p 0.05			
	Employee orientation				−0.06	NS
	Shareholder orientation				−0.05	NS
	Competitor orientation				0.41	0.01
	Consumer orientation				−0.28	NS
	Market growth				0.04	NS
	Competitive hostility				−0.19	0.02
	Market turbulence				0.17	0.05
Model 3	R^2 0.11	F 2.4	p 0.02			
	Employee orientation				−0.07	NS
	Shareholder orientation				−0.89	0.03
	Competitor orientation				0.37	0.02
	Consumer orientation				−0.21	NS
	Market growth				−0.85	0.04
	Competitive hostility				−0.16	0.04
	Market turbulence				0.15	NS
	Shareholder orientation* market growth				0.16	0.03

TABLE 19.7 Unstandardized regression coefficients on sales growth

					B	Sig
Model 1	R^2 0.05	F 2.7	p 0.03			
Model 2	R^2 0.12	F 4.2	p 0.00			
	Employee orientation				−0.19	NS
	Shareholder orientation				0.21	NS
	Competitor orientation				0.32	0.05
	Consumer orientation				−0.06	NS
	Market growth				0.33	0.00
	Competitive hostility				−0.03	NS
	Market turbulence				0.04	NS
Model 3	R^2 0.17	F 4.8	p 0.00			
	Employee orientation				−0.19	NS
	Shareholder orientation				0.18	NS
	Competitor orientation				0.38	0.02
	Consumer orientation				−1.08	0.08
	Market growth				1.1	0.00
	Competitive hostility				0.79	0.00
	Market turbulence				−2.2	0.02
	Consumer orientation* market turbulence				0.35	0.01

TABLE 19.8: Summary of moderator effects

	Competitor hostility	Market turbulence	Market growth
Competitor orientation		Market share; positive above 4.2 on the scale	
Consumer orientation		Sales growth; positive above 3.1 on the scale	
Employee orientation		New product success; positive above 5.4 on the scale	
Shareholder orientation	Market share; positive below 5.7		ROI; positive above 5.6 on the scale

Market share

In model 2 none of the measures of stakeholder orientation is significant. Two interaction terms entered model 3: shareholder orientation by competitive hostility and competitor orientation by market turbulence. For the former interaction term the partial derivative is:

$$dMS/dSHO = 1.2+(-0.21)CH = 0 \qquad (2)$$
$$CH = 5.7$$

where MS is market share, SHO is shareholder orientation and CH is competitive hostility. This value is the inflection point in the moderator effect. If values of competitive hostility above 5.7 are substituted into equation (2) the answers are negative, whereas values below 5.7 are positive. Thus the relationship is nonmonotonic; shareholder orientation is only positively associated with market share at medium to low levels of competitive hostility. For the second interaction term the partial derivative is:

$$dMS/dCOMO = -0.89+(+0.21)MT = 0 \qquad (3)$$
$$MT = 4.2$$

where MS is market share, COMO is competitor orientation and MT is market turbulence. This value is the inflection point of the moderator effect. If values of MT above 4.2 are substituted into equation (3) the answers are positive, whereas below 4.2 they are negative. Thus the relationship is nonmonotonic; competitor orientation is positively associated with market share at medium and high levels of market turbulence.

New product success rate

In model 2 none of the stakeholder orientations is significant. One interaction term entered model 3; employee orientation by market turbulence. The partial derivative of this effect is:

$$dNPS/dEO = -1.08+(+0.20)MT = 0 \qquad (4)$$
$$MT = 5.4$$

where NPS is new product success, EO is employee orientation and MT is market turbulence. This value is the inflection point of the moderator effect. If values of market turbulence above 5.4 are substituted into equation (4) the answers are positive, whereas below 5.4 they are negative. Thus the relationship is nonmonotonic; employee orientation is positively associated with new product success at high levels of market turbulence.

Return on investment

In model 2 competitor orientation, competitive hostility and market turbulence feature main effects. One interaction term entered model 3: shareholder orientation by market growth. The partial derivative of this effect is:

$$dROI/dSHO = -0.89+(0.16)MG = 0 \qquad (5)$$
$$MG = 5.6$$

where ROI is return on investment, SHO is shareholder orientation and MG is market growth. This value is the inflection point of the moderator effect. If values of market growth above 5.6 are substituted into equation (5) the answers are positive, whereas below 5.6 they are negative. Thus the relationship is nonmonotonic; shareholder orientation is positively associated with ROI at high levels of market growth.

Sales growth

In model 2 only consumer orientation and market growth demonstrate main effects. One interaction term entered model 3; consumer orientation by market turbulence. The partial derivative of this effect is:

$$dSG/dCONO = -1.08+(+0.35)MT = 0 \qquad (6)$$
$$MT = 3.1$$

where SG is sales growth, CONO is consumer orientation and MT is market turbulence. This value is the inflection point in the moderator effect. If values of market turbulence above 3.1 are substituted into equation (6) the answers are positive, whereas values below 3.1 are negative. Thus the relationship is nonmonotonic; consumer orientation is positively associated with sales growth at medium and high levels of market turbulence.

Discussion

Following calls for evidence about the association of stakeholder orientation with company performance (Clarkson, 1995; Donaldson and Preston, 1995; Kohli *et al.*, 1993; Slater and Narver, 1995), the study reported in this article has generated empirical evidence from a sample of UK companies. The results indicate that stakeholder orientation *per se* is not associated with performance *per se*, but that different types of stakeholder orientation are associated with different measures of performance, and that these associations are moderated by the external environment. Owing to the lack of previous empirical evidence the hypotheses in this study were exploratory in nature, and covered a wide range of combinations of stakeholder, performance and moderator variables. As to be expected in this type of study varying degrees of support for the range of hypotheses were found; for example, in the Slater and Narver (1994) investigation of potential moderator effects on the market orientation/ performance association twelve hypotheses were tested, but none was supported.

Consumer orientation

This orientation is associated with sales growth as a measure of performance, and the association is moderated by market turbulence. Indeed, the results indicate a positive association from quite low levels of change in consumer needs (at 3.1 on the market turbulence scale). This result demonstrates a fundamental but clearly crucial link between changes in marketplace consumer needs, internal consumer orientation and the achievement of sales growth. From fairly low levels of change in consumer needs the implication is that the greater the orientation to consumers the higher the sales growth. Although this demonstrates a propensity by firms to be responsive to consumer needs, it also shows that a certain level of change is likely to occur before consumer orientation is more actively addressed by companies. This result is consistent with the theoretical predictions.

Competitor orientation

Orientation to competitors features main effects on performance, when the latter is measured as ROI and sales growth, and these effects are not moderated by external variables. As the regression coefficients are positive the implication is that the greater the orientation to competitors the higher the sales growth and ROI. Given that competitive orientation is the only measure of stakeholder orientation that features main effects, the implication is that it is the most resilient to external influence. Competitor orientation is also associated with market share, but the association is moderated by market turbulence. This association is positive from the midpoint of the market turbulence scale, suggesting that at medium and high levels of change in consumer needs greater attention is given to competitors in order to sustain market share. This result demonstrates the influence of consumer power with respect to competitive action, when pursuing market share. Conversely, when there is little change in consumer needs the implication is that competitive orientation is key to sustaining market share. This result is consistent with the theoretical predictions.

Employee orientation

This orientation is only associated with new product success as a measure of performance. New product success clearly differs from the other measures of performance, in that it cannot be quantified in the same way and that it is a measure of a management process. Indeed, this result demonstrates the importance of the involvement of employees in achieving new product success. The result suggests that at high levels of market turbulence there is greater employee orientation (above 5.4 on the market turbulence scale), but that there is less attention at lower levels of turbulence. The implication is that the skills and expertise of employees become even more important in achieving new product success in a market environment of rapidly changing consumer needs. This result is consistent with the theoretical predictions.

Shareholder orientation

Here the orientation is associated with market share where competitive hostility is the moderator, and with ROI where market growth is the moderator. In the case of market share the implication is that less attention is given to shareholders in competitively hostile environments (above 5.7 on the competitive hostility scale), but that in medium to low hostility, market share will become more prevalent in pursuing shareholder interests. High hostility implies higher expenditure in order to sustain or gain market share, which means less availability of funds for dividend payments to shareholders. Alternatively, low hostility will mean more availability of funds for dividends and a higher orientation to shareholders. In the case of ROI the implication is that at high levels of market growth (above 5.6 on the market growth scale) greater attention is given to shareholders. The implication is that returns achieved as a consequence of high market growth are available for addressing the dividend interests of shareholders. Consequently, low market growth is likely to mean lower returns, which means that lower dividends will be available for shareholders. Both these results are consistent with the theoretical predictions.

Overall the results provide evidence that tests the general assumption in the literature that in order to be successful companies must address the interests of all stakeholders (Clarkson, 1995; Chakravarthy, 1986; Donaldson and Preston, 1995). The results infer that stakeholder orientation *per se* is not associated with performance *per se*, but that different types of orientation are associated with different measures of performance, and that the associations are moderated by the external environment. While the results have extended the results of the market orientation studies, they can also be compared to these studies. The present results are consistent with the UK market orientation studies, as both sets of results support the proposition that orientation/performance relationships are moderated by exogenous variables. However, they are inconsistent with the US studies, where it was concluded that the market orientation/performance relationship is sufficiently robust to not be influenced by other variables. They also challenge the results of Slater and Narver (1994), who, despite finding moderator effects, suggest that they are not significant.

Implications

There are a number of implications of these results. First, it seems that a crucial issue for stakeholder orientation is the definition of company success. If this is the extent to which internally planned performance objectives are achieved, then the relative balance for addressing the diverse interests of stakeholder groups should be based on performance objectives. If, however, the emphases among the performance objectives are to change over time, then it is likely that changes in emphases across the various stakeholder orientations will also be needed. For example, if a period of high ROI performance that has favoured shareholder orientation is to be followed by a period of sales growth, then more managerial attention and resources are likely to be directed to consumer and competitor orientations. Second, as the results show, these associations are complicated and confused by the influence of external variables, and therefore switching emphasis from one stakeholder to another may not be beneficial to overall performance unless the respective external influences have reached particular degrees of impact.

The third implication is that there may be lagged effects from the exogenous variables, and given that changing emphases in stakeholder orientations are likely to be subject to planned decision making, there may be delays before the new orientations have an appreciable impact on *gestalt* company performance. Fourth, as an added complication is likely to be that stakeholder/performance associations will also be moderated by other exogenous variables not investigated in this study, then additional moderator effects could be at work. Here the implication is that three or four way interaction effects may be evident, which will make decision making about the balance of orientations even more complex. The fifth implication is that planning stakeholder orientation with respect to performance objectives may be a limited option for some firms. Certain organizations have a particular stakeholder group that features an excessive amount of power and influence, with the implication that their interests will demand precedence over other stakeholders. For example, if the majority of shares are held by a single source then there may be a dictate to maximize short term profits for high dividend payouts. The sixth implication refers to firms where consumer power is relatively high, such as in business to business markets, where there may be few customers or even a single customer. Here there may be a requirement to minimize short term profits in order to maximize consumer value, to the detriment of shareholders' interests, giving more emphasis to market performance objectives than to financial objectives. The seventh implication refers to companies in which a scarcity of resources limits their options for addressing stakeholder interests. For example, resources for short term product modifications or for long term new product development may not be available with respect to consumer interests, or resources may not be available to enhance employee remuneration and working conditions. In these companies the setting of performance objectives will be determined and constrained by the necessity to prioritize stakeholder interests.

Study limitations and further research

As with all empirical investigations at an early stage of development, there is an opportunity in future research to broaden the investigation parameters, with the following directions:

1. The simultaneous investigation of stakeholder orientations can be extended to other groups of stakeholders, such as distributors, suppliers and other value-chain organizations.
2. The measures used to operationalize stakeholder orientation could be extended, with the objective of gaining further insights into company practices that are used in the pursuance of stakeholder orientation.
3. Other variables from the external environment could be tested for potential moderator effects, while potential moderation from the internal environment could also be tested.
4. As the current study used a cross-sectional research strategy, a longitudinal approach could monitor relative changes in orientation to various stakeholder groups with respect to environmental change, and consequential changes in performance. A related direction would be to focus on planned changes in performance objectives over a period of time, related changes in stakeholder orientation, environment changes, and subsequent trends in performance.
5. Another avenue would be to extend the unit of analysis to other executives in a number of different job functions and at different hierarchical levels, in order to investigate the incidence of different stakeholder subcultures. This approach could be incorporated into both cross-sectional and longitudinal studies.
6. A final direction would be to directly investigate managers' perceptions of the nature of stakeholder orientation/performance associations, their opinions about the relative importance of the different stakeholder orientations, and their views on how these orientations impact on performance.

References

Alvesson, M. (1989), Concepts of organizational culture and presumed links to efficiency, *Omega*, **17**, pp. 323–33

Amit, R. and Schoemaker, P. (1993), Strategic assets and organizational rent, *Strategic Management Journal*, **14**, pp. 33–46

Anderson, P.F. (1982), Marketing, strategic planning and the theory of the firm, *Journal of Marketing*, **46**, pp. 15–26

Armstrong, S.J. and Overton, T.S. (1977), Estimating non-response from mailed surveys, *Journal of Marketing Research*, **18**, pp. 263–64

Arnold, H. (1982), Moderator variables: a clarification on conceptual, analytical and psychometric issues, *Organizational Behavior and Human Performance*, **24**, 41–59

Aupperle, K.E., Carroll, A.B. and Hatfield, J.D. (1985), An empirical examination of the relationship between corporate social responsibility and profitability, *Academy of Management Journal*, **28**, 2, pp. 446–63

Barney, J.B. (1991), Firm resources and sustained competitive advantage, *Journal of Management*, **17**, pp. 99–120

Boyd, B.K., Dess, G.G. and Rasheed, A.M.A. (1993), Divergence between archival and perceptual measures of the environment: causes and consequences, *Academy of Management Review*, **18**, pp. 204–26

Campbell, A. and Tawadey, K. (1990), *Mission and Business Philosophy: Winning Employee Commitment*, Oxford: Heinemann

Campbell, A. and Yeung, S. (1991), Creating a sense of mission, *Long Range Planning*, **24**, 4, pp. 10–20

Canning, G. (1988), Is your company marketing oriented? *Journal of Business Strategy*, **9**, pp. 34–36

Chakravarthy, B.S. (1986), Measuring strategic performance, *Strategic Management Journal*, **7**, pp. 437–58

Churchill, G.A. (1979), A paradigm for developing better measures of marketing constructs, *Journal of Marketing Research*, **XVI** (February) pp. 64–73

Clark, T., Varadarajan, P.R. and Pride, W.M. (1994), Environmental management: the construct and research propositions, *Journal of Business Research*, **29**, pp. 23–38

Clarkson, M.B.E. (1995), A stakeholder framework for analysing and evaluating corporate social performance, *Academy of Management Review*, **20**, pp. 92–117

Cleland, D.I. and King, W.R. (1979), Developing a planning culture for more effective strategic planning, *Long Range Planning*, **7**, 3, pp. 70–74

Covin, J.G., Slevin, D.P. and Schulz, R.L. (1994), Implementing strategic mission: effective strategic, structural and tactical choices, *Journal of Management Studies*, **31**, pp. 481–505

Davis, D., Morris, M. and Allen, J. (1991), Perceived environmental turbulence and its effect on selected entrepreneurship, marketing, and organizational characteristics in industrial firms, *Journal of the Academy of Marketing Science*, **19**, pp. 43–51

Day, G.S. (1994), The capabilities of market driven organizations, *Journal of Marketing*, **58**, pp. 37–52

Day, G.S. and Nedungadi, P. (1994), Managerial representations of competitive advantage, *Journal of Marketing*, **58**, pp. 31–44

Day, G.S. and Wensley, R. (1988), Assessing advantage: a framework for diagnosing competitive superiority, *Journal of Marketing*, **52** (April), pp. 1–20

Deng, S. and Dart, J. (1994), Measuring market orientation: a multi-factor, multi-item approach, *Journal of Marketing Management*, **10**, pp. 725–42

Dess, G.G. (1987), Consensus on strategy formulation and organizational performance: competitors in fragmented industry, *Strategic Management Journal*, **8**, 259–77

Dess, G.G. and Robinson, R.B. (1984), Measuring organizational performance in the absence of objective measures, *Strategic Management Journal*, **5**, pp. 265–73

Deshpande, R., Farley, J.U. and Webster, F.E. (1993), Corporate culture, customer orientation and innovativeness in Japanese firms: a quadrad analysis, *Journal of Marketing*, **57** (January), pp. 23–37

Donaldson, T. and Preston, L.E. (1995), The stakeholder theory of the corporation: concepts, evidence and implications, *Academy of Management Review*, **20**, pp. 65–91

Doyle, P., Saunders, J. and Wright, L. (1989), A comparative study of US and Japanese marketing strategies in British markets, *International Journal of Research in Marketing*, **5**, 3, pp. 171–84

Dutton, J.E. and Duncan. R.B. (1987), The influence of the strategic planning process on strategic choice, *Strategic Management Journal*, **8**, 103–16

Dyson, R.G. and Foster, M.J. (1982), The relationship of participation and effectiveness in strategic planning, *Strategic Management Journal*, **3**, 77–88

Evan, W.M. and Freeman, R.E. (1993), A stakeholder theory of the modern corporation: Kantian capitalism, in T. Beauchamp and N. Bowie (Eds.), *Ethic Theory and Business*, Englewood Cliffs NJ: Prentice-Hall

Fisher, F.M. and McGowan, J.J. (1983), On the issues of accounting rates of return to infer monopoly profits, *American Economic Review*, March, pp. 82–97

Freeman, R.E. (1984), *Strategic Management; a Stakeholder Approach*, Boston MA: Pitman

Freeman, R.E. and Reed, D. (1983), Stockholders and stakeholders: a new perspective on corporate governance, in C. Huizinga (Ed.), *Corporate Governance: A Definitive Exploration of the Issues*, Los Angeles: University Press

Glick, W.H., Huber, G.P., Miller, C.C., Doty, D.H. and Sutcliffe, K.M. (1990), Studying changes in organizational design and effectiveness: retrospective event histories and periodic assessments, *Organizational Sciences*, **1**, pp. 293–312

Golden, B.R. (1992), SBU strategy and performance: the moderating effects of the corporate-SBU relationship, *Strategic Management Journal*, **13**, pp. 145–158

Gordon, G.G. and DiTomaso, N. (1992), Predicting corporate performance from organizational culture, *Journal of Management Studies*, **29**, 6, pp. 783–798

Grant, R.B. (1995), *Contemporary Strategic Analysis*, second, ed., Oxford: Blackwell

Greenley, G.E. (1994), Strategic planning and performance: an appraisal of the empirical evidence, *Scandinavian Journal of Management*, **10**, 4, pp. 383–96

Greenley, G.E. (1995), Market orientation and company performance: empirical evidence from UK companies, *British Journal of Management*, **6**, 1, pp. 1–13

Greenley, G.E. and Foxall, G.R. (1996), Consumer and nonconsumer stakeholder orientation in UK companies, *Journal of Business Research*, **32**, 2, pp. 105–16

Guth, W.D. and MacMillan, I.C. (1986), Strategy implementation versus middle management self interests, *Strategic Management Journal*, **7**, pp. 313–27

Hair, J.F., Anderson, R.E., Tatham, R.L. and Black, W.C. (1995), *Multivariate Data Analysis*, Fourth edn., New York: Macmillan

Hansen, G.S. and Wernerfelt, B. (1989), Determinants of firm performance: the relative importance of economic and organizational factors, *Strategic Management Journal*, **10**, pp. 399–411

Harrison, J.S. and St.John, C.H. (1994), *Strategic Management of Organizations and Stakeholders*, St.Paul MIN: West

Hart, S. and Banbury, C. (1994), How strategy-making processes can make a difference, *Strategic Management Journal*, **15**, pp. 251–269

Hart, S. and Diamantopoulos, A. (1993), Linking market orientation and company performance: preliminary work on Kohli and Jaworski's framework, *Journal of Strategic Marketing*, **1** (2), pp. 93–122

Hassard, J. and Shariffi, S. (1989), Corporate culture and strategic change, *Journal of General Management*, **15**, pp. 4–19

Hellevik, O. (1984), *Introduction to Causal Analysis*, London: Allen and Unwin

Hooley, G.J. and Saunders, J. (1991), Our five year mission – to boldly go where no man has been before, *Proceedings of the MEG Annual Conference*, Cardiff Business School, pp. 559–77

Hooley, G.J., Lynch, J.E. and Jobber, D. (1992), Generic marketing strategies, *International Journal of Research in Marketing*, **9**, pp. 75–89

Hill, C.W.L. and Jones, G.R. (1992), Stakeholder-agency theory, *Journal of Management Studies*, **29**, pp. 131–54

Huber, G.P. and Power, D.J. (1985), Retrospective reports of strategic-level managers: guidelines for increasing their accuracy, *Strategic Management Journal*, **6**, pp. 171–80

Hunt, S.D. and Morgan, R.M. (1995), The comparative advantage theory of competition, *Journal of Marketing*, **59**, pp. 1–15

Jaworski, B.J. and Kohli, A.K. (1992), Market orientation: antecedents and conse-quences, Working paper, Cambridge: Marketing Science Institute

Jaworski, B.J. and Kohli, A.K. (1993), Market orientation: antecedents and conse-quences, *Journal of Marketing*, **57**, pp. 53–70

Jones, J.M. (1995), Industrial stakeholder theory: a synthesis of ethics and economics, *Academy of Management Review*, **20**, pp. 404–37

Kelley, S.W. (1992), Developing customer orientation among service employees, *Journal of the Academy of Management Science*, **20**, 1, pp. 27–36

Kimberly, J., Norling, R. and Weiss, J.A. (1983), Pondering the performance puzzle: effectiveness in interorganizational settings, in R.H. Hall and R.E. Quinn (Eds.), *Organization and Public Policy*, Beverly Hills: Sage

King, W.R. and Cleland, D.I. (1978), *Strategic Planning*, New York: Van Nostrand Reinhold

Kohli, A.K. and Jaworski, B.J. (1990), Market orientation: the construct, research propositions, and managerial implications, *Journal of Marketing*, **54** (April), pp. 1–18

Kohli, A.K., Jaworski, B.J. and Kumar, A. (1993), MARKOR: a measure of market orientation *Journal of Marketing Research*, **XXX**, pp. 467–77

Kotter, J.P. (1990), *A Force for Change: How Leadership Differs from Management*, New York: Free Press

Kotter, J.P. and Heskett, J.L. (1992), *Corporate Culture and Performance*, New York: Free Press

Kukalis, S. (1991), Determinants of strategic planning system in large organizations: a contingency approach, *Journal of Management Studies*, **28**, pp. 143–59

Mahoney, J. and Pandian, J.R. (1992), The resource based view within the conversation of strategic management, *Strategic Management Journal*, **13**, pp. 363–80

Masiello, T. (1988), Responsiveness throughout your company, *Industrial Marketing Management*, **17**, pp. 85–93

McDonald, M. and Leppard, J.W. (1991), Marketing planning and corporate culture: a conceptual framework which examines management attitudes in the context of marketing planning, *Journal of Marketing Management*, **7**, 3, pp. 209–12

Miller, D. (1987), The structural and environmental correlates of business strategy, *Strategic Management Journal*, **8**, (1), pp. 55–76

Miller, R.L. and Lewis, W.F. (1991), A stakeholder approach to marketing management using the value exchange models, *European Journal of Marketing*, **25**, 8, pp. 55–68

Miller, R.L., Lewis, W.F. and Merenski, J.P. (1985), A value exchange model for the channel of distribution: implications for management and research, *Journal of the Academy of Marketing Science*, (Fall)

Mintzberg, H. (1983), *Power in and Around Organizations*, Englewood Cliffs NJ: Prentice-Hall

Mintzberg, H. (1990), The design school: reconsidering the basic premises of strategic management, *Strategic Management Journal*, **11**, pp. 171–95

Narver, J.C, and Slater, S.F. (1990), The effect of market orientation on business profitability, *Journal of Marketing*, **54** (October), pp. 20–35

Norusis, M.J. (1990), *SPSS Statistics Guide*, Chicago: SPSS

Nunnally, J. (1967), *Psychometric Theory*, New York: McGraw-Hill

Pearce, J.A. (1982), The company mission as a strategic tool, *Sloan Management Review*, Spring, pp. 15–24

Peterson, R. (1994), A Meta-analysis of Cronbach's coefficient alpha, *Journal of Consumer Research*, **21**, pp. 381–91

Pettigrew, A. and Whipp, R. (1991), *Management Change for Competitive Success*, Oxford: Blackwell

Podsakoff, P.M. and Organ, D.W. (1986), Self-reports in organizational research: problems and prospects, *Journal of Management*, **12**, pp. 531–44

Polonsky, M.J. (1995), Incorporating the natural environment in corporate strategy: a stakeholder approach, *Journal of Business Strategies*, **12**, 2, pp. 151–68

Posner, B.Z. and Schmidt, W.H. (1984), Values and the American manager: an update, *Californian Management Review*, **26**, 3, pp. 202–16

Powell, T.C. (1992), Organizational alignment as competitive advantage, *Strategic Management Journal*, **13**, pp. 119–34

Ramanujam, V. and Venkatraman, N. (1987), Planning system characteristics and planning effectiveness, *Strategic Management Journal*, **8**, pp. 453–68

Rhenman, E. (1968), *Industrial Democracy and Industrial Management*, London: Tavistock

Ruekert, R.W. (1992), Developing a market orientation: an organizational strategy perspective, *International Journal of Research in Marketing*, **9**, pp. 225–45

Samuels, J.M., Wilkes, F.M. and Brayshaw, R.E. (1990), *Management of Company Finance*, Fifth edition, London: Chapman and Hall

Schein, E. (1985), *Organizational Culture and Leadership*, San Francisco: Jossey Bass

Schoonhoven, C.B. (1981), Problems with contingency theory: testing assumptions hidden within the language of contingency theory, *Administrative Science Quarterly*, **26**, PP. 349–77

Shapiro, B.P. (1988), What the hell is market oriented? *Harvard Business Review*, **88**, 119–125

Sharma, S., Durand, R.M. and Gur-Arie, O. (1981), Identification and analysis of moderator variables, *Journal of Marketing Research*, **18**, pp. 291–300

Siguaw, J.A. and Diamantopoulos, A. (1995), Measuring market orientation: some evidence on Narver and Slater's three-component scale, *Journal of Strategic Marketing*, **3**, pp. 1–12

Sinha, D.K. (1990), The contribution of formal planning to decisions, *Strategic Management Journal*, **11**, pp. 479–92

Slater, S.F. (1996), Issues in conducting marketing strategy research, *Journal of Strategic Marketing*, **3**, 4, pp. 257–70

Slater, S.F. and Narver, J.C. (1994), Does competitive environment moderate the market orientation–performance relationship?, *Journal of Marketing*, **58**, pp. 46–55

Slater, S.F. and Narver, J.C. (1995), Market orientation and the learning organization, *Journal of Marketing*, **59**, pp. 63–74

Speed, R. (1991), 'Marketing strategy and performance in UK retail financial services', Unpublished Ph.D thesis: Loughborough University Business School, UK

Venkatraman, N. (1990), Performance implications of strategic coalignment: a methodological perspective, *Journal of Management Studies*, **27**, pp. 19–41

Venkatraman, N. and Ramanujam, V. (1986), Measurement of business performance in strategic research: a comparison of approaches, *Academy of Management Review*, **11**, 4, pp. 801–14

Verhage, B.J. and Waarts, E. (1988), Marketing planning for improved performance: a comparative analysis, *International Marketing Review*, **5**, 2, pp. 21–30

Webster, F.E. (1992), The changing role of marketing in the corporation, *Journal of Marketing*, **56**, pp. 1–17

Webster, F.E. (1994), Executing the new marketing concept, *Marketing Management*, **3**, pp. 9–16

Wong, V. and Saunders, J. (1993), Business orientations and corporate success, *Journal of Strategic Marketing*, **1**, 1, pp. 20–40

■ □ ■ ■ 20

The New Multivariate Jungle: Computer Intensive Methods in Database Marketing

David Coates, Neil Doherty and Alan French

The advent of powerful computers and relatively inexpensive disk storage has had a profound effect on marketing and market research. In particular, companies are now able to construct very large databases containing information about their customers. However, companies are now faced with the problem of how to use these vast sources of information to their advantage. Two typical problems discussed in this paper are data fusion and selecting those likely to respond to a particular marketing campaign, for example a particular mailshot. Such problems are difficult to solve exactly for all but the smallest of problem instances due to their complexity. There are a number of computer-based heuristic methods which have been successfully applied to problems outside the marketing domain, but for which there are relatively few examples of successful application within marketing. These techniques are reviewed in this paper and their application to large marketing databases discussed.

Introduction

The growth in computer power and the advances in computer-based techniques and methods over the last decade or so have led to major changes in marketing and market research. First, there has been a growth in large customer databases. The most impressive example of this is probably provided by Sears, Roebuck and Company in the States who have a database containing information on all of the households that do business with them. In the late 1980s this numbered 68.3 million households (Novek et al., 1990). Second, there has been a growth in the detail required of and provided by market research. This has led to a situation where respondents may be unwilling to provide all the data required on readership, holidays, financial holdings and so on (Baker *et al.*, 1989). Third, there has been a growth in computer intensive multivariate mathematical and statistical methods, providing alternatives to well established methods such as regression, cluster analysis and discriminant analysis.

This paper aims to provide a brief, non-technical introduction to these new computer intensive methods and to show their relevance to database marketing. Technical details of the methods have deliberately been omitted, these can be found in the references given.

Typically, these new methods are aimed at dealing effectively with the problem of combinatorial explosion. Broadly speaking, the combinatorial explosion is encountered in those situations where choices are sequentially compounded; a simple example is provided by the way the number of alternative routes through a maze increases as the size of the maze increases. Examples of situations where this type of compounding occurs in business generally include financial investment, manufacturing operations, inventory management, resource allocation and capital budgeting. Classical examples of where this type of compounding occurs in marketing include the travelling salesman problem and advertising budget allocation; examples in database marketing and data fusion are given in the sections on those topics. Such problems are said to be combinatorially complex.

The effect of the combinatorial explosion is that for such problems working out all the possible combinations rapidly becomes impractical, and alternative ways of finding the 'best' combination have to be explored. The process is complicated by the fact that having found a locally best combination, many classical methods are unable to move away from the local optimum to find the global optimum. One solution to this problem is to use a number of different starting combinations and take as the best combination the one with the best local optimum. This paper is concerned with recent developments of computer-based heuristic methods to solve this problem.

In spite of the development of such methods and the advances in computer power, conventional computers are still too slow for many combinatorially complex problems. One possible solution may be provided by parallel processing where many low-cost processors (such as the INMOS Transputer) are operated simultaneously (Trippi and Turban, 1990).

Very little has been published about most of the new computer intensive methods in the marketing journals. This paper introduces the methods in the context of database marketing and data fusion. First we will consider database marketing in general and the problem of classification of customers in particular. Some of the problems concerning data fusion will then be considered. Each of the new methods will then be introduced and discussed in a self-contained section. However, there will be strong links between the different sections as the various methods have strong links with each other. Simulated annealing will be covered first, followed by genetic algorithms, branch-and-bound and tabu search, and the paper concludes with an examination of artificial intelligence, expert systems and neural networks.

Database marketing

Stone and Shaw (1987) use the following definition of database marketing (DBM):

> DBM is an interactive approach to marketing communication, which uses addressable communications media (such as mail, telephone, and the sales force) to extend help to its target audience, to stimulate their demand, and to stay close to them by recording and keeping an electronic database memory of customer, prospect and all communication and commercial contacts, to help improve all future contacts.

The key to database marketing defined in this way is the immense processing capability and storage capacity of today's computers. However, the problem with so much data on actual and potential customers – even with the immense processing capability and storage capacity of today's computers – is using the data effectively. Specifically there is a need to classify those on the database into those 'likely' to respond and those 'unlikely' to respond to a particular marketing campaign, for example a particular mailshot. In other words, there is a need to select a 'best' subset of the database.

The way in which the number of possible subsets of a database increases with the size of the database provides a simple example of the combinatorial explosion; the total number of different subsets of a database of n customers is 2^n. Thus for a very small database of only 100 customers, for example, the total number of different subsets of the database is $2^{100} = 1.27 \times 10^{30}$. The problem of choosing the 'best' subset of the database for a particular marketing campaign is not, therefore, a simple problem.

Shaw and Stone (1988) describe the use of multiple regression, cell population analysis, cluster analysis and discriminant analysis as methods of analysing marketing databases. However, the problem can more naturally be defined in mathematical terms as an optimization problem. The problem can be defined as 'maximize the expected number of responses for a given marketing budget' in which case the objective function is the expected number of responses. Alternatively, the problem can be defined as 'minimize the marketing budget for a given expected number of responses' in which case the objective function is the marketing budget. Defined in either way, the problem of classifying those on the database most likely to respond to a particular marketing campaign can be analysed using many of the recent computer intensive mathematical and statistical methods of optimization described later in the chapter.

Data fusion

The ever increasing demand for detail in market research, especially in product and brand usage data, poses formidable data collection problems. In particular, the amount of data that can reasonably be expected from a single respondent is becoming more likely to be less than that ideally required by the company commissioning the market research. One solution to this problem is to fuse two surveys together so that the answers from one survey can be cross-tabulated with answers from the other survey. For example, one survey may be undertaken on readership (for example the National Readership Survey) and another survey may be undertaken on financial holdings (for example The NOP's Financial Research Survey). There are many cross-tabulations which are potentially of interest but which cannot be provided by the individual surveys as the data is split between the two surveys. However, if the data from the two surveys can be joined together then those cross-tabulations could be performed. This is the context of a major study on data fusion which has recently been reported by Baker *et al.* (1989).

At the heart of data fusion is the process of 'marrying' each respondent in one survey (the recipient survey) to the 'most similar' respondent in the other survey (the donor survey). The respondents are married on the basis of variables which are common to both surveys, and typically these variables will include (but not be restricted to) social class, age and gender. Once respondents have been matched, all of the data from the respondents in the donor survey is then added to the data in the recipient survey.

One of the fundamental statistical issues in data fusion is the method of statistically matching respondents. The fusion process depends on finding respondents who are very similar to each other based on a large number of variables. However, this process of matching respondents is typically complicated by the matching algorithm penalizing multiple use of a single respondent in the donor sample. Thus, there is considerable scope for advanced optimization methods in finding the 'best' fusion. The other fundamental statistical issues are measuring the quality of the data provided by the fusion and predicting the level of success of a fusion before carrying it out.

The way in which the number of possible marriages between respondents increases in data fusion as the survey size increases also provides a simple example of the combinatorial explosion. For example, if there are ten respondents in both the donor and recipient surveys, then there are 10^{10} possible fusions whereas if there are eleven respondents in both the donor and recipient surveys, then there are $11^{11} = 28.5 \times 10^{10}$ possible fusions.

Baker *et al.* (1989) conclude that 'fusion is potentially a very powerful and acceptable tool for market researchers' although not as good as a single data source. Perhaps critically, though, the accuracy of a fusion depends on the size of the donor survey. The larger the donor survey, the closer the matches and the greater the opportunity to use matching variables which are strongly related to the data being transferred between the surveys.

Simulated annealing

Simulated annealing was introduced by Kirkpatrick *et al.*, (1983) and Cerny (1985) and a review of the method including some modifications to improve the effectiveness of the basic algorithm has recently been written by Eglese (1990). The name 'simulated annealing' is used because the method is conceptually similar to annealing in engineering. When a piece of metal is annealed, its properties are altered by heating it until it is molten and then slowly cooling it. The aim of annealing is to reduce the piece of metal to its minimum energy or ground state. In simulated annealing, the analogy of the energy of the piece of metal is the value of the objective function and the aim of simulated annealing is to reduce the objective function to its minimum value.

Simulated annealing requires a neighbourhood structure to be defined so that what is meant by one solution being near another solution is well defined. For example, if a database contained information on age, gender, etc, then a possible solution would be (Under 30, Female, . . .). The nearest neighbours of such a solution would be defined as the set of solutions with one characteristic altered; (Under 30, Male, . . .), (30 to 50, Female, . . .) and so on. Simulated annealing proceeds by repeatedly generating new solutions (typically at random) in the neighbourhood of the current solution.

At any 'temperature' the components of the solution (for example the customers included in the subset) are allowed to change if the change reduces the value of the objective function (for example the expected cost per response). However the key feature of simulated annealing is that the components of the solution are sometimes allowed to change if the change increases the value of the objective function. At a 'high' temperature, the probability of a change which increases the value of the objective function is large (near one). However, as the temperature is reduced the probability of accepting such a change is also reduced until at a 'low' temperature the probability is very small (near zero). The probability of accepting a change which causes an increase in the objective function is called the acceptance function and is normally set to $\exp(-d/T)$ where d is the change in the objective function and T is a control parameter which corresponds to temperature in the analogy with physical annealing. This acceptance function implies that small increases in the objective function are more likely to be accepted than large increases. The algorithm is started with a large value for T (a high temperature) to avoid being trapped at a local optimum and proceeds by attempting a certain number of neighbourhood moves at each temperature. Key to the success of an implementation of simulated annealing is the correct choice of cooling schedule, that is the rate of decrease of the temperature. A great variety of cooling schedules have been suggested, some of these have been classified in Collins *et al.* (1988).

In conclusion, simulated annealing is a heuristic algorithm for obtaining good, though not necessarily optimal, solutions to optimization problems. It requires a neighbourhood structure to be specified and it requires a cooling schedule to be specified so that the probability of accepting a change which increases the objective value can be calculated. Simulated annealing can be applied to a wide range of optimization problems and can provide high quality solutions, given sufficient computer time. In their book, Aarts and Korst (1989) describe how an efficient massively parallel implementation of simulated annealing can be carried out in a neural network. Finally it should be noted that 'it is perhaps not surprising that an algorithm like [simulated annealing] which is very generally applicable does not always compete with algorithms specially designed to exploit features of the problem under consideration' (Eglese, 1990).

Genetic algorithms

Genetic algorithms (Holland, 1975) mimic the behaviour of genes, using Darwin's ideas of natural selection (survival of the fittest) in order to produce solutions to problems. For the case of genetic algorithms, the genes are in fact solutions. As with natural selection, each gene vies with other genes for survival. A fitter gene (better solution) will have a better chance of surviving to mate, thereby passing some of its genetic information onto its offspring. In doing this, the hope is that progressively fitter offspring will evolve over time leading eventually to extremely good solutions.

The mechanics of a genetic algorithm can be summarized as follows. An initial gene pool is produced and the relative fitness of each solution within the gene pool is calculated. Pairs of solutions are then picked from the gene pool for mating. The chance of a solution being selected to mate depends upon its relative fitness (i.e. the fitter solutions are more likely to be selected than weaker counterparts). After mating the gene pool will have expanded. The gene pool is returned to its original size. Again, relatively fit solutions stand a better chance of surviving. The process is then repeated.

As described above, there is a possibility of a gene pool evolving to such an extent that the processes of mating and reproduction have no further effect. Since the solutions in such a gene pool may well be suboptimal, there is a further process which prevents this stagnation occurring, i.e. mutation. Every so often, a solution in the gene pool is mutated which allows the possibility of locating other solutions.

Two solutions mate using a process known as crossover. This involves solutions aligning themselves and exchanging the parts of themselves which lie beyond a (randomly generated) crossover point. The result of this action is two new solutions to be added to the gene pool. It is important to note that crossover need not lead to good offspring solutions. However, since both the parents and offspring are in the gene pool, the relative fitnesses should ensure that fitter solutions survive.

The success of the genetic algorithm may depend upon the size of the gene pool, the initial genes in the pool and the rate of mutation. In reality, there will be huge numbers of genes vying with each other for survival. However, despite the large memories of modern computers, the size of the gene pool must be very small in comparison. A large gene pool is likely to lead to the discovery of good solutions, but will require more space and time to maintain. The initial gene pool can be generated randomly, but it may be worth spending some time generating reasonably good initial solutions. De Jong (1988) suggests that, for solutions encoded as bit-strings (series of 0s and 1s), each bit should mutate with probability 0.001 (one in every 1000).

There are a large number of successful applications of genetic algorithms, for example production scheduling and the travelling salesman problem. Many successful applications are cited in Goldberg (1989). One way in which a genetic algorithm could be applied to the mailshot problem already described would be to build the characteristics for each potential solution into a gene. Thus if a database contained information on age, gender etc., a possible gene would be (Under 30, Female, . . .). The fitness of each gene could be determined by selecting a random sample of records with these characteristics from the database and evaluating the objective function for this sample of records. At the end of the process, the gene pool would contain a number of solutions, providing a range of possible solutions.

Branch-and-bound

As was mentioned in the introduction, complete enumeration of all solutions for a combinatorially complex problem will only be possible for the smallest of problem instances. The application of branch-and-bound (Land and Doig, 1960) can obviate the necessity of checking whole groups of possible solutions. Branch-and-bound has been applied to a large number of applications. Perhaps its largest and most successful application has been in solving integer programming problems, i.e. linear programs with (some) integer variables. Such problems can have tens of thousands of constraints and variables. However, branch-and-bound is not restricted to solving integer programming problems.

Branch-and-bound works by acting upon a tree structure which represents the solution space for a problem. This means that branch-and-bound has great potential for parallelization since each processor could be given a different part of the solution tree to investigate. For example, the solution tree for tossing a coin twice is shown in Figure 20.1. The leaves at the bottom of the tree represent the possible solutions, i.e. HH, HT, TH, TT.

Branch-and-bound only investigates branches of the tree if there is a possibility of finding a better solution than the best solution so far found. This procedure can be repeated until every solution has either been enumerated or disregarded. At this stage the optimal solution will have been found. However, for large problems the solution space may be very large indeed, and it may be undesirable to complete the entire process. In such cases, branch-and-bound may be used as a heuristic with termination taking place when the current best

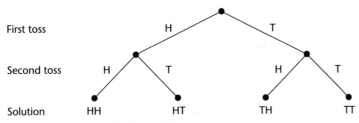

FIGURE 20.1 An example of a solution tree

solution is within some percentage of optimality (it should be noted that the optimal value may not be known).

The term branch-and-bound refers to a family of techniques rather than a single unique method. The differences between methods are how the tree of solutions is traversed. Excellent descriptions of the family of branch-and-bound techniques are given by Horowitz and Sahni (1978) and Turpin (1990). Applying branch-and-bound to the mailshot problem would involve constructing a tree. Figure 20.2 shows the top of a possible tree constructed by considering the possible classes for age and gender.

Tabu search

Tabu search was first introduced by Glover (1977, 1986). Although initially proposed as a method for solving a specific problem in computer science, it has been successfully applied to problem areas ranging from space planning (Glover *et al*, 1985) to character recognition (Hertz and de Werra, 1987). Glover (1990) provides an excellent introduction to the principles of tabu search, and to some of its successful applications. A relatively simplistic explanation of the ideas behind tabu search is presented below.

Tabu search has much in common with simulated annealing insofar as they are both local search heuristics and can employ as subroutines any procedure which can locate optima. Both techniques possess a mechanism which enables escape from local optima thereby increasing the chances of locating the global optimum. The concept of searching within a neighbourhood is also common to both techniques and the example of a neighbourhood given in the section on simulated annealing could also be used for tabu search. Tabu search proceeds by the iterative improvement of an initial feasible solution. The process is terminated upon reaching a set amount of computation time or a predetermined number of iterations of the procedure.

In order to be able to apply tabu search to a problem we require an objective function by which the relative worth of possible solutions may be compared and an initial solution. The algorithm then moves to the best

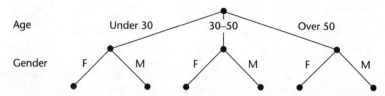

FIGURE 20.2 Part of a possible solution tree for the mailshot problem

solution it can find in the neighbourhood of the current solution, this may mean moving to a worse solution. At all times a record is kept of the best solution found so far. In order to enable the algorithm to escape from a local optimum, the algorithm maintains a tabu list of the most recently visited solutions which can not be revisited by the algorithm. This procedure of moving from solution to solution is repeated until one of the termination criteria is satisfied. The current best solution after termination is then accepted as the final best solution.

Since tabu search is a heuristic and takes very little account of the structure of a problem, we are not guaranteed to find good solutions every time. However, in most situations tabu search performs extremely well (reaching near-optimal solutions within a relatively short time). The performance of tabu search is dependent upon a number of factors including the initial solution, the length of the tabu list and the actual problem itself. Tabu search is extremely flexible and can be applied to a host of combinatorially complex problems. However, as also commented in the section on simulated annealing, this generality may lead to tabu search comparing less favourably with algorithms specifically designed to solve a particular problem.

Artificial intelligence

Since the late 1960s there has been great interest in developing computer systems that could in some way replicate intelligent human behaviour. Such systems are given the generic title of 'artificial intelligence'. Artificial intelligence is now a wide ranging discipline with many ongoing areas of research including natural language processing, visual perception, speech recognition, learning systems, robotics, theorem proving, game playing, general problem solving and expert systems (Turban, 1988). There has also been much interest recently in developing models which attempt to imitate explicitly the thought processes of the human brain. Such systems, known as neural networks, can either be viewed as another branch of artificial intelligence (Hart, 1992), or as a separate discipline which is closely related to artificial intelligence (Zahedi, 1991).

Most artificial intelligence problems can be formulated in terms of a large graph or tree of potential solutions, known as the state-space, which needs to be searched to derive one or more solutions. Exhaustive search strategies, which systematically search the entire state-space until a solution is found, are effective for small problems, but suffer from combinatorial explosion as the state-space becomes large. Because of the limitations of exhaustive search, heuristic techniques are often employed which allow acceptable solutions to be derived more speedily. Korf (1988) notes that in the artificial intelligence literature the term heuristic search has two somewhat different meanings. First, in the general sense the term heuristic means any technique or rule of thumb that is effective but does not necessarily produce optimal solutions. Second, in the more technical sense a heuristic is 'a function that returns an estimate of the cost of reaching a goal from a given state', often referred to as the 'heuristic evaluation function'. Of the many heuristic evaluation functions used in artificial intelligence applications it is those from the branch-and-bound family of techniques, previously described in this paper, that are likely to be of most relevance to the analysis of large marketing databases.

Of the numerous branches of artificial intelligence there are two, which can be classed as heuristic techniques in the more general sense, which will be of interest to the marketing manager. It is, therefore these two fields, namely expert systems and neural networks, which are explored in more detail in the following two sections. It should, however, be noted that whilst other branches of artificial intelligence are not directly applicable to database marketing, advances in natural language processing and speech recognition may dramatically affect the ways in which such databases are interrogated.

Expert systems

Currently most marketing related decisions are based upon the expertise and experience of the marketing manager. Consequently there is great potential to develop expert systems which can capture the relevant expertise and be used to facilitate the decision-making process. Expert systems have been defined as 'computer programs that . . . solve problems in a way that would be considered intelligent if done by a human' (Waterman, 1986). The principal components of such systems are a knowledge-base, typically containing IF <condition> THEN <action> rules, and an inference engine which manipulates the rules in order to derive one or more solution to a specific problem.

The condition components of a set of rules can be compared with facts, either stored in the knowledge-base or supplied by the user. Whenever a match between the two is made, the rule is said to have been 'fired' or 'executed' and the action component of that rule can be inferred. The process of matching and firing continues until a set of solutions has been generated.

Much of the interest in expert systems has been generated by the list of potential benefits that have been accredited to them. Turban (1988), for example, suggests that expert systems may provide cost, permanence, transference, consistency, output and response time advantages over the human expert. This list of potential benefits is given credibility because it is based upon a number of prominent and well documented successes. For example, the R1/XCON system (McDermott, 1982) has helped to reduce the error rate in the configuration of VAX computer systems from 35 per cent to 2 per cent. Despite the success of expert systems it has been recognized that they suffer from a number of limitations including: having a very narrow focus; providing inadequate explanation; and generally being unable to adapt to new experiences. Furthermore, it can be difficult to find an expert willing, and able to supply the required domain knowledge. As a result of such limitations, expert systems are not appropriate in all circumstances, and consequently it is important that application areas are chosen with great care.

Of all the techniques reviewed in this paper, expert systems have probably received the most attention from marketing researchers and practitioners, with many applications having already been developed and documented. Both Moutinho and Paton (1988) and Dubelaar *et al.* (1991), for example, provide reviews of the current and potential impact of expert systems within the marketing domain, whilst Stevenson *et al.* (1990) survey the use of expert systems specifically within industrial marketing, and Cook and Schleede (1988) explore the applications of expert systems within the field of advertising. It must be noted, however, that most marketing managers still have a limited understanding of expert systems. Morris *et al.* (1989), for example, discovered that out of 20 different computer-based techniques expert systems were the one with which marketing managers were least familiar.

Whilst there may be potential for applying expert knowledge to the analysis of marketing databases, it is also likely that expert systems will have an impact in other areas of the marketing domain. More specifically, in the near future it is likely that the application of expert systems to simple, well structured and repetitive problems is more likely to prove successful than attempting to develop highly complex applications (Stevenson, 1990). It is therefore necessary for the marketing managers and computer specialists to collaborate in objectively assessing which, if any, potential application areas are justifiable within their organizations.

Neural networks

Much interest has been generated recently in using computers to develop models, known as neural networks, of the neural and synaptic activity of the biological brain. An indication of strength of interest in neural networks can be gauged from the number of introductory textbooks on the subject which have been recently published, for example Nelson and Illingworth (1990), Beale and

Jackson (1990), Davlo and Naim (1991), and Ritter *et al.* (1992). The field of neural computing is multidisciplinary, with important contributions coming from mathematicians, computer scientists, biologists, psychologists and statisticians. Although many researchers are primarily interested in learning more about how the brain works, it is the use of neural networks as a problem solving tool that will be of most interest to the marketing manager.

Neural networks are primarily composed of processing elements, which are formed into a highly interconnected network. Each processing element has a number of weighted inputs, but just one output. On receipt of a set of input signals, the processing element will first sum the inputs, and then apply a transfer function which determines how the inputs are transformed into an output. In simple terms the transfer function determines whether the output signal will excite or inhibit all of the processing elements to which it is connected. The architecture of the neural network consists of layers of processing elements. Every neural network has an input layer, an output layer and one or more hidden layers connecting the input layer to the output layer.

Whilst both neural networks and knowledge-based systems have the common goal of simulating intelligent human behaviour, they use radically different methods (Zahedi, 1991). Neural networks, like biological brains, are required to function in parallel, whereas knowledge-based systems are typical of most computer systems in that they operate sequentially. Furthermore, neural networks do not require large knowledge bases, neither are they programmed to solve specific problems. Instead neural networks have been designed with a generalized capability to learn, and consequently they are trained to solve problems.

The training is conducted by applying a training set of inputs with their corresponding known outputs to the network. The network learns by applying learning rules which automatically adjust the weightings of the connections between the processing elements. Having trained the network it is necessary to test it by feeding it inputs and evaluating the resultant outputs. The ultimate performance of the trained network can only be guaranteed if it is supplied with good quality data for training and testing (Hart, 1992).

The development of a neural network, therefore, does not require the codification of computer algorithms, but rather necessitates the specification of the structure of the network, in terms of the number of processing elements and how they are formed into layers, and the specification of transfer functions and learning rules. Because neural networks are inherently parallel, and not designed for serial computation, they can be realized by creating them directly from electronic components (Glover, 1988). However, many neural networks have been simulated by writing traditional computer code, which can, therefore, be run on standard computer hardware.

It should be noted that there are several architectures of neural networks but they all have a great deal of commonality based upon a network of processing elements. The network architecture and training methods described in this section relate most closely to the multilayer perceptron (McClelland, 1986). A review of some of the more common architectures is provided by Dodd (1992), who emphasizes the importance of selecting a suitable architecture for a specific problem and if necessary combining two different architectures into a single application.

Neural networks have now been used on a wide variety of applications. They are best at solving classification problems, especially where it is necessary to recognize and match complicated, vague or incomplete patterns in data (Zahedi, 1991). Davlo and Naim (1991) suggest the following list of possible application areas for neural networks: 'pattern recognition, signal processing, vision, speech processing, forecasting and modelling, decision-making aids and robotics'. More specifically, Trippi and Turban (1990) suggest that neural networks should find many applications in the area of managerial decision making.

The ability of neural networks to learn from, and recognize patterns in, databases suggest that they should find many applications in the marketing domain, especially when it comes to the analysis of large-scale marketing databases. It should be possible to supply a neural network with sets of training data relating input variables such as age, sex, location, and earnings to an output variable which indicates whether in the past they have purchased a specific product. The neural network could then learn which are the important characteristics of potential customers, and only send mailshots to those individuals who match the characteristics.

Conclusions

The recent advances in computer-based methods reviewed in this paper should be of great interest to the marketing manager. Data fusion provides a method of marrying the results of two separate surveys together to provide a more detailed picture of potential customers. Simulated annealing, genetic algorithms, branch-and-bound, tabu search, expert systems and neural networks all have the potential to solve difficult problems by applying computer-based heuristic methods, allowing good, if not optimal, solutions to be derived. The key features of these methods are summarized in Table 20.1.

In many situations existing mathematical or statistical techniques, such as discriminant or regression analysis, will already provide acceptable

TABLE 20.1 Key features of the methods

Method	Key Features
Simulated annealing	Neighbourhood structure
	Depends on cooling schedule
	Improvement by random search
Genetic algorithms	Pool of solutions (genes)
	Improvement by crossover and mutation
Branch-and-bound	Tree structure
	Improvement by selective search of tree
Tabu search	Neighbourhood structure
	Depends on length of tabu list
Expert systems	Expert's knowledge typically encoded as rules
	Uses inferential reasoning
Neural networks	No underlying model
	Learns from training set of data
	Depends on architecture used

solutions. The techniques described in this paper will, therefore, be of greatest benefit in circumstances where the database is large and existing search methods cannot cope. One particularly promising application area for heuristic methods is in the identification of recipients for mailshots, so that the number of positive responses can be maximized. It should be noted that whilst each of these techniques already has great potential for applications in the analysis of marketing databases, they will all greatly benefit from the introduction of low cost parallel computing.

Although each of the techniques are quite distinct and have been addressed separately there is great potential to apply more than one of them to the solution of a specific problem. For example, it is possible to use neural networks to derive a set of rules which can then be incorporated in an expert system. Similarly, simulated annealing and tabu search can be jointly applied to the same problem, and it has been envisaged that genetic algorithms could be used to train neural networks (Glover, 1989). There is therefore great scope for researchers and practitioners specializing in one of these techniques to collaborate to evaluate the potential for developing synergistic relationships between them. Finally, it is of great importance that marketing managers, and market research specialists in particular, make themselves aware of these techniques and their potential for analysing large marketing databases so that the techniques can be applied and evaluated in practice.

Acknowledgements

Many thanks to John Saunders for his encouragement and constructive comments.

References

Aarts, E.H.L. and Korst, J.H.M. (1989), *Simulated Annealing and Boltzmann Machines*, Chichester, Wiley

Baker, K., Harris, P. and O'Brien, J. (1989), Data fusion: an appraisal and experimental evaluation, *Journal of the Market Research Society*, **31**, pp. 153–212

Beale, R. and Jackson, T. (1990), *Neural Computing: An Introduction*, Bristol, Adam Hilger

Cerny, V. (1985), Thermodynamical approach to the travelling salesman problem: an efficient simulation algorithm, *Journal of Optimisation Theory and Applications*, **45**, pp. 41–51

Collins, N.E., Eglese, R.W. and Golden, B.L. (1988), Simulated annealing – an annotated bibliography, *American Journal of Mathematical and Management Sciences*, **8**, pp. 209–307

Cook, R.L. and Schleede, J.M. (1988), Applications of expert systems to advertising, *Journal of Advertising Research*, **28**, No. 3, pp. 47–56

Davlo, E. and Naim, P. (1991), *Neural Networks*, London, Macmillan

De Jong, K.A. (1988), Learning with genetic algorithms: an overview, *Machine Learning*, **3**, pp. 121–138

Dodd, N. (1992), An Introduction to Neural Networks, in M.E. Mortimer (Ed.), *Operational Research Tutorial Papers*, The Operational Research Society

Dubelaar, C., Finlay, P.N. and Taylor, D. (1991), Expert systems: the cold fusion of marketing?, *Journal of Marketing Management*, **7**, pp. 371–82

Eglese, R.W. (1990), Simulated annealing: a tool for operational research, *European Journal of Operational Research*, **46**, pp. 271–81

Glover, F. (1977), Heuristics for integer programming using surrogate constraints, *Decision Sciences*, **8**, pp. 156–66

Glover, F. (1986), Future paths for integer programming and links to artificial intelligence, *Computers and Operations Research*, **13**, No. 5, pp. 533–49

Glover, F. (1990), Tabu search: a tutorial, *Interfaces*, **20**, No. 4, pp. 74–94

Glover, F., McMillan, C. and Novick, B. (1985), Interactive decision software and computer graphics for architectural and space planning, *Annals of Operations Research*, **5**, pp. 557–73

Goldberg, D.E. (1989), *Genetic Algorithms*, Reading, MA: Addison-Wesley

Hart, A. (1992), Using neural networks for classification tasks – some experiments on datasets and practical advice, *Journal of the Operations Research Society*, **43**, No. 3, pp. 215–226

Hertz, A. and de Werra, D. (1987), Using tabu search techniques for graph coloring, *Computing*, **29**, pp. 345–351

Holland, J.H. (1975), *Adaptation in Natural and Artificial Systems*, Ann Arbor MI:, University of Michigan Press

Horowitz, E. and Sahni, S. (1978), *Fundamentals of Computer Algorithms*, Rockville MD: Computer Science Press

Kirkpatrick, S., Gelatt, Jr., C. D. and Vecchi, M. P. (1983), Optimisation by simulated annealing, *Science*, **220**, pp. 671–680

Korf, R.E. (1988), Search: a survey of recent results, in *Exploring A.I.*, Shrobe, H. E., (Ed.) San Mateo CA: Morgan Kaufmann

Land, A.H. and Doig, A.G. (1960), An automatic method of solving discrete programming problems, *Econometrica*, **28**, pp. 497–520

McClelland, J.L. and Rumelhart, D.E. (1986), *Parallel Distributed Processing*: Volumes 1 & 2, Boston MA: MIT Press

McDermott, J. (1982), R1: a rule-based Ccnfigurer of computer systems, *Artificial Intelligence*, **9**, No. 1, pp. 39–88

Morris, H.M., Burns, A.C. and Avila, R.A. (1989), Computer awareness and usage by industrial marketers, *Industrial Marketing Management*, **18**, pp. 223–32

Moutinho, L. and Paton, R. (1988), Expert systems: a new tool in marketing, *The Quarterly Review of Marketing*, **13**, No. 2, pp. 5–13

Nelson, M.M. and Illingworth, W.T. (1991), *A Practical Guide to Neural Nets*, Reading MA: Addison-Wesley

Novek, E., Sinha, N. and Gandy, O. (1990), The value of your name, *Media, Culture and Society*, **12**, pp. 525–43

Ritter, H., Martinez, T. and Schulten, K. (1992), *Neural Computation and Self-Organizing Maps*, Reading MA: Addison-Wesley

Shaw, R. and Stone, M. (1988), *Database Marketing*, London: Gower

Stevenson, T.H., Plath, T.H. and Chandler, C.M. (1990), Using expert systems in industrial marketing, *Industrial Marketing Management*, **19**, pp. 243–49

Stone, M. and Shaw, R. (1987), Database marketing for competitive advantage, *Long Range Planning*, **20**, pp. 12–20

Trippi, R. and Turban, E. (1990), The impact of parallel and neural computing on managerial decision making, *Journal of Management Information Systems*, **6**, pp. 85–98

Turban, E. (1988), *Decision Support and Expert Systems*, New York: Macmillan

Turpin, H.J. (1990), 'The branch-and-bound paradigm', Ph.D. thesis, University of East Anglia, Norwich

Waterman, D.A. (1986), *A Guide to Expert Systems*, Reading: MA, Addison-Wesley

Zahedi, F. (1991), An Introduction to neural networks and a comparison with artificial intelligence and expert systems, *Interfaces*, **20**, No. 2, pp. 25–38

Using Chernoff Faces to Portray Service Quality Data

Deon Nel, Leyland Pitt and Trevor Webb

This paper presents an attempt to demonstrate the use of faces as a statistical data presentation technique in the portrayal of service quality data. The statistician Chernoff originally introduced a technique for the representation of multivariate data by means of the human face. It is helpful in that widely divergent facial features are shown, each of which can be associated with a different variable.

This study uses data obtained from an experimental research design, in an attempt to compare the facial presentation of multivariate service quality data. The data set was gathered across two grouping of customers which in turn was subdivided into users and non users of the service which served as input for the preparation of the Chernoff faces. The results offer a more concise and holistic interpretation of the service quality picture. It is almost certain that any individual would be able to identify the most pleasing face relative to the others.

In recent years much has been written about customer care, customer satisfaction and customer service quality. These concepts have been explained as perceptions of performance relative to customer expectations; consisting of various dimensions; incorporating functional qualities; described as attitudes and portrayed as the combination of various psychological attributes. Significant advances have been made in the measurement of customer service, but little innovation has been forthcoming in presenting multivariate service quality data in a more user-friendly format. While sophisticated measurement techniques may justify presentation to top management, and edified researchers, the need to communicate findings to lower management and operations staff is becoming essential. For it is at this level of customer contact where the service encounter has to be nurtured into a quality experience from the customer's point of view. Finding a means of communicating multivariate service quality data graphically, while at the same time ensuring comprehension, presents no mean challenge.

Several graphic display techniques including pie charts, histograms and scatter diagrams have been used to portray statistical data (Beniger and Robyn, 1978; Zelazny, 1972). The accessibility of user-friendly software and relatively inexpensive graphics plotters and printers, as well as other media-producing devices with which to create these displays, have greatly expedited the task of the manager in communicating numeric information. Unfortunately the ability of these displays to depict multi-dimensional data is severely constrained, particularly when a basis for generalizing and communicating relationships is desired. More recently researchers have developed icons for displaying multivariate data (Everitt, 1978; Cleveland, 1985). A variety of icons for representing multivariate data such as Fourier blobs (Fienberg, 1979), glyphs (Anderson, 1969) and faces (Chernoff, 1973) offer innovative ways of presenting complex data in a simple, interpretable picture.

This paper presents an attempt to demonstrate the use of Chernoff faces as a statistical data presentation technique in the portrayal of service quality data.

Theoretical background

Chernoff faces

Unlike most graphs, icons are not designed to communicate absolute numerical information. They are intended for recognizing clusters of similar variables and are useful for sorting or organizing variables that differ in many respects. Some theorists have found the use of icons subjective and ad hoc. Alternatively, cognitive science research on multiattribute visual processing, shows that people can accurately categorize multivariate data based on appropriate visual cues (Garner, 1974; Spoehr and Lehmkuhle, 1982). Faces are one of the most effective graphical icons for visually clustering multivariate data, particularly for long-term memory processing. Wang (1978) describes a number of papers on applications of faces to multivariate data, while Wilkenson (1982) showed that faces can be more effective than many other icons for similarity comparisons.

The facial technique was originally proposed by Chernoff (1973). It is helpful first, in that widely divergent facial features are shown, each of which can be associated with a different variable. Secondly, most people are accustomed to distinguishing accurately between faces with different features. As Chernoff (1973) has said, 'People grow up studying and reacting to faces all of the time. Small and barely measurable differences are easily detected and evoke emotional reactions from a long catalogue buried in the memory.' And in 1978:

> I believe that we learn very early to study and react to real faces. We perceive the face as a gestalt and our built-in computer is quick to pick out the relevant information and to filter out the noise when looking at a limited number of faces.

The procedure is both relatively lucid and adaptable and can be modified to suit the prerequisites of almost any data set. Chernoff (1973) describes its use in such diverse fields as the study of fossil data, in geology, and Huff *et al.* (1981) use the faces to illustrate progressions of business failure and success.

Essentially the procedure involves the assignment of variables in the data set to the features of a face. For example:

- Y_1 can be associated with the size or curvature of the mouth;
- Y_2 with the length of the mouth;
- Y_3 with the width of the nose; and
- Y_4 with the shape of the chin.

Chernoff's method (1973) can handle 18 variables at most. Flury and Riedwyl (1981) have expanded the procedure to handle up to 36 variables. This they have achieved by changing symmetrical features (e.g. nose, mouth, hair) to asymmetrical, which means that the left side of the mouth may look different from the right. It is seldom necessary, however, for 36 variables to be represented simultaneously in the type of marketing study under consideration. Doing so would seem to defeat the advantages of the original technique – which hinge chiefly on simplicity and the capacity to present pertinent data visually.

The procedure thus appears to be well suited to the depiction of strategic business data, with particular appurtenance to studies of a longitudinal nature (Huff, Mahajan and Black, 1981). The effects of product/business strategies can be facially represented, and the application of the technique to the monitoring of image (such as those of retail stores, and political candidates), sales response, competitor strategies, and environmental shifts is suggested (Huff, Mahajan and Black, 1981).

Chernoff faces are certainly not without drawbacks. A major problem is that the subjective assigning of features has a notable effect on the eventual shape of the face. Chernoff and Rizvi (1975) note that if the purpose of the data analysis is simply the classification in groups, permutations of the assigning of features can cause a percentage of error as high as 25 per cent. The most important variables, then, should obviously be assigned to the most prominent features. For example, facial representation of corporate financial performance would use curvature of the mouth (smile or frown) to describe a variable such as return on assets, and representation of strategic product data would use the mouth to portray share of the served market. Furthermore, features may change even though no data dimensions have been assigned to them because of interrelationships with other features. Thirdly, emotional responses of individuals will vary according to the location of data to features. As Huff *et al.* (1981) point out, one individual might focus on the mouth and another on the nose. The look of the face may also evoke certain feelings of emotion, while there may be nothing of an emotional nature inherent in the data.

Service quality

In applying a service quality measurement process, the well-documented 'gaps' model (Parasuraman, Zeithaml and Berry, 1985) serves as a conceptual framework for understanding service quality delivery. The model views service quality as five potential gaps where areas of service quality shortcomings can occur. These scholars conducted a series of customer focus groups and in-depth executive interviews on issues relating to service quality. This resulted in a conceptual model that defines service quality from the customer's viewpoint and from the point of view of a marketer of services. From the customer's standpoint, ten determinants of service quality were identified. Later empirical testing on the customer side of the model consolidated the determinants into five dimensions. The SERVQUAL instrument (Parasuraman, Zeithaml and Berry, 1988) focuses on measuring customer perceptions of service quality along the five dimensions: tangibles; reliability; responsiveness; assurance and empathy, known as gap 5 in the model. The validity and reliability of the SERVQUAL instrument have been the subjects of interest in a number of scientific studies. Generally these studies have found the instrument to be a most reliable one for the measurement of service quality (Brensinger and Lambert, 1990; Carman, 1990; Lambert and Lewis, 1990). Subsequent research focused on the service provider side of the model, building a rich set of constructs that could affect the delivery of service quality. The result was a detailed conceptual explication of the extended service quality model that was used to develop measures of the internal organizational gaps (Zeithaml, Parasuraman and Berry, 1990).

Methodology

Research design

The organization of the research described here resembled a 2×2 experimental design. This structure enabled the data to be captured across two different groupings of a large United Kingdom service provider, namely business and domestic customers. For each of the two groupings the data capture was subdivided into users and non users of the service. This provides a matrix of four categories which enables the comparison of (1) business users; (2) business non users; (3) domestic users; and (4) domestic non users on service quality as measured by SERVQUAL from the same data set.

The sample

Structured questionnaires were mailed to a total of 10000 customers of an electrical contracting company in the heart of England. The total was divided into 5000 each for business and domestic customers, which was again subdivided into 2500 users and 2500 non users of the company's services. Users and non users were identified by the frequency of use of services provided. Respondents were screened to determine whether they had used the company's services. Respondents that had not used services in the past five years were classified as non users.

A total of 2686 questionnaires were returned by the respondents, resulting in a response rate of 26.85 per cent. After elimination of incomplete questionnaires, a total of 2276 questionnaires were used in the analysis, an effective response rate of 22.76 per cent. Within the four categories the response rates were as follows (1) business users n=561; (2) business non users n = 79; (3) domestic users n = 1397; and (4) domestic non users n = 239.

Assignment of variables to facial features

In an attempt to simplify the presentation of the multivariate nature of service quality data, the four categories served as input for the preparation of the Chernoff faces.

The five dimensions and the composite service quality index were assigned to the facial features shown in Table 21.1. An attempt was made to assign variables in order of importance to the most visible facial features; for example, reliability was assigned to the curvature of the mouth. Reliability has been identified as the relative most important dimension (Parasuraman, Zeithaml and Berry, 1991).

TABLE 21.1 Facial features assigned to service quality dimensions

Service quality dimensions	Facial feature
Reliability	Curvature of the mouth
Assurance	Angle of brow
Empathy	Width of nose
Tangibles	Length of nose
Responsiveness	Length of mouth
Composite service quality index	Height of centre of mouth

Two faces were also constructed using the extreme points of the ranges to illustrate the basic relationships between the facial features and also to provide reference measures for the comparison of excellent and poor service quality. The Chernoff Faces in Figure 21.1 illustrate the effect of minimum and maximum values on the face. The melancholy face produced by the minimum values gives an indication of the worst service quality delivery, while the maximum values coalesce to yield the ecstatic face, or excellent service quality delivery.

Results

The dimensional scores and the composite service quality index for the four categories of respondents are illustrated in Table 21.2. After some perusal it is evident from Table 21.2 that the four groups of respondents differ with regard to service quality perceptions. Firstly, the users of both business and domestic users returned significantly more favourable scores than the non users. Secondly, domestic users have the most favourable SQI score at -1.273; followed by business users at -1.545; domestic non users at -1.975 and finally business non users at -2.138. Thirdly, the dimensional scores across all four categories follow a similar profile with tangibles being the less serious problem.

The problem with the presentation of these scores in this format is that they offer little immediate comprehension to some levels of managers, but more particularly to operating staff as to the actual interpretation and significance of the overall performance of service quality delivery. It is only after considerable thought and a deeper understanding of the SERVQUAL measurement methodology that the figures start to make sense.

The data in Table 21.2 were used as input to develop the Chernoff faces depicted in Figure 21.2. It is evident from Figure 21.2 that the four categories differ with regard to perceived service quality and it would not be presupposing

Maximum values

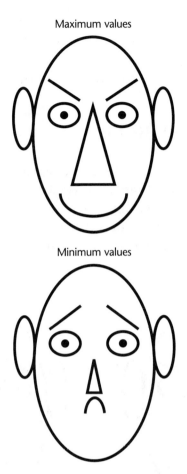

Minimum values

FIGURE 21.1 Effect of minimum and maximum values on the face

TABLE 21.2 SERVQUAL dimensional scores and composite SQI

	Business users	Business non users	Domestic users	Domestic non users
Tangibles	0.371	0.341	−0.028	−0.182
Reliability	−2.522	−3.314	−1.690	−2.618
Responsiveness	−2.307	−2.844	−1.608	−2.499
Assurance	−1.431	−2.445	−1.265	−2.201
Empathy	−1.813	−2.634	−1.599	−2.192
SQI	−1.545	−2.138	−1.273	−1.975

too much by saying that the face representing domestic users is the most pleasing. This is supported by the figures in Table 21.2. However, the faces in Figure 21.2 do offer a more concise and holistic interpretation of the service quality picture. It is almost certain that any individual would be able to identify the most pleasing face relative to the others.

Implications and some problems

Huff *et al.* (1981), have discussed some important aspects concerning the interpretation of faces which are also relevant to this study. Firstly, faces represent a method for comparing visually the similarities or differences among objects on a number of variables. Secondly, the detection of longitudinal trends is also facilitated by this type of multitudinal display. This

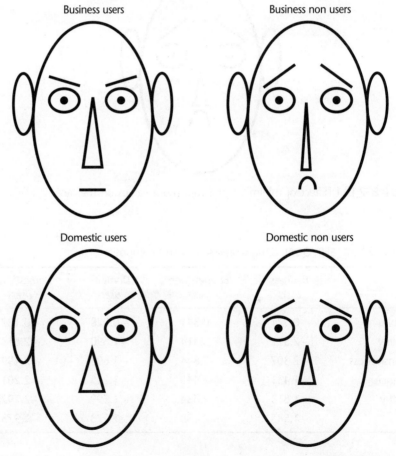

FIGURE 21.2: Chernoff faces representing the four categories of respondent

has already been briefly referred to. For example, the service quality manager can assess trends in the composite index by monitoring the acuteness of the smile on the face over a number of months or years. Not only can overall profile be portrayed, but also individual factors such as the dimensions of service quality.

Obviously the real advantage of this technique is that it enables the display of faces in the workplace so that contact personnel can constantly be informed and reminded of how their customers perceive the service they deliver. Certainly, fruitful, useful and interesting research can be done on the relative ease with which the average contact employee interprets faces, and service quality data.

The major problem in the use of faces lies in the fact that the relative importance of certain variables may be exaggerated because of the facial features to which they have been assigned. The fact that the look of a face may evoke certain feelings also presents somewhat of a problem – a happy face may evoke emotion while in fact there is nothing emotive in the data. A final problem which can also be overlooked is that some companies may not have access to the facilities (computer hardware and software) and skills (statistical and computer manipulation) with which to generate faces or other useful icons. Recent developments in the field of personal computers and user-friendly software may eventually alleviate this to some extent.

References

Anderson, E. (1969), A semigraphical method for the analysis of complex problems, *Technometrics*, **2**, No. 3, pp. 387–391

Beniger, J.R. and Robyn, D.L. (1978), Quantitative graphics in statistics: a brief history, *The American Statistician*, **32**, February pp. 1–10

Bresinger, R.P. and Lambert, D.M. (1990), Can the SERVQUAL scale be generalized to business-to business services?, *Proceedings of the Summer Educators' Conference*, Chicago IL: American Marketing Association

Carman, J.M. (1990), Consumer perceptions of service quality: an assessment of the SERVQUAL dimensions, *Journal of Retailing*, **66**, Spring, pp. 33–55

Chernoff, H. (1973), Using faces to represent points in K-dimensional space graphically, *Journal of the American Statistical Association*, **58**, June, pp. 361–368

Chernoff, H. (1978), Graphical representation as a discipline, in P.C. Wang, (Ed.) *Graphical Representation of Multivariate Data*, New York: Academic Press

Chernoff, H., and Rizvi, M.J. (1975), Effect on classification of random permutations of features in representing multivariate data by faces, *Journal of the American Statistical Association*, **70**, September, pp. 548–554

Cleveland, W.S. (1985), *The Elements of Graphing Data*, Monterey: CA: Wadsworth Advanced Books

Everitt, B. (1978), *Graphical Techniques for Multivariate Data*, London: Heineman Educational Books

Fienberg, S.E. (1979), Graphical methods in statistics, *The American Statistician*, **33**, November, pp. 165–178

Flury, B. and Riedwyl, H. (1981), Graphical representation of multivariate data by means of asymmetrical faces, *Journal of the American Statistical Association*, **76**, pp. 757–765

Garner, W.R. (1974), *The Processing of Information and Structure*, Hillside NJ: Lawrence Erlbaum

Huff, D.L., Mahajan, V. and Black, W.C. (1981), Facial representation of multivariate data, *Journal of Marketing*, **45**, Fall, 53–59

Lambert, D.M. and Lewis, M.C. (1990), A comparison of attribute importance and expectation scales for measuring service quality, *Proceedings of the Summer Educators' Conference*, Chicago IL: American Marketing Association

McNichols, T.J. (1983), *Executive Policy and Strategic Planning*, New York: McGraw-Hill

Parasuraman, A., Zeithaml, V.A. and Berry, L.L. (1985), A conceptual model of service quality and its implications for future research, *Journal of Marketing*, **49**, Fall, pp. 41–50

Parasuraman, A., Zeithaml, V.A. and Berry, L.L. (1988), SERVQUAL: a multiple-item scale for measuring consumer perceptions of service quality, *Journal of Retailing*, Spring, pp. 12–40

Parasuraman, A., Berry, L.L., and Zeithaml, V.A. (1991), Refinement and reassessment of the SERVQUAL scale, *Journal of Retailing*, Winter, pp. 420–450

Spoehr, K.T. and Lehmkuhle, S.W. (1982), *Visual Information Processing*, San Francisco: W.H. Freeman

Wang, P.C.C. (Ed.) (1978), *Graphical Representation of Multivariate Data*, New York: Academic Press

Wilkenson, L. (1982), An experimental evaluation of multivariate graphical point representation, *Human Factors in Computer Systems Proceedings*, Gaithersburg, MD, pp. 202–209

Zeithaml, V.A., Parasuraman, A. and Berry, L.L. (1990), *Delivering Quality Service: Balancing Customer Perceptions and Expectations*, New York: The Free Press

Zelazny, G. (1972), *Choosing and Using Charts*, New York: Video Arts

■ □ ▨ ■ 22

Validating Cross-National Research with LISREL: The Route to Initiation

Amanda J. Broderick

Examining the cross-national applicability of consumer behaviour constructs and models is becoming increasingly important. This paper illustrates confirmatory procedures for validating a measurement instrument across countries. The paper does not intend to provide comprehensive detail on cross-national approaches and equivalence issues, but provides a context in which confirmatory procedures across countries are illustrated. Specifically, the metric equivalence of consumer involvement in food in five European countries is tested. The results suggest that the model proposed in the paper is valid cross-nationally.

Introduction

Most traditional models of buyer behaviour are based on unicultural assumptions and, therefore, cannot be readily extended to the global marketplace. Conventional marketing models of consumption behaviour may not be universal across cultures, and with the rapid increase in internationalization it is paramount to identify and understand variants of consumer behaviour for developing international marketing strategy (Costa and Bamossy, 1995; Roth, 1995; McCarthy, 1989; Douglas and Isherwood, 1979; McCracken, 1988; Sahlins, 1976).

The construct of consumer involvement has received intensive and rapidly growing attention in consumer behaviour research since the late 1970s. Involvement is regarded as a primary determinant of consumer behaviour and explains the differences in the degree of both mental and physical effort a consumer is willing to devote to consumption related activities (Beharrell and Denison, 1995; Laaksonen, 1994; Foxall and Bhate, 1993; Burke, 1992; Jain and

Srinivasan, 1990; Maheswaren and Meyers-Levy, 1990; Beatty and Smith, 1987; Petty and Cacioppo, 1981; Chaiken, 1980). Although involvement has been one of the most heavily researched topics in the recent consumer behaviour literature, comparatively little research has been conducted on the cross-national generalizability of involvement as a mediating variable in decision making.

Comparability is a prerequisite for valid cross-national research, and comparability may be attained by demonstrating the equivalence of psychological concepts and data across groups. In other words, concepts and data from the cultures being compared must fall on some common baseline: that is, there must be dimensional identity (Frijda and Jahoda, 1966). Dimensional identity may be proved by demonstrating that the behaviour under investigation is equivalent in functional, conceptual and metric terms (Hui and Triandis, 1985).

Culture and nation have been used interchangeably throughout the paper. There are many definitions of culture and culture may be seen to not equate directly with nation-state. To operationalize culture for the purpose of investigating its effect on consumer behaviour, however, Triandis' (1972) definition has been adopted:

> Shared attitudes, beliefs, categorisations, expectations, norms, roles, self-definitions, values and other such elements of sub-jective culture found among individuals whose interactions were facilitated by shared language, historical period, and geographic region.

Extant literature in the cross-cultural psychology domain suggests that before any conclusions regarding the generalizability of a theory can be made cross-culturally, metric equivalence (i.e. measure dimensionality and internal consistency) must be established (Durvasula *et al.*, 1993). Metric equivalence is also viewed as a necessary prerequisite for testing mean differences on constructs across countries (Berry, 1980; Drasgow and Kanfer, 1985; Irvine and Carroll, 1980; Triandis, 1983). Whilst functional, conceptual and metric equivalence are necessary in cross-national research, this paper focuses primarily on metric equivalence, and demonstrates the role of confirmatory factor analysis in establishing metric equivalence across groups. Specifically, the process for establishing the metric equivalence of consumer involvement in food in five European countries is detailed.

Consumer involvement in food is particularly pertinent in the light of both increasing competition and internationalization in food retailing. Competitive advantage is constantly being sought (Humphries and Samways, 1993; Tordjman, 1995) and greater understanding of consumer markets in terms of global models of purchasing behaviour and strategic market planning is a potential source of advantage. Additionally, food retailing may be subject to the influence of consumer culture to a greater extent than other forms of retailing (Mennell *et al.*, 1992). As purchase behaviour comes into practice at the point of sale, cross-national purchasing disparities and commonalities are particularly relevant to food retail internationalization. To identify these, metric equivalence in purchasing constructs must be ensured.

Cross-national research approaches

Cross-national research may be approached from two perspectives; the emic approach or the etic approach (Pike, 1966; Berry, 1969). The emic approach holds that attitudinal or behavioural phenomena are expressed in a unique way in each culture. The approach works within a single culture to provide an intensive internal understanding of one particular culture. In contrast, the etic approach is primarily concerned with universals: it seeks to work extensively across cultures in order to produce cross-cultural generalizations (Berry, 1980). Market research measurement instruments adapted to each national culture (the emic approach) offer more reliability and provide data with greater internal validity than tests applicable to several cultures (etic). Adaptation, however, is at the expense of cross-national comparability and external validity: results are not transposable to other cultural contexts.

The international marketer is primarily interested in identifying similarities, since these offer the most attractive opportunities for the transfer of products and services and for the integration of strategies across markets. Consequently, adoption of an orientation reflecting an etic philosophy is likely to be preferable in international marketing research. Thus, the prime emphasis of this research is to identify and develop constructs and measures that are as comparable as possible across countries.

In order to ensure comparability between cultural groups a 'derived etic' framework should be adopted which encompasses necessary reliability in addition to external validity (Berry, 1969). Once initial research has been conducted in one's own culture, the researcher attempts to discover the concept in another culture. A comparison is made of emic A (home culture) and emic B (discovered culture). When a communality is evident (the derived etic), comparison between cultures is possible (Berry (1969) describes the procedure in more detail).

Cross-national equivalence

In order to integrate emic studies into a derived etic approach, functional, conceptual, and metric equivalence must exist (Hui and Triandis, 1985). Cross-cultural equivalence measures have been explored extensively in the extant literature (e.g. Green and Langeard, 1979; Douglas and Craig, 1983; Leung, 1989; Van Herk and Verhallen, 1995). Table 22.1 details categories of equivalence that must be achieved in order to ensure comparability in cross-cultural consumer research.

Conceptual equivalence is concerned with the interpretation that individuals place on objects, stimuli or behaviour, and whether these exist or are expressed in similar ways in different countries and cultures. Conceptual equivalence requires the constructs under investigation, and thus the measuring instruments or test materials, to have similar meaning across the social units studied. Conceptual equivalence is determined by investigating construct validity in each culture where cross-cultural research is undertaken. Construct validity is determined by following recognized procedures to ascertain the validity of the underlying constructs at the conceptual level and reliability at the empirical/measurement instrument level (e.g. Babin, 1994; Grunert *et al.*, 1993; Churchill, 1979).

TABLE 22.1 Categories of cross-cultural equivalence

Main categories	Subcategories
Conceptual equivalence	
Functional equivalence	
Translation equivalence	→ Lexical equivalence
	→ Idiomatic equivalence
	→ Grammatical–syntactical equivalence
	→ Experiential equivalence
Metric equivalence	
Sample equivalence	→ Sampling unit equivalence
	→ Sample representativeness
	→ Category equivalence
Data collection equivalence	→ Respondent cooperation equivalence
	→ Contextual equivalence
	→ Response style equivalence (scalar equivalence and item non-response pattern)

Source: adapted from Douglas and Craig (1983)

Functional equivalence is the confirmation that the researcher is measuring the same behaviour across societies. It exists when 'the behaviour in question has developed in response to a problem shared by two or more social/cultural groups, even though the behaviour in one society does not appear to be related to its counterpart in another society' (Berry, 1969). If similar activities perform different functions in different societies, their measures cannot be used for the purpose of comparison (Frijda and Jahoda, 1966).

The cross-national metric equivalence of a measure exists when the psychometric properties of measures (i.e. internal consistency and dimensionality) exhibit a similar pattern across nations. For subjects not belonging to the same culture, a different meaning may be attached to a given construct, in terms of the underlying variables over which the construct is extrapolated (Poortinga, 1989). If factors are to serve as useful theoretical constructs, it becomes crucial to establish the boundary conditions of factor invariance (Plummer, 1977). Metric equivalence exists when psychometric properties of two or more sets of data or observations from two or more cultural groups exhibit essentially the same coherence or structure (Berry, 1980). Unlike functional and conceptual equivalence, metric equivalence can only be determined after the data are analysed. Results should be investigated while simultaneously analysing and checking for the reliability measures of the rating scales. Thus, measurement unreliability is a threat to cross-national comparability (Davis *et al.*, 1981).

The cross-national equivalence of consumer involvement with food

The plethora of consumer behaviour and social psychology literature on involvement suggests considerable interest in this construct. There has not, however, been a common conceptual or methodological framework to its examination in either literature (Laaksonen, 1994; Jain and Srinivasen, 1990; Rothchild, 1984; Zaichkowsky, 1985; Traylor and Joseph, 1984). Despite the many and varied definitions of consumer involvement that have emerged in the literature, two common ideas predominate; involvement is a multi-dimensional construct (McQuarrie and Munson, 1986; Laurent and Kapferer, 1985), and a motivational force which can help explain various behavioural outcomes, (for example, number and type of choice criteria, extensiveness of information search, length of decision-making process, variety seeking, and brand switching). Various researchers uncover several underlying dimensions of the construct, including the most commonly cited:

- **normative involvement**: the importance of product class to values, emotions, and the ego (Higie and Feick, 1988; Lastovicka and Gardner, 1979);
- **enduring involvement**: the interest and familiarity with a product class as a whole over time (Beharrell and Denison, 1994; Jain and Srinivasan, 1990; Higie and Feick, 1988; Ratchford, 1987; Vaughn, 1986);
- **situational involvement**: the interest and commitment within a product class at a point in time, e.g. loyalty to the brand choice (Beharrell and Denison, 1994; Mittal, 1989);
- **hedonic involvement**: the level of arousal causing personal relevance (McQuarrie and Munson, 1986; Laurent and Kapferer, 1985); and
- **the subjective risk and probability of making a mispurchase**: (Knox *et al.*,1994; Jain and Srinivasan, 1990; Peter and Olsen, 1987).

Validation of the equivalence of involvement cross-nationally requires an instrument capable of capturing the latent dimensions. Goldsmith and Emmert (1991) have evaluated the various methods of measuring involvement, finding, for example, that Zaichkowsky's (1985) scale possesses good internal consistency, Laurent and Kapferer's (1985) scale is valid but exhibits lower internal consistency, and Mittal's (1989) scale is of short length, convenient and valid. Despite the multitude of involvement research, the construct of involvement has not been tested for cross-national generalizability. A small number of authors have applied their involvement scale cross-nationally (e.g. Zaichkowsky and Sood, 1989). They have, however, adopted an imposed etic approach where the scale developed in one country has simply been imposed on other countries without discovering whether equivalence exists.

Whilst conceptual and metric equivalence in consumer involvement across cultures has not been addressed, there is evidence of functional equivalence. A review of extant literature suggests that there may be food-related functional universals (Bareham, 1995). Food, for example has universal functional value in that it delivers calories, vitamins, and nutrition to the consumer, yet the form food takes, its availability, where food is available and its cost vary from culture to culture. Goldschmidt (1966) argues, however, that when evaluating functional equivalence it does not matter if institutions are the same, what may be compared is the solutions to these problems. For example, retail structures and availability of food products may differ in the EU, however, consumers universally perceive food shopping as a utilitarian function (in contrast, in developing countries, food shopping is perceived as a leisure activity, e.g. Mueller and Broderick, 1995). Involvement in food shopping, therefore, may be perceived as functionally equivalent across the

European Union. The conceptual and metric equivalence of the involvement construct are considered empirically below.

Method

Utilizing scale development paradigms within the psychometric literature (Nunnally, 1967; Churchill, 1979; Bearden *et al.*, 1993; Babin, 1994; Gerbing and Anderson, 1988), the author developed and validated a cross-national consumer involvement scale following a derived etic approach (Durvasula *et al.*, 1993; Albaum and Peterson, 1984; Douglas and Craig, 1983; Berry, 1969; Frijda and Jahoda, 1966). The procedure utilized is detailed in Figure 22.1 and summarized below.

Typically with primary data gathering, the problem of country selection is dealt with according to some combination of theoretical and pragmatic considerations (Elder, 1976). Much of previous cross-cultural research has used dramatically different cultures (e.g. Albaum and Peterson, 1984), thereby increasing the likelihood of finding differences. Although these research efforts are important for examining the generalizability of consumer behaviour constructs, it may be equally relevant to demonstrate the existence of differences in consumer decision making between cultures that are less dramatically different. For example, international business expansion often begins in countries fairly similar culturally to the country of origin. An inherent risk in developing into countries with similar cultures is that companies may erroneously assume consumer behaviour patterns will be the same. The European Union culture was, thus, deemed appropriate as a seemingly 'homogeneous' geographical area.

Countries have been selected in part on the basis of retail development and structure but also taking into account wider cultural patterns, processes and experiences; for example, volume of food consumption and food spending as a percentage of gross national product are significant variables for international development. Furthermore, it is interesting to compare North/South, and East/West geographical divides. Thus, the research has investigated the equivalence of the construct consumer involvement across five countries: the UK, France, Spain, Germany and Italy.

Scale development

Extant literature highlighted ten seminal involvement scales with 105 items in total which were selected to fulfil the identified subconstruct definitions. Scales developed by Knox *et al.* (see Chapter 13); Jain and Srinivasan (1990); Mittal

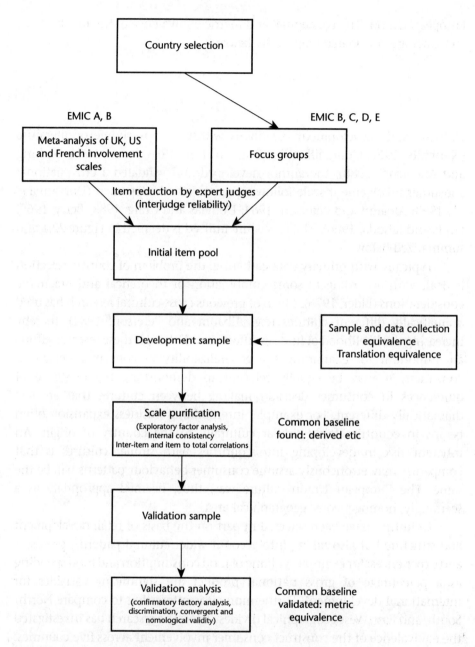

FIGURE 22.1 Procedure for establishing metric equivalence

(1989); Higie and Feick (1988); Ratchford (1987); Vaughn (1986); McQuarrie and Munson (1986); Zaichkowsky (1985); Laurent and Kapferer (1985); Traylor and Joseph (1984) and Lastovicka and Gardner (1979) were applied. These scales, together with statements created through a series of focus groups in each of the five countries, were combined into an initial 130 item pool measuring involvement. The initial item pool was screened and reduced by four expert judges as recommended by Bearden *et al.* (1993). Items chosen exhibited high inter-judge reliability and were consistent with the theoretical domain of the construct. The item pool thus exhibited content validity.

The sample

The measurement instrument (capturing consumer involvement with eight selected food products) was translated and back-translated by separate bilingual speakers of each of the four foreign countries under study to ensure translation equivalence (Douglas and Craig, 1983; Hui and Triandis, 1985; Campbell and Werner, 1970). The empirical investigation was based on two five-country samples: an interviewer surveyed students for the development sample, and food shoppers in selected mid-range supermarkets for the validation sample by means of a questionnaire in both cases.

The development sample consisted of 1000 undergraduate students from one business school in each of the five countries outlined (200 responses per country). The validation sample consisted of 2,727 responses, with approximately 600 respondents in each country. The questionnaires were administered in two regionally representative cities in each country (unfortunately, in Italy only 315 questionnaires could be collected in one city due to limited access to Italian-speaking interviewers). Multiple data screening methods were utilized and profile analysis was used to test for response set bias (Mullen, 1995).

Sample representativeness is essential, i.e., the sample is representative of the culture from which it is drawn. Douglas and Craig (1983) stress the limited availability of an exhaustive sampling framework which corresponds exactly to the characteristics of the population at a global (multi-country) level. They therefore suggest that an empirical method (non-probability sampling procedure) may prove as efficient as probability sampling, when researching cross-culturally. Data can be collected at a reasonable cost, compatible with the objectives of the survey. The basic criterion, therefore, for selecting the sampling procedure(s) will remain the comparability of results across countries. Thus the selection of observations was largely a convenience sample due to the lack of an accurate and comparable European sampling frame (Douglas and Craig, 1983). Food purchasing is influenced by gender, working status, age, income and marital status (Zeitaml, 1985). Quotas, therefore, of gender and age, were produced from published national statistics. Although quotas of working status and income could not be created, the respondents' profile on the questionnaire addressed these categories. The samples may not be considered totally representative of the populations of the different countries. They are, however, relatively homogeneous in a matched-samples sense (i.e. in terms of gender and age) and are considered appropriate for cross-national theory testing.

Results

The equivalence of measures were examined at a national level (i.e. each country's data were analysed separately) and a pooled-data level. Whilst all equivalence issues were considered in the study, this paper primarily focuses on metric equivalence.

A common baseline: derived etic

Exploratory factor analysis was implemented to summarize the interrelationships of variables as an aid to the conceptualization of involvement, and to test for metric equivalence. An analysis on the pooled data from the development sample utilized principal components with an orthogonal rotation. An orthogonal rotation is commonly used in factor analysis, which assumes that the factors are independent of each other, and provides ease of interpretation. The involvement scale, however, taps different facets of the same concept. The factors should not, therefore, be expected *a priori* to be orthogonal. An oblique factor rotation, which allows for correlations between the factors, was thus computed and compared to an orthogonal solution. Identical factor solutions and variance extracted were found, and therefore an orthogonal rotation was retained for ease of interpretation.

The process identified four dimensions which account for 70 per cent of the variance in the data (Table 22.2). A series of subsamples of 100 records were analysed to avoid artificially significant results from the large total sample (Hair *et al.*, 1993). When the data was analysed at the country level, the four factor solution was also evident. The four subconstructs of involvement, therefore, form a common baseline in the countries studied. Significantly, the four factors were consistent when scale data for each of the eight food products were analysed. The initial research, therefore, points to the finding that involvement is a universal construct exhibiting equivalent dimensions:

- **normative**: the relevance of a product to an individual's values and emotions;
- **enduring**: an interest/familiarity with the product class as a whole;
- **situational**: an interest between brands/types of products; and
- **risk**: the importance/probability of making an incorrect product choice.

TABLE 22.2 Empirically identified subconstructs of involvement

Subconstruct	Variable	Factor 1	Factor 2	Factor 3	Factor 4
Normative	I can tell a lot about a person by the type of ____ s/he chooses	0.93386			
	Buying ____ helps me express my personality	0.76836			
Situational	Buying ____ requires a lot of thought		0.82871		
	It is extremely important that I make the right choice of _____		0.81888		
	Choosing between _____ is a very important decision		0.77612		
Enduring	I attach great importance to ____			0.85650	
	I have a strong interest in _____			0.85166	
	I enjoy buying _____			0.63860	
Risk	All brands of _____ would not be equally enjoyable				0.82910
	I believe that differing brands of _____ would give different amounts of pleasure				0.68223
	In purchasing _____ I am certain of my choice				0.59584
	It is really annoying to make an unsuitable purchase of _____				0.58704

Nomological validity has been defined as the degree to which predictions from a formal theoretical network containing the concept under scrutiny are confirmed (Campbell and Fiske, 1959). Comparing the factor structure to previous studies, five key factors have been identified in the content analysis as broadly universal, four of these are evident in the current analysis. According to the literature review, enduring, normative, situational, hedonic and risk can be perceived as separate subconstructs of involvement. The current research has grouped together hedonic and normative statements into a single factor. The factor encompasses how related the product is to the respondent's values, emotions and feelings of pleasure and thus can be thought of as a distinct subconstruct. Nomological validity of the four factor solution is also investigated through confirmatory factor analysis in subsequent sections of this paper.

The reduced 12 item scale measuring the four dimensions of involvement possesses an overall Cronbach's alpha of 0.86 (Table 22.3), with all dimensions

TABLE 22.3 Cronbach's alpha by country and factor evidenced in empirical study

Data set	Total scale	Normative factor	Enduring factor	Situational factor	Risk factor
Pooled data	0.86	0.87	0.82	0.86	0.69
UK	0.86	0.83	0.86	0.89	0.87
France	0.84	0.82	0.88	0.87	0.85
Germany	0.93	0.91	0.93	0.95	0.89
Italy	0.96	0.92	0.98	0.96	0.96
Spain	0.80	0.80	0.82	0.82	0.83

exhibiting a high level of internal consistency and reliability (Murphy and Davidshofer, 1988). These results exceed the minimum α requisite of 0.7, for the research design used, as laid out by Peterson (1994).

The factor analysis detailed is an exploratory process which explored multiple solutions for the most meaningful factor structure. Yet a hypothesis testing procedure is needed in order to specify competing factor-analytic models, and to compare and test the models according to their goodness of fit to the validation sample. Additionally, verification of conceptual equivalence across the total five-country data was needed. A confirmatory factor analysis was executed, utilizing LISREL 7.0 software on the SPSS statistical package (Jöreskog and Sörbom, 1987; 1984), to confirm and validate the identified four factor structure.

Validating the common baseline: metric equivalence

Prior to the assessment of the confirmatory model, a number of assumptions for using this statistical tool need to be addressed, specifically, whether parametric statistics are appropriate to this data and what type of LISREL data matrix should be utilized given the research objectives.

Parametric tests rely on the assumption that the data has a distribution with known parameters/characteristics. According to the central limit theorem, a random sample will approximate a normal distribution as sample size increases (e.g. Morse, 1993). A normal distribution has known parameters, parametric tests can, therefore, be computed on large non-random samples (e.g. Townsend, 1990). When parameters of a population are not known, nonparametric tests are computed. Parametric tests, however, have been found, through Monte Carlo simulations, to be relatively robust in that there is no evidence that parametric tests falsely detect significant results that nonparametric tests would not (e.g. Townsend and Ashby, 1984).

The data from the five-country study can be tested for its approximation to the standard normal distribution by examining the kurtosis and skewness of the distribution of variables in the structural equation (Byrne *et al.*, 1989; Baumgartner and Steenkamp, 1996). The skewness of the variables range from −1.084 to +1.240, with a mean value of −0.43. The kurtosis ranges from −1.068 to +0.749, with a mean value of −0.18. These values are within an acceptable range from 0 providing sufficient evidence to suggest that the data approximates a normal distribution.

Parametric tests assume that data are interval level. The five-country study utilized likert scales which are ordinal in nature (for a classical discussion of these categories of data, see Stevens, 1962). This disparity may introduce measurement error. These data nevertheless can be analysed effectively using statistics that assume interval level measures if departures from intervalness are not extreme (Jaccard and Wan, 1996). Data from individual semantic scale items are clearly ordinal. The total score, however, is usually treated as interval, as when the arithmetic mean score, which assumes equality of intervals, is computed (Nunnally and Bernstein, 1994). The common practice by marketers, of averaging semantic scale data and utilizing metric statistical techniques indicates that many researchers, at least on a *de facto* basis, consider semantic data to be interval in nature (Holmes, 1974). Those who perform such operations thus implicitly use a scaling method to convert data from ordinal to interval level of measurement when they sum over items to obtain a total score.

Due to the large sample size of the five-country study, in addition to the tests conducted above, the data is assumed to be normally distributed, with a continuous interval measurement of consumer involvement with food. Parametric statistics using LISREL can therefore be computed.

Individual observations can not be input into the LISREL program. The raw data has to be converted into one of two types of matrices before estimation. Input for the program is a correlation or variance/covariance matrix of all indicators used in the model. Table 22.4 details the uses of the different types of matrices. Confirmatory factor analysis was initially formulated for use with the variance/covariance matrix. The covariance matrix has the advantage of providing valid comparisons between different populations or samples, something not possible when models are estimated with a correlation matrix. The correlation matrix, however, has gained widespread use in many applications (Hair *et al.*, 1995). Use of correlations is appropriate when the objective of the research is only to understand the pattern of relationships between constructs, but not to explain the total variance of a construct.

A confirmatory factor analysis, utilizing a covariance matrix, was computed first on the pooled five-country validation data set to determine

TABLE 22.4 A comparison of covariance and correlation matrices for LISREL

Covariance matrix	Correlation matrix
Valid comparisons between different populations.	
Difficult to interpret because coefficients must be interpreted in terms of the units of measure for the construct.	Common range that makes comparisons of the coefficients within a model possible.
	A standardized matrix that has often been used.
To explain the total variance of a construct.	To understand the pattern of relationships between constructs.
Validates causal relationships/satisfies assumptions of methodology.	Provides more conservative estimates of the significance of coefficients.

goodness of fit. Additionally, to confirm whether metric equivalence has been achieved, confirmatory factor analysis tested the model in each separate country (Figure 22.2) and tested multiple group models in which each country's sample served as a group. The results are summarized in Table 22.5. As both the individual country results and the pooled data results are deemed satisfactory, the following section details only the pooled data results. Finally the multiple-group results are detailed to assess the invariance of the factor structure.

The four factor confirmatory solution was assessed for 'overall model fit' to determine the degree to which the specified indicators represent the hypothesized construct. The overall model fit to the validation sample can be assessed statistically by the chi-square test, and heuristically by a number of goodness of fit indices. The chi-square statistic is, however, sensitive to sample size (Sharma, 1996; Hair *et al.*, 1993). For a large sample size, even small differences in the sample covariance matrix are statistically significant, although the differences may not be practically meaningful. The five-country

TABLE 22.5 Confirmatory factor analysis on pooled data and by country

Fit statistic	Pooled data	UK	France	Spain	Germany	Italy
GFI	0.944	0.897	0.937	0.935	0.906	0.920
RMSR	0.056	0.080	0.064	0.067	0.058	0.036
AGFI	0.910	0.832	0.898	0.894	0.848	0.880
RGFI	0.945	0.900	0.941	0.939	0.891	0.910

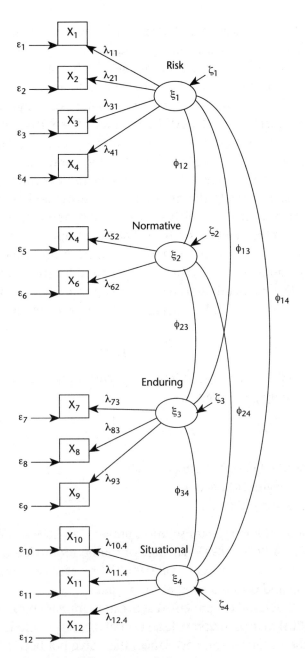

FIGURE 22.2 Path model of four factor solution

sample of 2,727 respondents is large enough to make the chi-square statistic significant even if extremely small relationships are present. It was deemed, therefore, to be an unacceptable test of model fit. Consequently, other methods are utilized for evaluating the fit of the model to the data (Bearden *et al.*, 1982). The fit indices applied are mainly provided by LISREL (Jöreskog and Sörbom, 1984), and are designed to provide a summary measure of the residual matrix; the difference between the sample and the estimated variance matrix. Fit indices utilized include: the goodness of fit index (GFI), the adjusted goodness of fit index (AGFI), the relative goodness of fit index (RGFI) and the root mean square residual (RMSR). Samples of less than 100 are likely to understate the fit of confirmatory-factor models (Bentler, 1990; Bollen, 1989). The comparative fit index (Bentler, 1990) is suggested for models estimated with smaller samples, to reflect the fit of these more accurately.

The GFI represents the amount of variances and covariances in the sample covariance matrix which are predicted by the model. The GFI for the four factor developed model on the validation sample is given as 0.944. It has been shown, however, that GFI and consequently the AGFI (0.910) are also affected by sample size and that the upper band for the GFI may not be one (Sharma, 1996). Rather than using GFI for large sample sizes, one should use a relative goodness of fit index (RGFI), which can be computed as:

$$RGFI \approx \frac{GFI}{EGFI}$$

Where the EGFI is the approximate expected value for the GFI (Maiti and Mukherjee, 1990), and is given by:

$$EGFI \approx \frac{1}{1 + (2df/pn)}$$

Where: p = number of indicators
df = degrees of freedom
n = sample size

Application to the four factor solution provides an EGFI=0.999, a GFI=0.944, and therefore a RGFI = 0.945. The rule of thumb for models with a good fit is that the GFI should be greater than 0.90. The four factor solution exceeds this specification and thus is a good fit to the data.

All of the fit indices presented above are summary measures of the fitted residuals (RES) matrix and provide an overall measure of model fit. This matrix contains the variances and covariances that have not been accounted for by the model. The larger the residuals, the worse the model fit, and vice versa. Residuals in the RES matrix are scale dependent. To overcome this problem, the RES matrix is standardized by their respective asymptotic standard errors. The resulting standardized residual matrix is also reported by LISREL. Standardized residuals that are greater than 1.96 (the critical z value for α = 0.05) are considered to be statistically significant, and, therefore, high. Ideally, no more than 5 per cent of standardized residuals should be greater than 1.96. For large samples, however, even small residuals will be statistically significant (Sharma, 1996). To compensate for sample size sensitivity, the root mean square residual (RMSR) has been used as a summary measure of the standardized fitted residual matrix (Sharma, 1996). The RMSR is the square root of the average of the square of the residuals. The larger the RMSR, the less is the fit between the model and the data and vice versa. The produced RMSR is 0.05. Only 5 per cent of the variances and covariances are not accounted for by the model and so it is a good fit to the data. The four factor solution therefore fulfils the minimum RMSR requirements.

To compare the four factor model against the null model (a baseline model that hypothesizes no relationship between the indicators and the factors), two incremental fit indices were calculated. The Tucker–Lewis measure (TLM) and the normed fit index (NFI) were calculated to determine the increase in model fit relative to the null model. Tucker–Lewis Index is expressed as:

$$TLI = \frac{(N\ CHI\text{-}SQUARE\ /\ N\ DF) - (P\ CHI\text{-}SQUARE/P\ DF)}{(N\ CHI\text{-}SQUARE\ /\ N\ DF) - 1}$$

Where N = the null model
    P = the proposed model
    DF = degrees of freedom

The normed fit index is calculated as:

$$NFI = \frac{(N\ CHI\text{-}SQUARE - P\ CHI\text{-}SQUARE)}{N\ CHI\text{-}SQUARE}$$

Where N = the null model
    P = the proposed model

Table 22.6 outlines the results. Values greater than 0.8 were produced providing an acceptable level of incremental fit (Carmines and McIver, 1981).

Construct validity is established by determining the extent to which the measure highly correlates with other measures designed to measure the same construct (convergent validity), and the extent to which the measure is distinct and is not simply a reflection of some other variable (discriminant validity). To test simultaneously convergent and discriminant validity, both exploratory factor analysis and multigroup confirmatory factor analysis can be computed. To have convergent validity, the scale of each subconstruct of involvement should correlate highly with each other. Although the dimensions are distinct they are still measuring the same construct. To ensure discriminant validity, a scale should not load on the same factor as another scale, i.e. the scale of each subconstruct should be unidimensional (Nunnally and Bernstein, 1994).

TABLE 22.6 Incremental fit of the model

Statistic	Pooled Data
Tucker–Lewis measure	0.88
Normed fit index	0.88

All factor loadings of the measurement instrument are significant (all t-values are larger than 6.0) and exceed the 0.4 level commonly considered meaningful in factor-analytic investigations (Ford *et al.*, 1986). These findings support the convergent validity of the items (Anderson and Gerbing, 1988). The four-factor model, detailed in Figure 22.2, was tested against a one-factor model (i.e. a unity correlation between all four constructs). Across the five samples, the four-factor model provided a significantly better chi-square fit to the data than did the one-factor model, providing evidence of discriminate validity. Item to total correlations, scree plots and factor loading results, as well as the LISREL results, provide support for the convergent and discriminant validity of the measurement instrument (Steenkamp and Van Trijp, 1991).

The various measures of overall goodness of fit lend sufficient support to deem the results to be an acceptable representation of the hypothesized construct. Once the overall model has been accepted, the measurement items can be assessed. Each of the scales can be evaluated separately by examining the indicator loadings for statistical significance and by assessing the constructs' reliability and variance extracted. Using the maximum likelihood parameter estimates for the squared multiple correlations (SMCs), the extent to which the variables are good or reliable indicators of the construct they purport to measure are calculated. The SMCs provide the communality of the indicator as reported in exploratory factor analysis programs. The SMC, therefore, can be used to assess how good or reliable an indicator is for measuring the construct it purports to measure. The minimum requirement of at least 0.5 is based on the logic that an indicator should have at least 50 per cent of its variance in common with the construct. This requirement is met by ten of the twelve indicators, which therefore may be perceived as reliable (Table 22.7).

The total coefficient of determination (TCD) assesses the extent to which the indicators as a group measure the construct. A common cut-off value for TCD is 0.80, but figures as low as 0.50 have been used (Sharma, 1996). The four factor solution (TCD = 0.999) greatly exceeds the minimum requirements and, therefore, the internal consistency of the group of indicators is high.

The modification indices of the LISREL output can be used to respecify the hypothesized model. The modification index of a fixed parameter gives the

TABLE 22.7 Reliability of involvement model parameters (squared multiple correlations for independent variables)

Scale 1	Scale 2	Scale 3	Scale 4	Scale 5	Scale 6	Scale 7	Scale 8	Scale 9	Scale 10	Scale 11	Scale 12
0.838	0.875	0.706	0.296	0.652	0.731	0.653	0.584	0.384	0.700	0.624	0.825

approximate decrease in the χ^2 if the fixed parameter is freed (i.e. it is estimated). None of the modification indices for the loading of an item on the nonhypothesized factor were significant at the 0.05 level, and none of the estimated changes reported by LISREL exceeded 0.2 (Baumgartner and Steenkamp, 1996). Modification of the model, therefore, would not increase the fit to the data.

As a final test of metric equivalence, multiple group analysis was conducted. An unconstrained model, in which the factor structure (item to factor loadings) and the correlations among the four involvement factors are allowed to vary across the five country samples, is estimated. This model is then compared to a constrained model, in which the factor structure is declared invariant across samples (Durvasula *et al.*, 1993; Bollen, 1989; Jöreskog and Sörbom, 1984). For the four factor model of risk, normative, situational and enduring involvement, the unconstrained model's chi-square was 188.32 (df = 35), and the constrained model's chi-square was 233.93 (df = 59). The fit of the unconstrained model (as given by chi-square) is not significantly different from the fit of the constrained model (chi-square difference = 45.61, df = 24). This result suggests that the factor structure is invariant across samples. As the measurement invariance holds, any remaining differences between country groups are manifest by differences in the distributions of the latent variable rather than inconsistent scoring and response set bias (Mullen, 1995). Thus, the measurement appears to be universal across the five countries and a comparison of means using the model presented will capture 'true' cultural differences rather than measurement and scaling prejudices.

Conclusions

This paper illustrates the use of confirmatory factor analysis for the purposes of testing for metric equivalence. Validating the cross-national generalizability of a consumer behaviour construct allows true comparisons to be made between countries. This is crucial information for the internationalizing organization. The results from the confirmatory factor analysis show a four factor model that is valid and reliable across five countries. This positive evidence of psychometric equivalence suggests that there is much commonality as measured by involvement in the five countries studied. It can be seen that this four factor involvement model provides an appropriate perspective in which intercultural consumer markets can be assessed.

References

Albaum, G. and Peterson, R.A. (1984), Empirical research in international marketing: 1976–1982, *Journal of International Business Studies*, **15** (1), Spring/Summer, pp. 161–173

Anderson, J.C. and Gerbing, D.W. (1988), Structural equation modelling in practice: a review and recommended two-step approach, *Psychological Bulletin*, **103**, pp. 411–23

Babin, L. (1994), Guidelines for state-of-the-art scale development, *Proceedings of the Southern Marketing Association Annual Conference*: New Orleans, pp. 198–201

Bareham, J. (1995), *Consumer Behaviour in the Food Industry. A European Perpsective*, Oxford: Butterworth-Heinemann

Baumgartner, H. and Steenkamp, J-B.E.M. (1996), Exploratory consumer buying behaviour: conceptualization and measurement, *International Journal of Research in Marketing*, **13**, pp. 121–37

Bearden, W.O., Netemeyer, R.G. and Mobley, M.F. (1993), *Handbook of Marketing Scales*, Newbury Park: Sage Publications

Beatty, S.B. and Smith, S.M. (1987), Involvement, search and satisfaction: a path analytic model, in W. Darden and K. Monroe (Eds.), *Research Methods and Causal Modeling in Marketing*, Chicago: AMA

Beharrell, B. and Dennison, T.J. (1995), Involvement in a routine food shopping context, *British Food Journal*, **97** (4), pp. 24–9

Bentler, P.M. (1990), Comparative fit indices in structural models, *Psychological Bulletin*, **107** (2), pp. 238–46

Berry, J.W. (1969), On cross-cultural comparability, *International Journal of Psychology*, **4**, pp. 119–28

Berry, J.W. (1980), Introduction to methodology, in H.C. Triandis and J.W. Berry (Eds.) *The Handbook of Cross-Cultural Psychology*, Vol 2, Boston: Allyn and Bacon

Bollen, K.A. (1989), *Structural Equations with Latent Constructs*, New York: Wiley

Burke, R.E. (1992), Comparing dynamic consumer choice in the real and computer-simulated environments, *Journal of Consumer Research*, **19**, pp. 1–10

Byrne, B.B., Shavelson, R.J. and Muthén, B. (1989), Testing for the equivalence of factor covariance and mean structures: the issue of partial measurement invariance, *Psychological Bulletin*, **105** (3), pp. 456–66

Campbell, D.T. and Fiske, D.W. (1959), Convergent and discriminant validity by the multitrait–multimethod matrix, *Psychological Bulletin*, **56**, March, pp. 81–105

Campbell, D.T. and Werner, O. (1970), Translating, working through interpreters and the problem of decentering, in R. Naroll and R. Cohen (Eds.), *A Handbook of Method in Cultural Anthropology*, New York: The Natural History Press

Carmines, E. and McIver, J. (1981), Analysing models with unobserved variables: analysis of covariance structures, in G. Bohrnstedt and E. Borgatta (Eds.) *Social Measurement: Current Issues*, Beverly Hills: Sage

Chaiken, S. (1980), Heuristic versus systematic information processing and the use of source versus message cue persuasion, *Journal of Personality and Social Psychology*, **39**, November, pp. 752–56

Churchill, G.A. (1979), A paradigm for developing better measures of marketing constructs, *Journal of Marketing Research*, **XVI**, February, pp. 64–73

Costa, J.A. and Bamossy, G.J. (1995), *Marketing in a Multicultural World*, Thousand Oaks CA: Sage

Davis, H.L., Douglas, S.P. and Silk, A.J. (1981), 'Measure unreliability: a hidden threat to cross-national research?', American Marketing Association Attitude Research Conference, (March), Carlsbad, CA, pp. 1–40

Douglas, M. and Isherwood, B. (1979), *The World of Goods: Towards an Anthropology of Consumption*, New York: Norton

Douglas, S. and Craig, C.S. (1983), 'International Marketing Research', Englewood Cliffs NJ: Prentice-Hall

Durvasula, S., Andrews, J.C., Lysonski, S., and Netemeyer, R.G. (1993), Assessing the cross-national applicability of consumer behaviour models: a model of attitude toward advertising in general, *Journal of Consumer Research*, **19**, March, pp. 626–36

Elder, J.W. (1976), Comparative cross-national methodology, *Annual Review of Sociology*, **2**, pp. 209–30

Ford, J.K., MacCallum, R.C. and Tait, M. (1986), The application of exploratory factor analysis in applied psychology: a critical review and analysis, *Personnel Psychology*, **39**, pp. 291–314

Foxall, G.R. and Bhate, S. (1993), Cognitive styles and personal involvement as explicators of innovative purchasing of 'healthy' food brands, *European Journal of Marketing*, **27** (2), pp. 5–16

Frijda, N.H. and Jahoda, G. (1966), On the scope and methods of cross-cultural research, *International Journal of Psychology*, **1**, pp. 110–27

Gerbing, D.W. and Anderson, J.C. (1988), An updated paradigm for scale development incorporating unidimensionality and it's assessment, *Journal of Marketing Research*, **25**, May, pp. 186–92

Goldschmidt, W. (1966), *Comparative Functionalism*, Berkeley CA: University of California Press

Green, R.T. and Langeard, E. (1979), 'Comments and recommendations on the practice of cross-cultural marketing research', Paper presented at the International Marketing Workshop, EIASM (November) Brussels

Grunert, S., Grunert, K.G. and Kristensen, K. (1993), Une méthode d'estimation de la validité interculturelle des instruments de mesure: le cas de la mesure des valeurs des consommateurs par la liste des valeurs LOV, *Recherche et Applications en Marketing*, **8** (4), pp. 5–28

Hair, J.F. Jr., Anderson, R.E., Tatham, R.L. and Black, W.C. (1993), *Multivariate Data Analysis*, New York: MacMillan Publishing Co

Higie, R.A. and Feick, L.F. (1988), Enduring Involvement: Conceptual & Methodological Issues, in T. Srull (Ed.) *Advances in Consumer Research*, 16, Provo UT: Association for Consumer Research

Holmes, C. (1974), A statistical evaluation of rating scales, *Journal of the Market Research Society*, **16** (2), pp. 28–107

Hui, C.H. and Triandis, H.C. (1985), Measurement in cross-cultural psychology: a review and comparison of strategies, *Journal of Cross-Cultural Psychology*, **16**, June, pp. 131–152

Humphries, G. and Samways, A. (1993), The outlook for UK retailing in the 1990's, *Financial Times Management Reports*, p. 14

Irvine, S.H. and Carroll, W.K. (1980), Testing and assessment across cultures: issues in methodology and theory, in H.C. Triandis and J.W. Berry (Eds.), *The Handbook of Cross-Cultural Psychology*, Vol 2, Boston MA: Allyn and Bacon

Jaccard, J. and Wan, C.K. (1996), LISREL approaches to interaction effects in multiple regression, Series: *Quantitative Applications in the Social Sciences*, London: Sage Publications

Jain, K. and Srinivasan, N. (1990), An empirical assessment of multiple operationalisations of involvement, in M. Goldberg, G. Gorn and R. Pollay (Eds.) *Advances in Consumer Research*, 17, Provo UT: Association for Consumer Research

Jöreskog, K.G. and Sörbom, D. (1984), *LISREL: Analysis of Linear Structural Relationships by the Method of Maximum Likelihood*, Chicago: SPSS Inc.

Jöreskog, K.G. and Sörbom, D. (1987), *LISREL 7: A Guide to the Program and Applications*, Chicago SPSS Inc.

Laaksonen, P. (1994), *Consumer Involvement: Concepts and Research*, London: Routledge

Lastovicka, J.L. and Gardner, D. M. (1979), Components of involvement, in J.C. Malony and B. Silverman (Eds.) *Attitude Research Plays for High Stakes*, Chicago: American Marketing Association

Laurent, G. and Kapferer, J.N. (1985), Measuring consumer involvement profiles, *Journal of Marketing Research*, 22, February, pp. 41–53

Leung, K. (1989), Cross-cultural differences: individual level versus culture level analysis, *International Journal of Psychology*, 24, pp. 703–19

Maheswaren, D. and Meyers-Levy, J. (1990), The influences of message framing and involvement, *Journal of Marketing Research*, 27, August, pp. 361–67

Maiti, S.S. and Mukherjee, B.N. (1990), A note on distributional properties of the Jöreskog and Sörbom fit indices, *Psychometrika*, 55, December, pp. 721–26

McCracken, G. (1988), *Culture and Consumption*, Bloomington IL: Indiana Press

McQuarrie, E.F. and Munson, J.M. (1986), The Zaichkowsky personal involvement inventory: modification & extension, in P. Anderson and M. Wallendorf (Eds.), *Advances in Consumer Research*, Provo UT: Association for Consumer Research

Mennell, S., Murcott, A., and Otterloo, A.H. van (1992), *The Sociology of Food*, London: Sage

Mittal, B. (1989), Measuring purchase-decision involvement, *Psychology & Marketing*, 6, Summer, pp. 147–62

Morse, L.B. (1993), *Statistics for Business and Economics*, New York: Harper Collins College Publishers

Mueller, R.D. and Broderick, A.J. (1995), East European retailing: a consumer perspective, *International Journal of Retail and Distribution Management*, 23 (1), pp. 32–40

Mullen, M.R. (1995), Diagnosing measurement equivalence in cross-national research, *Journal of International Business Studies*, Third Quarter, pp. 573–96

Nunnally, J.C. (1967), *Psychometric Theory*, New York: McGraw-Hill Book Company

Nunnally, J.C. and Bernstein, I.H. (1994), *Psychometric Theory*, Third edition, New York: McGraw-Hill

Peter, J.P. and Olsen, J.C. (1987), *Consumer Behaviour: Marketing Strategy Perspectives*, Homewood: Irwin

Peterson, R.A. (1994), A meta-analysis of Cronbach's coefficient alpha, *Journal of Consumer Research*, 21, September, pp. 381–91

Petty, R.E. and Cacioppo, J.T. (1981), *Attitudes and Persuasion: Classic and Contemporary Approaches*, Dubuque IA: C. Brown Company Publishers

Pike, K.L. (1966), *Language in Relation to a Unified Theory of the Structure of Human Behaviour*, The Hague: Mouton

Plummer, J. (1977), Consumer focus in cross-national research, *Journal of Advertising Research*, **6**, Spring, pp. 5–15

Poortinga, Y.H. (1989), Equivalence in cross-national data: an overview of basic issues, *International Journal of Psychology*, **24**, pp. 737–56

Ratchford, B.T. (1987), New insights about the FCB grid, *Journal of Advertising Research*, **27**, August-September, pp. 24–38

Roth, M.S. (1995), The effects of culture and socio-economics on the performance of global brand image strategies, *Journal of Marketing Research*, **32**, May, pp. 163–75

Rothschild, M.L. (1984), Perspectives on involvement: current problems and future directions, T. Kinnear (Ed.), *Advances in Consumer Research*, **11**, pp. 216–17

Sahlins, M. (1976), *Culture and Practical Reason*, Chicago: University of Chicago Press

Sharma, S. (1996), *Applied Multivariate Techniques*, New York: John Wiley & Sons

Steenkamp, J-B.E.M. and Van Trijp, H.C.M. (1991), The use of LISREL in validating marketing constructs, *International Journal of Research in Marketing*, **8**, pp. 283–99

Stevens, S.S. (1962), Mathematics, measurement, and psychophysics', in S.S. Stevens (Ed.), *Handbook of Experimental Psychology*, New York: John Wiley and Sons

Tordjman, A. (1995), European retailing: convergences, differences and perspectives, in P.J. McGoldrick and G. Davies (Eds.), *International Retailing: Trends and Strategies*, London: Pitman Publishing

Townsend, J.T. (1990), Truth and consequences of ordinal differences in statistical distributions: toward a theory of hierarchical inference, *Psychological Bulletin*, **108**, pp. 551–69

Townsend, J.T. and Ashby, F. (1984), Measurement scales and statistics: the misconception misconceived, *Psychological Bulletin*, **96**, pp. 394–401

Traylor, M.B. and Joseph, W.B. (1984), Measuring consumer involvement with products: developing a general scale, *Psychology & Marketing*, **1**, pp. 65–77

Triandis, H.C. (1983), Dimensions of cultural variation as parameters of organisational theories, *International Studies of Management and Organisation*, **XII** (4), pp. 139–69

Van Herk, H. and Verhallen, T.M. (1995), 'Equivalence in empirical international research in the food area, *Proceedings of the 2nd Conference on the Cultural Dimension of International Marketing*, Odense

Vaughn, R. (1986), How advertising works: a planning model revisited, *Journal of Advertising Research*, **27**, February–March, pp. 57–66

Zaichkowsky, J.L. (1985), Measuring the involvement construct, *Journal of Consumer Research*, **12**, December, pp. 341–35

Zaichkowsky, J.L. and Sood, J.H. (1989), A global look at consumer involvement and use of products, *International Marketing Review*, **6** (1), pp. 20–34

Zeitaml, V. (1985), The new demographics and market fragmentation, *Journal of Marketing*, **49**, Summer, pp. 64–75

Index

NOTE: Page numbers in italic indicate information is to be found only in a figure or table.

Powell, T.C. 385
Pras, B. 295–6
preference structures 295, 297, 300, 306–10, 313
PRELIS 228
Prendergast, G. 352, 353
presentation of data *see* data presentation
Preston, L.E. 372, 373, 374–5
pricing decisions:
    conjoint analysis used 80–2, 86
    forecasting prices 101, 103, 109
    modelling application 28, *29*
principal component factor analysis *208*, 322–4, 334, 386, 440
product decisions:
    conjoint analysis used 76–80, 83, 86
    forecasting new product sales 105–8
    see also new products
product involvement 265
    see also consumer involvement
PROFIT program 341, 344
promotional decisions 82–3, 86
purchasing involvement 265
    see also consumer involvement

Q-factor analysis 55
Q-plot of residuals 246–7, *248*
quantitative methods:
    applications 1–3
    diffusion of 18–40
    good practice 204–5
    ten commandments for 15–17

R1/XCON expert system 415
Ramajuman, V. 385
Rao, V. 69, 86
regression analysis *29*, 30, *35*, 37, 417–18
    linear additive model 306–7, 310, 314
    preference regression 306–10, 313
    ratio effects 212, 217, *219*
    robustness of techniques 205, 211
    and small sample size 13, 204–19
    stepwise regression 306–7
    two-variable linear regression 24, 25, *29*, 30, *31*
    validation with small samples 211, 213–18
    see also canonical correlation analysis; hierarchical moderated regression analysis; logistic regression; multiple discriminant analysis; multiple regression analysis; principal componenets analysis
re-interviewing *see* attitude variation
reliability 181, 273–4, 277, 375, 389, 433
research as stakeholder orientation *380*, 383, *388*
residual analysis 63, 67, 246–7, *248*

retail location study 11, 14, 317–36
    design of study 321–2
    factor analysis use 322–32
    gravitational theory 318, 332
    method used 322–4
    questionnaire 321–2, *326*, 335–6
    results 324–32
    see also shopping centre studies
retail scanner data 97, 114
RGFI (relative goodness of fit index) *444*, 446
Richins, M. 270
Riedwyl, H. 423
risk management 109–11
Ritchie, B.J.R. 339
Rivett, P. 19
Rizvi, M.J. 423–4
RMSR (root mean squared residual) 246, 250–1, *444*, 446, 447
Robinson, R.B. 385
role playing 94, *95*, 101, 102, *113*, 114, 117
Rosenbaum, H.F. 78–9, 84
Rosko, M.D. 85
Ruekert, R.W. *376*
rule-based forecasting *95*, 98, 112, *113*, 115–16
Rumelhart, D.E. 367
Rush, 109

Saaty, T.L. 122, 126, 138–9
Sahni, S. 412
St. John, C.H. 378
sales forecasting 92, 93, 104–8, 114, 115, 117
    modelling application 28–9
    new product sales 105–8
sample size:
    for LISREL modelling 254, 444–5, 446, 447
    test power affected by 205, 206–7, 212, 218
    see also small samples
sampling:
    opportunity sampling 322, 335
    reuse techniques 214, 217, 218
    see also sample size; small samples
Sanderson, S. 92
Sands, S. 75, 77
Sasaki, M.S. 170
SAS software 26, 37
Saunders, J. 9, 12, 46, 53–4
scale development paradigms 437–9
scanner data 97, 114
scenarios 116, 117
Schleede, J.M. 415
Schnaars, S.P. 105
Schoonhoven, C.B. 172, 390
Schram, J. 369
Schweikl, H. 85
scree plots 9, 51, 324–5, *327*, 335
Sears, Roebuck customer database 404